A Commentary on Selected Speeches of Isaios

Mnemosyne

Supplements

Monographs on Greek and Latin Language and Literature

VOLUME 364

The titles published in this series are listed at brill.com/mns

A Commentary on Selected Speeches of Isaios

By

Brenda Griffith-Williams

BRILL

LEIDEN • BOSTON
2013

Library of Congress Cataloging-in-Publication Data

Isaeus, approximately 420 B.C.–approximately 350 B.C., author.
A commentary on selected speeches of Isaios / by Brenda Griffith-Williams.
pages cm. — (Mnemosyne, Supplements. Monographs on Greek and Latin Language and Literature, ISSN 0169-8958 ; 364)
Revision of the author's doctoral thesis, University of London—2009.
Includes bibliographical references and index.
ISBN 978-90-04-25857-0 (hardback : alk. paper) — ISBN 978-90-04-26018-4 (e-book)
1. Inheritance and succession (Greek law) 2. Inheritance and succession—Greece—Athens—History—To 1500. 3. Forensic orations—Greece—Athens—History—To 1500. 4. Isaeus, approximately 420 B.C.–approximately 350 B.C.—Translations into English. 5. Speeches, addresses, etc., Greek—Translations into English. I. Griffith-Williams, Brenda, writer of added commentary. II. Title.

KL4196.I825 2013
340.5'38—dc23

2013026804

This publication has been typeset in the multilingual "Brill" typeface. With over 5,100 characters covering Latin, IPA, Greek, and Cyrillic, this typeface is especially suitable for use in the humanities. For more information, please see www.brill.com/brill-typeface.

ISSN 0169-8958
ISBN 978-90-04-25857-0 (hardback)
ISBN 978-90-04-26018-4 (e-book)

This book is printed on acid-free paper.

In loving memory of Jill Valerie Stanley (née Millard), 1934–2009.

CONTENTS

LIST OF DIAGRAMS

PREFACE

The speeches of Isaios are our principal source of information on Athenian inheritance law in the fifth and fourth centuries BC, and they also provide a unique insight into property acquisition strategies, religious observance and domestic life in classical Athens. So they are of interest to legal, social and economic historians as well as to students of Athenian law, oratory and rhetoric, and to those reading the work of the Athenian orators as literature. Yet despite the renaissance in the study of the Attic orators over the last twenty to thirty years, Isaios has attracted relatively little attention from commentators, especially in English. The only comprehensive English language commentary is still that of William Wyse (1904), whose influence on subsequent scholarship has been largely negative.

A new commentary is clearly needed, both to correct Wyse's bias and to take account of more recent developments in the study of oratory and law. A commentary on all of Isaios's speeches would have been beyond the scope of the doctoral thesis on which this book is based, so a selection had to be made. The selection gains cohesion from the fact that each of the chosen speeches was written for delivery in court by a claimant in a *diadikasia*, the (supposedly) non-adversarial procedure used to determine contested inheritance claims. The commentary focuses mainly on the legal and factual issues in dispute, and on logographic strategy. Modern parallels are adduced, wherever relevant, to illustrate the resemblances as well as the differences between ancient and modern legal procedures and advocacy techniques. Textual problems are discussed, as are questions of language and style, where they have significant implications for interpretation and for the understanding of rhetorical strategy. Comments on historical issues, prosopography, and *realia* are limited mainly to points which have not been adequately discussed in the public domain, or where some adjustment is needed to the received opinion. The General Introduction provides a brief discussion of Isaios and his work, and an overview of aspects of the Athenian inheritance system (substantive law, procedure, sources of dispute, evidence and argumentation) insofar as these are relevant to the speeches covered by the commentary. It concludes with an account of Isaios's reception from antiquity to the twenty-first century. An appendix (pp. 247–252) catalogues all the inheritance disputes, known from the work of the Attic orators, in which there was at least one court hearing.

The Greek text used as the basis for this commentary is that of E. S. Forster in the Loeb edition (1927). Given that there is as yet no OCT edition of Isaios, the other options were the editions of C. Scheibe (Bibiotheca Teubneriana, 1860) and W. Wyse (1904), both of which include a more extensive critical apparatus, and P. Roussel's Budé edition (1926). In fact, the choice of text is of relatively little consequence, given that there are few significant differences, so the Loeb edition was chosen mainly because it is the most widely available to Anglophone readers. For the same reason, English versions of the lemmata are based on Forster's translation, but I have adapted it fairly freely to meet the needs of the commentary. I have not consulted the manuscripts independently, but the most important textual differences are discussed in the commentary as they arise. Readers who are interested in the manuscript tradition will find a full account in Wyse's Critical Introduction.

In adapting the thesis for publication, my aim has been to make the book as accessible as possible to readers who do not know Greek, by keeping the use of Greek script to a mininum. In practice this has, perhaps inevitably, resulted in some inconsistency, but the general principles I have followed are outlined here.

Greek lemmata of more than one line in length have been abbreviated, but translations are always given in full so that each lemma is intelligible without reference to the Greek text. Citations from other classical Greek sources have also been translated into English. Individual Greek words and short phrases used in the commentary are transliterated unless the context makes Greek script more appropriate (as, for example, in discussion of textual variants). I have followed this principle even in citations from earlier works of modern scholarship where Greek script is used more extensively; so, for example, where Harrison writes 'one or other party was bound to forfeit the παρακαταβολή', I have rendered the Greek word for 'deposit' as *parakatabolē*. The names of Greek people and places are generally transliterated (so Isaios, not Isaeus), but Latinized forms are used for those most widely familiar to English readers (e.g. Socrates, Aeschylus, Corinth).

I have also translated all quotations from French, German and Italian scholars into English, but retained the original text for the convenience of those who would prefer to read it for themselves.

My policy on legal terminology requires some explanation. Many features of the Athenian legal system have no exact equivalent in terms of modern institutions and procedures. For example, the functions of an Athenian *dikastēs* combined those of a judge and juror, so to translate it by either of these words is misleading. Similarly, the use of words such as 'protestation' for *diamarturia*, 'adjudication' for *epidikasia* or 'heiress' for *epiklēros* can only approximate to the meaning of the original. For this reason I have chosen to transliterate rather than translate the Greek terms, which are defined briefly on their first occurrence in the General Introduction and explained more fully in the Glossary (pp. 253–255), which also includes rhetorical and other technical terminology.

Words included in the glossary are marked with an asterisk (*) on their first occurrence in the introductions to each of the speeches, and (for the benefit of readers consulting the commentary for guidance on individual passages) on their first occurrence in each note in the lemmatic commentary.

Brenda Griffith-Williams
London, June 2013

ACKNOWLEDGEMENTS

The original version of this commentary was a University of London Ph.D. thesis, completed in 2009. Part of my research, from 1 October 2006 to 30 September 2008, was carried out with the support of the Arts and Humanities Research Council (doctoral award no. 06/124509), which I acknowledge with thanks.

The work has evolved over a number of years, with a considerable amount of help from others. I am hugely indebted to my Ph.D. supervisor at UCL, Professor Chris Carey, for enabling me to find my own voice as a commentator on Isaios. This would not have been possible without his constant encouragement, wise advice, and constructive criticism. And, by no means least, I am grateful to him for making the project so much fun. I am also deeply grateful to the examiners, Professor Mike Edwards and Professor Stephen Todd, for their perceptive and detailed comments, which have helped enormously in the task of converting the thesis into a book. Caroline van Erp and her colleagues, at Brill, have provided guidance and support throughout the publication process, and the two anonymous readers have suggested numerous improvements as well as alerting me to some errors and inconsistencies. Any remaining errors are, of course, my own responsibility.

Finally, I want to record my warm thanks to the many friends—especially Valerie Smith, Roy Walmsley, and the late Jill Stanley—who have encouraged and supported my return to academic work.

ABBREVIATIONS

Ancient Authors and Works

Aesch. *Kho.*	Aeschylus *Khoephoroi*
Aiskhin.	Aiskhines
Andok.	Andokides
Antiph.	Antiphon
Arist.	Aristotle
Nic. Eth.	*Nicomachean Ethics*
Pr.	*Problemata*
Rh.	*Rhetoric*
Aristoph.	Aristophanes
Ath. Pol.	[Aristotle] *Athēnaiōn Politeia*
Dein.	Deinarkhos
Dem.	Demosthenes
Dion. Hal.	Dionysios of Halikarnassos
Eur. *El.*	Euripides *Elektra*
Hdt.	Herodotos
Hermog.	Hermogenes
Hes. *Theog.*	Hesiod *Theogony*
Hyp.	Hypereides
Isa.	Isaios
Isok.	Isokrates
Lyk.	Lykourgos
Lys.	Lysias
Men.	Menander
Dys.	*Dyskolos*
Epit.	*Epitrepontes*
Plato *Euthyd.*	Plato *Euthydemus*
Quint.	Quintilian
Rh. Al.	*Rhetorica ad Alexandrum*
Xen.	Xenophon
An.	*Anabasis*
Oik.	*Oikonomikos*

Modern Publications

D. Tel.	*Daily Telegraph*
IG	*Inscriptiones Graecae*
LGPN Attica	*A Lexicon of Greek Personal Names*, vol. 2, Attica, ed. M. J. Osborne and S. G. Byrne, Oxford, 1994.
OCT	Oxford Classical Texts
PA	*Prosopographia Attica*, ed. J. Kirchner, 2 vols., Berlin, 1901–1903

Modern Court Judgments

References to modern English court judgments follow the neutral citation system, in which a citation comprises the relevant year in [], followed by the name of the court in abbreviated form, and a unique number assigned by the court to each judgment. Thus judgments of the England & Wales Court of Appeal (Civil Division) issued in 2000 are numbered [2000] EWCA Civ 1, 2, 3, etc. Judgments of the England & Wales High Court (Chancery Division) are numbered [2000] EWHC 1, 2, 3, etc. (Ch).

General

fr. (pl. frr.)	fragment
Gk.	Greek
lit.	literally
ms. (pl. mss.)	manuscript
pl.	plur

GENERAL INTRODUCTION

Isaios and His Work

Biographical information about Isaios is sparse and unreliable. Given that he appears to have played no part in the political life of Athens, he was probably a metic (resident alien), although according to one source he was born in Athens. His career as a logographer (professional speechwriter) appears to have started in the early 380s and continued until the late 340s, so it is possible that he was born around 415–410 BC.[1] The corpus of his work that was known to later antiquity comprised a rhetorical handbook (*tekhnē*), which may have been a collection of commonplaces, and sixty-four forensic speeches, of which fifty were accepted as genuine. All the speeches that can now be identified were almost certainly forensic,[2] and a large majority were from private actions. Speeches concerning family matters, including inheritance, the epiklerate and guardianship, and other property disputes, predominate. Dionysios of Halikarnassos expresses the view that some speeches by Isaios were mistakenly attributed in his day to Lysias, or *vice versa*,[3] but the attribution of the speeches that have survived through the manuscript tradition has not been seriously questioned by modern scholars. Blass[4] lists fifty-six speeches which have either survived in full or as fragments transmitted by Dionysios, or are known by citations of their titles in the grammarians. The list below follows Blass's classification with some modification.

thirteen inheritance cases (*klērikoi*),[5] including those now known as Isa. 1–11;
three cases concerning *epiklēroi* or 'heiresses' (*epiklērikoi*);
two guardianship disputes (*epitropikoi*);

---

[1] For a fuller summary of the available biographical data, see, e.g., Edwards (2007), 1–2.

[2] Jebb (1876), 312–313, n. 3, notes that the speech recorded under the title 'Concerning what was said in Macedonia' περὶ τῶν ἐν Μακεδονίᾳ ῥηθέντων may have been an exception, but is more likely to have been concerned with a *parapresbeias graphē* (prosecution for a false or dishonest embassy), perhaps arising from the negotiations about Amphipolis in 358 BC.

[3] Dion. Hal., *De Isaeo*, 2.

[4] Blass (1892), 492–496.

[5] This class is defined by subject matter, not by legal procedure; it includes speeches from *dikai pseudomarturiōn* and other types of *dikai*, as well as *diadikasiai*.

eight disputes over land (listed by Blass as *diadikasiai*);
three actions for ejectment from property (*dikai exoulēs*), of which one is of doubtful attribution;
four cases of desertion of a patron by an ex-slave (*dikai apostasiou*), of which one is of doubtful attribution;
one contract case (*dikē enguēs*);
one 'preliminary oath' (*antōmosia*);
two appeals from the decision of a deme in cases of disputed citizenship (*epheseis*), one of which is the substantial fragment now known as Isa. 12;
four public speeches (*dēmosioi logoi*), of which one is of doubtful attribution; and
fifteen cases of uncertain class.

In addition to these, a papyrus fragment previously attributed to Lysias, apparently from a citizenship dispute, has now been tentatively ascribed to Isaios.[6]

Thus, for a man whose logographic career spanned some fifty years, it would appear that Isaios's output was not large, unless there was a substantial number of speeches unknown in later antiquity. Lysias, whose career was half as long, left a corpus of 425 speeches, of which 233 were considered genuine by Dionysios and Caecilius.[7] The difference can only partly be explained by the broader range of Lysias, who, unlike Isaios, wrote deliberative and epideictic as well as forensic speeches, and was also engaged in at least one court case on his own account. Demosthenes, whose main career was in politics, was less prolific as a logographer: sixty-five speeches were attributed to him, and considered genuine, in later antiquity.[8] In the extant Demosthenic corpus there are only forty-one forensic speeches, including sixteen of doubtful authenticity, as well as several delivered by Demosthenes himself as prosecutor. Despite this relatively small output, Demosthenes was said to have grown rich as a logographer before achieving fame in the political arena;[9] but in the absence of any firmer information about the fees charged by logographers, it seems unlikely that Isaios could have supported himself exclusively from his forensic activity, and apart from the *tekhnē* and the tradition that Demosthenes was his pupil, there is no direct evidence that he worked as a teacher of rhetoric. If he was a metic, he could not have owned land in Attica, but it is possible that he had an income from trade.

---

6 Carey (2005).
7 Edwards (1994), 21.
8 Edwards (1994), 42.
9 Dein. 1.111.

The Athenian Inheritance System

Any society in which private property is recognized needs rules for its transmission after the death of the person last in possession,[10] to prevent forcible seizure and provide a framework for the resolution of disputes. In many ancient cultures, including classical Athens, the idea of succession and inheritance was also strongly associated with a desire to continue the religious observances associated with the household and to perpetuate the existence of the family itself.[11] It is possible, in fact, that laws permitting the adoption of a son as universal heir predated the testamentary disposition of property.

While it is helpful to place Isaios's speeches in their historical context, a complete history of Athenian inheritance law would be beyond the scope of this commentary. In the absence of documentary evidence for the period before Solon, and between the sixth and fourth centuries, any conclusions must, in any event, be conjectural. Much of the published work, especially by continental European scholars, needs to be treated with caution because it starts from a perspective based on Roman law which may not be appropriate in the Athenian context. So, except where the contrary is indicated, all references are to Athenian law as it stood in the fourth century BC.

Substantive Law

After the death of an Athenian citizen, his inheritance was transmitted in one of three ways: ideally by lineal descent through the male bloodline, with the female line acting as substitute in default of male heirs; or in accordance with his stated wishes, if he left no lineal descendants but had made a will; or to his next of kin if he had neither left descendants nor made a will.

The principle of succession by lineal descent, which is probably a universal feature of the various inheritance systems operating at different

[10] It is questionable whether the concept of 'ownership', as distinct from 'possession', was recognized in Athenian law. For a summary of the scholarly debate, see Todd (1993), 227–234.

[11] Cf. Harrison (1968), 123: "... we must constantly be on our guard against the anachronism of regarding succession in classical Athens as a purely economic matter.... It may well be that Athenian ideas were unconsciously moving in that direction, but there is ample evidence to show that a man's heir was looked upon as owing to him a primary duty to preserve the *sacra* of the house, and that this aspect of succeeding to a dead man was seldom far from the minds of those who had to determine disputes as to succession."

times and in different cultures,[12] was well established in Athens by the time of Solon, when legitimate sons had an unquestioned right to inherit their paternal estate (in equal shares, if there was more than one such son). This may not have been the subject of an explicit enactment, since the extant laws only prescribe what should happen in cases where there were no surviving descendants through a male line. An Athenian with no legitimate sons could choose his own heir by adopting a son, either *inter vivos* (i.e. during the adoptive father's lifetime) or by will. A law attributed to Solon permitted those leaving no legitimate sons to dispose freely of their estates, but its precise scope and effect are unclear.[13] In the surviving fourth century forensic speeches it is cited in support of testamentary adoption as well as adoption *inter vivos*, but it may originally have applied only to the latter.[14] There was a third possibility, known by modern scholars as 'posthumous adoption', which appears to have been a matter of custom rather than law; this did not necessarily involve the expressed wishes of the deceased, but was negotiated between the surviving family members.[15]

When the only surviving descendants of the deceased were daughters and their issue, the position was less straightforward. A girl or woman who was left without a father or brothers (or brothers' descendants) was subject to the rules of the epiklerate, which appears to have been a peculiarly Greek (though not exclusively Athenian) institution. Its principal feature was that a female did not inherit her father's property in her own right, but acted as a conduit through which it was transmitted to her sons, so it would be misleading to translate the word *epiklēros* as 'heiress'. The sons of a woman who had predeceased her father were also entitled to the estate of their maternal grandfather, but it is not clear from the sources whether they enjoyed the same procedural protection as did sons of sons.

---

[12] Cf. 'Inheritance', in *Encyclopaedia Britannica* 2007. Retrieved from Encyclopaedia Britannica Online, 27 Sept. 2007.

[13] The law is cited in full at [Dem.] 46.14: Ὅσοι μὴ ἐπεποίηντο, ὥστε μήτε ἀπειπεῖν μήτ' ἐπιδικάσασθαι, ὅτε Σόλων εἰσήει τὴν ἀρχήν, τὰ ἑαυτοῦ διαθέσθαι εἶναι, ὅπως ἂν ἐθέλῃ, ἂν μὴ παῖδες ὦσι γνήσιοι ἄρρενες, ἂν μὴ μανιῶν ἢ γήρως ἢ φαρμάκων ἢ νόσου ἕνεκα, ἢ γυναικὶ πειθόμενος, ὑπὸ τούτων του παρανοῶν, ἢ ὑπ' ἀνάγκης ἢ ὑπὸ δεσμοῦ καταληφθεῖς. "Anyone who had not been adopted, so that he could neither renounce nor claim [an inheritance], when Solon took office, may dispose of his property as he wishes, provided he has no legitimate sons and is not mentally incapable through madness, old age, drugs or illness, or under the influence of a woman or acting under compulsion or deprived of his liberty." Cf., e.g., Isa. 2.13; 3.68; 6.9; and, for discussion, see Harrison (1968), 150.

[14] As argued by Gernet (1930), 125.

[15] For a more detailed discussion of posthumous adoption, see pp. 203–205.

The fact that inheritance through a female line is an issue in so many of the surviving speeches may reflect a lack of clarity in the law, or perhaps simply the fact that a female citizen's status was more vulnerable to attack than a man's.[16]

When an Athenian died leaving no legitimate descendants or testamentary heir, his estate passed to the members of his kinship group (*ankhisteia*) in the order prescribed by the law. Males were preferred to females at every degree of kinship, and there was a strong patrilineal bias, with matrilineal kinsmen, including half-brothers by the same mother, admitted only in the absence of any patrilineal kin up to second cousins.[17] The origin of this law, which is discussed in Isa. 11 and cited at [Dem.] 43.51, is uncertain. It may have predated the Solonian law on freedom of disposition, but it is conceivable, if ultimately unprovable, that at some stage during the archaic period the estate of a man who died without issue simply reverted to the collective ownership of his *genos*, or was divided among his collateral kinsmen with no fixed order of priority.[18]

Procedure

All claimants, apart from natural legitimate sons and sons adopted *inter vivos*, were required to apply to a court for authority to take possession of the property (*epidikasia*). This applied to sons adopted by will and to collateral kinsmen claiming under the law of intestate succession, and perhaps also to a daughter's sons if the daughter had not been *epiklēros*. Legitimate sons (including those adopted *inter vivos*) and their issue had the right of direct entry onto the estate (*embateusis*) without the authority of the court. A legitimate son enjoyed the protection afforded by the *dikē exoulēs* (prosecution for ejectment from the property) in cases of violation. He could also block a rival's claim for *epidikasia* by issuing a formal statement (*diamarturia*) to the effect that the estate was not

---

[16] See p. 132.

[17] Or possibly first cousins once removed, according to how one interprets the phrase "up to the children of cousins" (μέχρι ἀνεψιῶν παίδων, Isa. 11.2 and [Dem.] 43.51. For a summary of the scholarly debate, see Thompson (1976), 4–7.

[18] Ar. *Birds*, 1665–1666, attributes to Solon a law providing that when a man dies without legitimate issue, his property is shared by his next of kin. Hes. *Theog.* 603–607 deplores the situation of the man who dies childless so that his property goes to his collateral relations. This clearly refers to a context where there was no power of testamentary disposition, but the passage does not reveal whether there was a fixed order of intestate succession. (For the difficulty of using archaic verse texts as a basis for conjecture about early Athenian law, see Todd (1993), 33–35.)

subject to adjudication, but this would give rise to adversarial litigation if the rival retaliated by initiating a prosecution for false testimony (*dikē pseudomarturiōn*). It appears that uncontested claims were dealt with summarily and expeditiously, but there are differing scholarly views as to whether *epidikasia* was a purely administrative procedure under the control of the presiding court official (*arkhōn*) or whether a judicial decision was required.[19]

When a claim for *epidikasia* was contested, the procedure used was known as *diadikasia*. Six of Isaios's eleven extant inheritance speeches (1, 4, 7, 8, 9 and 10) are from *diadikasiai*.[20] There could be any number of claimants in such a case, although nearly all those of which we have any knowledge involved only two parties.[21] All parties were, in principle, on an equal footing, since the procedure was not adversarial; there was no inherent allegation of wrong, and no penalty for the loser(s) apart from the loss of a deposit.[22] Recent scholarly work on litigation strategies in classical Athens[23] has focused primarily on the adversarial procedures of *dikai* (private cases) and *graphai* (public cases). One of the aims of this commentary is to explore both the similarities and the differences between the strategies deployed by claimants in *diadikasiai* and those engaged in formally adversarial proceedings.

As one would expect, it was the prosecutor who made the first speech in a *dikē* or *graphē*,[24] but the principle underlying the order of presentation in a *diadikasia* is unclear. In Isaios's *diadikasia* speeches there are usually linguistic clues as to whether his client spoke first or second. In particular, a first speaker may use the future tense to anticipate his opponent's argument (for example, at 9.10). The speaker of Isa. 8 makes it clear that his opponents have already spoken when he promises to begin his account at the same point as they did (8.6). There is, however, no direct evidence for the method by which the order of speakers was determined.

---

19 Karabélias (1992), 84–85, summarizes the evidence and arguments on both sides.

20 Isa. 2, 3 and 6 are from *dikai pseudomarturiōn* arising when a witness has been prosecuted for giving false testimony in a *diamarturia*. Both Isa. 5 and Isa. 11 are from subsidiary proceedings in long-running inheritance disputes.

21 [Dem.] 43.8–10 describes a *diadikasia* in which there were five claimants, and there appear to have been at least four in the case mentioned at [Dem.] 48.30, the details of which are more obscure.

22 See p. 101, n. 36.

23 See, e.g., Johnstone (1999), Rubinstein (2004), and Rubinstein (2005).

24 In modern English procedure, a criminal trial is invariably opened by the prosecution, and a civil trial normally by the claimant (formerly known as 'plaintiff'). This follows the principle that 'whoever asserts a wrong must prove it' (Du Cann (1993), 73).

One possibility is that the parties spoke in the order in which they had submitted their claims. The speakers of Isa. 1, 9 and 10, each of whom was challenging a will, all spoke before their opponents,[25] but the evidence of only three speeches is not enough to infer a general rule. An alternative possibility is that the parties were allocated their turn by lot. If so, this was presumably done before the day of the trial so that speakers (or their advisers) had sufficient time to prepare an appropriate speech. The limited evidence from the speeches supports this supposition: although the formula at Isa. 8.6 might have been inserted at the last minute, since there is nothing in the rest of the speech that would have made it unsuitable to be delivered first, Isa. 10 relies extensively on anticipation of the opponent's argument (*prokatalēpsis*), and could not have been used as the second speech without substantial rewriting.[26] The time allowed for each speaker appears to have been changed at some time in the course of the fourth century. [Dem.] 43.8 mentions an allocation of one amphora (12 *khoes*) for the main speech and three *khoes* for the second speech. By the time of the *Ath. Pol.* the allocation was 6 *khoes*, and there was no second speech.[27]

Despite the supposedly non-adversarial nature of the *diadikasia* it must have been difficult, if not impossible, for an Athenian litigant to sustain his own claim to an estate without undermining, or even directly attacking, his opponent's arguments. It is hardly surprising, then, to find the competing parties in Isaios's cases engaged in an adversarial contest in which their respective rôles, according to the circumstances of each case, quite closely resemble those of prosecutor and defendant in other litigation. This polarization may have been encouraged by the deep-seated and protracted nature of many of the disputes, as well as by the relative inflexibility of inheritance law. It may also account for the apparent rarity of 'multi-party' *diadikasiai*, since a potential claimant whose case was weak would have come under strong pressure to withdraw before the dispute reached court.[28]

---

[25] As noted by Blass (1892), 529, 561 and 564.

[26] See commentary on 10.8–17.

[27] *Ath. Pol.* 67.2, with Rhodes's commentary.

[28] Isa. 4.7–10 names five potential claimants to the estate of Nikostratos, in addition to the two parties who eventually contested the estate in court. Cohen (1995), 169 appears to see this as an indication that the Athenian procedure for claiming an inheritance was effectively a lottery in which anyone had a chance of success. In reality, the fact that the number of claimants was eventually narrowed down to two suggests that the system could be very effective at filtering out the more hopeless claims.

The dynamics of a *diadikasia* were, nevertheless, different from those of an adversarial *dikē* or *graphē*, where one party (the prosecutor) was seeking redress for a wrong allegedly done by the other (the defendant). In formally adversarial litigation it was the prosecutor who made the decision to litigate, giving the defendant no choice but to defend himself in court if he was unable, or unwilling, to achieve a negotiated settlement. Thus it was the prosecutor who had the upper hand in any pre-trial negotiations, because he had the option of withdrawing at any stage. But no-one was obliged to litigate in consequence of a wrong that had been done (or perceived to have been done); it was open to a potential prosecutor, within limits, to come to a private agreement with the wrongdoer, or simply to overlook the wrong.[29]

In an inheritance claim the balance of power did not lie so clearly with one or other of the parties. When the deceased left no direct descendants, litigation was in one sense unavoidable, because no-one could legally take possession of the estate without first going to court.[30] But no-one was obliged to contest a claim that had already been made, and if a claim did became contested it was open to any of the parties, not just the first claimant, to withdraw. So, albeit at the price of losing the inheritance, no-one involved in a *diadikasia* was actually forced to defend his position like the defendant in an adversarial trial. This is not always apparent, however, from the rhetorical strategies of the litigants; the speaker of Isa. 8, for example, presents himself as having been forced to defend his legitimacy, when in fact it was he who challenged his opponent's claim to Kiron's estate.

Despite any resemblances, there are some features that distinguish the rhetorical strategies employed by speakers in *diadikasiai* from those used in *dikai* and *graphai*. There is, in particular, a tendency for Isaios's clients in *diadikasiai* to avoid direct personal attacks against their opponents.[31] In

[29] In this respect the Athenian model is much closer to modern civil litigation, where the conduct of the proceedings is largely in the hands of the parties, than to criminal procedure where control is largely taken away from the parties by agencies of the state.

[30] The position is similar under modern English law, where, unless an estate is very small and does not include land, the heirs or legatees of a deceased person cannot take over his property until the court has made a 'grant of representation' (either probate of a will or letters of administration for the estate of an intestate). In the vast majority of cases application for such a grant is a purely administrative procedure, with no judicial involvement and no requirement to attend court if the applicant is legally represented.

[31] Rubinstein (2005), 134–135, points to the compulsory nature of litigation to claim an estate, suggesting that "the decision to litigate in inheritance cases did not presuppose a deep-seated personal conflict between the opposing claimants". She finds three main

two of the speeches the speaker's hostility is directed against a third party (Diokles in Isa. 8 and Hierokles in Isa. 9) while the legal opponent remains a shadowy figure. In other speeches the opponents are sometimes criticized for their conduct of the litigation or their behaviour towards the deceased, but where there is a direct attack on an opponent's character it may, as at 7.38 and 10.25, take the form of a 'glancing blow' rather than a sustained diatribe. In a society where litigation against kin was evidently viewed with distaste, it is likely that this restraint has more to do with the relationships between the parties to a *diadikasia* than with the nature of the procedure itself.[32] The speaker of Isa. 1 may or may not be sincere when he talks of his embarrassment at finding himself opposing his kinsmen in court (1.6), but he is certainly taking a stance that would have helped him secure the good will of his audience, the *dikastai*. Isa. 4.28–29 shows, on the other hand, that more extended character assassination (*diabolē*) was not completely unacceptable in a *diadikasia*. This speech was delivered by a *sunēgoros* (supporting speaker) who may not have been related to the claimants for whom he appears; but the more significant point is that their opponent, the object of the *diabolē*, was not a kinsman of the deceased Nikostratos but a complete stranger to the family who claimed to have been adopted by will.

The characteristically more restrained tone of a *diadikasia* is illustrated by the fact that Isaios's clients in these cases do not engage in direct confrontation with their opponents (the rhetorical device known as apostrophe), whereas Isaios does apostrophize individuals in four of his five inheritance speeches from ancillary proceedings.[33] In Isa. 3, the prosecution speech from a *dikē pseudomarturiōn*, the speaker directs a string of hostile questions, first, to his opponent Nikodemos, then to the uncles of Pyrrhos, who have testified on Nikodemos's behalf (3.40, 69, 70, 71). The speaker of Isa. 6, also the prosecutor in a *dikē pseudomarturiōn*, apostrophizes his

---

distinctions. In summary: speakers in *diadikasiai* never explicitly incite the judges to anger or hatred at the behaviour of their opponents; they never represent the judges' decision in terms of a penalty or punishment inflicted on their opponents; and they never claim that the outcome of an inheritance dispute could influence the future behaviour of other members of the community.

32 Nowadays people involved in inheritance disputes sometimes express their distaste for the exposure of private family matters in public. For instance a friend of the Birley family, members of which were contemplating litigation about the estate of the late Mark Birley, was reported as saying: "Mark would be spinning in his grave at the thought this might go to court. It would be the ultimate airing of dirty linen in public so we are all hoping they can reach a settlement" (*D. Tel.* 10 November 2007).

33 The references in this paragraph are cited by Denommé (1974b), 137–138.

opponent, Androkles, twice (6.25, 53).[34] Isa. 5 concludes with a savage piece of *diabolē* against Dikaiogenes III (the speaker's opponent in the substantive dispute over the estate of Dikaiogenes II, though not formally a party to the present action), including a series of ironic questions addressed to him by name (5.43, 45, 46, 47). Theopompos, the speaker of Isa. 11 and the defendant in the case, avoids the use of his opponent's name but twice addresses him in the second person singular (11.4, 5). It would appear, then, that the need for restraint was perceived as less pressing in these explicitly adversarial cases, where in any event the relationship between the speaker and his opponent was not always close. It also seems that Isaios was not following rigid rules, but was flexible enough to adapt his rhetorical strategy to the circumstances of the individual case. Thus the only example of apostrophe to an individual in one of his *diadikasia* speeches is at 9.23, where the person addressed is Hierokles, the maternal uncle of the speaker as well as of the deceased Astyphilos but not a party to the proceedings.

The Prevalence of Inheritance Disputes in Classical Athens

It has sometimes been suggested that inadequacies in the Athenian legal system led to a 'proliferation of forged wills' or to an unseemly 'pursuit of inheritances'.[35] In a society as reputedly litigious as classical Athens, and where remarriage, promoting complex kinship patterns, was common, it would not be surprising if wills were frequently challenged, especially when a substantial estate was in issue.[36] A procedural factor which

---

[34] Todd (2007), 470, commenting on Lys. 6.49, describes the use of the vocative to address an opponent as "a characteristic of prosecution speeches and often a sign that the speaker wishes to be confrontational".

[35] Caillemer (1879), 5, takes Isa. 4.7–9 at face value, concluding that "Le mal était si grand que... l'orateur Isée proposait de condamner tout individu, qui succombait dans une pétition d'hérédité, à payer... une somme égale à la valeur de la succession injustement réclamée" ("The evil was so great that... the orator Isaios suggested that the losing party to an inheritance claim should be fined a sum equal to the value of the falsely claimed estate."). Karabélias (1992), 103, refers to "la prolifération de faux testaments et les nombreuses contestations du contenu des actes de dernière volonté" ("the proliferation of forged wills and the numerous disputes about their contents' ", which he attributes to three features of the Athenian system: the reliance on witnesses for the validation of wills; the major rôle of the *dikastai* in validating wills; and the absence of judicial sanctions for forgery. He concludes (p. 106) that "la chasse aux héritages par le moyen de faux testaments est génératrice d'un malaise visible dans la Société d'Athènes" ("the pursuit of inheritances by means of forged wills generates a visible unease in Athenian society").

[36] Cf. *D. Tel.* 3 January 2008, 'Sharp rise in contested wills': "One law firm based in north-west England said that its caseload had tripled in the past three years, as people

may have encouraged litigation is the generous time limit for starting or reopening an inheritance claim (throughout the lifetime of the last heir or within five years of his death, Isa. 3.58). It is likely, too, that there was less scope for informal settlement than in the types of dispute where litigation was not compulsory. On the other hand, despite the apparent lack of a prosecution for forgery of wills,[37] both the risk of losing the deposit and the possibility of prosecution for *pseudomarturia*, which, on a third conviction, led to *atimia* (loss of civic rights), must have deterred at least the most hopeless and frivolous claims. Moreover, since freedom of testamentary disposition was significantly restricted in Athens because of the privilege accorded to legitimate sons, the overall number of wills would have been limited. And we cannot know how many beneficiaries of Athenian wills, or sons adopted *inter vivos*, were already the adopter's next of kin (i.e. the person(s) who would have inherited in any event if he had died intestate), precisely because such cases are the least likely to have been contested. In some cases, also, other family members would have benefited rather than suffered as the result of an adoption, as when a son inherited the whole of his natural father's estate after his brother had been adopted into a different family.[38]

We do not have enough evidence to support any meaningful conclusions about the number of Athenian inheritance cases. The fourteen extant speeches from such cases,[39] of which eleven are by Isaios and the remaining three among those doubtfully attributed to Demosthenes, form about thirteen percent of some 105[40] forensic speeches surviving from the work of all the Attic orators. Internal evidence from the work of the orators suggests a total of thirty-three Athenians (listed in the Appendix, pp. 247–252) whose estates became the subject of forensic disputes. Some of these cases involved more than one trial; the total number of attested hearings is forty-three, rising to forty-seven with the inclusion of four other

---

become more litigious, inheritances swell in size and families become more complex because of remarriage."

37 Cf. [Dem] 43.4, where the speaker says that Glaukos, Glaukon and Theopompos, having produced a spurious will in court, not only lost their case but left the court in disgrace. This is cited by Karabélias (1992), 107 as an indication that there was no prosecution for forgery or altering the contents of a will.

38 Cf. Rubinstein (1993), 79–80.

39 This classification is based on the subject matter of the dispute—an inheritance—not on the legal procedure adopted, which may be either a *diadikasia*, a *dikē pseudomarturiōn* following a *diamarturia* in which it was claimed that the estate was not adjudicable, or some other form of *dikē* ancillary to the original claim.

40 Cf. the catalogue of speeches (excluding fragments) in Edwards (1994), 74–79.

'lost' speeches in which the identity of the deceased is unknown. By way of comparison, there appear to be some sixteen attested cases of homicide or violence, and fourteen actions for damages (*dikai blabēs*).[41] We have no means of knowing whether the surviving sample is representative of the actual distribution of lawsuits, but these figures may, nevertheless, imply that the incidence of disputed inheritance claims among the business of the Athenian courts was relatively high.[42]

Kinship Patterns in Athenian Inheritance Disputes

With the exception of Isa. 4, all of Isaios's eleven surviving inheritance speeches derive from disputes between rival claimants within the deceased's own family. In two cases (Isa. 5 and 11) we know that there had been a history of previous litigation; but some of the other speeches also reflect long-lasting family feuds, involving deep-seated hostility between different branches of a family which originated before the present claimant's lifetime (Isa.7, 9 and 10) or rivalry between the families of the deceased by different marriages (Isa. 8).

The privileged position of legitimate sons and their issue, combined with the principle of partible inheritance, obviously created the potential for fraternal conflict over inheritance.[43] Examples of such conflict, though not numerous, occur in Greek literature as early as Hesiod's *Works and Days*. The speaker of Isa. 9 refers to a fight between two brothers over their paternal estate as the source of a long-running family feud. Rivalry between half-brothers with the same father appears to have been the

---

41 Listed by Osborne (1985b), 55–58. The sixteen cases of homicide or violence comprise two *graphai hubreōs*, four *dikai aikeias*, seven *dikai phonou* and three *dikai traumatos ek pronoias*. These figures are not, however, directly comparable with those given for inheritance disputes, because Osborne's catalogue of *dikai* and *graphai*, while it includes fragments and cases known only from references in extant speeches, excludes cases attested only by speech titles "because of the unreliability of titular classifications".

42 Litigation over contested wills (contentious probate) in England and Wales is very rare. In 2008, 267,500 grants of representation (of which 215,000 involved wills) were made by the Family Division of the High Court, while only 106 contentious probate claims were issued in the Chancery Division in London (*Judicial and Court Statistics 2008*; London, 2009, Cm7697). These cases would have included claims made under family provision legislation, as well as challenges on the grounds that the testator lacked testamentary intention or capacity, or that there was a failure to comply with the proper formalities. (Cf. Sawyer (1998), 360.) No separate figures are recorded for contentious probate claims in the eight provincial High Court centres with Chancery jurisdiction. If there were any such claims, the number is likely to have been minimal.

43 Cf. Cox (1988), 391: "The Athenian sources ... confirm the tendencies toward fraternal conflict found in partible systems elsewhere in Europe at later times."

cause of litigation in two of the cases known to us from the corpus of forensic speeches: the attack in Isa. 6 on the legitimacy of Euktemon's sons from his supposed second marriage, and the dispute in Dem. 39 and [Dem.] 40 between two sons of Mantias by different wives, one of whom disputes the other's legitimacy. (In the latter case, however, the inheritance itself was not in dispute since Mantitheos had agreed to share Mantias's estate with his two half-brothers after Mantias acknowledged them.[44]) In Isaios's speeches there are stronger indications that the rigidly prescriptive order of intestate succession, with its preference for those related to the deceased on his father's side, could in some circumstances lead to a perception that a strict application of the law would be unfair. For example, a half-brother by the same mother who had enjoyed a close relationship with the deceased might feel aggrieved at being outranked by a patrilineal cousin who (as he claims) was not even on speaking terms with the deceased (Isa. 9). The son of a half-sister by the same mother, who claimed to have been adopted by his half-uncle, might come under attack from the adoptive father's patrilineal cousins (Isa. 7). A daughter's son could argue that his mother's claim to her paternal estate had been overlooked in favour of her father's male kin (Isa. 10).

Wills

It is perhaps not surprising that disputed wills or adoptions *inter vivos*, where the succession was determined not by legal prescription but by the choice of the deceased himself, feature in all but one of Isaios's inheritance speeches. (The exception is Isa. 8.) A testator may, for various reasons, make his will in favour of his next of kin,[45] but the essence of testamentary freedom is that it enables the testator to disrupt the order of intestate succession by leaving his estate to a more distant relation, or even to someone who was not a member of his family at all. In some cases, inevitably, this will lead to disappointed expectations, and sometimes to disputes that need to be resolved by litigation.

Some modern commentators have suggested that Athenian juries were, as a matter of principle, prejudiced against wills and in favour of the next

[44] Dem. 39.6.

[45] In classical Athens this option would have been particularly attractive to someone who wanted not just to dispose of his property but also to ensure the continuation of his *oikos* by appointing an heir to take his place in carrying out the family cults. Cf. Rubinstein (1993), 78.

of kin,[46] or even that an Athenian will was not a legally binding document.[47] These views derive, at least in part, from Philokleon's account of his experience as a juror in Aristoph. *Wasps*:

> And if a dying father bequeaths his heiress daughter to someone we tell that last will and testament to go soak its head, and the same to the clasp sitting so pretty over its seals, and we award that girl to whoever talks us into it.[48]

But it would be a mistake to take this passage too literally; it is true that *Wasps* replicates many features of the Athenian legal system, but, just like any modern political satire, it depends for its comic effect on some wild exaggerations and distortions.

Some of the argumentation in Isa. 1 and 4 has similarly been taken to support the notion of an Athenian prejudice against wills, but that interpretation is not supported by a careful reading of the text. When the speaker of Isa. 1 refers to previous decisions of the *dikastai* (1.38), he is not claiming that they have always voted in favour of the next of kin, but *either* the next of kin *or* those who were closest in affection to the deceased (whom the deceased has therefore singled out as his heirs in preference to the next of kin). It is certainly possible, although neither speaker makes such a claim, that in the majority of cases where a will was contested, the court decided in favour of the intestate heirs. If so, the reasons are more likely to have been concerned with the difficulty of proving the authenticity of a specific will than with a general prejudice against testamentary disposition in favour of kinship. Given the Athenians' suspicion of written documents, it would have been easier to cast doubt into the minds of the *dikastai* about

[46] See, especially, Wyse, 177: "The judges took the greatest liberties with testaments, and did not hesitate to substitute their own sympathies and preferences in place of the intentions of the deceased." Harrison (1968), 153, refers to a "general prejudice against wills". Hunter (1993), 105, thinks that "a deeply ingrained negative attitude to adoption encouraged Athenians to challenge a deceased relative's choice of a son". On the other hand, Karabélias (1992), 106 takes a more nuanced view of the judges 'suspicion' of wills, and the traditional approach is directly challenged by Thompson (1981), 14: the argumentation in Isa. 1 and 4 "does not rely on a prejudice which the jurors already had; instead, it seeks to inspire one in them. And, of course, it does not suggest that wills are a bad thing in themselves, merely that it is too easy to forge them."

[47] Wohl (2010), 259, describes the Athenian will as "a tenuous document, without the clear legal force it has today".

[48] κἂν ἀποθνῄσκων ὁ πατήρ τῳ δῷ καταλείπων παῖδ' ἐπίκληρον | κλάειν ἡμεῖς μακρὰ τὴν κεφαλὴν εἰπόντες τῇ διαθήκῃ | καὶ τῇ κόγχῃ τῇ πάνυ σεμνῶς τοῖς σημείοισιν ἐποίσῃ | ἔδομεν ταύτην ὅστις ἂν ἡμᾶς ἀντιβολήσας ἀναπείσῃ. | καὶ ταῦτ' ἀνυπεύθυνοι δρῶμεν·τῶν δ' ἄλλων οὐδεμί' αρχή (Aristoph. *Wasps* 583–587, Loeb trans.) This passage is taken literally by Wyse, 222–3. Lanni (2006), 42, describes it more sensitively as a "recognizable though exaggerated account of the ploys litigants use to win over the jury".

the authenticity of a particular will than to prove beyond doubt that it was genuine.[49] It is noteworthy that the speakers of both Isa. 9 and 10, each of whom contests the validity of a particular will, are careful to express their respect for the Solonian law on freedom of testamentary disposition.[50]

When an Athenian court was called on to adjudicate in the case of a disputed will, the key issue, as it is for the courts today, was whether the document produced by the claimant genuinely represented the wishes of the testator. The specific questions for consideration were also essentially the same as in the modern context. Did the testator really make the will, and did he know and fully understand its contents? Was he in his right mind? Was he acting under coercion or in the heat of the moment? The underlying problem, in modern as well as ancient legal systems, is how to determine whether the disputed document genuinely represents the wishes of someone who, in the nature of things, is not available to present his views in person to the court.[51]

Under modern English law a valid will must comply with certain legal formalities.[52] It must, in particular, be signed by the testator in the presence of at least two independent witnesses, who must themselves sign the document in the presence of the testator and of one another. Stricter formalities apply in some of the civil law jurisdictions in continental Europe, where a will must be notarized in order to be valid. The aim is to provide a safeguard against forgery, undue influence, or dispositions made in the heat of the moment; but the disadvantage is that a will that genuinely represents the wishes of the testator may be found to be invalid if it fails

---

49 [Arist.] *Pr.* 29.3, which Wyse adduces in support of the supposed bias of the *dikastai* in favour of kinship, suggests no more than that they were suspicious of wills because of the numerous forgeries produced in court: "Why do they vote in some *dikastēria* for kinsmen rather than wills? Is it because kinship cannot be invented, but is clearly evident, whereas many wills have been exposed as false?" The verbal echoes of Isa. 1.41 may suggest that this line of reasoning had become commonplace in inheritance speeches.

50 See on κωλῦσαι…, 9.11 and οἶμαι…, 10.22.

51 "Probate proceedings peculiarly pose problems for the court because the protagonist, the testator, is dead and those who wish to challenge the will are often not able to give evidence of the circumstances of the will." *Fuller v Strum* [2001] EWCA Civ 1879 (7 December 2001). Cf. Isa. 4.12: περὶ δὲ τῶν διαθηκων πῶς ἄν τις γνοίη τοὺς μὴ τἀληθῆ λέγοντας, εἰ μὴ πάνυ μεγάλα τὰ διαφεροντα εἴη, αὐτοῦ μὲν καθ᾽οὗ μαρτυροῦσι τεθνεῶτος, τῶν δὲ συγγενῶν μηδὲν τῶν πεπραγμένων εἰδότων, τοῦ δὲ ἐλέγχου μηδαμῶς ἀκριβοῦς γιγνομένου; "But concerning wills, how can one know which party is not telling the truth, unless there are major discrepancies, since the man against whom they are testifying is dead, the relatives know nothing about what happened, and there is no obvious way of refuting their evidence?"

52 §9 Wills Act 1837, as amended; discussed by Sawyer (1998), 77–108.

to comply with the formalities. Modern jurisdictions vary as to the extent of judicial discretion they allow to validate a will that does not comply with all the legal requirements. Some flexibility may be seen to prevent what would otherwise be seen as an unfair result; but, on the other hand, too wide a discretion may lead to uncertainty as to how the law applies to a particular situation. The inevitable lack of legal formalities in classical Athens, where there were no characteristic signatures or cursive handwriting, contributed, among other factors, to a degree of flexibility that has been viewed by some modern critics as undesirable or even inimical to justice. It is arguable, however, that this flexibility was not merely a defining characteristic, but actually a strength, of the Athenian legal system, as compared with the more narrowly legalistic approach favoured in many modern jurisdictions.

In modern litigation, where cases can be won or lost on legal technicalities, strict application of legal rules sometimes conflicts with public perceptions of the 'justice' or 'morality' of a particular case. The potential for conflict between 'legal' and 'moral' values in inheritance claims is implicitly recognized in a judgment of the English Court of Appeal which makes it clear that a court cannot uphold or refuse a challenge to a will on moral rather than legal grounds.[53] Formally, the Athenian *dikastai*, who swore to decide cases in accordance with the law, had no more discretion than a modern court to decide a case on the basis of their own moral judgment, but in the nature of the system they did have greater flexibility to interpret and apply the law. In Isa. 1, for example, the speaker attempts to overturn Kleonymos's will on the grounds that Kleonymos had intended to revoke it but died before he could put his wishes into effect. Nowadays, unless there were exceptional circumstances, an attempt to overturn a valid will on this basis would be unlikely to succeed;[54] but there is no reason to suppose that an Athenian court could not legitimately allow such

[53] "The question is not whether the court approves of the circumstances in which the document was executed or of its contents. The question is whether the court is satisfied that the contents do truly represent the testator's testamentary intentions. That is not, of course, to suggest that the circumstances of execution or the contents may not, in the particular case, be of the greatest materiality in reaching a conclusion whether or not the testator did know and approve of the contents of the document—and did intend that they should have testamentary effect. But their importance is evidential. There is no over-riding requirement of morality." *Fuller and Strum* [2001] EWCA Civ 1879, 65.

[54] It is sometimes possible to circumvent the normal requirements under modern English law, e.g. through the equitable doctrine of proprietary estoppel. In one such case, *Thorner v Curtis & Ors* [2007] EWHC 2422 (Ch), David Thorner successfully challenged the intestate heirs of his cousin Peter Thorner on the basis that he had been encouraged

a claim, provided the claimant had convincing evidence of the testator's change of mind. (It is the absence of such evidence, rather than the basis of his claim, that makes the speaker's case in Isa. 1 appear weak.) In a case such as this the exercise of judicial discretion would not have required the *dikastai* to ignore the law, or form their decisions in accordance with a competing code of 'moral' or 'extra-legal' values, but rather to apply the general principles of the law in order to reach a just result in a particular set of circumstances.

Evidence and Argumentation[55]

It is clear from the speeches that an Athenian litigant could not successfully contest a claim by someone acknowledged to be the legitimate or testamentary heir, or the next of kin of the deceased, on the basis that he was more deserving than his opponent, or had been on better terms with the deceased.[56] Whatever the true nature and causes of the dispute between the parties, once it became the subject of litigation the case always had to be presented from a 'legal perspective',[57] taking the form of an attack on a rival claimant's legitimacy (Isa. 8), a challenge to the validity of a will or an adoption (Isa. 7, 9 and 10), or an allegation that an opponent had lost his place in the order of intestate succession in consequence of an adoption into a different *oikos* (Isa. 9).

In the absence of such modern resources as archival records, and scientific techniques of document analysis or blood testing, Athenian courts and litigants relied on the same means of persuasion (*pisteis*) in inheritance cases as in other areas of litigation: testimony, laws, arguments from probability, and (in appropriate cases) character. Establishing a claim to an inheritance typically involved genealogical and other information about the claimant's relationship to the deceased, with testimony on relevant factual matters such as the introduction of an adopted son to the phratry or deme of the deceased. In addition, litigants frequently deployed evidence of hostile or friendly relations within the family, observance of

---

to expect that Peter would make a will in his favour, and had acted 'to his considerable detriment' in reliance on that expectation over 15 years.

55 This topic is developed more fully in Griffith-Williams (2012).

56 Cf. Carey (1994), 182: "It is … important to note that we do not find speakers in court admitting that their case is weak and asking for a verdict in their favour on the basis of factors outside the case." A similar point is made by Tangri (2004), 62.

57 Johnstone (1999), 47. Johnstone's chapter on 'Law and narrative' (46–69) focuses on explicitly adversarial litigation (*dikai* and *graphai*), but much of his discussion is relevant also to inheritance claims (*diadikasiai*).

burial rites and other religious customs, and the character of the rival claimants.[58] Such evidence has been characterized by some modern commentators as 'non-legal', 'extra-legal' or 'irrelevant'. with the implication that the speaker was seeking to find favour with the *dikastai* on moral rather than legal grounds, or trying to disguise a weak legal case by milking the audience's sympathy.[59]

According to the 'social competition' model of Athenian litigation, 'non-legal' evidence was inevitably determinative in inheritance cases because 'structural factors' in the Athenian system (including the absence of professional lawyers and judges, the individual basis of decision-making by the *dikastai*, the reliance on testimony rather than documentary evidence, and the brevity of the trial) made it impossible for a court to get at the 'truth'.[60] This, as I shall seek to demonstrate, is a simplification, not supported by the sources: lacking an adequate understanding of 'relevance', it both underestimates the capacity of the Athenian courts to deal with evidential problems and exaggerates the supposed superiority of modern legal systems, where, in many cases, a judge or jury still has to assess the credibility of witnesses and decide between conflicting versions of fact which are uncorroborated by documentary or scientific evidence. A more helpful and less simplistic analysis is provided by Lanni, who recognizes the Athenians' highly 'contextualized' or 'case-specific' approach to justice, but rightly rejects the 'social competition' model. Crucially, however, she, too, fails to recognize the legal significance of some of the supposedly 'extra-legal' evidence.[61]

In modern English law there is no specifically legal test of relevance; whether a particular fact is relevant to a particular case is determined by

---

[58] Cf. Hardcastle (1980).

[59] The twentieth century debate on 'relevance' was foreshadowed by Jones (1779), xxxiv: "...we must never forget that the *dikastai* were judges of fact, law, and equity, with ample powers of deciding according to the justice of every case; so that the parties were permitted in general to prove whatever tended to place them in a favourable light." Cf. Lanni (2006), 42: "...Athenian juries aimed at reaching a just verdict taking into account the particular circumstances of the individual case...".

[60] See, e.g. Cohen (1995), 106–107: "How could the Athenian court, forced to rely solely upon the presentation of facts and issues adopted by the litigants, within the extremely limited time frame and scope of a trial, and with the limited and unreliable means of proof available, resolve such conflicting claims except on the basis of a general judgment about their reputation, character and status as citizens?"

[61] Lanni (2006), 51: "Discussion of the circumstances and context of the contested event is most prominent in suits involving a challenge to a will. Litigants often appeal to a variety of arguments rooted in notions of fairness and justice *unrelated to the formal issue of the validity of the will.*" (Italics added.)

ordinary inferential reasoning based on logic and general experience. On one view:

> ...an evidentiary fact is relevant or potentially relevant to a *probandum* (i.e. a fact to be proved)...if it has some connection with it—the test is: does it tend to support (or negate) the *probandum* at all? On what basis do we establish the connection? The answer is largely on the basis of 'the available stock of social knowledge' in a given society.[62]

It is worth considering the various categories of supposedly 'non-legal' Athenian evidence in the light of this analysis, and comparing its use with actual forensic practice in some modern cases. To start with family relations: the argumentation used in Isaios's speeches indicates that an Athenian litigant attacking a will would have been expected to show that he was closer to the deceased than his opponent, not only in terms of blood relationship, but also of intimacy and affection. For instance, the speaker of Isa. 9, in describing the deceased Astyphilos's hostility towards Kleon and good relations with Theophrastos and the speaker himself, is not (ostensibly, at least) inviting the *dikastai* to award the estate to him because he is more morally deserving than his opponent. He does not suggest that the *dikastai* should ignore Astyphilos's wishes but seeks to demonstrate that the will produced by his opponents cannot be valid because it is unlikely that Astyphilos, in his right mind, would have made a will adopting the son of his sworn enemy. (A similar line is taken by the speaker of Isa. 1, though with a much more perfunctory narrative and greater reliance on argumentation from probability.) There is no surviving Attic oration in which the speaker defends a will against an attack by the next of kin,[63] but it is reasonable to assume that a litigant in that position would have used similar argumentation to explain why the testator had chosen to disrupt the order of intestate succession. This, indeed, is the line taken by the speaker of Isok. 19, who defends a testamentary adoption under the law of Aegina.

In modern contested probate cases, evidence about a testator's relationships with his beneficiaries and others is frequently deployed because

[62] Twining (2006), 121, summarizing the view taken by one school of legal theorists. He adds (p. 154, n. 134) that others "maintain that the evidence has to be 'sufficiently relevant', thereby incorporating other tests. The difference is probably one of semantics, not substance."

[63] Isa. 6, the prosecution speech from a *dikē pseudomarturiōn*, was delivered on behalf of a son adopted by will, but the argumentation focuses on the legitimacy of the rival claimants rather than the validity of the will.

it may arouse suspicion about the authenticity of a will. For example, in the case of *Franks v Sinclair*[64] the court heard extensive evidence about the character of the testatrix and her relations with members of the family, before deciding that the will produced by the claimant (her son) did not represent her true intentions and that an earlier will in favour of her grandson (a daughter's son) should stand. The later will had been drafted, at the testatrix's request, by her son, who was a solicitor. There was no suggestion that the document he produced was a forgery, but he was suspected of having framed some of the provisions to his own advantage, against her instructions and in obscure language that she was unlikely to have understood. The overall picture of the testatrix was of a rather cantankerous and mistrustful old woman, who changed her will several times after falling out with various relatives, but who developed a lasting rapport with the grandson whom she trusted above anyone else. The evidence on relations within the family was not, in itself, determinative, but it roused serious suspicion as to whether the testatrix fully understood the contents of the later will, a suspicion which was confirmed when the court considered the circumstances in which the will had been executed.

The relevance of character might, in at least some cases, be considered more doubtful. In adversarial Athenian litigation (*dikai* and *graphai*), extended references to the speaker's character are most commonly found in defence speeches, where a defendant would typically make use of his conduct, especially his services to the community, in attempt to persuade the *dikastai* that he could not possibly be guilty of the offences of which the prosecutor has accused him.[65] In inheritance disputes the character of a claimant is typically contrasted with that of his opponent, in order to show that he would be the more deserving recipient of the estate. When the estate at issue is sufficiently large, the speaker may suggest that, whereas he would use it for the benefit of the community as a whole, the rival claimant would squander it for personal use (Isa. 4.27–30, 6.60–61; cf. also 10.25).

Most of Isaios's clients do not recite their liturgies (public services), perhaps because they were not in a position to do so. Thrasyllos, the speaker of Isa. 7, is one of the exceptions. He speaks at some length about his own record of public service and generally good character, as seen through the eyes of the deceased Apollodoros, but his purpose is (again, ostensibly)

64 [2006] EWHC 3365 (Ch).

65 See Johnstone (1999), 95–96, for examples and discussion.

not to claim that he has a stronger moral entitlement to the estate than his opponent, but to demonstrate the likelihood that Apollodoros would have chosen such an exemplary citizen as his adopted son.[66]

In other speeches Isaios attacks the character of his clients' opponents or their associates, either with a 'glancing blow' or more extended *diabolē*. As will be discussed in the commentary, the relevance of these attacks is problematic because of its link with the truth value of the narratives, which is impossible for the modern reader to determine with certainty.[67]

It is worth noting that in today's very different social conditions and legal culture, a claimant's conduct in financial matters may still sometimes be considered relevant to a claim for maintenance against a deceased person's estate. In one such case before the English High Court, the judge found that the testatrix had in her lifetime been "exceptionally generous" towards the claimant, who had squandered the money given to her and whose "current financial plight" was "largely of her own making". The judge also found that the claimant had "exploited the testatrix's generosity", and he accepted the testimony of witnesses that the testatrix had been "pressurised, if not bullied" to pay off the claimant's debts and make provision for her future. "This," he observed, "is not conduct which, in my judgment, should be rewarded."[68]

Some of the other arguments put forward in Isaios's *diadikasia* speeches appeal to Athenian religious custom in support of the speaker's case.[69] For example, participation in family cults or attendance at festivals is sometimes used as evidence of a claimant's close relationship with the deceased (Isa. 8.17; 9.30). The frequent references to the burial of the dead and conduct of the funeral rites are of particular interest. It appears that in some ancient cultures the performance of these duties had a precise legal significance. According to Maine, for example:

> Among the Hindoos, the right to inherit a dead man's property is exactly co-extensive with the duty of performing his obsequies. If the rites are not properly performed or are performed by the wrong person, no relation is

[66] *Pace* Rhodes (2004), 146: "[Isa. 7] has a section towards the end in which the speaker claims that the public services of himself and his connections justify their receiving the inheritance (34–42), and returns to the points at issue in the conclusion (43–6)."

[67] See, especially, pp. 95–96.

[68] *Baynes v. Hedger and others* [2008] EWHC 1587 (Ch) (14 July 2008), a claim under the Inheritance (Family and Dependants) Act 1975. The published judgment includes a section headed 'Any other relevant matters including conduct'.

[69] For a modern discussion of the relationship between custom and law, see Hart (1994), 44–48.

> considered as established between the deceased and anybody surviving him; the law of Succession does not apply, and nobody can inherit the property.[70]

This led to a strong obligation on the childless Hindu to adopt, so that an heir would be in place to carry out the funeral rites. There was no corresponding legal requirement in fourth century Athens, but it is clear that there was a strong expectation that the customary rites (*ta nomizomena*) would be performed by the person(s) entitled to inherit the estate of the deceased. Consquently a litigant could boost his claim to an estate by pointing out that he had taken responsibility for the funeral, or that his opponents had not; and if he had not done so himself, he would be expected to explain why not (Isa. 9.4).

It is clear that in the Athenian context, evidence on family relations, character and observance of religious customs could, at least in some circumstances, support or negate a proposition such as the validity of a will or the legitimacy of a claimant's relationship to the deceased. A fact that would probably not be considered relevant by a modern court—for example, that a claimant either did or did not bury the deceased—might have been seen as supporting a case in the different cultural context of classical Athens. A fact that might be considered relevant in both ancient and modern litigation—for example, that a testator was not on speaking terms with the supposed beneficiary of his will—would inevitably carry greater weight[71] in the ancient world, where scientific means of proof were not available. The Athenians had neither legal rules on admissibility[72] nor procedural means of excluding irrelevant evidence, but they did understand that forensic evidence or argumentation might be 'off the point' (*exō tou pragmatos*).[73] It was up to the *dikastai* to consider, on a case by case basis, the relevance and cogency of all the evidence put before them.

In a system where each *dikastēs* formed his own judgment independently of the others, and with no guidance from a legally qualified judge or clerk, all that was required was for a majority of the individual *dikastai*

---

70 Maine (1861), 159.

71 Twining (2006), 193: "The 'weight' or 'cogency' or 'probative force' of a single evidentiary proposition, or of a mass of evidence, refers to the strength or weakness of the support or negation. Questions of relevance (is there any connection?) and of weight (how strong is the connection?) are intimately related, but it is useful to keep them conceptually distinct."

72 The main rule of evidence, in English law, is that all irrelevant evidence is inadmissible.

73 See, e.g., Dem. 57.63 and 66, where the speaker argues that the misdeeds of his fellow demesmen are relevant to his case against them although the *dikastai* might consider them *exō tou pragmatos*.

to be more convinced by one party's case than the other's. It might, of course, be in the interest of a litigant, especially one with a weak case, to adduce evidence of doubtful relevance, and to exaggerate its probative force. Indeed, it is not unknown for modern advocates to deploy such tactics, to the extent that the rules allow.[74] So it would hardly be surprising if some of the Athenian *dikastai* were sometimes taken in, or if they were on occasions swayed by a logographer's appeals to their emotions rather than their intellect, but that is no reason to conclude that cases in the Athenian courts were regularly decided on moral rather than legal grounds, or that modern legal systems, with their greater professionalism, are necessarily superior. Excessive legalism may, in fact, lead to a sense of dissatisfaction with, or even alienation from, a legal system which is seen to be out of touch with the needs and values of ordinary people. In the very different legal culture of classical Athens, with all the supposedly negative features identified by its critics, it is doubtful whether a conflict between moral and legal values would have been recognized.

Persuasion: The Rôle of the Logographer

Given that the 'profession' had no official status, it is hardly surprising that the primary sources reveal little about the rôle of the logographer; but it is reasonable to assume that, while he may on occasions have acted as an adviser or agent to his client, his primary function (as the Greek word *logographos* itself implies) was to provide a speech, based on facts supplied at a preliminary consultation by the client, for the client to learn and deliver in court.[75]

An Athenian logographer, like a modern professional advocate, was paid to win cases for his clients. In an adversarial system such as that of classical Athens, or those of common law jurisdictions today, winning a

[74] Cf. Lanni (2006), 9: "A skilful trial attorney will exploit the flexibility in the rules of evidence to his advantage, and may even be able to suggest surreptitiously in his opening and closing statements that the verdict should hinge on legally irrelevant factors—from the race or class of one of the parties to the relative importance of a money judgment to the family of a poor tort victim as opposed to a wealthy corporate defendant." Similarly, Rubinstein (2004), 108–109, points out that, although they are reluctant to admit it, modern advocates also use emotional arguments as a means of persuasion; there is a fine line between acceptable and unacceptable behaviour.

[75] This is the traditional view, propounded by Lavency (1964), 36–45. Dover's theory of "composite authorship" by "client and consultant" (Dover (1968a), 148–174), has not gained widespread acceptance, and was convincingly refuted by Usher, who, after reviewing the primary evidence, concludes that "Dover's hypothesis would have surprised Dionysios and Plutarch and astounded Plato" (Usher (1976), 40).

case requires the litigant or his representative to persuade an independent tribunal that his own case is factually as well as legally stronger than his opponent's. So, despite some significant differences between the ancient and the modern systems, the fundamental need to tell a convincing story is common to both professions, and many of the rhetorical techniques used by the Athenian logographers have parallels in the theory and practice of modern advocacy.[76] An effective story is not merely an objective account of the facts but a form of persuasion that engages the audience's imagination and inclines them to believe the speaker's version of the facts in dispute.[77] The subjective aspect of persuasion was explicitly recognized in Aristotle's *Rhetoric*, where the 'artificial means of persuasion' (*entekhnoi pisteis*) include 'character' (*ēthos*) and 'emotion' (*pathos*) as well as the more rational forms of argumentation from probability.[78]

Accordingly, many of Isaios's narratives do not simply convey facts but operate simultaneously at a less rational level, soliciting the sympathy of the *dikastai* and encouraging them to see the case from his client's point of view.[79] A man who wanted to take away his grandfather's body for burial appeals to Athenian sentiment in explaining that he did not do so because he was unable to resist the pleas of the grieving widow (8.22). The same speaker, trying to demonstrate that Kiron looked on him and his brother as legitimate grandsons, vividly describes how as children they always accompanied him at festivals and family sacrifices (8.16). A speaker portraying his mother as a defrauded *epiklēros*, probably some years after her death, explains that her husband did not press her claim to her paternal estate because her father's next of kin threatened to claim her in marriage, and he would have let them keep an estate of twice the value rather than lose her (10.19). Thrasyllos criticizes his opponents because they allowed their brother's *oikos* to become empty instead of giving him a son by posthumous adoption (7.31).

Unlike his modern counterpart, an Athenian logographer had considerable latitude to exaggerate, suppress and even invent aspects of his story

[76] See Inns of Court School of Law (2006), chapter 14: 'The advocate as storyteller'.

[77] Cf. Inns of Court School of Law (2006), 99: "your audience is always more likely to accept a story which fits in with their beliefs, knowledge, experiences and prejudices."

[78] Arist. *Rh.* 1356a. Cf. Carey (1994), 184: "as ancient rhetoricians realized, the task of persuasion is a complex one, involving the emotional response of the hearer as well as the cognitive faculties".

[79] *Pace* Usher (1999), 128, who describes the purpose of Isaios's narratives as "not so much to tell a story which creates an atmosphere and constructs a picture of character, as to provide the essential material for proof".

in order to make the best of his client's case.[80] Even when the case was legally and factually strong, he might see the need to embellish some elements of the story to make it more convincing, or to undermine his opponent's case more effectively.[81] We have no means of knowing, in any of Isaios's speeches, to what extent the facts have been manipulated to conform with cultural stereotypes, but it is significant that he takes care to present his clients as compliant with accepted Athenian values, from which their opponents are invariably shown to have deviated.

In a speech before a *dikastērion*, aspects of the 'story' in the broader sense might be presented in the course of the argumentation, as well as in the formal narrative sections and the introduction (proem) and epilogue. This commentary provides numerous examples of techniques used by Isaios to enhance the credibility of his story and focus the attention of the *dikastai* on those aspects that he particularly wanted them to remember.[82] Examples of such techniques are the inclusion or omission of inessential detail (for instance in the naming and non-naming of individuals); the repetition of key words or phrases; the planting of seeds; changes of *focalization; rhetorical questions; and direct addresses to the *dikastai* in the second person.

The Reception of Isaios's Work from Antiquity to the Twenty-First Century

Antiquity

Although there are no surviving references to Isaios from the fourth century, we have an indirect indication of his fame (or perhaps notoriety) in his lifetime, in the tradition that he was mentioned, presumably as an object of satire, in Theopompos's comedy *Theseus*, which has been dated to 390–380 BC.[83] Only one of Isaios's surviving speeches, on the estate of Dikaiogones (Isa. 5), can be dated with certainty to this decade, and nine

80 An English barrister's conduct of proceedings in court is governed by the Bar Standards Board's Code of Conduct, which forbids him, *inter alia*, to "adduce evidence obtained otherwise than from or through the client or devise facts which will assist in advancing the lay client's case" (rule 708(e)), retrieved from www.barstandardsboard.org.uk, 18 January 2009.

81 See the introduction to Isa. 7, pp. 40–41.

82 Cf. Inns of Court School of Law (2006), 97: "If the 'story' is the evidence at a trial, then the advocate may want to ensure that the listener does indeed recall only bits and further that only those bits that favour the client are recalled."

83 The tradition stems from the pseudo-Plutarchian *Vitae decem oratorum*, cited by Jebb (1876), 270. On the dating of Theopompos's comedies, see Webster (1952), 13–26.

of the remaining eleven are certainly later. We do not, of course, know the dates of the lost speeches, but the implication is that he had established a reputation at a very early stage of his logographic career, perhaps on the basis of no more than one or two high profile cases.

Apart from Dionysios of Halikarnassos (first century BC), the only ancient rhetorician to comment substantively on Isaios's speeches was Hermogenes (second century AD).[84] Otherwise, Isaios is mentioned only in passing by Quintilian, among a number of Attic orators whom he does not place in the first rank.[85] The reasons for this comparative neglect are unclear, but it may be partly attributable to Isaios's lack of involvement in public affairs, and to the complexity and obscurity of Athenian inheritance law, which makes his speeches less accessible than those of other Attic orators.[86]

As the only sustained analysis of Isaios's work to survive from antiquity, Dionysios's essay has exercised a profound, and perhaps disproportionate, influence on the modern reception of Isaios, in two particular respects. First, Dionysios characterizes Isaios as an imitator of Lysias and forerunner of Demosthenes, attributing his lasting reputation mainly to the tradition that he was the teacher of Demosthenes.[87] Dionysios's detailed stylistic and rhetorical analysis brings out many of the strengths of Isaios's speeches, and shows him in some respects to be an innovator. Isaios, nevertheless, is inevitably overshadowed by Demosthenes, and suffers from being constantly compared with Lysias, whose simplicity was more admired by Dionysios and his contemporaries than Isaios's rhetorical artifice.[88] This approach has contributed to the continuing neglect, and sometimes underestimation, of Isaios in more recent times.

---

84 Hermog. *peri ideōn*, B. c. 11, cited by Jebb (1876), 298–299. Jebb describes the passage as an "incomplete" but "careful and respectful" estimation of Isaios's strengths and weaknesses in comparison with Lysias and Demosthenes.

85 "Transeo plurimos, Lycurgum, Aristogeitona, et his priores Isaeum, Antiphontem ..." "I pass over many, Lykourgos, Aristogeiton, and before them Isaios, Antiphon ..." (Quint. 12.10.22). Jebb (1876), 299, comments: "The truth is that Quint. made no careful study of the Greek orators, except Isokrates, Demosthenes, and (in a measure) Lysias; but this treatment of Isaeus is especially remarkable."

86 As suggested by Jones (1779), iii, v.

87 Jones (1779), vii, disagrees with this assessment; in his opinion, Isaios was not a "mere imitator" of Lysias and would, without Demosthenes, have been the greatest of the Attic orators, or at least second to Hypereides.

88 Moy (1876), 130–131, comments that Dionysios "immole [Isée] dans la gloire de Lysias, et semble ne l'admettre en son livre que par faveur" ("immolates [Isaios] in the glory of Lysias, and seems to admit him into his book only as a favour").

Secondly, Dionysios tells us that Isaios had a reputation among his contemporaries for "chicanery and deception" and for his skill at "devising speeches for the worse cause".[89] It is not clear whether this judgment derives from reliable fourth century sources, but it is consistent with the classical Athenian attitude that "the just man has no need of skill; if he is in the right his case speaks for itself, and it is only the man in the wrong who needs artifice".[90] So Isaios's reputation rested solely on his rhetorical technique, with no implication that he was actually more dishonest or deceptive than other logographers.[91] Dionysios's words have, nevertheless, laid the foundation for the hostile moral assessment of some modern scholars.

Modern Scholarship

Suspicion of rhetorical cleverness is not, of course, confined to the ancient world. As the first English translator of Isaios, Sir William Jones, himself a barrister and later a judge, observed:

> ... it is certain that both Isaeus and Demosthenes had the reputation of being extremely subtle advocates, a reputation by no means favourable at the bar, as it always diminishes and frequently destroys the confidence of the jury, who, through a fear of being deluded, are apt to suspect a snare in every argument of such a speaker ...[92]

Jones's assessment of Isaios is, nevertheless, essentially positive, reflecting, without moral disapproval, a professional appreciation of the logographer's efforts to win cases. Some later scholars, notably Wyse, would have done well to follow Jones's perceptive advice to the reader to "place himself at Athens, and to drop for a time all thoughts of our own forensick dialect", and to "read an Attick orator with the mind, and, as it were, the eyes, of an Athenian".[93]

Wyse's work on Isaios has two great strengths: his minute attention to textual detail and his recognition that a corpus of forensic speeches cannot be treated as if it were a legal textbook aiming to give an objective account of the law. This latter perception enabled him to correct

---

89 Dion. Hal., *De Isaeo* 4, trans. Usher.

90 Dover (1968a), 155.

91 Cf. Usher (1999), 128, n. 6: "[Isaios] was too careful to rely routinely on blatant falsehood. His 'reputation' ... was earned purely by his technical skills. Lysias, no less adept at deceit, escapes critical censure by parading his skills less overtly."

92 Jones (1779), ix.

93 Jones (1779), xxiii–xxiv.

some of the over-literal readings of nineteenth century classicists and legal historians,[94] but it led him to an extreme mistrust of everything that Isaios said, whether on Athenian law or on the facts of a particular case. Underlying his interpretation is a negative assessment of the Athenian legal system as one in which untrained adjudicators were easily outwitted by unscrupulous logographers who had no regard for the truth. The ethical standards by which he judges Isaios are anachronistic, and the influence of Roman law led him to an inappropriate assumption that Athenian inheritance law was consistent and comprehensive.

Some of these limitations were apparent to Wyse's contemporaries. One reviewer, while commending him for his recognition that forensic speeches are not an impartial source, confesses to "grave misgivings":

> Did Isaeus never have a case in which the jury might equitably have given a verdict in his favour? Are the twelve speeches preserved for us without exception specimens of what he could do in a bad case? If not, ought we not to understand that in most suits there is an element of justice in each side, and that something not merely specious, but sound and equitable can be urged by both litigants? Mr. Wyse writes as though every speech was throughout dishonest, and, without stating it plainly, hints at every point that the fact was otherwise than it is represented, or admitted of another explanation or complexion, that the law was unmistakably against the speaker, and that he is bluffing the jury and inciting them to override it. Reflexion will show that the most straightforward speeches of the most upright orator could not support so riddling an attack.[95]

Like that of Dionysios, Wyse's assessment of Isaios has proved impossible for later scholars to ignore. Despite the early recognition of his methodological bias, there has, more than 100 years after Wyse's commentary was published, been no fundamental reassessment of Isaios's work. This seems to reflect, at least in part, a perception that Wyse's work has left little or no scope for further scholarship.[96] Some scholars have accepted Wyse's views as the basis of their own work, and some have deliberately chosen

[94] Todd (1990a), 161–162, sees the publication of Wyse's commentary as the culmination of a trend, starting in the later half of the nineteenth century, towards a more sceptical reading of the Attic orators as historical source material.

[95] Nicklin, (1905), 306; cf. Seymour (1906), 187–190.

[96] Lewis (1959), 162, refers to "a feeling... that Wyse's edition with its minute text criticism and exhaustive commentary has left little more to be done."

not to comment further on the legal aspect of the speeches,[97] while only a few have directly challenged Wyse's method and conclusions.

The only comprehensive later editions, those of Roussel (1922) and Forster (1927) provide, respectively, a French and an English translation, but the commentary in both is limited in scope and largely based on Wyse. The German translator Münscher, whose interest in the speeches is predominantly legal, echoes Wyse in his contemptuous prefatory account of the non-specialist Athenian legal culture in which he sees the law as playing little part and litigants as motivated purely by self-interest and greed. Isaios, in his view, stands out among the Attic orators as "master of the most unscrupulous and insidious distortion of the law".[98] Lentzsch (1932) offers some new insights into the four speeches covered in his study (Isa. 3, 6, 8 and 10) but does not challenge Wyse's basic method.

An obvious reason why Wyse's work is in need of revision is that some aspects of his commentary have been superseded by later scholarly developments, including several studies on the historical background to some of Isaios's speeches, especially 6, 7 and 9.[99] The discovery of Menander's plays has, in addition, cast new light on the legal problems that feature in the speeches, especially in relation to the epiklerate,[100] although the precise value of New Comedy as source of information on Athenian law is a matter of controversy.[101] As will be discussed in the individual commentaries, these developments not only enhance our understanding of the speeches but also tend to corroborate Isaios's presentation of legal and factual details, against Wyse's interpretation.

---

[97] See, e.g., Wevers (1969), Preface, explaining why he has confined his study of Isaios to chronology, prosopography and social history: "Since these two fields [of rhetoric and law] have already received careful study it has seemed best that in this work these traditional areas of Isaean scholarship be bypassed…".

[98] "Meister … im skrupellosesten, perfidesten Verdrehen des Rechts". Münscher (1919/1920), 41.

[99] See, e.g., Labarbe (1953), Kamps (1938), and Thompson (1970) on Isa. 6; Boëthius (1918) and Parke (1939) on Isa. 7; Wade-Gery and Merritt (1936), Bourriot (1982), Welsh (1991), and Rosivach (2005) on Isa. 9.

[100] See, e.g., Brown (1983), Karabélias (1975), Karabélias (2005), MacDowell (1982).

[101] Cf. Mossé (1989), 130: "… la fonction du théâtre comique n'est pas de refléter les réalités de la société contemporaine, mais, partant de ces réalités, de faire rire en les exagérant" ("… the function of the comic theatre is not to reflect the realities of contemporary society, but, starting from those realities, to make people laugh by exaggerating them"); and see the introduction to Isa. 10, p. 203.

Harrison, in his influential work on the law of Athens, explicitly distances himself from Wyse's scepticism about Isaios as a legal source.[102] Harrison (1947), Lewis (1959) and Thompson (1976) have all challenged Wyse's view that Theopompos, the speaker of Isa. 11, owed his victory against Sositheos to Isaios's legal chicanery and distortion of fact. A Serbian legal historian, Sima Avramovič, has also sought to rehabilitate Isaios, both in an article on Isa. 9[103] and in a more extensive monograph on Isaios and Athenian law. Publication of the latter in an Italian translation[104] has made Avramovič's work accessible to Western scholars, and, in particular, influenced the commentaries of Cobetto Ghiggia on Isa. 5 and Ferrucci on Isa. 8.[105] Arguably, however, Avramovič's challenge to the scepticism of Wyse goes too far in the direction of accepting Isaios's version of factual and legal details.[106]

There is a separate scholarly tradition, dating from late antiquity, of reading Attic oratory purely as a literary genre, without regard to the legal content of the speeches or their value as a historical source. Nineteenth century adherents to this tradition, including predominantly Blass and Jebb, were able to form a positive assessment of the orators on the basis of their stylistic and rhetorical skills, without becoming involved in controversy about the moral dimension of their work.[107] The tradition has continued into the latter half of the twentieth century and beyond, with, for example, the work of Usher on Greek oratory and Edwards on narratology in the orators similarly focusing on the speeches as literary rather than legal documents. In relation specifically to Isaios, Denommé's work on language and style[108] led him to a positive assessment of the literary value of the speeches, without regard to their legal context.[109] Edwards's

102 Harrison (1968), 122, n. 1: "Throughout his commentary Wyse atempts to discredit Isaios' statements as to what was the law. This scepticism has been much overdone; it is unlikely that Athenian juries were so gullible or so ignorant of the law as it implies."

103 Avramovič (1990).

104 Avramovič (1997).

105 Cobetto Ghiggia (2002); Ferrucci (2005).

106 For examples, see the introduction to and commentary on Isa. 9.

107 Todd (1990a), 162.

108 See Bibliography.

109 Denommé (1974b), 4–5: "Nous nous abstiendrons aussi de porter des jugements de valeur sur les arguments, sur les faits, sur la sincérité et le souci d'honnêteté de l'auteur.... D'ailleurs W. Wyse les a scrupuleusement analysés dans ses copieuses notes sur les discours d'Isée." ("We shall abstain, too, from making value judgments on the arguments, on the facts, and on the writer's sincerity and concern for integrity.... W. Wyse has, in any case, scrupulously analysed these factors in his copious notes on the speeches of Isaios.") Other work on the stylistic and rhetorical features of Isaios's speeches includes, e.g.,

new (2007) translation of Isaios into English includes introductory essays and notes in which due weight is given to recent work on the historical background. But despite the translator's declared aim of providing a "more balanced view" than Wyse, his main interest is in rhetoric and he does not attempt a detailed legal analysis of the speeches.[110]

While it is perfectly legitimate to focus on the rhetorical aspects of forensic oratory, this approach carries the risk of missing an important dimension. It is difficult to arrive at a full and balanced appreciation of the rhetorical qualities of the speeches, or of the orator's logographic skills, without exploring the legal and factual dimensions. The last word on these aspects of Isaios's work has so far, in effect, been left to Wyse, and there remains a need for a holistic approach to the interpretation of the speeches which is not driven by anachronistic moral value judgments and does not seek to impose principles derived from Roman law onto a radically different legal system. My aim in this commentary is, by addressing the complex interplay of factual, legal, and rhetorical issues in Isaios's work, to reach a more nuanced view of the qualities of the speaker's case and the dynamics of the forensic contest.

Robinson (1901), Seymour (1901a) and Seymour (1901b), Baden (1906), Miller (1936), Theodorakopoulos (1972), Cooper (1974), and Renehan (1980).

[110] Edwards (2007), 4–5: "In my Introduction and Notes to the speeches I attempt to give a more balanced view, and if legal historians are destined to be frustrated by what many will continue to regard as Isaean chicanery it is hoped that the brilliant rhetoric in which Isaeus entangles his readers will come to be recognized in its own right."

ISAIOS 7: ON THE ESTATE OF APOLLODOROS

Introduction

Background and Chronology

Apollodoros, whose estate is claimed by Isaios's client, belonged to a wealthy and distinguished Athenian family. The earliest generation mentioned in the speech is that of Apollodoros's father, Thrasyllos, who had two brothers, Eupolis and Mneson, each of whose share in their father's estate is said to have been large enough to make them liable to perform *liturgies. Epigraphic evidence discovered during the twentieth century has extended the family tree back by two, or perhaps three, further generations, and placed the family in the *deme Leukonoion. The earliest known ancestor of Apollodoros is now Mneson of Leukonoion, named in an Akropolis dedication to Athena, dated to around 480 BC, by his sons Thrasyllos and Gnathios.[1] Davies, in his discussion of the evidence, argues that there must have been a further generation between Thrasyllos the dedicator[2] and Thrasyllos the father of Apollodoros.[3] He plausibly suggests that the 'missing' ancestor, who may have been the son of either of the dedicators Thrasyllos and Gnathios, was another Apollodoros.

The location of the deme Leukonoion is uncertain, but the traditional view that it was to the northwest of the city has been challenged by epigraphic evidence that it may have been in southern Attica. That would be consistent with the suggestion that Apollodoros's *phratry could have been the Akhniadai, who had a shrine to Apollo near Kephale.[4] It is possible to date the speech, with reasonable certainty, to about 354 BC, on the basis of internal references to the system of contributions to the trierarchy by symmories, and to the pilgrimage to Delphi (Pythaïs) in which the speaker Thrasyllos participated in the year before the court hearing.[5]

Diagram 1 shows the family of Apollodoros, the **de cuius* of the speech, assuming him to have been a descendant of the dedicator Thrasyllos.

---

1 Raubitschek (1949), 116, no. 112; discussed by Davies (1971), 43–44.

2 Listed in *LGPN Attica* as Θράσυλλος (29).

3 Listed in *LGPN Attica* as Θράσυλλος (30).

4 See commentary on καὶ ἐπειδὴ …, §15.

5 See commentary on πρὶν γὰρ …, §27 and οὐκ ἐκ συμμορίας …, §38.

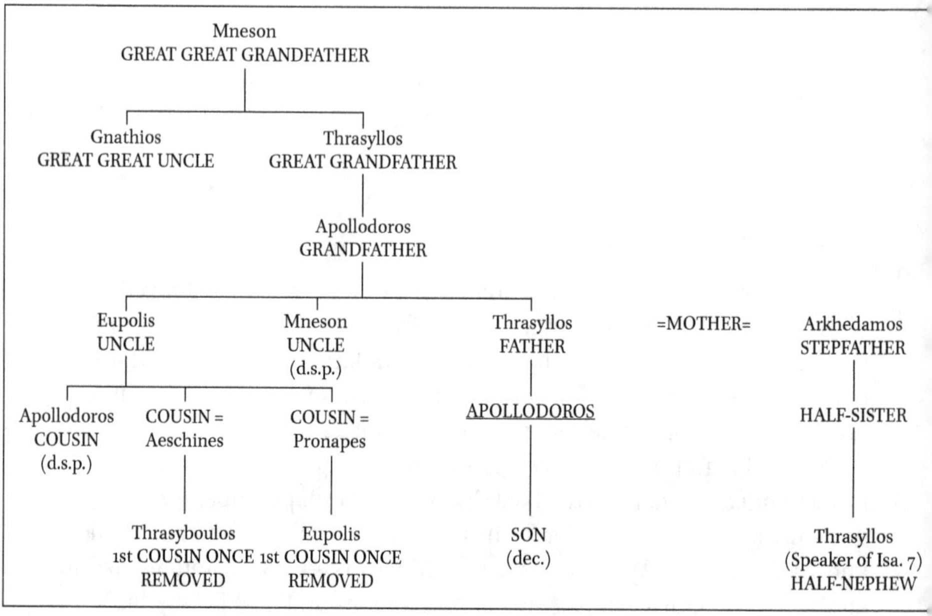

Diagram 1: The family of Apollodoros

The 'Facts' and the Issues in Dispute

According to the speaker, the Apollodoros whose estate is in dispute was a minor when his father, Thrasyllos, died while serving as a trierarch on the Sicilian expedition of 415/413 BC. One of his paternal uncles, Mneson, died unmarried and childless at around the same time. The surviving uncle, Eupolis, became Apollodoros's guardian, but cheated him of his share in Mneson's estate and squandered the rest of his fortune. Apollodoros's mother, in the meantime, had married her second husband, Arkhedamos, to whom she bore a daughter. Seeing Eupolis's abuse of his position as guardian, Arkhedamos took the boy Apollodoros into his own household, and, when he came of age, helped him to recover his fortune by winning two lawsuits against Eupolis. Apollodoros repaid this kindness by securing Arkhedamos's release after he became a prisoner of war, and sharing his own property with him when he was financially embarrassed.

Isaios's client is a son of Apollodoros's *uterine sister, who claims to have been adopted **inter vivos* by Apollodoros and inscribed by the **phrateres* and demesmen as Thrasyllos Apollodorou ('Thrasyllos, son of Apollodoros'). His opponent, who contests the adoption and claims the estate as next of kin, is a first cousin of Apollodoros, the wife of Pronapes of Aixone who represents her in the litigation. She is one of the three children of Apollodoros's uncle, Eupolis, the others being Apollodoros Eupolidos[6] and another daughter who married Aiskhines of Lousia. Apollodoros Eupolidos has died without issue. The wife of Aiskhines is also dead, but she is survived by a son, Thrasyboulos.

In his attempt to persuade the court that Thrasyllos had been legally adopted *inter vivos* by his uncle Apollodoros, Isaios describes three discrete stages in the adoption process. First, after the death of his own legitimate son, Apollodoros approached his half-sister and sought her permission to adopt her son. With her blessing, he installed Thrasyllos in his household, and, considering himself too old and frail to manage for himself, handed over the conduct of his financial affairs to his new 'son'. The second stage of the process was the introduction of Thrasyllos to Apollodoros's **gennētai* and *phrateres*. Apollodoros duly carried this out, swearing the appropriate oath, the members voted in his favour, and his 'son' was inscribed in the register as Thrasyllos Apollodorou. All that remained was the third and final stage, the enrolment of Thrasyllos in Apollodoros's deme.

Isaios tells us that Apollodoros feared, because of his age and frailty, that he might not survive until the deme meeting (probably a regular annual event), at which Thrasyllos was to be enrolled. So he told his fellow demesmen that he had adopted his nephew and registered him with the phratry and **genos*, urging them, whatever happened, to inscribe his adopted son in their register as Thrasyllos Apollodorou. Then Apollodoros died, and it appears that Thrasyllos was away from Athens at the time of the meeting. The demesmen, nevertheless, carried out Apollodoros's wishes by inscribing Thrasyllos in their register, in the face of objections to the adoption from those who later became Thrasyllos's opponents in the litigation.

Some modern scholars have assumed that the adoption was not legally valid because the formalities were not completed by Apollodoros in his lifetime. Isaios, on this view, does his best to conceal the irregularity of the proceedings by omissions and evasions designed to mislead the audience.[7] That interpretation needs to be questioned, on the basis of

[6] I use the patronymic Eupolidos ('son of Eupolis') to distinguish this Apollodoros from the *de cuius*, Apollodoros Thrasyllou ('son of Thrasyllos').

[7] See, especially, Wyse, 549: "When Apollodoros died, the adoption was certainly incomplete.... Isaeus' policy is to slur over the irregularity as if it were a thing of no consequence...". Theodorakopoulos (1972), 18–26, bases his rhetorical analysis of Isa. 7 on

what we know about the Athenian legal system in general as well as the circumstantial details of this speech.

We do not know the exact basis of the opponent's case, but there are indications in the speech that Pronapes and his wife attacked the adoption as invalid on the grounds that Apollodoros was acting under the influence of a woman, that Thrasyllos was not recognized by the *phrateres* and *gennētai* as the son of Apollodoros's sister, and that it was Thrasyllos himself, and not Apollodoros, who urged the demesmen to carry out the enrolment in the event of Apollodoros's death. Pronapes and his wife may also have said that they were willing to give Apollodoros a son of their own by adoption, but were thwarted by the intervention of Thrasyllos and his mother.[8]

Thrasyllos's account of the adoption implies that it became effective after his introduction to the phratry and *genos*. The demesmen were informed of the adoption as a *fait accompli* which they were required simply to ratify by inscribing Thrasyllos in their register. He describes the phratry procedure in considerable detail, then postpones any reference to the deme registration until after a lengthy excursus on legal issues. His account of the deme registration is brief, emphasizing that the demesmen were acting in accordance with Apollodoros's known wishes, and playing down the objections of his opponents.

Clearly, Thrasyllos's version of events cannot be taken as impartial. In particular, the emphasis he places on his acceptance by Apollodoros's phratry was very much in his own interest, but perhaps it also accorded with contemporary perceptions of what constituted (or might, in the appropriate circumstances, constitute) a valid adoption *inter vivos*. We do not know what normally happened if an adoptive father died without completing all the formalities of the adoption, but the case of Apollodoros and Thrasyllos can hardly have been unique. Perhaps the closest parallel from the extant sources is to be found in Dem. 39, an account of a long-running dispute between Mantitheos son of Mantias and his (possibly

---

Wyse's assessment of Thrasyllos's claim as "not strong". Earlier scholars did not always take this view; for Jones (1779), 195, the speech is a "clear and full commentary" on adoption *inter vivos*. Cf. Moy (1876), 218: "Nous avons l'occasion de voir, dans ce plaidoyer, quelles étaient les formalités nécessaires pour la validité de l'adoption." ("We have the opportunity to see, in this speech, what were the necessary formalities for a valid adoption.") Wyse is strongly challenged by Avramovič (1997), 163, emphasizing the difference between Greek and Roman law.

8 See commentary on ἐλθὼν …, §14, ἐκείνῳ … γεγονω§ς, 17, ἔλεγε …, 27, παρά του …, 33, and τὶς <ἂν> …, 36.

illegitimate) half-brother Boiotos. Mantitheos says that after Mantias was forced to acknowledge paternity[9] of Boiotos and his brother Pamphilos, he introduced them to his phratry but died without enrolling them in his deme. Boiotos then presented himself to the deme and enrolled himself[10] under the name of Mantitheos instead of Boiotos. Mantitheos the speaker objects to his brother's usurpation of his own name, but makes no suggestion that the self-enrolment was illegal *per se*.

There is some further support for the suggestion that the main, or perhaps the only, formal requirement for at least some types of adoption was the introduction of the adopted son into his adopted father's phratry. In Isa. 10, where an (apparently) posthumous adoption is under attack, there is no mention at all of deme enrolment; it appears that the adoption had been accepted as valid on the basis that the phratry had admitted the new member without objection. A less direct analogy is provided by Isa. 8, where the speaker, who is not an adopted son but is defending a challenge to his legitimacy, describes in some detail how he and his brother were introduced to their father's phratry, but does not refer to their enrolment in the deme. In the case of an adoption *inter vivos* it would, nevertheless, have been normal for the adoptive father to complete the deme enrolment himself. The absence of this formality may (as Thrasyllos's emphasis on the known wishes of Apollodoros suggests) have given his opponents the loophole they needed to question his narrative of the preceding events.

So far as we know, the only legal basis for adoption *inter vivos* was the Solonian law on the disposal of property by those with no legitimate descendants.[11] (This is cited in Isa. 2, where a long-standing adoption *inter vivos* is disputed, and in other speeches as the authority for testamentary adoption.) It is unlikely that the detailed procedure was spelt out in written legislation, although the phratries and demes would have had their own procedural rules. Thrasyllos implies that the private arrangement between himself, his mother and Apollodoros constituted a *de facto* adoption. On that basis the formalities of introduction to the phratry and

[9] The term used is *epoiēsato* (Dem. 39.4), but in this context it cannot be translated as 'adopted' since Mantias already had a legitimate son and could not, in any event, have adopted his own offspring. Cf. Rudhardt (1962), 53–56.

[10] ἐλθὼν εἰς τοὺς δημότας ... ἐνέγραψεν ἑαυτόν, Dem. 39.5.

[11] See General Introduction, p. 4, and cf. Rubinstein (1993), 17: "The institution of an heir by means of adoption *inter vivos* could be conceived of as one way of 'disposing of one's property', and the fact that the law is appealed to in the lawcourt speeches as the law permitting adoption *inter vivos* indicates that there was no other law which warranted this procedure in particular."

enrolment in the deme would have been necessary to ensure that the adopted son was publicly and legally recognized as the legitimate heir of his adoptive father, but in one sense they could be seen as the ratification of an act that had already taken place.[12]

Moreover, in a society that recognized posthumous adoption, with no active participation at all by the adoptive 'father', it is entirely plausible that the deme would have had discretion to enrol a son on behalf of a fellow demesman who had died before the formal process was completed, although there may have been no explicit legal basis for such discretion. At worst, it may be that someone in Thrasyllos's position was required, like a testamentary adoptee, to apply to the court for **epidikasia* instead of entering directly onto the estate. In the event of a dispute, the known wishes of the deceased adopter are likely to have been crucial.[13] On this analysis, it would have been the accuracy of Thrasyllos's account of the facts that was in issue, not the validity of the adoption procedure he describes.

The Legal Procedure

Isaios does not explain the process by which the dispute came to court. However, since Thrasyllos had already been installed in Apollodoros's household and given control of his affairs, it is reasonable to assume that he was in *de facto* possession of the estate at the time of Apollodoros's death. (Thrasyllos's absence from Athens might have given his opponents the opportunity to seize possession, but he makes no mention of such an illegal action.) He evidently relied on his rights as a son adopted *inter vivos*, and did not apply to the court for *epidikasia*; but his occupation of the estate was challenged by Pronapes, who submitted a claim on behalf of his wife as Apollodoros's next of kin.

Thrasyllos claims that he could, as a son legally adopted *inter vivos*, have blocked the rival claim by issuing a **diamarturia*. He did not do so because he knew that the court would prefer to have the full facts of the

[12] This would accord with Gernet's view that, in the classical period, introduction to the phratry was a formal element of the adoption, but no longer a legal requirement (Gernet (1930), 159).

[13] The wishes of the deceased 'adopter' do not appear to have been an essential feature of posthumous adoption, but could usefully be adduced in a case where there was disagreement among the surviving members of the family. Sositheos, in his account of the posthumous adoption of Euboulides III, emphasizes that it had been the dearest wish of the adoptive father, Euboulides II, that his daughter might produce a son to continue his *oikos* ([Dem.] 43.12).

case expounded in an 'immediate trial' (*euthudikia*, §3). His reasoning appears disingenuous, not least because of the equivocal circumstances of his adoption, and we cannot be sure that he really did enjoy the full rights of a son adopted *inter vivos*. Even if he did, he must have known that a *diamarturia* would have been challenged by his opponents, with the result that he or the witness who had issued the *diamarturia* would have become the defendant in a *dikē* **pseudomarturiōn*. To avoid that disadvantage, his best course would have been to proceed by way of *epidikasia*, whereby his claim would be heard on an equal footing with that of his opponent.[14]

The Structure of the Speech and Means of Persuasion

In the main body of the speech (§§5–36) the narrative is broken down into three discrete sections, each followed by the relevant testimony.[15] Also interwoven with the 'factual' narrative and supporting testimony are four separate arguments from probability. The sequence can be analysed as follows.

1(a) Narrative: The family history, up to and including Apollodoros's successful lawsuits against his guardian, Eupolis (§§5–10).
1(b) Testimony.
1(c) Argument: Apollodoros would have wanted his estate to go to the descendants of his benefactor, Arkhedamos, not to those of his lifelong enemy, Eupolis (§§11–12).
2(a) Narrative: The adoption: private arrangement and phratry introduction (§§13–17).
2(b) Testimony.
2(c) Argument (with supporting law and testimony): Thrasyboulos, Apollodoros's first cousin once removed (patrilineal female cousin's son) has a better claim to the estate than Thrasyllos's opponent, the wife of Pronapes. She, as a patrilineal first cousin, is more closely related to Apollodoros than is Thrasyboulos, but she is outranked by him in the **ankhisteia* because of the principle of male precedence. Despite this Thrasyboulos has made no claim to the estate, thus demonstrating by his conduct that he accepts Thrasyllos's title as adopted son (§§18–26).
3(a) Narrative: The adoption: deme enrolment (§§27–28).

---

[14] Rubinstein (1993), 54, argues that it would have been risky for Thrasyllos to issue a *diamarturia* because he would have been required to pay a deposit of ten percent of the value of the estate. We cannot be certain, however, that he would not have had to pay the deposit in any event. (Cf. the introduction to Isa. 8, p. 101, n. 36.)

[15] This structural technique is identified by Dion. Hal., *De Isaeo* 14, as being characteristic of Isaios, as distinct from Lysias.

3(b) Testimony.
3(c) Argument: Apollodoros Thrasyllou saw how shamefully his female first cousins behaved after the death of their brother, Apollodoros Eupolidos, neglecting to give him a son by posthumous adoption and allowing his **oikos* to become empty. Apollodoros Thrasyllou would naturally have taken steps to avoid letting his inheritance fall into the hands of such people (§§29–32).
4 Argument from character: Thrasyllos's exemplary conduct towards his natural parents, and record of service to the **polis*, made him the obvious choice for Apollodoros when seeking to adopt an heir (§§33–36).

The Strength of the Speaker's Case

Thrasyllos appears to have a good claim to the estate of Apollodoros as his son adopted *inter vivos*, despite the irregularity in the adoption procedure caused by the death of Apollodoros before the formality of Thrasyllos's enrolment in the deme. It is unlikely that the *dikastai* would have perceived the irregularity as fatal to his case, provided he could persuade them that the adoption was indeed carried out in accordance with Apollodoros's wishes. Isaios puts his client's case in a coherent and convincing narrative, of which the essential points are supported by testimony. His argumentation repeatedly plays to the prevailing mistrust of mere words or speeches (*logoi*) citing the conduct or actions (*erga*) of the family members in support of Thrasyllos's case. Argument 1(c), drawn from the enmity between Apollodoros and Eupolis, is similar to the argument in Isa. 9 that Astyphilos would never have wanted to leave his estate to the son of his father's sworn enemy, Kleon. Unlike the speaker of Isa. 9, however, Thrasyllos does not rely on this argument as the main plank of his case, and the origin of the quarrel is attested by witnesses. In fact, both of the arguments 1(c) and 4, drawn from the character of the speaker Thrasyllos, are straightforward, and plausible enough. Although they do not in any sense prove the validity of the adoption, they do support the speaker's case by explaining why Apollodoros would choose to adopt his sister's son.[16]

As the commentary will show, however, the argumentation at 3(c) appears to involve some misrepresentation of the factual situation. Why, then, in a case where his client's position seems to have been factually and legally strong, did Isaios think it necessary to deploy these arguments? It is hardly surprising that he compresses the narrative to emphasize the strengths of his client's case and play down its weaknesses, especially

[16] Cf. the defintion of 'relevance' discussed at pp. 18–23.

given that economy of language is a regular feature of his speeches. What is surprising, at least to the modern reader, is that he does not simply leave the facts of the adoption to speak for themselves, but seeks to bolster the factual case with argumentation from probability involving some distortion of facts which are not crucial to his case, denigration of his opponents, and an apparently irrelevant eulogy of Apollodoros and his father. Such tactics inevitably arouse suspicion about the real strength of his case, but a closer reading of the speech indicates that he may have seen the need to embellish his case in anticipation of a strong counterattack from an unscrupulous opponent.[17]

Commentary

*Proem (1–4)

In a relatively short introduction Thrasyllos adopts the confident and businesslike tone that prevails throughout the speech. Without going into the factual details of his case, he plunges straight into an argument about the relative merits of testamentary and *inter vivos* adoption, followed by a justification for the procedure he has adopted and a brief statement of the basis of his claim. The proem ends with a conventional plea for the good will of the **dikastai.*

1 Ὤιμην μέν, ὦ ἄνδρες ('I would have thought, gentlemen)'. Three of Isaios's other speeches open with an expression of the speaker's opinion, combined with an address to the **dikastai*: 'I think, gentlemen', 2.1; 'We thought, gentlemen', 5.1; 'I could wish, gentlemen', 10.1. Cf., e.g., Lys. 14.1; 31.1.

An address to the *dikastai* at the beginning of a speech, to solicit their attention, is an almost universal feature of Athenian forensic oratory. (One of the rare exceptions is Isa. 11.) It is characteristic of Isaios's speeches from inheritance cases that his preferred form of address is *ō andres* ('gentlemen'). In Isa. 12, a citizenship case, he consistently uses *ō andres dikastai* ('judges', equivalent to 'gentlemen of the jury' in modern English), but this mode of address occurs only four times in all his other speeches

[17] Cf. Todd (1993), 38: "It is often possible to show (as Wyse does) that a speaker is lying, but it is dangerous to infer from this that his opponent is telling the truth; even when you have a case that is both legally strong and likely to win the favour of the jury, it may be worth 'improving' it...".

(in addition to one instance of *andres dikastai* without the interjection, the opening words of Isa. 3). His preference for *ō andres* clearly differentiates his style from that of Lysias, who almost without exception uses *ō andres dikastai* in speeches before a **dikastērion*. The only forms of address used in the Demosthenic corpus are *ō andres dikastai* and *ō andres Athēnaioi* ('men of Athens').

Isaios's clients address the *dikastai* in the vocative 162 times in his twelve extant speeches. The frequency of such addresses within each speech is variable, ranging from five in Isa. 3 (his longest speech) to twenty-two in Isa. 10 (his shortest). In this speech the *dikastai* are addressed only eight times.

In addition to its conventional function in the opening sentence, an address could also be used to mark a transitional point in a speech, especially between the *proem and main narrative (§5; cf. §13) or the resumption of the speech after the reading of testimony or other evidence (§§18 and 29). An address in the course of argumentation or narrative may have a more meaningful function in signalling a point which the speaker particularly wants to emphasize, or as a means of engaging the *dikastai* in his argument (§§37, 45). In particular, it is often associated with a plea for the sympathy or good will of the *dikastai* (§4). Cf. Denommé (1974b), 136: "... ces apostrophes ne se bornent pas à solliciter discrètement l'attention des membres du tribunal; elles veulent aussi les associer intimement à l'argumentation de l'orateur." ("... these addresses do not just solicit discreetly the attention of the tribunal members; they also seek to associate them closely with the orator's argumentation.")

On addresses to the *dikastai* in the Attic orators generally, see Dickey (1996), 177–181.

προσήκειν οὐ τὰς τοιαύτας ἀμφισβητεῖσθαι ποιήσεις ('that it was not appropriate for adoptions of this kind to be disputed'). This is one of only two extant speeches in which an adoption **inter vivos* is contested. (The other is Isa. 2, where an adoption that had, according to the speaker, subsisted for twenty-three years is challenged after the adoptive father's death.) This compares with at least ten known disputes about testamentary or posthumous adoptions, details of which can be found in Rubinstein (1993), 117–125. It is impossible to tell whether this tiny sample is representative of Athenian inheritance cases, but there may be some substance in Thrasyllos's assertion that an adoption *inter vivos* was less likely to become the subject of litigation. When an Athenian adopted a son during his lifetime, any questions about the adopter's mental capacity or the son's eligibility for adoption should have been considered by the *phratry and *deme, with the adopter himself available for questioning, before the adoption was completed. These formalities would have filtered out the most doubtful cases. On the other hand, a claimant to an estate on the basis of a testamentary adoption would have to go to court before the formalities were carried out, providing an opportunity for questions to be raised by rival claimants. Isaios makes Thrasyllos's argument sound authoritative by framing it in general terms, omitting to mention the specific features of his case which may have provided an opening for his opponents.

ζῶν καὶ εὖ φρονῶν ('while alive and in his right mind'). An adoption, whether **inter vivos* or testamentary, was not valid unless the adopter was in his right mind and free from undue influence. It is likely that Apollodoros's state of mind when he adopted Thrasyllos was an issue in this case, here prejudged by Thrasyllos. The phrase 'alive and in his right mind' recurs at §43, and cf. on ἐλθὼν ὡς τὴν ἐμὴν μητέρα…, §14. The state of mind of the adopter, Menekles, is also at issue in Isa. 2, where the speaker, who claims to be his adopted son, describes him three times as 'in his right mind'. (2.14, 19, 43).

ἐπὶ τὰ ἱερὰ ἀγαγὼν εἰς τοὺς συγγενεῖς ἀπέδειξε ('after he has led his adopted son to the domestic shrines and presented him to his kinsmen'). Although ostensibly speaking in general terms about the formalities required for a valid adoption, Thrasyllos is clearly anticipating the more detailed account of his introduction to Apollodoros's *phratry and **genos*, at §§15–17.

καὶ εἰς τὰ κοινὰ γραμματεῖα ἐνέγραψεν ('and inscribed him into the common registers'). Wyse suggests three possible explanations of the plural 'registers': a) that the *phratry kept two lists, or b) that the phratry and **genos* kept separate registers, or c) that the speaker is referring to the register of the *deme as well as that of the *genos* and/or phratry. Lambert (1993), 176, n. 182, suggests that the plural need not be significant but could be used of a single register of the *genos* and/or phratry. Cf. on εἰς τὸ κοινὸν γραμματεῖον, §16. It remains possible that Isaios intended to include the deme register, which is later mentioned separately (cf. on ἐγγράψουσι με…, §27.) If so, this would carry the misleading implication that Apollodoros himself enrolled Thrasyllos into his deme as well as his phratry.

ἅπανθ' ὅσα προσῆκεν αὐτὸς ποιήσας ('and carried out all the proper formalities himself'). Following the ambiguity of 'register(s)' in the preceding clause, this might imply either that Apollodoros completed the *deme enrolment himself, or that the *phratry introduction was the only part of the formal adoption procedure which the adoptive father was required to carry out in person. The latter would be consistent with Isaios's presentation of the phratry introduction later in the speech. Cf. on ποιησαμένου με ἐκείνου…, §17.

εἴ τι πάθοι ('if anything should happen to him', lit. 'if he should suffer anything'). A euphemism commonly used by the orators with reference to the disposition of a person's property in the event of his death. It recurs twice in this speech, §§9 and 27, and cf. Isa. 1.4; 6.5; 11.8; Isok. 17.6; Lys. 32.6; Dem. 23.7, [Dem.] 52.24; [Dem.] 59.58.

2 φανερὰς κατέστησε τὰς αὑτοῦ βουλήσεις ('has made his wishes clear'). This, too, is taken up later in the speech; the fact that Apollodoros had made his wishes clear to his fellow *demesmen is an important feature of Thrasyllos's case.

δόντων αὐτῷ τῶν νόμων ('as the laws allow him to do'). This appeal to 'the laws', in the plural, is a general statement of the legality of adoption *inter vivos*, not a reference to any specific law. Significantly, it is not repeated later in the paragraph, in relation to testamentary adoption. Isaios deploys a variety of terminology to emphasize the legality of the specific procedure carried out by Apollodoros. The formulation used here emphasizes the rights of the adoptive father, rather than those of the adopted son, like 'as the laws have empowered him to do', §17; cf. 'in accordance with the laws', §§3, 18, 26; 'legally', §4; 'correctly', §18; 'valid', §26.

ἀδήλους ἐποίησε ('has made [his wishes] secret'). Someone who chooses testamentary adoption as the means of disposing of his property makes his wishes 'unclear' or 'secret' in the sense that they are not publicly known until after his death, when they may easily be disputed.

διὸ πολλοὶ ... ποιηθέντας ('with the result that many people decide to contest the succession against adopted sons, alleging that the will is a forgery'). Contested wills feature in eight of Isaios's eleven inheritance speeches, but we have no means of knowing whether these cases were typical, or what proportion of all Athenian testamentary adoptions were contested. Cf. General Introduction, pp. 10–12.

ὑπὲρ τῆς θυγατρὸς τῆς Εὐπόλιδος ('on behalf of Eupolis's daughter'). Thrasyllos has not yet explained his opponent's relationship to Apollodoros, describing her only as the daughter of Eupolis. Cf. on ταύτην τε ..., §18.

3 τὰς εὐθυδικίας ('immediate trials'). Instead of blocking a rival claim by **diamarturia*, a legitimate heir could opt for an immediate trial of the disputed issues (*euthudikia*). As Harrison, (1968), 117, observes, "There are occasional suggestions, perhaps mere rhetoric, that procedure by *euthudikia* showed a greater reliance on the justice of one's claim." The reality may have been that the speaker had difficulty in finding a witness who was prepared to take the risk of testifying by way of a *diamarturia*.

Cf. Isa. 6.3, 43, 52, 59; also Dem. 34.4 and [Dem.] 45.6, where *euthudikia* is discussed as an alternative to *paragraphē* (a procedure enabling the defendant in an adversarial action to bring a charge of illegal prosecution against the prosecutor).

μὴ ἐπίδικον εἶναι τὸν κλῆρον ('that the estate was not subject to adjudication'). The standard formula used in a **diamarturia*; the estate was said to be 'not subject to adjudication' by the court because of the existence of a direct descendant who had the right of **embateusis*. Cf. Isa. 3.3, 43; 5.16; 6.4, 59; [Dem.] 44.46.

ὡς ποιησαμένου … κατὰ τοὺς νόμους ('since Apollodoros adopted me in accordance with the laws'). Cf. on δόντων αὐτῷ τῶν νόμων, §2.

4 ἀποδείξω δὲ ('I shall prove to you'). Isaios anticipates the two main strands of the speech: the enmity between Apollodoros and Eupolis, and Apollodoros's adoption of his nephew Thrasyllos. He appears to have a good case on the strength of the facts about the adoption, but it is noteworthy that he does not rely solely on this. To persuade the **dikastai* of the justice of his client's case, he must also explain why Apollodoros was likely to have adopted Thrasyllos, not only adducing witnesses to the principal facts but also drawing inferences from their testimony.

πολλὰ καὶ δεινὰ … ὑφ' ἡμῶν ('having suffered many injuries at my opponents' hands … having received great benefits from my family'). The contrast between the behaviour of the two parties towards Apollodoros, first mentioned here, will become a major theme of the speech. In the second half of the antithesis the pronoun, expressing the agent of the benefaction, is placed in the prominent position. Just as 'by them' associates Eupolis's daughter with the actions of her father, so 'by us' associates Thrasyllos with those of Arkhedamos. Isaios repeatedly uses the first person plural with this effect (cf. §§9 and 11), even though Thrasyllos was formally a member of his father's **oikos*, not that of his maternal grandfather, and the events in question happened before his lifetime.

δικαίως ('legally'). Cf. on δόντων αὐτῷ τῶν νόμων, §2.

ὄντα ἀδελφιδοῦν ('being his nephew'). This is the first reference to Thrasyllos's blood relationship with Apollodoros. Their kinship does not affect the validity of the adoption, but, according to Thrasyllos's reasoning, it does provide a motive for Apollodoros to have adopted him. Cf. on ἐκείνῳ … γεγονώς, §17, οὐδὲ ἀλλότριον ἀλλ' ὄντα ἀδελφιδοῦν, §35, and ἀδελφιδοῦς ὤν, §43. There is also an implied contrast between his position as Apollodoros's nephew and that of his opponent, a cousin, which becomes explicit at §45.

δέομαι … παρασχεῖν ('I beg you all, gentlemen, to show me good will'). The introductions to five of Isaios's speeches include a plea to the **dikastai* to listen to the speaker's case with good will (*eunoia*). The verb *deomai* ('I beg') is typically associated with such pleas; cf. 6.2; 8.5; and 2.2, where it is combined with *hiketeuō* ('I beseech') and *antibolō* ('I entreat'). Cf. Johnstone (1999), 174, n. 3: "The combination of *deomai, antibolō*, and *hiketeuō* seems to have been a conventional appeal. It appears 11 times in the orations; two of the three words appear in combination another 18 times." (Exceptionally, the wording of Isa. 10.3, 'if you are willing to listen to me with good will', avoids verbs of pleading or supplication altogether.) Here, as at Isa. 2.44; 5.20; 6.57, 62; 8.5 and 9.34, the verb of entreaty is reinforced by an address to the *dikastai* in the vocative.

Johnstone (1999), 61–62, argues that pleas for *eunoia*, in Athenian oratory generally, are used by speakers, most often defendants, who want to present themselves as being at a disadvantage. *Eunoia* was "thought to equalize the trial"; it was "not a recompense for any previous benefit but restored the equality that was part of the Athenian ideology of citizenship". In the context of a **diadikasia*, that analysis requires some modification. Thrasyllos's position is analogous to that of a defendant, but only to the extent that he has been disadvantaged by a rival claim to an estate that he regards as his. There is no sense that he is the weaker or less experienced party, and his tone throughout the speech is one of confident authority rather than apology or pleading.

βοηθεῖν μοι τὰ δίκαια ('to help me obtain justice'). The conventional request for the assistance of the **dikastai*, naturally coupled at the beginning of a speech with a plea for their good will, recurs at §37. Cf. Isa. 2.47; 4.31; 5.20; 8.9, 45; 9.35.

ποιήσομαι … διδάσκων ὑμᾶς ('I shall speak as briefly as possible, telling you all that has happened from the beginning'). A typical metanarrative narratorial intervention, forming a bridge between the end of the *proem and the beginning of the first passage of narrative (cf. Edwards (2004), 352). In other speeches Isaios's clients promise to tell their story 'from the point where you will most quickly understand the facts' (1.8, using almost exactly the same words as Isok. 19.4); 'from the point at which my opponents began their speech' (8.6); or 'from the point where you will understand the facts most clearly' (10.3).

A promise to put one's case, or deal with a particular issue, 'as briefly as possible' is a commonplace of Athenian forensic oratory, showing respect for the **dikastai* and demonstrating a businesslike approach on the part of the litigant (who may in some cases also be aware that he is running out of time). Cf. Isa. 6.19; Isok. 21.2; Lys. 12.62; 24.4; Dem. 27.3, 12; 36.3; 37.3; 43.18; 45.2; 54.2.

Telling one's story 'from the beginning' is another commonplace, often conveying a willingness to 'tell the whole truth' and found very frequently in the orators: cf., e.g., Isa. 2.2; Andok. 1.8; Dem. 34.5; 37.3; 40.5; 43.1; 45.2; 49.4; 54.2; Isok. 17.3; 18.4; Lys. 1.5; 7.3; 12.3; 32.3. Typically in an inheritance case, and as the next section shows, the 'beginning' is not the death of the **de cuius*; the origins of the dispute lie a generation further back in the family history.

Narrative, Testimony and Argument: The Quarrel between Apollodoros and Eupolis (*5–13*)

In the opening section of the narrative Isaios first establishes the extent of the family's wealth: Apollodoros's father, Thrasyllos, shared his paternal inheritance with two brothers, but they each had enough property to make them members of the *liturgical class. Next, he explains the origins of Apollodoros's estrangement from his uncle Eupolis and his descendants. Eupolis, who became Apollodoros's guardian after the death of Thrasyllos senior, deprived him of all his fortune; and it was Arkhedamos, Apollodoros's stepfather and the maternal grandfather of the speaker Thrasyllos, who helped Apollodoros to recover his property in two successful lawsuits against Eupolis. Apollodoros reciprocated this kindness, and became **kurios* of Arkhedamos's daughter after the latter's death.

Apollodoros's situation, as presented by Isaios, might be compared with that of Phrastor, who wanted to avoid dying childless so that his property would not go to his collateral relations, with whom he had quarrelled ([Dem.] 59.55). A closer parallel is the family feud described in Isa. 9, where Thoudippos allegedly caused the death of Astyphilos's father in a fight; in both speeches Isaios argues that the **de cuius* would never have wanted his estate to go to the descendants of his lifelong enemy. In each case the origins of the feud go back forty or fifty years, before the speaker's lifetime, but Thrasyllos makes a more convincing claim to Apollodoros's estate than the speaker of Isa. 9 to that of Astyphilos: the outcome of the two lawsuits resulting from Eupolis's fraud or financial mismanagement is more easily verifiable than the fight between the two brothers, and Thrasyllos (unlike the speaker of Isa. 9) appears to have no difficulty in producing witnesses to support his account.

5 Εὔπολις γάρ… καὶ ὁμοπάτριοι ('For Eupolis, Thrasyllos and Mneson were brothers, gentlemen, sons of the same father and mother'). Thrasyllos, the father of Apollodoros, had two brothers of the full blood, so each was entitled to an equal share of their father's estate. Isaios does not need to spell this out to his audience, who would have been familiar with the Athenian system of partible inheritance.

The explanatory particle *gar* ('for'), coupled with the address to the **dikastai*, marks the transition to narrative after an introduction in which the main issues in the case have been set out. (See on Ὤιμην…, §1.) Cf. Isa. 2.3; 8.7; 10.4; 11.8; and, for *gar* without the address to the *dikastai*, 1.9; 6.3. The transitional use of *gar* to introduce the first narrative is regularly found in the Athenian orators after Antiphon, who does not use it in the first narratives of his surviving three forensic speeches, although it does mark the beginning of a subsequent narrative section at Antiph. 1.18 (Edwards (2004), 318–319). In this speech the particle also marks the transition to narrative at §§7, 14, 18 and 27.

ὥστε καὶ λῃτουργεῖν ἕκαστον ἀξιοῦσθαι παρ' ὑμῖν ('so that each of them was considered able to perform *liturgies on behalf of the city'). We have no precise information on the minimum financial requirement for the liturgical class, but it appears to have been at least three talents. Davies (1971), xxiii–xxiv, reviews the evidence from the orators, concluding that it "suggests that during the fourth century men whose property was worth less than 3 *tal.* were free from liturgical obligations, while men whose property was worth over 4 *tal.* were very unlikely to escape such obligations in the long run." That is consistent with the claim (§6) that Apollodoros recovered three talents from Eupolis in his guardianship action.

περὶ τὸν αὐτὸν χρόνον ('at about the same time'). Isaios does not yet specify whether Mneson or Thrasyllos died first.

ἐνθάδε ('here). Mneson died 'here in Athens'.

ἄγαμος καὶ ἄπαις ('unmarried and childless'). This indicates that Mneson's estate should have been shared equally among his next of kin: Eupolis, his surviving brother, and Apollodoros, the son of his deceased brother Thrasyllos.

ὁ δὲ Θράσυλλος… τριηράρχων ('Thrasyllos [died] in Sicily, having been chosen as one of the trierarchs'). By the late fifth century, the function of a trierarch included the payment of a ship's running costs as well as commanding it in the fleet (Rhodes (1981), 680). The trierarchs were appointed by the generals (*Ath. Pol.* 61.1, with Rhodes's commentary). The trierarchy became the most prestigious and expensive of the *liturgies, costing up to a talent for a year's service.

The disastrous Sicilian expedition of 415–413 BC cast a long shadow over the fourth century, when many Athenians would have remembered their ancestors and fellow citizens who fought, and many of whom died, there. (See, e.g., Isa. 6.14 and Dem. 57.37.) The reference to the death of Apollodoros's father, Thrasyllos, in Sicily solicits the respect of the **dikastai* (cf. the eulogy of Thrasyllos, §38), but we are not explicitly told that he was killed in action, so it is perhaps more likely that he died of natural causes or accidentally.

καταλιπὼν ὑόν Ἀπολλόδωρον ('leaving a son Apollodoros'). It appears that Apollodoros was his father's only son and heir.

6 οὗ καὶ Ἀπολλοδώρῳ προσῆκε τὸ ἡμικλήριον ('half of which belonged to Apollodoros'). Thrasyllos apparently died before his brother Mneson, leaving his whole estate to Apollodoros as his legitimate heir. When Mneson died, his estate ought to have been shared equally **per stirpes* between his next of kin (i.e. half to Eupolis or his heirs and half to Thrasyllos or his), but Eupolis claimed the entirety for himself.

φάσκων αὐτῷ δοῦναι τὸν ἀδελφόν ('asserting that his brother had given it to him'). Presumably Apollodoros claimed his share of Mneson's estate in a **diadikasia*, in which Eupolis's defence was that the property at issue had been given to him by Mneson. Thompson (1981), 22, suggests that this passage "may refer to an arrangement whereby a man gave his estate to his brother with the stipulation that the brother would someday [*sic*] introduce his own son as the testator's heir by posthumous adoption". There is no evidence of such a transaction in the available sources, and it is unlikely to have been legally valid if it deprived another collateral kinsman of his share in the estate. So, if it did happen in this case, Apollodoros would have had a strong claim against Eupolis. Isaios's account of Eupolis's alleged transgressions is, however, very brief, and, although the reference to the lawsuits gives an appearance of truth, it may well have been exaggerated.

ἐπιτροπεύων ('acting as guardian'). Eupolis, the only survivor of the three brothers, would have been the obvious choice of guardian for his nephew Apollodoros after the death of Thrasyllos senior, whether or not he had been explicitly appointed by Thrasyllos; in the absence of such an appointment, it is likely that the duty of guardianship fell to the deceased's next of kin. Cf. Harrison (1968), 100.

ὥστε τριῶν αὐτῷ ταλάντων δίκην ὀφλεῖν ('so that he was ordered to restore three talents to him'). The sum that Eupolis was required to repay to Apollodoros, equal in itself to a *liturgical estate, indicates the scale of his alleged misconduct. It also confirms Thrasyllos senior's status as a member of the liturgical class. Cf. on ὥστε καὶ λητουργεῖν…, §5.

7 ’Αρχέδαμος γὰρ…(‘For Arkhedamos…’). For the particle *gar*, see on Εὔπολις γάρ…, §5. In an extremely economical piece of narrative, Isaios introduces his client's maternal grandfather, Arkhedamos, one of the key figures in the family feud. Arkhedamos is presented, like Theophrastos in Isa. 9, as the beneficent stepfather, with whom his stepson forms strong bonds of gratitude and affection after becoming estranged from his own father's surviving family.

ὁ πάππος οὑμός (‘my grandfather’). Thrasyllos takes the earliest opportunity to establish his own relationship with Arkhedamos, which he will later exploit to associate himself with the mutual good will between Arkhedamos and Apollodoros. Cf. on ὁ δὲ πάππος…, §8.

ὁρῶν αὐτὸν πάντων ἀποστερούμενον (‘seeing that he was being robbed of all his fortune’). See on ἀποστερῶν, 8.3. The present tense of the participles indicates that Arkhedamos did not just take action after Apollodoros had been deprived of his property, but intervened while Eupolis's allegedly criminal activity was still going on.

παῖδα ὄνθ’ (‘while he was a child’). The words emphasize Apollodoros's vulnerability when Arkhedamos ‘rescued’ him from Eupolis, but even if he was still a minor he could not have been a small child (unlike Astyphilos when Theophrastos took him in; cf. μικρὸν ὄντα, 9.27). We are told (§8) that, after he had come of age and won two court cases against his guardian, Apollodoros helped secure the release of Arkhedamos when he was taken prisoner of war. If this happened in the later years of the Peloponnesian War, which ended in 404 BC, it is probably reasonable to assume that Apollodoros was born no later than 425 BC, so that he would have been at least ten or eleven when his father Thrasyllos died, and reached eighteen no later than 407. On the assumption that the speech can be dated to 355 BC, he would then have been at least seventy at the time of his death.

ἀνδρί τε γενομένῳ (‘when he became a man’). An orphan was entitled to sue his guardian(s) within five years after coming of age (Dem. 38.17, cited by Rubinstein (2000), 68).

συνηγωνίσατο (‘assisted him in bringing a legal action’). On the activities and level of participation implied by the verb *sunagōnizesthai*, see on τοῦ πάππου συνηγωνισμένου καὶ λέγοντος, §10. Arkhedamos almost certainly bore all or most of the financial cost of the litigation, perhaps including the fee of a *logographer. As Rubinstein (2000), 68, points out, the participation of **sunēgoroi* in cases concerning guardianship is hardly surprising, given the youth and inexperience of the litigants; other attested guardianship cases in which a *sunēgoros* spoke on behalf of the prosecutor include Lys. 32 and Lys. fr. XXXVII (OCT).

δίκας δύο ἑλών ('winning two lawsuits'). The grammatical subject is Arkhedamos, giving the impression that he was the active prosecutor of the litigation. For the nature of the two lawsuits, see on τὴν μὲν ἐπιτροπῆς..., §10.

καὶ τὴν οὐσίαν... πᾶσαν ('and enabled Apollodoros to recover his entire property'). If Apollodoros inherited the whole of his father's estate and half that of his uncle Mneson, his personal fortune must originally have been in the order of four and a half talents, but in the aftermath of the Peloponnesian War, with its severe impact on the Athenian economy, it is likely that the value of the estate would have depreciated. Eupolis, therefore, may not have been entirely to blame for Apollodoros's losses.

8 τὸν πάντα χρόνον ('all the time'). Cf. on τὸν ἅπαντα χρόνον, 9.20.

ὁ δὲ πάππος οὑμὸς καὶ Ἀπολλόδωρος φιλικῶς ('whereas my grandfather and Apollodoros were close friends'). In the second half of the antithesis, Thrasyllos refers to Arkhedamos as 'my grandfather' instead of using his name, in order to emphasize the relationship and associate himself with the friendship between Arkhedamos and Apollodoros. Cf. on ὁ πάππος οὑμός, §7. On Isaios's use of relationship terms instead of names, cf. on Κίρων ὁ πάππος, 8.3 and τῶν τἀδελφοῦ, 9.2.

τοῖς δ' ἔργοις ἄν τις τεκμήραιτο μάλιστα ('The actions of Apollodoros provide the best evidence'). The superior evidential weight of actions (*erga*) over words (*logoi*) is a recurrent theme of this speech. Cf. §§11, 12, 18, 19, 26, 38. Isaios's use of the *motif* is often tendentious, since the agents themselves might not have recognized the motivation he imputes to them.

9 εἰς Κόρινθόν τε στρατεύεσθαι μέλλων ('about to set off for Corinth on military service'). This apparently refers to the Corinthian War of 395–386 BC. Apollodoros was probably in his early thirties at the beginning of the war (cf. on παῖδα ὄνθ', §7), but his service may have started later.

εἴ τι πάθοι ('in case anything should happen to him'). Cf. on εἴ τι πάθοι, §1.

διέθετο τὴν οὐσίαν ('bequeathed his property'). On the frequency of wills made before military campaigns or journeys abroad, see on καὶ οὐδ' ἐν μιᾷ..., 9.14. It has sometimes been inferred (e.g. by Wyse) that Apollodoros adopted his half-sister, but nothing in the text suggests that his will involved an adoption. It is perhaps more likely that by the time he set off for Corinth, he had become her **kurios* after the death of her father, Arkhedamos. On wills without adoption, see Rubinstein (1993), 81–86.

τῇ ἐκείνου μὲν θυγατρί, ἐμῇ δὲ μητρί, αὑτοῦ δὲ ἀδελφῇ ('Arkhedamos's daughter, his own sister and my mother'). This is the first reference to Arkhedamos's daughter, the half-sister of Apollodoros and mother of Thrasyllos the speaker. (For the accumulation of kinship words, which heightens the emotional tone of the passage, cf., e.g., Lys. 32.12.) Since she was unmarried when Apollodoros set off for the Corinthian War (395 BC at the earliest) it is unlikely that she was born before about 410, when Apollodoros was already about fifteen. So, despite the emphasis placed in the speech on the bonds of affection between them, they were not actually brought up together as small children. They might, nevertheless, have become close after the death of Arkhedamos, when Apollodoros would have become his sister's **kurios*.

διδοὺς αὐτὴν Λακρατίδῃ τῷ νῦν ἱεροφάντῃ γεγενημένῳ ('providing for her marriage to Lakratides, who has now become hierophant'). The hierophant, a member of the house of the Eumolpidae, was the high priest of the cult of Demeter at Eleusis, who displayed the sacred emblems at the Eleusinian mysteries. Cf. 6.33, the only other reference to this office in Isaios's surviving speeches. Since Apollodoros survived the war, his will did not come into effect, and presumably his sister did not marry Lakratides. (Her eventual husband, the father of Thrasyllos the speaker, is not named in the speech.) A votive relief dedicated by a priest named Lakratides features among the remains of the Ploutonion at Eleusis, the construction of which is dated to the *arkhonship of Kephisophon, 329/8 BC (Mylonas (1962), 147). The office of hierophant was held for life, but it is implausible that the dedicator was the Lakratides mentioned here, who was presumably of marriageable age in the late 390s. He may, nevertheless, have belonged to a later generation of the same family.

περὶ ἡμᾶς τοὺς ἐξ ἀρχῆς αὐτὸν σώσαντας ('towards us who had originally saved him from ruin'). Cf. on πολλὰ καὶ δεινὰ…, §4.

10 ὡς δ' ἀληθῆ λέγω ('and to prove that I am telling the truth'). At this point the specific 'facts' to which the witnesses will testify are summarized. This is unusual in Isaios's speeches, but cf. on κάλει μοι…, §32.

τὴν μὲν ἐπιτροπῆς τὴν δὲ ἡμικληρίου ('one in respect of his guardianship and the other concerning the half-share [of Mneson's estate]'). Cf. on δίκας δύο ἑλών, §7. It now becomes clear that the two legal actions were a *dikē epitropēs* to recover the money embezzled by Eupolis as guardian and a *diadikasia* to claim Apollodoros's share of the estate of Mneson.

τοῦ πάππου συνηγωνισμένου καὶ λέγοντος ('my grandfather having supported his case and speaking on his behalf'). Cf. on ὁ δὲ πάππος…, §8. A *sunēgoros* could either present the whole case on behalf of the litigant or make a supplementary speech in support of the litigant's own presentation. In a case such as this, where the litigant was young and inexperienced, it is likely that his *sunēgoros* would have delivered the main speech.

δι' ἡμᾶς…ἀνταπέδωκε ('that it was thanks to us that he recovered his fortune, and that he repaid our good services'). Cf. on πολλὰ καὶ δεινὰ…, §4.

τούτων πρῶτον βούλομαι παρασχέσθαι τοὺς μάρτυρας. καί μοι κάλει δεῦρο αὐτούς ('on all these points I want first to produce the witnesses; please call them forward'). Six pieces of witness testimony are introduced in this speech, each following the section of narrative to which it relates. Some of the witnesses were Apollodoros's **phrateres* and *demesmen, but none are identified more closely, so they were probably not related to him. Humphreys (1986), 69, argues that the speaker's father is likely to have been among those testifying to the good relations between Apollodoros and his step-kin, citing this as one of four cases where a father probably testified on behalf of his son. There is, however, no support for this in the text, and in fact it seems unlikely that the speaker's father was still alive (cf. on καὶ ᾔτησε καὶ ἔτυχεν, §14).

Five of the six witness statements in this speech are introduced with formulae including the verbs *kalein* ('call') or *parekhesthai* ('produce'), both of which have the witnesses themselves as objects (cf. §§25, 28, 32, 36). The formula introducing the remaining witness statement (§17) refers to the testimony rather than the person giving it: 'take the depositions for me'. As discussed by Bonner (1905), 46–52, this reflects the change from oral to written witness testimony in the Athenian courts in the early fourth century. Formulae relating to the witnesses continued to be appropriate after the change, because they were still required to appear in court, but Isaios was the first of the orators to use formulae relating specifically to the testimony. Bonner dates the procedural change after 380 BC, and Calhoun (1919), 192–193, argues plausibly for 378/7 as the year of a general reform of the Athenian legal system, including a requirement for both pleadings and witness testimony to be in writing, and a change in the method of selecting **dikastai*. There is a potential difficulty with this date, so far as testimony is concerned, because a direction to the court clerk to 'read the testimony for me' occurs at Isa. 5.2, in a speech which is generally dated by modern scholars, at the latest, to the year 389. Bonner (1905), 47 follows Jebb in suggesting that Isa. 5 "may be as late as 372". Calhoun, 191, accepts the earlier date for the speech, but argues that witness statements may occasionally have been presented in writing before written testimony became a legal requirement.

Thomas (1989), 38–45, discusses the transition to written pleadings and testimony in the Athenian courts in the wider context of a society in which documentary evidence was gradually becoming more acceptable.

11 παρ' ἡμῶν ('from us'). Cf. on πολλὰ καὶ δεινὰ…, §4.

περὶ τοσούτων χρημάτων ('about such large amounts of money'). Thrasyllos's explanation forestalls any suggestion from his opponents that there might have been a reconciliation between Apollodoros and Eupolis or his descendants. The large sum involved is a convincing reason why they never became reconciled.

μεγάλα γὰρ τεκμήρια ('convincing proofs'). A *tekmērion* (pl. *tekmēria*) may, typically in dramatic recognition scenes, be a physical sign or token such as a lock of hair or a ring. (See, e.g., Aesch. *Kho.* 205, Eur. *El.* 575, Men. *Epit.* 456.) In forensic oratory a *tekmērion* may be any fact or piece of evidence from which inferences may be drawn in support of a proposition which the speaker seeks to prove (as, in this instance, Thrasyllos wants to prove that Apollodoros and Eupolis were bitter enemies; cf. 8.6, 15; 9.10, 16, 26). Arist. *Rh.* 1357b defines *tekmērion* as a form of 'sign' (*sēmeion*) which is 'necessary' (*anankaion*), in the sense that it forms the basis of a syllogism leading to an irrefutable conclusion. In practice, speechwriters tend to overstate the probative value of their *tekmēria*, which are often (at best) indications that a particular conclusion is probable rather than necessary.

As Thrasyllos is about to reveal, the *tekmēria* he has in mind are the actions (*erga*) of Eupolis and Apollodoros (cf. on τοῖς δ' ἔργοις…, §8).

Εὔπολις γὰρ…ἔδωκε ('although Eupolis had two daughters and was descended from the same ancestors as Apollodoros and saw that he had acquired money, yet he gave neither of them to him in marriage)'. Osborne (1985a), 136, describes this as an argument "of rather curious logic", reflecting "some popular support for marriage to kin". The fact that Eupolis did not marry one of his daughters to Apollodoros does not, of course, prove that the normal ties of kinship between them had broken down, but Isaios's argument may have been quite persuasive in a society where endogamous marriage was commonplace. Thompson (1967) and (1972), 211, identifies, from literary sources, sixteen marriages between first cousins in classical Athens. An endogamous marriage might be motivated by such factors as a desire to strengthen family bonds, keep a family estate intact, or provide an heir for a branch of the family that would otherwise have died out. But in appropriate circumstances (as discussed by Osborne (1985a), 128–138) marriage strategies might be determined by location of property rather than kinship. We know that Eupolis in fact married both of his daughters out of his *deme, to Aiskhines of Lousia and Pronapes of Aixone (§18). It may be assumed that Apollodoros's eventual marriage was exogamous, although no information is given about it in the speech.

Eupolis was 'descended from the same ancestors' as his nephew Apollodoros: their common ancestor was the father of Eupolis and grandfather of Apollodoros. The phrase is used in a similar sense, referring to the obligations of kinship, at 10.23. For its meaning in the context of inheritance law, see on κρατεῖν δὲ…, §20.

The negative ('gave neither of them') conveys the idea of an unfulfilled expectation, after a build-up of three reasons why Eupolis should have seen a marriage between one of his daughters and his nephew Apollodoros as an attractive option. (For presentation through negation, see on ἐκείνῳ…, §17.) The detail that Eupolis had two daughters seems to imply that he had all the more reason to marry one of them to Apollodoros, but there is no legal basis for this. Cf. on ἐκείνῳ δ'οὐκ εἰσποιουόσας, §31.

12 καίτοι δοκοῦσιν ἐπιγαμίαι…μεγάλης διαφορᾶς ('Yet it is generally thought that marriages reconcile serious animosities'). After considering the specifics of Eupolis's situation, Isaios now puts the argument in more general terms, as is usual in argumentation from probability in Athenian forensic oratory. Thompson (1981), 17, takes this passage as an illustration of the point that Athenian marriage was a social institution, not merely a property transaction.

13 οἶδα γὰρ ὅτι καὶ ὑμῶν ὅσοι πρεσβύτεροι μνημονεύουσιν ('for I know that the older ones among you remember'). It is possible that, as Thrasyllos implies, the litigation between Apollodoros and Eupolis became a *cause célèbre* in Athens because of the large sums of money involved, and even fifty years later some of the older **dikastai* might have remembered it. In the absence of court records in Athens, Thrasyllos could only appeal to their collective memory, although it is possible that one or both parties employed a *logographer who circulated the speeches to advertise his services. In any event, this use of the second person plural is an effective way of engaging the audience with the speaker's argument. For appeals to the memory specifically of the older *dikastai*, cf., e.g., Antiph. 5.71 (on the release of Sosias from the custody of the Eleven) and Lyk. 1.93.

καὶ διότι πολὺ αὐτὸν Αρχέδαμος εἷλεν ('and because Arkhedamos obtained heavy damages'). Cf. on δίκας δύο ἑλῶν, §7.

ζῶν αὐτός ('during his lifetime'). As the narrative moves on from the enmity of Eupolis and Apollodoros, Thrasyllos summarizes the ground he is about to cover in the next section. He starts with his strongest point by emphasizing again that Apollodoros adopted him in his own lifetime.

καὶ εἰς τοὺς γεννήτας καὶ εἰς τοὺς φράτορας ἐνέγραψε ('and entered me in the registers of his *genos* and phratry'). On the relationship between **genos* and *phratry, see on εἰς τοὺς γεννήτας τε καὶ φράτορας, §15. Thrasyllos does not yet mention his enrolment in Apollodoros's *deme, which Apollodoros did not carry out himself.

Narrative and Testimony: Apollodoros's Adoption of Thrasyllos (14–17)

In this key section of the speech, Thrasyllos explains how Apollodoros decided to adopt him after the death of his legitimate son, took him into his household, and introduced him to his *phratry and **genos*. He treats the adoption as complete at that stage, postponing his account of the *deme enrolment until after a lengthy argument on male precedence in the law of intestate succession.

14 Ἀπολλοδώρῳ γὰρ ἦν ὑός ('For Apollodoros had a son'). For the explanatory *gar*, see on Εὔπολις γάρ…, §5. Thrasyllos explains the timing of his adoption by pointing out that Apollodoros naturally expected his legitimate son to take over his property and continue his line of succession after his death.

ἐπειδὴ δὲ ἐτελεύτησε νοσήσας ('but when he became ill and died'). As usual Isaios's narrative is extremely compressed, but he presumably intended his audience to infer that the illness and death of Apollodoros's son were sudden and unexpected.

τοῦ ἐξελθόντος ἐνιαυτοῦ μηνὸς Μαιμακτηριῶνος ('in the month of Maimakterion last year'). Maimakterion was the fifth month of the Athenian year (October–November), so the case must have come to court within at most eighteen months after the death of Apollodoros's son.

ἐπὶ τοῖς παροῦσιν… καταμεμψάμενος ('depressed by his misfortunes and viewing his advancing age with regret'). This is the only section of the speech in which Isaios relies on **pathos*, evoking, first, a picture of Apollodoros as an old man grieving at the death of his only son.

ὑφ' ὧν καὶ ἐξ ἀρχῆς εὖ πεπονθὼς ἦν ('from whom he had in earlier years received kindness'). It would, in any event, have been natural for Apollodoros to turn to his sister for help in his distress, but Isaios links this explicitly with the kindness bestowed by her father Arkhedamos on the younger Apollodoros.

ἐλθὼν ὡς τὴν ἐμὴν μητέρα ἑαυτοῦ δὲ ἀδελφήν ('he came to my mother, his own sister'). Continuing his use of **pathos*, Isaios appeals to the Athenians' sentimentality about women, emphasizing Apollodoros's affection for his half-sister and respect for her wishes. More importantly, however, this passage stresses that it was Apollodoros who took the initiative in proposing the adoption, undermining any suggestion from Thrasyllos's opponents that it was invalid because he was acting under the influence of a woman. Cf. on ζῶν καὶ εὖ φρονῶν, §1.

καὶ ᾔτησε καὶ ἔτυχεν ('and asked her permission, which was granted'). Presumably Thrasyllos's natural father was dead by this time, otherwise Apollodoros would have sought his permission for the adoption. The extent of the mother's authority is unclear; as Thrasyllos presents the story, Apollodoros sought and obtained her permission, but he could probably have proceeded even without her agreement. Although Thrasyllos does not mention any siblings, he probably had at least one brother who remained in their father's **oikos* after the adoption. Presumably, too, Thrasyllos retained his share of his natural father's estate, which would have been consolidated with that of Apollodoros after the latter's death. Cf. on ἐκποίητος, §23.

15 καὶ ἐπειδὴ Θαργήλια ἦν ('and when the Thargelia came round'). The regular time for the introduction of a natural or adopted son to his father's *phratry was "the great ancestral festival of Apatouria" (Parker (1996), 105), which took place in the month of Pyanepsion. Apart from Isa. 7, there is no other evidence for a link between phratry activity and the Thargelia, an ancient Ionian festival celebrating the birth of Apollo on the seventh day of the eleventh month. Since Apollodoros's own son had died in Maimakterion, the month immediately after Pyanepsion, he would have had to wait almost a year for the next Apatouria. It is tempting to conclude (with Parker (1996), 107) that the phratry made a special arrangement for Apollodoros to introduce Thrasyllos as his adopted son, because he knew that he might not survive until the Apatouria. But there was still an interval of about five months before the Thargelia, and it is possible that the phratry in question held one of its regular meetings then. Lambert (1993), 216, argues persuasively that there is a 'good case' for identifying Apollodoros's phratry as the Akhniadai, which had a cult of Apollo Hebdomeios and may have met regularly at the Thargelia. This phratry apparently had a

centre at Kephale in southern Attica, which may also have been the location of Apollodoros's *deme, Leukonoion.

εἰς τοὺς γεννήτας τε καὶ φράτορας ('to the members of his *genos* and phratry'). The exact nature of the Athenian **genos*, and its relation to the *phratry, have been the subject of scholarly debate. The evidence is reviewed by Lambert (1993), 59–74, who concludes that the *genē* were probably well established by the late fifth century as groups associated with phratries but with a separate institutional identity. A *genos*, normally a sub-group of a phratry, was "a group of the same type as the *deme and phratry themselves, with hereditary membership and local associations, but not consisting of persons of any particular status" (Lambert (1993), 61). Not every citizen was a member of a *genos*, but membership could be used as evidence of legitimacy or descent in disputes concerning inheritance or citizenship.

Thrasyllos claims to have been admitted to two distinct groups, but describes only one procedure. This is consistent with the law of Philokhoros *FGrH* 328 F 32 (discussed by Lambert (1993), 67), under which the procedure of swearing and voting took place in the *genos*, and was followed by automatic entry to the phratry. It is possible that entry to the *genos* actually took place at the phratry meeting. For further discussion of the system of *genē*, and their association with the phratries, see Parker (1996), 64–65.

16 ἔστι δ'αὐτοῖς νόμος ὁ αὐτός ('and these bodies have the same rule'). These words are generally taken to mean that Apollodoros's *phratry and **genos* applied the same rules whether it was a natural or an adopted son who was being introduced (Wyse, *ad loc.*; Andrewes (1961), 5; Lambert (1993), 66, n. 37). An alternative interpretation is that the phratry and *genos* had the same rule, but this, as Lambert observes, seems forced.

ἐξ ἀστῆς ... καὶ γεγονότα ὀρθῶς ('lawfully born of an Athenian mother'). From the fact that this rule apparently applied to adopted as well as natural sons, Wyse, *ad loc.*, reasonably infers that a bastard could not be legitimated by adoption. But Harrison (1968), 68, thought there was "no good reason to believe that [bastards] were ineligible for adoption, by which means they could, if the occasion arose, be brought back into the stream, as it were, of full life in an *oikos*".

εἰς τὸ κοινὸν γραμματεῖον ('in the common register'). Lambert (1993), 67, considers the possibility that the **genos* and *phratry had a joint register, or that Isaios is here referring elliptically to the registers of *genos* and phratry respectively. Pointing out that there are no parallels for either usage, he suggests that the 'common register' might more naturally be taken as 'the register of a single institution, i.e. of a *genos* that was also a whole phratry'.

In itself an imprecise term, *grammateion* may refer to any document, including a will or other testamentary disposition (e.g. Isa. 1.25; 4.13; 6.29, 31; 9.12, 18, 25) or a written agreement (e.g. Isa. 5.25). With reference to the documentation of an organization such as a *deme or phratry it is regularly translated as 'register', but, as Lambert (1993), 175, points out, it "could also function more widely as the minutes of an organization. It was not simply a list of members whose names were entered once and for all." The purpose of maintaining a list of current members was to determine who was entitled to the privileges or subject to the obligations of membership (including, in the case of a deme, liability for payments or services to the **polis*). The registers were probably never considered as a permanent, archival record, and it is plausible that members' names were erased at death, as in Plato's theoretical state (*Laws* 6.785a–b, discussed by Lambert (1993), 174–175). Cf. Thomas (1989), 40, on "the crucial difference between documents and archives and between the use of documents and their systematic preservation".

τοιαύτας ἀκριβείας ἔχει τὰ δίκαια παρ' αὐτοῖς ('such is the exactitude with which they carry out their formalities'). Thrasyllos is not the only forensic speaker to emphasize the thoroughness of the scrutiny conducted by his *phratry before he was accepted as a member; cf. Isa. 8.19 (cited by Lambert (1993), 173). This may have been pure rhetoric, but it is possible that some phratries were more conscientious than others in carrying out these formalities.

17 ἐκείνῳ ... γεγονώς ('having full confidence in him and not being unaware that I was his sister's son'). Thrasyllos again stresses his blood relationship with Apollodoros (cf. on ὄντα ἀδελφιδοῦν, §4), but it would have been more natural for him to make a positive statement: 'The *phrateres* and *gennētai* trusted Apollodoros, and knew that I was his nephew'. The emphatic negation seems to imply that he is rebutting an allegation from his opponents that his enrolment in the *phratry and **genos* was disputed because he was an outsider to the family, unknown to Apollodoros's associates.

In her narratological analysis of the *Iliad*, De Jong (2004), 61–68, discusses 'presentation through negation' as a technique used to contradict the expectations of the poet's audience (which may be based on contextual knowledge, historical knowledge, or general knowledge of the world). Hornblower (1994), 166 adds that, in historiography, a negative statement may also be "a polemical way of flagging a controversy". In forensic oratory, where both types of negation are used, it is not always easy to distinguish one from the other. Further examples in Isaios include, e.g., 7.34, 38; 8.23, 36, 37; 9.1, 4, 5.

ἐγγράφουσί... καθ' ἱερῶν ('inscribe my name in the common register, after Apollodoros had sworn with his hand on the victims'). Thrasyllos has already described, in general terms, the formalities required for the introduction of a natural or adopted son to his father's **genos* and *phratry (§16). Now, in a compressed but vivid account (note the historic present) he confirms that all the requirements were met in his own case, with Apollodoros himself participating as the introducer.

καὶ οὕτω μὲν ὑπὸ ζῶντος ἐποιήθην ('and in this way I was adopted by him in his lifetime'). Thrasyllos presents the adoption as complete after his introduction to the *phratry and **genos*. Cf. on ὅτι πεποιημένος..., §27.

εἰς τὸ κοινὸν γραμματεῖον ἐνεγράφην Θράσυλλος Ἀπολλοδώρου ('I was inscribed in the common register as Thrasyllos son of Apollodoros'). Cf. on εἰς τὸ κοινὸν γραμματεῖον, §16. Thrasyllos has now twice referred specifically to the entry of his name in the register. In a modern court case one would expect the register itself, or a certified copy of the relevant entry, to be produced as evidence, but a preference for testimony over documentary evidence was firmly embedded in the Athenian legal culture. On the persistent mistrust of documentation, even into the period when Athens was in transition from orality to literacy, see, e.g., Thomas (1989), 41–42.

As Wyse notes, Thrasyllos probably took this name after the adoption; Apollodoros would have been following established custom in naming his (adopted) son after his own father.

ποιησαμένου με ἐκείνου τοῦτον τὸν τρόπον ('after he had adopted my in this way'). Thrasyllos again implies that the adoption had been completed by Apollodoros in person.

τῶν νόμων αὐτῷ δεδωκότων ('as the laws have empowered him to do'). Cf. on δόντων αὐτῷ τῶν νόμων, §2.

ὡς δ' ἀληθῆ λέγω, λαβέ μοι τὰς μαρτυρίας ('to prove that I am telling the truth, please take the depositions'). This testimony relates to Apollodoros's adoption of Thrasyllos and introduction into his *phratry and **genos*. On the formulae used to introduce testimony in this speech, see on τούτων πρῶτον..., §10.

Narrative, Argument, Laws and Testimony: The Order of Intestate Succession (18–26)

After Thrasyllos's account of his introduction to Apollodoros's *phratry, the narrative is interrupted by legal argument. In a digression from the central issue, Thrasyllos claims that if Apollodoros had not left an adopted son, it was not the wife of Pronapes who would have had first claim to his estate as next of kin, but her nephew, Thrasyboulos. Interpreting the law of intestate succession in a way which has been questioned by modern scholars, Isaios argues that, despite being more distantly related to Apollodoros (as first cousin once removed), Thrasyboulos ranked above the wife of Pronapes in the **ankhisteia* because of the principle of male precedence. Wyse, 560, typically, characterizes Isaios's argumentation as "dishonest" and "ugly", while Harrison (1968), 148, n. 2, describes it more neutrally as "probably a misrepresentation of the law". These conclusions are worth re-examining.

Isaios's starting point is uncontentious: if a deceased Athenian left no descendants or brothers, and had not adopted a son, his surviving sister would share the estate equally with a nephew born of another sister who was already dead. This, as he observes, is what happened when Apollodoros Eupolidos died: half of his estate went to his surviving sister, the wife of Pronapes, and the other half to Thrasyboulos, the son of his deceased sister the wife of Aiskhines. But Isaios goes on to say that if the next of kin are not siblings but cousins of the deceased (as were the daughters of Eupolis to Apollodoros Thrasyllou), then the law provides that 'males and the descendants of males have precedence, if they are descended from the same ancestors, even if they are more distantly related'. (See the commentary on §20, below, for a more detailed explanation.) So, if Thrasyboulos had claimed the estate as Apollodoros's intestate heir, the wife of Pronapes would not have been entitled even to a share of it, whereas in fact she is claiming the whole estate while Thrasyboulos has made no claim at all.

Wyse, seeing "no sufficient reason" for the differential treatment of siblings and cousins, argues that the preference given by the law to males and their descendants over females and their descendants operated in the same way at each degree of kinship. Thus (as Isaios acknowledges) a deceased brother's son would exclude a surviving sister, and a male cousin's son would exclude a female cousin (his aunt) because the male cousin would have excluded the female cousin (his sister). But a female cousin's son would not exclude a female cousin (his aunt) because the two female cousins (each other's sisters) would have taken equal shares, so that Thrasyboulos and his aunt would each have been entitled to half of Apollodoros's estate: she in her right as the surviving first cousin of Apollodoros, and he as the representative of his deceased mother who was also a first cousin. So Isaios, in Wyse's view, is deliberately exploiting the supposed ignorance of the Athenian **dikastai* in order to strengthen the case against his client's opponents.

Wyse's argument makes good sense from the perspective of modern inheritance law, but that is no reason to doubt Isaios's account of the Athenian system, which may well have been different. Although it is not explicitly corroborated by other ancient sources, neither is it contradicted by them; the principle of male precedence is well attested, but its precise application is not clearly stated elsewhere (see on κρατεῖν δὲ…, §20). In fact, the rule is perfectly plausible in a system designed to transfer a deceased citizen's estate to his closest male relative; as Lacey (1968), 139 points out, its effect would have been to restrict the accumulation of property by women. So it would seem that the only basis for scepticism is an expectation based on modern inheritance systems, combined with a general reluctance to trust Isaios as a source of information on Athenian law.

But even if we accept that Isaios's argument about male precedence is legally correct, we may still wonder why he deployed it at all, given that it is not central to his client's case and relates only to a hypothetical situation. The real point of this discussion, in its rhetorical context, is to enable Isaios to assert on behalf of his client that Thrasyboulos, by refraining from asserting his own claim to the estate, has indicated his acquiescence in the adoption of Thrasyllos. (For an alternative explanation of Thrasyboulos's silence, see on ἔργοις φανερῶς μεμαρτυρήκασιν, §18.) It also enables him to put the wife of Pronapes in a bad light (although she was not actually acting illegally, given that the function of the court was not to establish who was Apollodoros's next of kin, but simply to decide whether she had a better claim to the estate than Thrasyllos). But, as Roussel (1922), 127, observes, Isaios could have made these points by showing that Thrasyboulos had an equal claim with the wife of Pronapes. He might have gained some rhetorical advantage by exaggerating the alleged greed and opportunism of the latter, but it is difficult to believe that he would have thought it worth misrepresenting the law in order to achieve this, given the risk of discredit to his client if even some of the *dikastai* noticed the error.

18 Οἶμαι τοίνυν, ὦ ἄνδρες ('I imagine, gentlemen'). See on ὦ ἄνδρες, §1.

ἔργοις φανερῶς μεμαρτυρήκασιν ('have clearly attested by their conduct'). See on τοῖς δ'ἔγροις..., §8. Isaios tries to enlist Thrasyboulos as an additional 'witness', claiming that he has shown support for Thrasyllos through his conduct, but there are other possible explanations of Thrasyboulos's silence. Humphreys (1986), 72, points out that he had already inherited his natural father's estate and half that of his maternal uncle, and stood to inherit from his adoptive father: "He would have cut a poor figure in court if he had claimed Apollodorus' estate as well."

ὀρθῶς καὶ κατὰ τοὺς νόμους ('correctly and in a legal manner'). Cf. on δόντων αὐτῷ τῶν νόμων, §2.

κατέλιπε γὰρ Εὔπολις θυγατέρας δύο ('For Eupolis left two daughters'). See on Εὔπολις γάρ..., §5.

ταύτην τε ἣ νῦν ἀμφισβητεῖ καὶ Προνάπει συνοικεῖ ('the one who is the present claimant and is married to Pronapes'). Epigraphic evidence suggests that Pronapes was a member of the deme Aixone: a Eupolis, son of Pronapes of Aixone, is mentioned at *IG* ii[2] 1623, 60–61; cf. *IG* ii[2] 1626, 7–8. Aiskhines, the other son-in-law of Eupolis, is identified as belonging to the deme Lousia.

The verb *sunoikein* (lit. 'live with') denotes "the factual cohabitation of a man and woman" (Harrison (1968), 2), often, but not necessarily, referring to a formal marriage by **enguē* (for which see on τοὺς ἐγγυησαμένους..., 8.14). For the conventions on the naming of women in Athenian forensic oratory, see on Κυρωνίδης καὶ..., 10.4. Thrasyllos's opponent, described at §2 as the daughter of Eupolis, is now identified as the wife of Pronapes. In the rest of the speech Thrasyllos refers to her either with the demonstrative pronoun *hautē* alone (§§23, 24, 25) or as 'the disputant', §43. The pronoun *houtoi* ('they') is similarly used for 'my opponents' (§28). This use of the demonstrative pronoun, to avoid referring to an opponent by name, is a very common feature of Athenian forensic oratory, which has the effect of depersonalizing the opponent. Similar tactics are recommended to modern students of advocacy: "decide on the best way to minimise any empathy the court may have for the opposing party—for example, you may want to try to depersonalise them by using only a title when referring to them (e.g. 'the claimant')." (Inns of Court School of Law (2006), 117).

19 ἔστι δὲ νόμος...καθίστησι ('There is a law which provides that if a brother by the same father dies childless and intestate, his property is to be divided equally between the surviving sister and any nephew born of another sister'). This, as Isaios goes on to explain, was the position when

Apollodoros Eupolidos died, leaving his estate to be shared by his nephew Thrasyboulos and the wife of Pronapes. As noted by Karabélias (2002), 45, a *uterine sister would have no claim to her half-brother's estate, because she belonged to a different **oikos*, that of her father.

ἔργῳ γὰρ οὗτοι φανερὸν τοῦτο πεποιήκασι ('for they have made this clear by their conduct'). See on τοῖς δ'ἔργοις . . . , §8.

τοῦ γὰρ Εὐπόλιδος . . . εἴληφεν ('for Eupolis's son Apollodoros died without issue, and Thrasyboulos received half his estate'). As usual, Isaios's chronology is vague, but there is a clear implication that the wife of Aiskhines died before her brother Apollodoros, leaving Thrasyboulos to inherit what would have been her share of the estate. This is difficult to square with Thrasyllos's later accusations about the behaviour of Apollodoros Eupolidos's sisters (plural) after his death, although it might be possible to reconcile the two accounts if Thrasyboulos's share of the estate of Apollodoros Eupolidos came to him only on the death of his mother. Cf. the introductory note to §§29–32.

20 ἀνεψιοῦ δέ . . . ('but when a cousin dies . . .'). Isaios elaborates his explanation of the law on intestate succession: when the next of kin are first cousins or more distant relations of the deceased, rather than siblings, males have precedence over females.

"κρατεῖν δὲ . . . ὄντες" ('Males and the descendants of males have precedence, if they are descended from the same ancestors [as the females], even if their degree of kinship [to the deceased] is more remote'). Cf. the law cited at [Dem.] 43.51, where the principle of male precedence is expressed in substantively the same words, but the application of the principle is unclear because the text of the citation is lacunose. The same words, 'males and the descendants of males have precedence', also occur at [Dem.] 43.78 and [Dem] 44.62, and cf. 'males have precedence' at Isa. 11.17.

The phrase *ek tōn autōn* was translated at §11 as 'descended from the same ancestors'. Here, in a more narrowly legal context, it must have a more precise meaning. The inheritance rights of collateral kin under Athenian law may be explained in terms of 'inheritance classes' (the term preferred by Thompson (1976), 28 to Wyse's 'stocks'). The presence of any member of a higher class excluded any member of a lower class. Within each class, members having the same relationship to the deceased were entitled to equal shares of the estate, subject to the principles of representation and of male precedence.

Those in the first inheritance class were descended from the deceased's father, i.e. his brothers and sisters, nephews and nieces (and their descendants). The second class comprised those more distantly related who were descended from the deceased's paternal grandfather: his first cousins and their children (first cousins once removed, descending). (It is unlikely that the uncles and aunts of the deceased, who were also descended from his grandparents, had any inheritance rights in the Athenian system. For a discussion of the evidence on the inheritance rights of ascendants, and a summary of the earlier scholarly debate, see Harrison (1968), 138–142.) The deceased's first cousins once removed (ascending) and second cousins, who were descended from his paternal great grandfather, belonged to the third class, but the **ankhisteia* did not extend to their children. Any two or more members of the same class were *ek tōn autōn*, i.e. descended from the same common ancestor as one another. (The same system of 'inheritance classes' could be applied to the collateral kin of the deceased on his mother's side, but that is not relevant to the present discussion because all the *ankhisteis* on the father's side had priority over those on the mother's.)

22 ὁμοίως καὶ ἀδελφὴ καὶ ἀδελφιδοῦς ἰσόμοιροι κατὰ τὸν νόμον εἰσί ('under this clause of the law the sister and the nephew have equal shares'). If an Athenian died childless and intestate, leaving no brothers or brothers' descendants but only sisters or sisters' descendants, then a surviving sister would share the inheritance equally with her nephew, the son of a deceased sister. That, according to Thrasyllos, was the position of Thrasyboulos and the wife of Pronapes after the death of Apollodoros Eupolidos. The order of intestate succession, giving preference to brothers and their offspring over sisters and their offspring, is spelt out more fully at Isa. 11.1–2.

Ἐὰν μὴ ὦσιν ἀνεψιοὶ … κρατεῖν ('If there are no first cousins or their children or other relatives on the father's side, the law gives the right to inherit to those on the mother's side, specifying the right of succession'). Again, this is consistent with Isa. 11.2; presumably the clause of the law read out to the court gave fuller details of the order of matrilineal succession.

Thrasyllos stresses several times that he was Apollodoros's nephew, without specifying that, since their relationship was matrilineal, he was outranked in the **ankhisteia* by the wife of Pronapes, a patrilineal first cousin. It seems surprising that Isaios refers to this clause of the law at all, given that it was not relevant to the present case and in any event would not have worked in his client's favour. Perhaps he wanted to impress the **dikastai* by giving a full and accurate account of the law of intestate succession.

23 Ταῦτα τῶν νόμων κελευόντων ('Since this is what the laws provide'). Thrasyllos appeals both to 'the laws' in general and to the specific laws just read out to the court, not in order to justify his own or Apollodoros's conduct (as at §§2 and 17) but to condemn that of his opponents. Cf. on δόντων αὐτῷ τῶν νόμων, §2.

ὁ μὲν ἀνὴρ ὢν ('he, being a man'). Thrasyboulos has not claimed even a share of the estate, let alone the entirety, to which he, as a man, would have been entitled as intestate heir. On the other hand, the representatives of this woman have claimed the whole of the estate.

τολμήσουσι ('they will have the impudence'). The future tense suggests that Thrasyllos is the first speaker, anticipating an argument to be put forward by his opponents. It cannot, however, be taken for granted that his version of the opposing case is correct. Cf. on Isaios's use of **prokatalēpsis*, 10.8–17.

ἐκποίητος ('adopted out'). The verb *ekpoiēsthai* was regularly used of a person adopted out of his natural father's **oikos*. Under Athenian law an adopted son lost his legal relationship with his natural father, so after the adoption he was excluded from inheriting either directly from the father or from any of his paternal kin. (See Isa. 9.33; 10.4, 7, 8, 26; 11.45 (cited by Wyse, 569)). Harrison (1968), 93, n.2, points out that Phainippos apparently retained his natural father's estate as well as that of his adoptive father ([Dem.] 42.21), suggesting that this might have been a special case because Phainippos was adopted by his maternal grandfather: "... it is conceivable that he had been posthumously adopted and that, by an exception, the law allowed the son of an *epiklēros* who was thus adopted into her father's house to remain also his own father's heir". A simpler explanation would be that an adopted son was allowed to retain whatever he had inherited from his natural kin before the adoption; cf. on καὶ ᾔτησε καὶ ἔτυχεν, §14.

The effect of adoption on an individual's claim to inherit from his natural family is an issue in Isa. 9 and 10.

εἰς τὸν οἶκον τὸν Ἱππολοχίδου ('into the *oikos* of Hippolokhides'). The adoptive father is listed in *LGPN Attica* as Ἱππολοχίδης (2), son of Thrasymedes of Lousia. A son of Hippolokhides, known as Hippolokhides (II), is recorded as a trierarch before 334/3 BC. As Davies (1971), 45–46, suggests, it is likely that this was the name taken by Thrasyboulos after his adoption, since Hippolokhides (I) could not have adopted him if he already had a legitimate son. An alternative possibility is that Hippolokhides (II) was a natural son born to Hippolokhides (I) after the adoption of Thrasyboulos. The name of the adoptive father is not relevant to Thrasyllos's case, but Isaios presumably names him to enhance the credibility of the story. This contrasts with his perfunctory treatment of the supposed adoption of Thoudippos in Isa. 9, which is far more central to his client's case. Cf. on εἰς ἄλλον οἶκον, 9.2.

λέγοντες τοῦτο μὲν ἀληθές, ἐκεῖνο δ' ου προσῆκον ('While what they say is true, the conclusion drawn from it does not apply'). Thrasyllos accuses his opponent of an error of logic which he himself commits more than once. Cf., e.g., on εἴπερ τὰ πεπραγμένα, §24.

24 ὄντι προτέρῳ ταύτης ('since he has a prior claim to that of this woman'). See on ταύτην τε . . . , §18.

εἴπερ τὰ πεπραγμένα μὴ κυρίως ἔχειν ἐνόμιζεν ('if he did not think the adoption was valid'). It may be that Thrasyllos is here committing the logical error of which he has just accused his opponents: even if it was true that Thrasyboulos was entitled to claim either the whole or a share of Apollodoros Thrasyllou's estate, the fact that he refrained from doing so does not prove that he supported Thrasyllos's claim to have been adopted by Apollodoros.

ἀλλ' οὐκ ἔστιν ἀναίσχυντος ('but he is not shameless'). By commenting that Thrasyboulos is not 'shameless' enough to contest the adoption and claim the estate, Thrasyllos implicitly criticizes his opponents for doing so.

25 μητρὸς δ'οὐδείς ἐστιν ἐκποιήτος ('but no-one is adopted out of his mother's family'). See on ἐκποιήτος, §23. Thrasyllos anticipates his opponent's explanation, that Thrasyboulos had no claim to the estate of Apollodoros Thrasyllou because of his adoption by Hippolokhides, by asserting that adoption, while removing the adoptee from the **oikos* of his natural father, does not deprive him of his legal relationship with his mother. Thrasyboulos, therefore, could still have claimed the estate as next of kin, since his relationship to Apollodoros was through his mother, the daughter of Eupolis and wife of Aiskhines.

The rule cited by Isaios, which must have been a significant feature of the Athenian inheritance system, has a degree of plausibility in the context of a legal system which permitted inheritance through a female line. As Harrison (1968), 93–94, points out, there is some support for the existence of the rule at [Dem.] 43.15, where the speaker has had one of his sons posthumously adopted, as Euboulides III, into the *oikos* of his wife's deceased brother Euboulides II. When the boy's claim to the estate of Hagnias was submitted to the **arkhōn*, it was his older brother, not his natural father, who was inscribed as his **kurios*. As Harrison argues, the reasoning behind this would be that the two brothers retained their blood relationship through their mother, after one of them had been adopted out of the paternal *oikos*.

In the absence of more direct supporting evidence a sceptical commentator might, nevertheless, question the reliability of Isaios's version of the rule, given that it seems to operate so conveniently in favour of his client. How, in particular, could the two rival claimants disagree about the application of the rule in the present case, if it was really an established feature of Athenian law? It has to be remembered that Pronapes may not, in fact, have put forward the argument attributed to him by Thrasyllos. Whatever reasons Thrasyboulos may have had for distancing himself from the litigation, there was no need for Pronapes to explain them in order to make good his wife's claim to the estate. He might, indeed, have been wiser to ignore what was essentially a diversionary tactic on Isaios's part, designed to make his client's opponents look foolish or dishonest by imputing to them either ignorance or disregard of the law.

διὸ . . . μέρους ('Therefore [Thrasyboulos] was not deprived of his share'). This refers to to the estate of Apollodoros Eupolidos, Thrasyboulos's uncle, which, according to Isaios, was shared between Thrasyboulos and his aunt, the wife of Pronapes and rival claimant to Thrasyllos for the estate of Apollodoros Thrasyllou. Isaios gives no indication of the date of either the death of Apollodoros Eupolidos or the adoption of Thrasyboulos by Hippolokhides, so it is impossible to assess the validity of the argument that the adoption did not prevent Thrasyboulos from taking his share of the inheritance. Cf. Wyse, 569.

ὡς δ'ἀληθῆ λέγω, κάλει μοι τούτων τοὺς μάρτυρας ('And to prove that I am telling the truth, please call the witnesses to these facts'). The witnesses presumably confirmed that Thrasyboulos inherited half of the estate of Apollodoros Eupolidos, sharing it with the wife of Pronapes. Cf. on τούτων πρῶτον . . . , §10.

26 οὐκ ἀμφισβητῶν αὐτὸς ἔργῳ δεδήλωκεν ('has made it clear by his conduct in not claiming the estate himself'). Cf. on τοῖς δ'ἔργοις . . . , §8, and ἐργοῖς φανερῶς μεμαρτυτήκασιν, §18.

κυρίως . . . καὶ κατὰ τοὺς νόμους ('valid and in accordance with the laws') See on δόντων αὐτῷ τῶν νόμων, §2. Here, 'in accordance with the laws' is not just an expression of Thrasyllos's own opinion but is attributed to Thrasyboulos.

Narrative and Testimony: The Enrolment of Thrasyllos in Apollodoros's Deme (27–28)

It appears that Thrasyllos had evidence of his enrolment in Apollodoros's *deme that would have been very difficult for his opponents to refute. Proof of his admission would weigh heavily with the **dikastai*, especially since it would have enhanced the credibility of his account of the *phratry procedure. The account of the deme enrolment in these two sections is, nevertheless, more than usually compressed, even by the standards of such a habitually economical writer as Isaios. In the context of a narrative which is generally clear and precise, this section passes rapidly over events and leaves some significant details obscure.

This is in marked contrast with Dem. 57.9–13, where Euxitheos gives a detailed account of the proceedings, and his opponents' tactics, at the meeting at which he was expelled from his deme. It would, however, be a mistake to take this as an indication of the relative strength of the two speakers' cases, or to assume that Thrasyllos was hiding something that would have been seriously detrimental to his case. Euxitheos, who is disputing the outcome of the deme's vote, has an interest in exposing his opponents' machinations at length. For Thrasyllos, on the other hand, the vote was favourable, so Isaios focuses on the outcome and 'edits out' any details that might distract attention from it.

27 πρὶν γὰρ ἐμὲ ἥκειν ἐκ τῆς Πυθαΐδος ('For before I returned from the Pythaïs'). See on Εὔπολις γάρ…, §5. Isaios resumes the narrative as if it followed directly after the interruption following §17, although there was no indication in the earlier section that Thrasyllos left Athens after being introduced to Apollodoros's *phratry. The significance of his absence is that it enables him to rebut his opponent's allegation that it was Thrasyllos himself rather than Apollodoros who persuaded the *demesmen to enrol him. (See below on ἔλεγε πρὸς τοὺς δημότας Ἀπολλόδωρος.)

Wyse, following earlier scholarship, emends the ms. Πυθαΐδος to Πυθίαδος. On that reading, the reference would be to the Pan-Hellenic Pythian Festival (the Pythia), which was celebrated in the third year of the Olympiad, so that possible dates for the speech would be 354/53 or 350/49 BC. The Pythia fell in the Delphic month of Boukatios, equivalent to the Athenian Metageitnion. On the assumption that Thrasyllos left Athens for Delphi early in Metageitnion, Wyse points out that nearly three months (most of Thargelion and the whole of Skirophorion and Hekatombaion) would have elapsed since his introduction to Apollodoros's phratry.

Wyse considers it suspicious that Thrasyllos was not enrolled in the deme during this time, especially given the likelihood that a general meeting of the deme would have been held in Hekatombaion, the first month of the Athenian year. This argument becomes untenable, however, once it is recognized that the text refers not to the Pythia but to the Pythaïs, an occasional pilgrimage from Athens to Delphi held in one of the three summer months (Skirophorion, Hekatombaion and Metageitnion). So it is possible that Thrasyllos left Athens as early as Skirophorion and was enrolled at a deme meeting in Hekatombaion, almost certainly while he was still away from Athens.

Boëthius's research on the Pythaïs (summarized by Parke (1939) and by Parker (2005), 83–87) shows that the procession was sent to Delphi at irregular intervals, only after lightning flashes, which were perceived as an omen from Zeus, had been observed over Harma on Mount Parnes. The Pythaïsts mounted a vigil for three days and nights in each of the three summer months. The vigil was probably held every year, but the pilgrimage did not take place unless the omen was observed.

As to the particular year in which Thrasyllos took part in the Pythaïs, Parke (1939) argues persuasively for 355 BC, on the grounds that it would have been impossible for a procession to reach Delphi by land from Athens during the Third Sacred War (autumn 355–346 BC), and that a later date is unlikely because the Athenians would not have sent a pilgrimage devoted to the Pythian Apollo at a time when they were estranged from Delphi. In any event, Thrasyllos was probably born in the late 390s and still in his thirties when he delivered the speech, so a date in the mid 350s is more plausible than one ten years later.

Below is a possible reconstruction of the sequence of events from the death of Apollodoros's son (Maimakterion 356/355 BC) to the court hearing some time in the following year.

Maimakterion 356/5: Apollodoros's son dies.

Between Poseideion and Mounikhion 356/5: Apollodoros takes Thrasyllos, his sister's son, into his *oikos* and gives him control of his affairs.

Thargelion 356/5: At the Thargelia, Apollodoros introduces his adopted son to his phratry and *genos*, who inscribe him as Thrasyllos Apollodorou.

Skirophorion 356/5: Thrasyllos joins the Pythaïs, a pilgrimage to Delphi. In Thrasyllos's absence, Apollodoros urges his fellow demesmen to enrol Thrasyllos as his adopted son. Apollodoros dies.

Hekatombaion 355/4: Thrasyllos is enrolled by the demesmen of Leukonoion as the adopted son of Apollodoros.

Later in 355/4: Thrasyllos Apollodorou serves as *gymnasiarch at the Prometheia. The inheritance dispute between the wife of Pronapes and Thrasyllos comes to court.

ἔλεγε πρὸς τοὺς δημότας Ἀπολλόδωρος ('Apollodoros told the demesmen'). The emphatic position of the subject confirms the impression that Thrasyllos is rebutting an allegation from his opponent that Apollodoros took no active or willing part in the adoption: 'It was [not I but] Apollodoros himself who …'. The wording here implies a formal meeting of the whole *deme, unlike [Dem.] 44. 37, where Leokhares is said to have tried to persuade some of the demesmen to enrol him as the adopted son of Arkhiades 'having gathered together a few of the Otrynians'.

ὅτι πεποιημένος … φράτορας ('that he had adopted me as his son and had registered me with the members of his **genos* and *phratry'). Taken at their face value (which of course suits the speaker's case), these words indicate that Apollodoros considered the adoption to be complete before Thrasyllos was registered in his *deme. Cf. on καὶ οὕτω …, §17. Otherwise, he could have said that he had made the introduction 'with a view to adopting' (*hōs poiēsamenos*) Thrasyllos, or he could simply have told his fellow demesmen about the introduction, leaving them to infer that this was the first step in the adoption procedure, which he wanted them to complete.

ἄν τι πάθῃ ('if anything should happen to him'). See on εἴ τι πάθοι, §1.

πρότερον ('before'). I take this (*pace* Wyse and Forster, but following Boëthius (1918), 16) to mean not 'before Thrasyllos's return to Athens', but 'before the meeting where the *demesmen were to inscribe Thrasyllos in their register'. Roussel's concise formulation, "s'il lui arrivait auparavant malheur" ("if anything should happen to him beforehand"), conveys this sense without losing the economy of the Greek.

ἐγγράψουσι με εἰς τὸ ληξιαρχικὸν γραμματεῖον Θράσυλλον Ἀπολλοδώρου ('they were to enrol me in the public register as Thrasyllos son of Apollodoros'). Cf. on εἰς τὸ κοινὸν …, §17. Thrasyllos's new identity as the son of Apollodoros is now confirmed by his enrolment in the *deme.

28 τούτων ἐν ἀρχαιρεσίαις … ὑόν ('although my opponents complained at the electoral meeting of the deme, and claimed that he had not adopted me'). Thrasyllos was enrolled as a member of the *deme at the meeting at which the deme officials were appointed. This was also the occasion when Leokhares made his final attempt to gain admission to the deme of Arkhiades 'at the last elections of the officials' ([Dem.] 44.39), so it may have been a common or regular practice to deal with both of these items of business together. In any event the officials would have been appointed annually, probably at the beginning of the year. Whitehead (1986), 290, n. 145, points out that, on the basis of these two passages, the term *arkhairesiai* ('electoral meeting') appears to have continued in use after sortition had replaced election as the method of appointing deme officials.

The nature of the opponents' objections is not explicitly stated, but it appears that the object of their attack was not the supposed irregularily of the deme enrolment but the validity of the procedure carried out by Apollodoros himself, or perhaps they were disputing the fact of the introduction to the *phratry.

καθάπερ ἐκεῖνος ἐκέλευε ('in accordance with his instructions'). The fact that Thrasyllos's enrolment in the *deme took place in accordance with Apollodoros's instructions is likely to have been a significant point in his favour.

ὡς δ' αληθῆ λέγω, κάλει μοι τούτων τοὺς μάρτυρας ('And to prove that I am telling the truth, please call the witnesses to these facts'). Cf. on τούτων πρῶτον…, §10.

Argument and Testimony: The Succession of Apollodoros Eupolidos (29–32)

Isaios introduces a new argument from probability, which he uses, like the argument at §§18–26, not only to enhance the credibility of Thrasyllos's adoption, but also to blacken the character of his opponents: after the death of Apollodoros Eupolidos, his sisters and their husbands were happy to share his estate but neglected to give him a son by posthumous adoption, thus leaving his **oikos* shamefully desolate. Seeing how they treated their own brother, their cousin, Apollodoros Thrasyllou, realized that he could expect nothing better from them if he allowed his estate to devolve to them.

Wyse, 573, observes that these paragraphs "do not harmonise" with the rest of the speech. Not all of his objections are sustainable, but, as the notes below reveal, there is indeed some inconsistency between what Isaios says here and in §19 about the succession of Apollodoros Eupolidos. In a modern adversarial trial, any such discrepancies would be likely to be identified by the opposing advocate and exposed in cross-examination, but the Athenian trial format gave the speechwriter greater latitude to distort the facts. Isaios's willingness to do so here appears to be a measure of the importance he attached to undermining the case of Thrasyllos's opponent by blackening her character. Possibly he was anticipating a claim that Pronapes and his wife wanted Apollodoros to adopt a son of their own, and that his decision instead to adopt Thrasyllos was invalid because he had acted under the influence of a woman (his half-sister).

29 Ἐπὶ μὲν τοσούτων μαρτύρων, ὦ ἄνδρες ('before so many witnesses, gentlemen'). See on Ὤιμην…, §1. The fact that a significant number of

*demesmen were prepared to testify to his enrolment must have been a strong point in Thrasyllos's favour.

ἡ ποίησις ('the adoption'). The regular term for 'adoption' seems here to refer specifically to the *deme enrolment, in contrast to §§17 and 26, where it is implied that the adoption was complete after the introduction to Apollodoros's *phratry and **genos*. This may suggest that there was some uncertainty as to the precise point at which an adoption was formally complete, which is consistent with the suggestion that the effect of the formalities was to ratify rather than create an adoption. (See the introduction to this speech, pp. 36–38.)

ἔχθρας μὲν παλαιᾶς...ὑπαρχούσης ('when there was an inveterate enmity between Apollodoros and my opponent, but a close friendship as well as kinship between Apollodoros and us'). Thrasyllos does not rely solely on the testimony of witnesses to his adoption, but supports it with the implicit argument from probability that Apollodoros would have been more likely to adopt him than to leave his property to his enemies.

30 ὅπως μὴ ἐξερημώσουσι τοὺς σφετέρους αὐτῶν οἴκους ('to prevent their families from becoming extinct'). A childless Athenian contemplating his own death would be concerned not only about the disposal of his property, but also to ensure that his **oikos* did not 'become empty' or die out.

ὁ ἐναγιῶν ('someone to perform sacrifices'). The performance of sacrifices on behalf of a dead father is also mentioned at Isa. 2.46, where it is specifically described as an annual obligation, and at 6.51 and 65, where it is combined with the offering of libations. Elsewhere, Isaios refers more generally to the 'customary rites', on which see the following note.

καὶ πάντα τὰ νομιζόμενα ('and all the customary rites'). As well as the annual commemorative sacrifices and libations, the 'customary rites' for the dead included the laying out and burial of the body, the funeral feast and the 30 days of mourning with offerings at the grave on the third and ninth days. (For a detailed account of Athenian funeral rites in the classical period, see Kurtz and Boardman (1971), 142–48.) All the rites, both immediately after the funeral and in subsequent years, were carried out at the family tombs. In the absence of lineal descendants, responsibility for the funeral would have fallen to the next of kin, or, in an extreme case, to any available friends of the deceased (as in Isa. 9, where Astyphilos was buried by his friends and fellow soldiers.) A claimant to a deceased person's estate would be expected to have carried out the funeral, or, as in Isa. 8 and 9, to explain why he had been unable to do so. Cf. also

Isa. 4.19, where the speaker points out that his opponent, who claims to be the adopted son of Nikostratos, did not carry out any of the funeral rites.

It has been suggested that only direct descendants were obliged to perform the commemorative rites in subsequent years, especially in view of the possibility that all Athenian families commemorated their ancestors on the same day, at the public festival of *Genesia* on the fifth day of Boedromion. If that was the case then, as is argued by Rubinstein (1993), 71, an Athenian could not have been held responsible for the tomb cult of his collateral kin as well as his own ascendants, unless all the family tombs were in the same place. According to Parker (2005), 27–28, on the other hand, it is not clear whether there was in fact a single annual occasion on which all Athenian families commemorated their dead, or whether private *Genesia* were performed by individual families on the anniversary of the ancestor's death or another appropriate date. (See Parker (2005), chapter 1, for a full account of Athenian funeral practices.)

The wish for a son to carry out *ta *nomizomena* is attributed to Apollodoros as a motive for adoption, which might appear to support the view that the task could not be performed by collaterals. The same motive is imputed to Kleonymos at Isa. 1.10, to Menekles at 2.10, and, at 9.7, to Astyphilos, who is said to have wanted the customary rites carried out on behalf of his ancestors as well as himself. In all these cases the obligation is probably envisaged as an ongoing one, to include sacrifices repeated every year until the son's own death. Cf. Isa. 6.65, where the speaker, seeking proof that Euktemon was legally married to Kallippe, asks whether anyone saw Euktemon performing *ta nomizomena* on her behalf, and whether her sons still carry out the appropriate sacrifices and libations. In Isa. 1, 7 and 9, however, the deceased is portrayed as having had a deep-seated grudge against his next of kin (or, in Isa. 1, against the guardian of his next of kin, who were minors), so that the more natural interpretation of the wish to adopt is either a fear that the next of kin would neglect to carry out *ta nomizomena* or antipathy to the idea of the commemorative rites being performed by an enemy. Cf. on τυχεῖν τῶν νομιζομένων…, §32. There may also have been a more general perception that the obligation to one's parents was stronger than to collateral relatives, so that direct descendants were more likely to carry out their duties conscientiously.

καὶ οὐ μόνον ἰδίᾳ… ἀλλὰ καὶ δημοσίᾳ ('And there is not merely a personal feeling in favour of this, but the state has taken public measures'). Isaios seeks to add weight to his client's case with the assertion that there is a public as well as a private interest in the continuation of an **oikos*.

νόμῳ γὰρ … ἐπιμέλειαν ('since it entrusts the *arkhōn* with the duty of preventing families from dying out'). The law cited at [Dem.] 43.75, which may be the same as that to which Isaios refers here, charges the **arkhōn* with a duty to 'take care of' orphans, **epiklēroi*, and 'empty' **oikoi*, and to punish anyone who commits an offence against them. Some commentators have interpreted Isaios's words as a more positive injunction actively to prevent the extinction of *oikoi* by initiating posthumous adoptions. It would, however, be unwise to read too much into his precise wording, given that his account at §31 of what happened to the estate of Apollodoros Eupolidos gives no indication that the *arkhōn* was, or might have been, involved.

Harrison (1968), 92–93, summarizes the earlier scholarly debate on the exact nature and extent of the *arkhōn*'s power, concluding that it probably did not extend to forcing a posthumous adoption in a case where the deceased's family was reluctant to provide an adopted son. The issue is re-examined by Rubinstein (1993), 106–109, who finds no positive evidence that the *arkhōn* ever took the initiative in arranging a posthumous adoption, and sees the speakers' arguments in both Isa. 7 and [Dem.] 43 as "a strong indication that it was entirely up to the intestate heirs to initiate posthumous adoptions, and that there was no centralised attempt to guarantee that it would indeed happen". She concludes that a legal obligation on intestate heirs to provide an adopted son would be incompatible with the law permitting an inheritance case to be reopened by means of a new **epidikasia*, so that if the *arkhōn* ever had been empowered to initiate posthumous adoptions, the power must have lapsed by the fourth century.

31 ἐκείνῳ δὲ πρόδηλον ἦν … ('Now it was quite clear to him …'). Having explained in general terms the considerations that might motivate a man who knew he was about to die, Isaios moves on to the specific circumstances in which Apollodoros found himself. He makes the whole argument more persuasive by making Apollodoros the *focalizer: it is not Thrasyllos but Apollodoros himself who has drawn the appropriate conclusions from the behaviour which Thrasyllos imputes to Eupolis's daughters.

ἐκείνῳ δ' οὐκ εἰσποιούσας ὄντων αὐταῖς παίδων ('but never gave him a son by adoption, although they had sons of their own'). We need not doubt that this statement is factually true, but neither of the sisters could realistically have been expected to provide a son for Apollodoros Eupolidos by posthumous adoption unless she and her husband had another son who could remain in his father's **oikos*. Isaios does not make it clear whether this was the case, and his vagueness here contrasts with §11, where he says specifically that Eupolis had two daughters, neither of whom he gave in marriage to Apollodoros. Pronapes is known to have had at least one son, Eupolis, who is not mentioned in the speech; he is attested as a trierarch before 334/3 BC, and was probably still a minor at the time of the court case (Davies (1971), 45). Aiskhines's son Thrasyboulos was adopted by Hippolokhides, but we cannot be sure whether this happened before or after the death of Apollodoros Eupolidos.

Wyse, 574, acknowledges the evidence that Eupolis the son of Pronapes served as a trierarch before 334/3 BC, but argues that the existence of a son of Pronapes and his wife at the time of the trial would be inconsistent with Isaios's reasoning in §§18–25. It would appear, however, that Wyse is trying too hard to find fault with Isaios. The proposition in §§18–25 is that the son of a deceased female first cousin of the **de cuius* would exclude another female first cousin, his aunt; Isaios does not necessarily imply that a male first cousin once removed of the *de cuius* would exclude a female first cousin who was his own mother, during her lifetime.

ταύτας τὰς ἀδελφὰς τὸν μὲν Ἀπολλοδώρου τοῦ ἀδελφοῦ κλῆρον ἐχούσας ('that these sisters of Apollodoros inherited their brother's estate'). The impression given here, that both of Eupolis's daughters outlived their brother Apollodoros and shared his estate between them, appears to conflict with the statement at §25 that the estate of Apollodoros Eupolidos was shared between one of his sisters, the wife of Pronapes, and Thrasyboulos, the son of his other sister. It might be possible to reconcile the two accounts on the basis that both sisters were still alive when their brother Apollodoros died, and that Thrasyboulos came into his share of the estate only after his mother's subsequent death, but some inconsistencies would still remain.

τὸν δὲ οἶκον αἰσχρῶς οὕτω καὶ δεινῶς ἐξηρημωμένον ('but that his house was left shamefully and disgracefully without heirs'). The adverbs convey a tone of strong moral condemnation, implying that posthumous adoption into an **oikos* that would otherwise remain empty may have been considered a moral obligation, even if it was not actually a legal requirement. Rubinstein (1993), 111–112 points out that there could be more than one reason for a posthumous adoption, including the avoidance of *liturgies, of which Theopompos had apparently been accused by his opponent in Isa. 11. (Cf. on οὐχ ὥσπερ Προνάπης..., §39.) She concludes that the moral obligation was "far from strong enough to allow the assumption that most intestate heirs would provide for such an adoption—for moral reasons, at any rate".

32 τυχεῖν τῶν νομιζομένων ὑπ' αὐτῶν ('receive the customary rites from them'). If it is correct that only direct descendants could carry out the annual commemorative rites for the dead (cf. on καὶ πάντα…, §30), then *ta *nomizomena* in this context must refer only to the burial and the thirty days of mourning. That explanation would not, however, account for the reference at Isa. 1.10, where the speaker says that Kleonymos was afraid he might die while his next of kin, his nephews, were still minors, and did not want their guardian, his enemy Deinias, to be responsible for *ta nomizomena* until they came of age.

ἀνεψιὸς ὢν ἀλλ' οὐκ ἀδελφὸς αὐταῖς ('being their cousin, not their brother'). The gist of Thrasyllos's argument is 'If this is how the daughters of Eupolis behaved towards their brother, how could a mere cousin expect better treatment from them?' It is not unreasonable to suppose that the bond of kinship was perceived as being closer between siblings than between cousins.

τριηραρχοῦντα ('serving as trierarch'). Wevers (1969), 115, rightly points out that the extinction of families capable of paying for a trierarchy would have been a matter of concern to the **polis* (cf. on καὶ οὐ μόνον ἰδίᾳ…, §30), but his general conclusions about a "trend towards childlessness" as "proof of social irresponsibility, of an element of decay in society" are not justified by the sources.

κάλει μοι καὶ τούτων τοὺς μάρτυρας ('please call the witnesses to these facts, too'). Cf. on τούτων πρῶτον…, §10. Here, too (see on ὡς δ' ἀληθῆ λέγω, §10), Isaios specifies precisely the 'facts' which are confirmed by this testimony.

Argument and Testimony: The Character of the Speaker (33–36)

A striking feature of this speech is that ten sections, almost a quarter of the whole length, are devoted to character, including not only that of the speaker but also of Apollodoros and his father, with occasional blows against the opponent. First, in §§33–36, Thrasyllos presents his own credentials as a dutiful son and model citizen, deploying as part of his legal 'proof' an argument from probability using his own character to support Apollodoros's choice of him as an adopted son. It seems that such an explanation was needed to rebut a claim by Pronapes and his wife that they had been willing to let Apollodoros adopt a young son of theirs, but that he had rejected their offer under pressure from his half-sister, agreeing instead to adopt her son who was little more than a stranger to him.

33 τί βέλτιον ἂν ἔπραξεν ('how could he have done better?'). Thrasyllos strives to present Apollodoros's decision to adopt him as a positive choice, but he gives no indication of a close personal relationship between them. If, nevertheless, Apollodoros really wanted to avoid letting his property fall into the hands of any descendant of Eupolis, he may have had little choice but to adopt his half-sister's son, whether or not there were real ties of affection between them.

εἰ... παιδίον ἐποιήσατο λαβὼν παρά του τῶν φίλων ὄντων ('if... he had adopted a child from the family of one of his friends'). Wyse and Forster follow Reiske and others in accepting the mss. παρά του τῶν rather than adopting Bekker's παρὰ τούτων, which would change the meaning of the phrase to 'from these people, who were his friends'. There is no strong reason to retain the word division and accentuation used by the mediaeval scribe if the alternative makes better sense, but, on either reading, the passage is problematic. On the one hand, why should Thrasyllos introduce the idea, inherently improbable, that Apollodoros might have considered adopting the young son of one of his friends? (Lincke (1884), cited by Wyse, argues with some force that 'child' (παιδίον) seems odd in this context, since Apollodoros was an old man who must have had friends with adult sons.) The passage as a whole reads like a refutation of an argument put forward by (or expected from) the opponents, who are unlikely to have suggested that Apollodoros could have adopted a friend's child, but may well have claimed that they had offered him a son of their own. That would be consistent with the fact that Pronapes is known to have had a son who was probably a child at the time of the speech (see on ἐκείνῳ δ' οὐκ εἰσποιούσας..., §31). In the wider context, it would also account for Thrasyllos's attack on the behaviour of Eupolis's daughters after the death of their brother. (See introductory note to §§29–32.)

The difficulty with this interpretation lies with the words 'being friends' (φίλων ὄντων), given that, on Thrasyllos's account, Pronapes and his wife were emphatically not on friendly terms with Apollodoros. But they will undoubtedly have claimed that they were his friends, and so the difficulty is perhaps best resolved if (*pace* Wyse) Isaios's words are taken to be ironic.

νὴ Δία ('by Zeus'). On invocations to the gods in Isaios's speeches, see on μὰ τοὺς θεοὺς τοὺς Ὀλυμπίους, 8.29.

ἀλλὰ … ἔσεσθαι ('But even such a child's parents would not have known whether he would be a good man, or worthless'). For the idea that it is impossible to predict what a child's character will be like when it grows up, cf. Lys. 2.13; 20.34 (cited by Dover (1974), 92). This is one of only two extant cases of adoption **inter vivos* where the age of the adoptee is known, and in both cases he was an adult. The other is that of Menekles, whose adopted son had already served as a soldier (Isa. 2.6, cited by Rubinstein (1993), 22). A preference for adopting an adult would, in the Athenian context, be entirely plausible: a child would not have been able to take on the responsibilities of caring for his adoptive father in old age if adopted *inter vivos*, or, whether the adoption was *inter vivos* or testamentary, to conduct the funeral and commemorative rites. And, as Isager (1982), 89, points out, the prospects of a child's survival would have been uncertain. (There are some attested cases of a son adopted by will or posthumously who was probably a child, such as Kleon's son in Isa. 9 and the son of Sositheos in [Dem.] 43, but it may be that this was a last resort because no suitable adult was available.) In the present case, if Apollodoros did reject an offer from the wife of Pronapes to give him an adopted son, his preference for Thrasyllos might have been based on the respective ages of the candidates rather than the more personal motives put forward by Thrasyllos.

34 δοκιμασίαν ἱκανὴν λαβών ('having sufficiently tested me'). The word *dokimasia* is here used in a non-technical sense, meaning 'proof' or 'test'; but it also carries overtones of the formal scrutiny which an Athenian had to undergo before being admitted to public office, pointing forward to Thrasyllos's reference in the next sentence to his service as a **thesmothetēs*.

εἴς τε γὰρ τὸν πατέρα καὶ τὴν μητέρα ('towards my father and mother'). This is the only reference in the speech to Thrasyllos's natural father, who is not named. It is noticeable that Thrasyllos, unlike some of Isaios's other clients, gives no details of his own relationship with the **de cuius*, relying instead on what Apollodoros knew of his conduct towards his parents and of his record of public service. This might appear unsurprising, given that an uncle and nephew might not be expected to be as close as the two half-brothers in Isa. 9 or the brothers and their grandfather in Isa. 8, but there is evidence of a traditionally strong bond between mother's brother and sister's son in ancient Greece. (See Bremmer (1983), 179–182 for references, which include four from the orators: Aiskhin. 2.78; Andok. 3.29; [Dem.] 59.12; and Isa. 3.26, 29.) It need not follow from Isaios's silence that the relationship between Apollodoros and Thrasyllos was actually hostile, but it does appear that the absence of a positive bond enabled Thrasyllos's opponents to portray him as an outsider who had taken advantage of Apollodoros at a time when he was vulnerable.

θεσμοθετήσας ('having served as a *thesmothetēs*'). On the duties of the six **thesmothetai* in the fourth century, see *Ath. Pol.* 3.4 and 59.1, with Rhodes's commentary.

οὐκ ἀγνοῶν ἀλλὰ σαφῶς εἰδὼς ('not in ignorance, but with full knowledge'). For the presentation through negation, cf. on ἐκείνῳ . . . , §17.

35 οὐδὲ ἀλλότριον ἀλλ' ὄντα ἀδελφιδοῦν ('no stranger, but his own nephew'). Cf. on ὄντα ἀδελφιδοῦν, §4.

ὥσπερ οὗτοι τὰ τοῦ κλήρου πεποιήκασιν ('as they have squandered the property composing the estate'). While using his own character as evidence in support of Apollodoros's decision to adopt him, Thrasyllos strikes a 'glancing blow' against his opponents, claiming that he will make better use of the estate than they did of that of Apollodoros Eupolidos. Cf. on οὐχ ὥσπερ Προνάπης . . . , §39.

ἀλλὰ βουλησόμενον καὶ τριηραρχεῖν . . . ὥσπερ κἀκεῖνος ('but wanting to act as a trierarch and go on military service and act as **khorēgos* . . . as he himself had done'). Thrasyllos does not yet have an extensive record of public service with which to impress the **dikastai*, so he refers instead to the duties he aspires to perform, identifying himself with Apollodoros who actually did so. The piling up of infinitives linked by *kai* ('and') gives emphasis to each of the *liturgies in his list.

36 καὶ συγγενὴς . . . τοιοῦτος εἶναι ('his kinsman, and his friend, and his benefactor, and a man of public spirit approved as such'). Thrasyllos summarizes his qualifications to receive the estate of Apollodoros, again using *kai* for emphasis in his list of attributes. Here, *dedokimasmenos* ('approved of') refers to the *dokimasia* undergone by Thrasyllos before he became a **thesmothetēs*. Cf. on δοκιμασίαν ἱκανὴν λαβών, §34.

τίς <ἂν> ἀμφισβητήσειε . . . ποίησιν; ('who could dispute that my adoption was the act of a man of sound judgment?'). See on ζῶν καὶ εὖ φρονῶν, §1. This is perhaps the strongest indication in the speech that Thrasyllos's opponents had attacked the adoption on the grounds that Apollodoros was not mentally capable.

τῶν ὑπ' ἐκείνου δοκιμασθέντων ('the promise of which had won his approval'). By emphasizing that he gained the approval of Apollodoros for the *liturgies he intended to perform as his adopted son, Thrasyllos creates the impression of a relationship between them which may not, in fact, have been very deep-rooted.

γεγυμνασιάρχηκα γὰρ εἰς Προμήθεια τοῦδε τοῦ ἐνιαυτοῦ ('for I have served as *gymnasiarch at the festival of Prometheus in the present year'). See Parker (2005), 479, on the Prometheia, and cf. Lys. 21.3.

ὡς οἱ φυλέται πάντες ἴσασιν ('as all my fellow-tribesmen know'). Thrasyllos capitalizes on the public nature of the festival by calling on his fellow-tribesmen to testify to his service as *gymnasiarch. While this might have made a good impression on the **dikastai*, the evidential value of their testimony in terms of his legal claim to the estate was not very high.

ὡς δ' ἀληθῆ λέγω, κάλει μοι τούτων τοὺς μάρτυρας ('To prove that I am telling the truth, please call the witnesses to these facts'). Cf. on τούτων πρῶτον . . . , §10. This final piece of testimony confirms Thrasyllos's account of his own services to the **polis*.

Argument: The Character of Apollodoros and His Father (37–42)

Thrasyllos moves on from the legal 'proofs' of his claim to the estate to a plea for the support of the **dikastai* on behalf of Apollodoros and his father, Thrasyllos senior, with whom the speaker takes the opportunity to align himself. Such an extended eulogy of the deceased and his father is unparallelled in Isaios's other speeches, which perhaps reflects this particular family's genuinely outstanding record of public service. On the face of it, there is no reason why the achievements of the deceased or his ancestors should weigh in favour of one claimant rather than another in a **diadikasia*. In this case, however, it would be difficult for Pronapes to take a similar stance on behalf of his wife, in the face of Thrasyllos's attack on her father as the negligent guardian and lifelong enemy of Apollodoros.

37 Τὰ μὲν ἡμέτερα δίκαια . . . ὦ ἄνδρες ('These, gentlemen, are the legal grounds on which we claim that we are entitled to keep the estate'). See on ὦ ἄνδρες, §1. This sentence formally concludes the legal presentation of Thrasyllos's case, indicating that the eulogy of Apollodoros and his father is not part of the formal evidence.

δεόμεθα δ' ὑμῶν βοηθεῖν ἡμῖν ('and we beg you to help us'). See on βοηθεῖν μοι τὰ δίκαια, §4.

οὐ γὰρ ἀχρήστους αὐτοὺς εὑρήσετε πολίτας ('for you will not find that they were unprofitable citizens'). The record of Thrasyllos senior, in particular, provides an opportunity for the speaker to appeal to the patriotism of his audience, evoking their collective memory of the Sicilian expedition (cf. on ὁ δὲ Θράσυλλος…, §5) and reminding them of an era when standards of public service were more rigorous and demanding. Cf. Isa. 4.27, where the speaker describes his clients Hagnon and Hagnotheos as 'not unprofitable to the state', and 11.50, where Theopompos complains that his opponent has slandered him as 'wealthy but unprofitable'.

38 οὐκ ἐκ συμμορίας…ὥσπερ οἱ νῦν ('not contributing through symmories, as is the practice nowadays'). For the presentation through negation, see on ἐκείνῳ…, §17. This begins a sequence of four negative statements designed to show, *per contrariam*, how admirably and conscientiously Thrasyllos senior carried out his duties as trierarch. The reference is to Periander's law, in force from the early 350s until 340 BC, which provides the starting point for the dating of the speech. (Gabrielsen (1994), 182, dates the law to 358/7.) Part of a series of fourth century reforms of the trierarchic system, Periander's law created a group of 1200 citizens, known as *sunteleis*, who were liable for an annual contribution to the trierarchy. The group as a whole was subdivided into 20 subgroups or 'symmories' of 60 each. The detailed operation of the system has been the subject of scholarly debate, summarized by Gabrielsen (1994), 182–199.

[τὴν ναῦν ποιησάμενος] ('building the ship'). These words were treated as inauthentic by early editors, since neither an individual trierarch nor a symmory was required literally to 'build' a ship. Suggested alternatives to *poiēsamenos* ('building'), cited by Wyse, are *porisamenos* ('providing') (Naber), *paraskeuazomenos* ('kitting out', 'equipping') (Herwerden) and *plērosamenos* ('manning') (Thalheim). Wyse himself rejects the phrase completely, considering that it "may conceivably be a gloss added to explain οὐκ ἐκ συμμορίας ἀλλ' ἐκ τῶν αὐτοῦ δαπανῶν, where δαπανῶν was not seen to be a participle". Gabrielsen (1994), 195–196, considers the assumptions made by all these editors to be "unsatisfactory", pointing out that the wording of the ms. may not have been intended literally: "One area in which a group of *synteleis* would have collaborated was that of making one or more ships from their symmory ready for a journey. The expression 'to make a ship' in Isaeus 7.38 may refer specifically to that duty." This is hardly persuasive, given the more specific vocabulary that would have been available to Isaios if what he had in mind was the 'making ready' of a ship. On balance, Wyse's judgment appears to be sound: the bracketed words are syntactically awkward, and add nothing to the meaning that a contemporary audience would not have understood without them.

οὐδὲ δεύτερος αὐτὸς ὢν ἀλλὰ κατὰ μόνας ('and not jointly with one other but by himself'). The system of syntrierarchy, which enabled two men to share the expense of a trireme, is mentioned at Lys. 32.24 and was probably introduced in the late fifth century (Gabrielsen (1994), 173–176).

οὐδὲ δύο ἔτη διαλιπὼν ἀλλὰ συνεχῶς ('and not at intervals of two years, but continuously'). At an unknown date, perhaps near the beginning of the Peloponnesian War, a concession was introduced allowing a respite from the responsibility of the trierarchy. It is possible that the period of intermission was originally one year, later extended to two because of the heavy financial burden (Gabrielsen (1994), 86). As Gabrielsen points out, this reference does not prove that the two years' respite existed either at the time of the Sicilian expedition or after Apollodoros's death in the 350s. We cannot, therefore, be sure whether Thrasyllos senior's commitment is singled out for praise because it exceeded the standard in force in his time, or simply because that standard was higher than in later years. As Gabrielsen concludes, however, the reference "does not go counter to the supposition that the rule was effective both before 413 and in 354."

Three further references in the orators to the length of trierarchic service are discussed by Gabrielsen, *loc. cit.*: Lys. 19.29 and 21.2; Isa. 5.41.

ἀνθ' ὧν ὑμεῖς κἀκεῖνον ἐτιμᾶτε ('for which reasons you honoured him'). Thrasyllos links the public record of Apollodoros's father with the decision of the earlier **dikastērion* in favour of Apollodoros and against Eupolis.

μεμνημένοι τούτων τῶν ἔργων ('mindful of these actions'). See on τοῖς δ'ἔγροις…, §8.

39 καὶ μὴν καὶ αὐτὸς Ἀπολλόδωρος ('and, indeed, Apollodoros himself'). Thrasyllos now turns to the public record of Apollodoros himself, using the emphatic combination of particles *kai mēn kai* to imply that it was not inferior to that of his father.

οὐχ ὥσπερ Προνάπης ('not, like Pronapes'). At the beginning of his eulogy of Apollodoros, Thrasyllos condemns Pronapes with a 'glancing blow'. Cf. Usher (1999), 140: "Thumb-nail character contrasts are a distinguishing Isaean feature." For other examples of the 'glancing blow' technique, see 7.35 and 10.25. The implication is that Pronapes, unlike Apollodoros, did conceal the extent of his property in order to avoid the performance of *liturgies. On the rhetorical use of liturgy avoidance to slander an opponent, see Christ (1990), 159: "While the boasts and slanders of individual litigants obviously deserve close scrutiny, it is significant that speakers regularly play off the popular belief that the rich conceal their assets to avoid public service."

οὐδὲ βίᾳ μὲν ἐζήτει τὰ ἀλλότρι' ἔχειν ('nor did he seek to take possession by force of the property of others'). This apparently refers to Eupolis's misappropriation of Apollodoros's share of the estate of Mneson.

40 κἀκ τούτων τίνα λητουργίαν οὐκ ἐξελητούργησεν; ('As a result of these principles, what liturgy did he fail perfectly to discharge?'). This is one of five speeches in which Isaios uses the vocabulary of *liturgies to emphasize the merits of his clients. Cf. 4.27; 5.36; 6.60; 11.50. In a series of three questions, Thrasyllos seeks the admiration of his audience for Apollodoros's record of public service. The form of this first question invites the listener to conclude that Apollodoros performed every possible liturgy, although the conclusion is not actually justified by Thrasyllos's reply.

ἢ τίνα εἰσφορὰν οὐκ ἐν πρώτοις εἰσήνεγκεν; ('Or to what war-tax was he not among the first to contribute?'). The second question appears to imply that Apollodoros was one of the 300 richest Athenians who, by Demosthenes's time, were required to pay the *proeisphora*. (See ἐν τοῖς τριακοσίοις, Isa. 6.60, with Wyse's note.) Wyse, on the other hand, thinks that Thrasyllos "only means that Apollodoros was always one of the earliest to pay his taxes."

ἢ τί παραλέλοιπεν ὧν προσῆκεν; ('What duty has he ever failed to perform?'). The third, purely rhetorical question invites the answer 'none', but is too vague to convey any substantive information about Apollodoros's actions.

ὁ τρίπους ἐκεῖνος ἕστηκε ('the well-known tripod still stands'). Having implied that Apollodoros had performed every possible *liturgy, Thrasyllos singles out one example, his service as **khorēgos*, presumably because the tripod stood as a public memorial of which his audience would be aware. On the significance of the khoregic tripod as a public statement of wealth and civic virtue, see Wilson (2000), 201–208.

41 ταύτην τὴν χάριν ἀποδοίητε ('you would repay this benefaction'). For the ideology of *kharis* as a reciprocal obligation, see on οὐδετέρῳ..., 9.23.

τὴν ἐκείνου γνώμην ('his intentions'). Thrasyllos again emphasizes his claim that the adoption was in accordance with Apollodoros's wishes, by asking the **dikastai* to award him the estate not only for his own sake but in order to honour Apollodoros by carrying out his intentions.

καὶ μὴν καὶ ἐμέ γε ('As for myself'). Cf. on καὶ μὴν καὶ αὐτὸς Ἀπολλόδωρος, §39. Reverting to his own character, Thrasyllos again uses the emphatic particles *kai mēn kai*, with the effect of placing himself in the same category as Apollodoros and Thrasyllos senior. At this stage he is no longer using his record to justify Apollodoros's decision to adopt him, but more openly seeking to make a favourable impression on the **dikastai.*

κατὰ τὴν ἐμὴν ἡλικίαν ('[I have performed the civic duties] appropriate to my age'). This seems to imply that Thrasyllos had not yet reached the qualifying age for some of the public offices in Athens. Since he had already served as a **thesmothetēs* and a *gymnasiarch, he was presumably over thirty, which is likely to have been the minimum age for most such offices. Cf. Rhodes (1981), 389–390. Certain offices, including that of *proboulos* (*Ath. Pol.* 29.2) and, at least in the fourth century, *khorēgos* (*Ath. Pol.* 56.3) were reserved for men of at least forty. A birthdate in the late 390s, which would place him in his late thirties at the time of the speech, is consistent with the fact that his mother was not yet married when Apollodoros set off for the Corinthian War. Cf. on τῇ ἐκείνου μὲν θυγατρὶ . . ., §9.

42 τὴν Ἀπολλοδώρου γνώμην ('the intentions of Apollodoros'). Cf. on τὴν ἐκείνου γνώμην, §41.

ἀποδόντες ἡμῖν τοῦτον τὸν κλῆρον ('by restoring this estate to us'). The language is tendentious, since there has been no suggestion that Thrasyllos's opponents have taken the estate away from him. He may be obliquely alluding to the history of enmity between the descendants of Eupolis and those of Thrasyllos senior.

Epilogue (*43–45*)

Thrasyllos concludes with a tendentious summary of his own case and that of his opponent, followed by a conventional appeal to the **dikastai* to cast their votes in accordance with justice.

43 Ἵνα δὲ μὴ δοκῶ διατρίβειν ('But in order that I may not seem to be wasting time'). This contributes to the impression of Thrasyllos as a confident and businesslike litigant, while showing due respect for the **dikastai.*

ἀδελφιδοῦς ὢν ('being his nephew'). Thrasyllos, as nephew, was more closely related to Apollodoros than was the wife of Pronapes (first cousin), but he could not claim to be Apollodoros's next of kin because their relationship was matrilineal. Cf. on ὄντα ἀδελφιδοῦν, §4.

ζῶντος καὶ εὖ φρονοῦντος ('while he was alive and in his right mind'). See on ζῶν καὶ εὖ φρονῶν, §1, and ἐλθὼν ὡς τὴν ἐμὴν μητέρα . . ., §14.

καὶ εἰς τοὺς γεννήτας καὶ φράτορας ἐγγραφείς ('and having been registered with the members of his *genos* and phratry'). Isaios apparently did not think it important at this point to mention Thrasyllos's enrolment in Apollodoros's *deme, as well as his introduction to the **genos* and *phratry. This could be taken as an indication that acceptance by the phratry was in fact the crucial element of a valid adoption. He may, on the other hand, have been reluctant to remind the **dikastai* that Apollodoros did not carry out the deme enrolment in person.

Προνάπης δὲ τί ὑπὲρ τῆς ἀμφισβητούσης; ('What does Pronapes claim on behalf of my opponent?'). See on ταύτην τε…, §18.

44 ἔχειν μὲν τοῦ τῆς γυναικὸς ἀδελφοῦ τιμὴν τοῦ ἡμικληρίου ('to keep half of his wife's brother's estate'). Thrasyllos is putting words into his opponent's mouth: it was not part of Pronapes's case that he claimed to keep his wife's inheritance from her brother, but Isaios plays to what appears to have been an Athenian prejudice against those who took possession of more than one estate. Cf. on ἀλλὰ καὶ τόνδε προσλήψονται, 10.23.

πένθ' ἡμιτάλαντα ('five half-talents'). Isaios does not mention the exact value of the estate at issue in the case, but by specifying that the wife of Pronapes has already inherited the substantial sum of two and a half talents from her brother, he reinforces his attack on his opponents' greed. Moreover, it appears that Thrasyllos's natural father was already dead (cf. on καὶ ᾔτησε καὶ ἔτυχεν, §14), so he may be anticipating an attack on similar lines from his opponent. But his inheritance from his father may well have been less than two and a half talents, especially if it was shared among several brothers, in which case he could claim a moral victory over Pronapes and his wife.

ἑτέρων ταῖς ἀγχιστείαις προτέρων αὐτοῦ τῆς γυναικὸς ὄντων ('although there are others more closely related to Apollodoros than his wife'). This recalls the argument at §20, that Thrasyboulos outranked the wife of Pronapes in the order of intestate succession, and the inference that, because he had made no claim to the estate, Thrasyboulos implicitly supported Thrasyllos's claim as the adopted son of Apollodoros. (Thrasyllos himself, despite pointing out that he was a nephew of Apollodoros while his opponent was only a cousin, cannot claim to be closer in the order of succession because his relationship with Apollodoros was through his mother.)

οὔτ' ἐκείνῳ παῖδα εἰσπεποιηκὼς ('but he has not given him a son by posthumous adoption'). On the verb *eispoiein* ('to adopt') in the active voice, see on ὃν εἰσποιεῖ ἐκείνῳ, 9.2. Thrasyllos has already criticized the daughters of Eupolis for not giving their brother Apollodoros a son by posthumous adoption (§§29–32).

οὔτε τούτῳ ἂν εἰσποιήσας ἀλλ' ὁμοίως ἂν καὶ τοῦτον ἐξερημώσας ('and he would similarly fail to give Apollodoros a son by adoption and would leave his house without heirs'). Thrasyllos's message to the **dikastai* is that if they award the estate to the wife of Pronapes, she and her husband will allow Apollodoros's **oikos* to die out, just as they did with that of her brother. Irrespective of whether they were to blame for this, or whether they simply did not have a son who was available for adoption, the outcome would be equally undesirable; the *dikastai* would be better advised to vote for Thrasyllos, who as an adopted son will not only inherit Apollodoros's material estate but also continue his *oikos*.

καὶ ἔχθρας μὲν τηλικαύτης ὑπαρχούσης ('although such enmity existed'). Apollodoros's quarrel with Eupolis probably started more than fifty years before his death, but it is plausible that the enmity continued, and that Apollodoros would have wanted to avoid leaving his property to the descendants of the man who had defrauded him.

διαλλαγῆς δὲ οὐδεμιᾶς πώποτε ὕστερον γενομένης ('and there was no subsequent recociliation'). This emphatic denial of a reconciliation perhaps anticipates a contrary argument from Pronapes.

45 ταῦτα χρὴ σκοπεῖν, ὦ ἄνδρες ('You must take these points into consideration, gentlemen'). See on Ὤιμην . . ., §1, and cf. 4.22: ἀλλ' ὑμᾶς χρή, ὦ ἄνδρες, πρῶτον μὲν τὰς διαθήκας σκοπεῖν.

ὅτι ἐγὼ μὲν ἀδελφιδοῦς αὐτῷ, ἡ δὲ ἀνεψιὰ τοῦ τελευτήσαντος ('that I am the nephew of the deceased, while my opponent is his cousin'). Thrasyllos has referred several times to his blood relationship with Apollodoros as a reason why it was appropriate for Apollodoros to adopt him. Cf. on ὄντα ἀδελφιδοῦν, §4. He has not previously compared his degree of kinship directly with that of his opponent, who, despite being only a cousin, ranked higher in the **ankhisteia* of Apollodoros because of her patrilineal relationship (cf. on Ἐὰν μὴ ὦσιν ἀνεψιοὶ . . ., §22). He now appears to be hedging his bets by staking a claim to the inheritance on grounds of closer kinship as well as adoption. It would have been difficult to sustain this argument at any length without exposing its weakness, but Isaios no doubt hoped that a hint would be enough to have put the idea into the minds of any of the **dikastai* who were unconvinced about the validity of the adoption.

καὶ ὅτι ἡ μὲν δύ' ἔχειν ἀξιοῖ κλήρους ('and that she claims two estates'). See on ἔχειν μὲν . . ., §44.

ἐγὼ δὲ τοῦτον μόνον εἰς ὅνπερ εἰσεποιήθην ('but I claim only this one, to which I am entitled by adoption'). Cf. on πενθ' ἡμιτάλαντα, §44.

καὶ ὅτι αὕτη μὲν οὐκ εὔνους τῷ καταλιπόντι τὸν κλῆρον ('that she was not on good terms with the man who left the property'). Thrasyllos has not really shown that the wife of Pronapes was herself on bad terms with Apollodoros, but only that there was a lasting enmity between Apollodoros and her father, Eupolis. He has also argued that Apollodoros was unimpressed by her treatment of her brother's estate, but that, again, does not necessarily amount to personal enmity. It is likely, nevertheless, that his argument would have appeared plausible in a culture where enmity was inherited.

ἐγὼ δὲ καὶ ὁ ἐμὸς πάππος εὐεργέται γεγόναμεν αὐτοῦ ('whereas my grandfather and I have been his benefactors'). Cf. on ὁ δὲ πάππος…, §8.

τίθεσθε τὴν ψῆφον ᾗ δίκαιόν ἐστι ('cast your vote in accordance with justice'). Isaios uses an almost identical formula at 8.46, and expresses similar ideas in different words at 4.31 and 6.65.

Οὐκ οἶδ' ὅτι δεῖ πλείω λέγειν…εἰρημένων ('I do not know of anything more that I need to say, for I think that no part of my speech has escaped your attention'). The same formula is used at Isa. 8.46, and cf. Dem. 20.167; 36.62; 38.28; 54.44.

ISAIOS 8: ON THE ESTATE OF KIRON

Introduction

Background and Chronology

Kiron has died leaving property to the value of about ninety minas (a talent and a half), plus an unspecified amount of money out on loan at interest. His two sons have predeceased him, dying young and without issue. His nephew (brother's son) has submitted a claim to the estate as next of kin. This is contested by Isaios's client, who claims the estate as the son of Kiron's deceased daughter and therefore his legitimate heir.[1] The speaker and his opponent are thus first cousins once removed. The estate appears to have been in the occupation of Kiron's brother-in-law, Diokles, who may have lived in Kiron's house during the latter's lifetime.

Nothing is definitely known about Kiron and his family. Given that the name is an unusual one, and that the speaker and his father were members of the *deme Pithos,[2] it is possible that (as shown in Diagram 2)[3] the speaker was also called Kiron, the father of the Mnesikles Kironos who is named on an ephebic list from Pithos dated to "somewhere in the ten years before 326".[4] Kiron himself was not necessarily a member of the same deme as his son-in-law.

On the assumption that the speaker was aged at least twenty at the time of the court case, the earliest possible date for the speech is about 383 BC, since he tells the **dikastai* that he and his brother were born after the *arkhonship of Eukleides.[5] It is generally accepted that it must have been written by 363 BC, when Demosthenes delivered his speeches

---

[1] The pattern of kinship in this dispute is similar to that in Isa. 10, where the speaker (who is the son of Aristarkhos senior's daughter) claims that his mother was deprived of her rightful inheritance by her father's brother and the brother's son.

[2] Cf. on μετὰ τῆς Διοκλέους γυναικὸς τοῦ Πιθέως, §19. It has commonly been assumed that the speaker must have been the older of Kiron's two grandsons; and, as Edwards (2007), 134, points out, the name of a maternal grandfather is more likely to have been given to a younger son. There is, however, no firm evidence that the speaker's brother was living at the time of the speech (see on ἀλλ' ἡμᾶς . . ., §1) so the identification cannot be ruled out.

[3] For the sake of simplicity, the husbands of Kiron's daughter, whose identity is not relevant to the dispute, are not shown on the diagram.

[4] Davies (1971), 316, referring to *IG* ii^2 2385, 101.

[5] 403 BC; for the significance of this date, see on μετ' Εὐκλείδην . . ., §43.

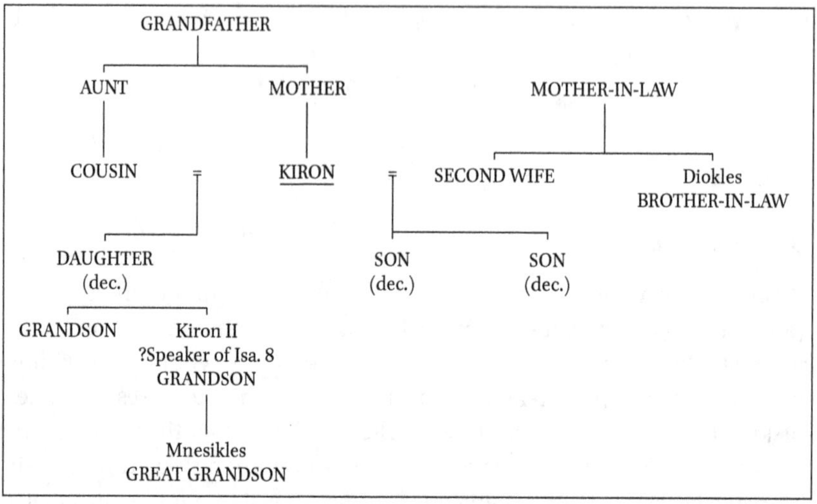

Diagram 2: The family of Kiron

against his guardians, Aphobos and Onetor, in which several passages appear to have been 'borrowed' from Isa. 8. In fact, we cannot reliably infer that Demosthenes was directly imitating Isaios, since both writers may have been using common rhetorical **topoi*; but it remains unlikely, given the speaker's apparent youth, that Isa. 8 was written significantly later than 363 BC.

In the chronology suggested below, the sequence of events and, so far as possible, the intervals between them, are based on information given in the speech. Other intervals are based on conjecture (for example, that Kiron first married at the age of thirty, and his daughter at sixteen). The conjectural dates assume that the speech was delivered in about 370 BC, and that the speaker was then in his late twenties.[6]

Birth of Kiron, c452.
Kiron's first marriage, to his cousin (§7), c422.
Birth of Kiron's daughter (§7), c421.
Death of Kiron's first wife (four years[7] after daughter's birth, §7), c417.
Kiron's second marriage, to the sister of Diokles (§7), c416.
Births of Kiron's two sons (§7), c415–413.
First marriage of Kiron's daughter, to Nausimenes of Kholargos (§8), c405.

---

[6] Since the speaker does not refer to his own youth, Davies (1971), 315, plausibly infers that he was 'probably nearer 30 than 20'.

[7] Or possibly thirty days; see on μετὰ ἐνιαυτοὺς τέτταρας . . ., §7.

Death of Nausimenes of Kholargos (three or four years after the marriage, §8), c401.
Second marriage of Kiron's daughter, to the speaker's father (§8), c400.
Births of two sons, the speaker and his brother, to Kiron's daughter, c399–397.
Death of Kiron, c370.

It is impossible to suggest precise dates for the deaths of Kiron's two sons, who may have died at some time between 400 and 390. Similarly, Kiron's daughter and her second husband (the speaker's parents) may have died at any time between 397 and 370.

The Speaker's Story and the Structure of Isaios's Narrative

The litigation over Kiron's inheritance appears to be the latest stage in a long-running feud between two branches of his family. On the one side, the speaker himself was apparently the only surviving kinsman of Kiron from his first marriage. On the other side are Kiron's second wife and her brother Diokles, with whom the son of Kiron's brother is aligned.

This speech illustrates clearly how a supposedly non-adversarial **diadikasia* could, in practice, take on the characteristics of an adversarial **dikē* or **graphē.*[8] Kiron's nephew spoke first at the trial, apparently relying on the legal argument that a brother's son takes precedence over a daughter's son in the order of intestate succession, as well as on the allegation that the mother of Isaios's client was not a legitimate daughter of Kiron. The nephew's highly damaging attack on the grandson's status, like an accusation in a criminal trial, demands a response, and his position as first speaker accentuates his quasi-prosecutorial rôle. Isaios thus finds his client forced into the position of defendant, and his first task must have been to neutralize any disadvantage attaching to that position. As the detailed commentary will show, he succeeds not merely in doing so, but in positively exploiting the situation for the benefit of his client. We can only speculate as to how different his approach might have been if his client had spoken first, but one of the themes of this commentary is to examine how Isaios's rhetorical strategy in this speech differs from those written for the first speaker in a *diadikasia.*

[8] Cf. General Introduction, pp. 7–10.

According to the speaker, Kiron's first wife was a blood relation, his first cousin (mother's sister's daughter).[9] She died not long after the birth of her only child, a daughter, who became the speaker's mother. Kiron remarried, and brought up his daughter alongside his two sons by his second wife. The daughter's first husband was Nausimenes of Kholargos, who died after a few years leaving no issue. She remarried, and was selected by the wives of her husband's fellow demesmen as a candidate for the presiding rôle at the Thesmophoria, a festival in which only women of citizen status were allowed to participate. She had two sons (the speaker and his brother) by her second husband, who is not named in the speech, and they were introduced into their father's *phratry as his legitimate offspring. Kiron cherished these grandsons, and, after his own sons had died, always took them with him to sacrifices and festivals.

The speaker claims that, after the deaths of Kiron's sons, Diokles and his sister started plotting to take control of Kiron's estate. By staging a series of faked pregnancies and miscarriages, she deceived Kiron into thinking that he might father another son, in order to prevent him from adopting the speaker or his brother. Diokles persuaded Kiron to let him handle his money and manage his real property, while at the same time accusing the speaker's father of trying to take over the estate. After Kiron died, the speaker tried to remove his body and take it to his own house for the funeral. The intercession of Kiron's grieving widow, who wanted to help lay out the body, persuaded him to conduct the funeral from Kiron's house. Diokles started making, and paying for, some of the funeral arrangements, then demanded payment from the speaker, but later refused to let the speaker pay and claimed to have recovered the money from Kiron's nephew (although the speaker says the money for the funeral actually came from Kiron's estate). The quarrel continued at the burial itself, where the speaker denounced Diokles in his speech at the graveside. Diokles, who was already in illegal occupation of Kiron's property, had all along been grooming Kiron's nephew to submit a formal claim to the estate, offering

9 According to Cox (1998), 33, "marriage to a kinswoman through the matriline could leave the offspring from that union at a severe disadvantage legally: Ciron's grandson from Ciron's first marriage to his mother's sister's son [*sic*] was prevented from inheriting by Ciron's agnate, his brother's son." There is nothing in the text, or in other sources of Athenian law, to support this view. Kiron's grandson is at a disadvantage legally through being a daughter's son rather than a son's son, and more particularly the son of a daughter married by *enguē* rather than *epidikasia*. The nature of his grandparents' marriage has no bearing on his position.

to share it with him but playing down its real value so that the nephew would get only a tiny proportion.

What exactly the opponent had said is largely a matter of conjecture, although, as the commentary shows, some parts of his version of events may be inferred from Isaios's narrative and argumentation. Whatever the precise details, it is clear that his account must have been highly damaging to the speaker. As the first speaker at the trial, Kiron's nephew would have had the opportunity to undermine Isaios's client by making false or irrelevant allegations.[10] The story that Isaios chose to present in response is not a direct refutation of the opponent's narrative, which might have served only to reinforce the opponent's credibility with the *dikastai*, but a counternarrative of his own.[11] His narrative is carefully structured not only to focus on the strongest points in his own client's case, but also, apparently, to deflect attention from the strengths of the opponent's account.

The early events, up to the births of Kiron's grandsons and their introduction into their father's phratry, are succinctly narrated in chronological sequence. After the description of Kiron's funeral, in which the speaker struggles to convince his audience that he, and not his opponents, was in control of events, the rest of the narrative is devoted mainly to the alleged rôle of Diokles in seeking to deprive the speaker of his rightful inheritance. As the narrative moves further away from events that have a direct bearing on the status of the speaker and his mother, it becomes more detailed and expansive. It is also, however, considerably vaguer as to chronology, and there are some obvious omissions and evasions.

Most significantly, Isaios tells us nothing at all about the speaker's mother, beyond the basic 'facts' of her birth, upbringing in Kiron's household, two marriages, and eligibility to preside over the Thesmophoria. If she had any rôle in the family feud, it is not mentioned. This is in marked contrast with Isa. 10, where he solicits the sympathy of the *dikastai* by portraying the speaker's mother as a wronged heiress, victim of a fraud

[10] Cf. Hyp. 1.8–10 (cited by Rhodes (2004), 147) where the speaker describes the advantages enjoyed by prosecutors, who have the first word at trials. These include "making all the statements and lies they please", and "depriving the defendants of their defence by the lying abuse they have cooked up about them". So, as the speaker complains, defendants are faced with a dilemma: they can either "defend themselves against the irrelevant slanders to the detriment of their defence in the matter at issue, or else ... forget the accusations that have already been made and thereby leave the jurors with the impression that what has been said is true" (trans. Whitehead).

[11] Cf. Johnstone (1999), 54–60, on counternarrative as a common feature of defence speeches in adversarial Athenian trials.

by her uncle and cousin. In the present case, even if Kiron's daughter died at a relatively early stage, it would still have been possible to present her as a victim, abused or intimidated by her stepmother and half-brothers. As it is, Isaios apparently wanted the speaker to say as little as possible about his mother's upbringing, taking refuge in the assertion that Kiron's household slaves could have told the true story, if only his opponent had been willing to produce them for torture. Perhaps he feared that, by engaging too closely with the opponent's allegations against his client, he might give them additional credibility or encourage the *dikastai* to consider them more seriously.

The speaker's father, as well as his mother, may have played a larger part in the feud than Isaios admits;[12] the opponents probably presented him as an outsider trying to insinuate himself into Kiron's household, and perhaps claimed that Kiron resented his interference, preferring to rely on Diokles for support. The speaker says nothing about his own or his father's social standing or financial affairs, although there is a hint of the father's status in the fact that his wife was considered eligible to preside at the Thesmophoria. There may well have been a property qualification for such an honour, in view of the expenditure that is likely to have been involved.[13] It is possible that the speaker had already inherited a substantial estate from his father, and that Kiron's nephew, pleading poverty on his own part, had argued that it would be unfair to let him have Kiron's estate as well.[14] If that was the case, Isaios might well have decided that the matter was best passed over in silence. In any event he mentions nothing about the father's financial affairs, and neither does he give any indication of the timing of his death.

Nor does Isaios tell us exactly when Kiron's sons died. We know that they were still alive when the speaker's mother married her first husband (§8), and probably at least one of them was living at the time of her second marriage, since it is unlikely that Kiron would have married her exogamously if he had no surviving sons. When Kiron took his two grandsons to the festivals and sacrifices, he treated them as his only surviving lineal descendants (§17), from which we may infer that Kiron's sons died either before his grandsons were born or while they were small children. Isaios

[12] See on πάλιν ἐκδίδωσι…, §8 and καὶ τὸν πατέρα…, §36.

[13] Cf. Parker (2005), 279.

[14] For the Athenian prejudice against the inheritance of more than one estate, see on ἔχειν μὲν…, 7.44.

has thus provided sufficient information to establish that Kiron's sons predeceased their father, and, at least implicitly, that they died without issue. These points were important because the speaker, as a daughter's son, would have had no claim to the estate during their lifetime or that of any offspring of theirs.

The chronological imprecision may, therefore, be regarded as an example of Isaios's characteristically economical style, rather than deliberate evasion, but his vagueness does also serve a rhetorical purpose. In the key section of his narrative, dealing with the machinations of Diokles and his sister to take control of Kiron's estate, Isaios says that they started plotting 'as soon as Kiron's sons had died' (§36). It is possible for a reader of the speech to work out that this must have been at least twenty years before Kiron's own death (as suggested in the chronology on p. 90) but Isaios must have hoped that the length of this interval would not be apparent to the audience when the speech was delivered orally. If they had noticed it, they might have asked questions about the credibility of his narrative and how much Isaios was leaving out; it would not, in particular, have been possible for Kiron's wife to sustain her pretence of aborted pregnancies over such a long period.

The Significance of Character

The account of Diokles's criminal record (§§40–42) is brief, but inextricably linked with his alleged rôle in the family dispute: his character is blackened from the start, and he is presented throughout the speech as the mastermind behind the illegal seizure of Kiron's property. A listener or reader is invited to draw the obvious inference: a man who could rob his half-sisters of their rightful inheritance, killing or imprisoning their husbands in the process, is clearly capable of defrauding an elderly brother-in-law and manipulating his nephew. In fact, the account of Diokles's plot to take over Kiron's estate, in combination with the character assassination, is the most persuasive weapon in the speaker's armoury, but its evidential value is questionable.

There may have been an element of exaggeration in what the speaker says about Diokles's crimes against his sisters, but the credibility of his account is enhanced by the support of testimony. There are, however, no witnesses to events within Kiron's household, perhaps because there was no-one available to testify on the speaker's behalf. Whatever the reason, the lack of testimony leads to the suspicion that Isaios made use of Diokles's known bad character in order to invent, or at least exaggerate, his rôle in the family feud, as a means of distracting attention from the weaker elements of his client's case. Even if it was true, however, the account of the feud has no direct bearing on the speaker's legitimacy, or on the relative claims of a daughter's son and a brother's son.

So Isaios's portrayal of Diokles may suggest that Athenian litigants sometimes wanted the *dikastai* to pay more attention to character, and to marginally relevant 'facts', than to legal issues and argumentation. It does not, nevertheless, support the view that a litigant could safely rely on character alone.[15] Had that been the case, the speaker might simply have admitted that his mother was illegitimate, or that it was impossible for him to prove her status, and invited the *dikastai* to award him the inheritance because he was more deserving than his opponent. Instead, he deploys a range of different types of 'proof' (witness testimony, challenge to torture, laws), of which he is careful to remind the *dikastai* at the conclusion of his speech (§45). It is clear from his emphasis on formal 'proofs' that he did not expect the *dikastai* openly to disregard the legal issues, but they would undoubtedly have accepted character evidence as part of the 'larger story' of relevant facts.[16]

The Legal Issue: The Inheritance Rights of a Daughter's Son

We have no evidence for an explicit provision in Athenian law on the particular issue raised in the present case: the inheritance rights of a daughter's son when the daughter in question was not **epiklēros* but had been married by **enguē* to a husband outside the family.[17] There is, however, no doubt that an inheritance could be transmitted through a female line, both lineally and collaterally.

If an Athenian died leaving no sons but a daughter or daughters, she or they became *epiklēros*, and could be claimed in marriage by the father's next of kin, who had to claim the 'heiress' along with the estate by **epidikasia*. Neither the *epiklēros* herself nor her husband legally owned the estate, which passed to any son(s) of their marriage two years after puberty. So a woman in this position did not herself inherit her father's estate, but became the channel through which it passed to her son. One effect

[15] See pp. 20–21.
[16] Cf. Rhodes, 2004, 146.
[17] Lawless, whose Ph.D. thesis explores Isaios's use of "emerging ideas of legal equity" to deal with situations not explicitly covered by the law, finds examples of equity argument in Isa. 1, 2, 6 and 8, "where a significant gap or obscurity in statute law appears to elicit this line of argumentation" (Lawless (1991), 134–135).

(perhaps the intended one) of this arrangement was to create an heir for the deceased to whom he was related, albeit only collaterally, through a male as well as a female line.

Isaios does not address the opponent's argument directly, so we do not know the exact basis of Kiron's nephew's claim to be closer in the line of succession than his daughter's sons. It is possible that, as the writer of the hypothesis to the speech assumes, he relied on the precedence of males over females. If so, there is nothing in the available sources to support his interpretation of the law. The only evidence we have for a doctrine of male precedence in Athenian inheritance law occurs in the context of the order of distribution of intestates' estates among collateral relations.[18] According to this law, a male collateral can exclude a female even if she is in a closer degree of consanguinity with the deceased. So not only would a brother's son exclude a sister, and an uncle's son an aunt, but the son of the uncle's son would exclude the uncle's daughters and the son of the aunt's son would exclude the aunt's daughters.[19] It cannot, however, be inferred from this that a brother's son would exclude a daughter's son, who was not a collateral but a lineal descendant. Indeed, the fact that a woman could inherit from her *homopatric brother, if he died leaving no descendants or male siblings,[20] makes it all the more likely that a daughter could inherit from her father, whether she was *epiklēros* or not.

Isaios bases his reply on the precedence of lineal descendants over collaterals. In principle this is entirely plausible, but his argumentation appears evasive to modern readers because he does not cite a law that would explicitly support his case, relying instead on references by analogy to the laws dealing with the inheritance rights of the sons of *epiklēroi*, and with the duty to maintain elderly relations.[21] There is a certain naïveté

---

18 See on κρατεῖν δὲ ..., 7.20.

19 Lipsius (1905), 558. Cf. commentary on 7.18–26.

20 Under the law cited at Isa. 11.1–2. Examples of women inheriting in these circumstances occur in Isa. 7 and 11, and in Men. *Aspis*.

21 Cf. Körte (1906), 391: "Hätte es ein Gesetz gegeben, das den Töchtersöhnen den Vorzug vor den Brudersöhnen sicherte, so würde es Isaios natürlich angeführt haben, aber das tut er *nicht*, und grade die Art, wie er diesen schwachen Punkt zu verdecken strebt, läßt deutlich erkennen, daß er sich im Widerspruch zum geltenden Recht befindet." ("Had there been a law which gave daughters' sons priority over brothers' sons, Isaios would naturally have cited it, but that is what he does *not* do, and it is precisely the way in which he strives to conceal this weakness which makes it clear that he is in the wrong.") Wyse, 609, thinks that the "general considerations" adduced by Isaios are "a poor substitute for a quotation from a law". Usher (1999), 143, finds Isaios's argument "convincing", but adds that "the matter might have been put beyond doubt by the citing of a specific law."

in this critical response; had there been a law that explicitly gave the daughter's son a better claim than the brother's son, it is unlikely that the speaker's opponent would have bothered to raise the issue at all. We cannot, of course, be sure that the opponent did not cite a law in his own favour, which Isaios conveniently omits to mention, but the assumption that Athenian law was complete and comprehensive is anachronistic. It is at least equally likely that the position of a daughter's son, when the daughter had been married by *enguē* rather than by *epidikasia*, was not specifically covered by the law at all. It was, however, always important for an Athenian litigant to demonstrate that he had the law on his side, and in this situation Isaios may simply be doing the best he can by drawing analogies from laws that can be plausibly presented as having some relevance to his case. Perhaps the speaker had been challenged by his opponent to produce the law dealing with the claim of a daughter's son to an estate—just as the speaker of Isa. 10 (knowing, apparently, that there was no law explicitly authorizing posthumous adoption) challenged his opponent to say under what law Aristarkhos junior had been adopted.[22]

Isa. 8, uniquely among Isaios's inheritance speeches, does not involve a disputed will or adoption. In fact, Isaios tells an elaborate story to explain why Kiron did *not* adopt either the speaker or his brother. He was probably responding to a point made by his opponent, who may have implied that Kiron could not adopt one of his grandsons because they were illegitimate and therefore not eligible for adoption.[23] If we reject the speaker's explanation as being too far-fetched, the real reason why Kiron did not adopt one of his grandsons, or another preferred heir, such as his nephew or Diokles, remains unclear. Even if he did have hopes of producing another natural son, he could have made a provisional adoption by will, as the speaker of Isa. 6 asserts that Philoktemon did (§§6–7).

Kiron's failure to adopt one of his grandsons has been interpreted by some scholars as evidence that the son of a daughter married by *enguē* could not inherit from his maternal grandfather at all unless the grandfather adopted him.[24] This view relies chiefly on the point that a daughter's son, being a member of his father's **oikos*, was outside the line of succes-

[22] See. on νόμον κελεύετε δεῖξαι . . ., 10.14.

[23] As suggested by Rubinstein (1993), 104.

[24] See, e.g., Lipsius (1905), 546, n. 27, where he argues that Diokles's efforts to prevent Kiron from adopting one of his grandsons would have had no real purpose if their entitlement to inherit from Kiron had been beyond doubt.

sion of his maternal grandfather.[25] The argument is not persuasive, first because it ignores the right to inherit of a sister's son, who would equally be outside his maternal uncle's line of succession. It also overlooks the more general point that a legitimate claim to an inheritance is not quite the same as a right of succession. It is clear that the perpetuation of an *oikos* was important to the Athenians, but it is equally clear that some *oikoi* were allowed to remain empty, after the death of an intestate whose estate was taken by his next of kin in default of natural or adopted descendants. Was Kiron, then, so confident of the legal position of his preferred successor that he saw no need for adoption? This seems improbable since, given the state of conflict within the family, he might have guessed that a claim by either the grandson or the nephew would be challenged by the other. A more likely explanation, consistent with the speaker's story though not explicitly mentioned, is that Kiron was not mentally competent to make a will.

It has to be remembered that the purpose of adopting an heir under Athenian law was not only to dispose of an estate, but to ensure the continuation of an *oikos* that would otherwise have become empty. This could be achieved not only by the adoption of a daughter's son,[26] but also by that of a collateral relative who would, if not adopted, have been the intestate heir of his adoptive father.[27] Posthumous adoption was a possibility when the deceased had left neither a will nor a son adopted **inter vivos*, but in the present case it was clearly not an option because of the dissension within the family. There are, as Wyse points out, no known adoptions of a son's son,[28] but that is because a man was already in his paternal grandfather's line of succession without the need for adoption. Wyse's inference that the inheritance rights of a daughter's son depended on his being adopted by his grandfather is not justified,[29] although such an adoption would certainly have given the grandson a degree of protection against rival claims, as well as providing a male heir for the grandfather.

---

[25] See, especially, Lentzsch (1932), 31, who follows Körte (n. 21) on this point.

[26] Examples are Kyronides, adopted by Xenainetos senior (Isa. 10), Euboulides II, posthumously adopted by Euboulides I ([Dem] 43), the unnamed grandson of Arkhimakhos ([Dem.] 43. 37), and Diokles, adopted by Lysandros (Plut. *Them.* 32); discussed by Rubinstein (1993), 79.

[27] Examples include Endios (son of Pyrrhos's sister) in Isa. 3 and Khairestratos (son of Philoktemon's sister) in Isa. 6; discussed by Rubinstein (1993), 78–80.

[28] In Isa. 10, Aristarkhos senior was by blood the paternal grandfather of his posthumously adopted son, Aristarkhos junior, but *de jure* the brother of Aristarkhos junior's maternal grandfather.

[29] Wyse, 609.

A related argument is that the institution of the epiklerate would be meaningless if a daughter's son could inherit from his grandfather even if the daughter had been married by *enguē* and not by *epidikasia*.[30] This, too, is an unconvincing objection. The purpose and functioning of the epiklerate are not fully understood, but its rules came into operation in a particular situation: when a man died leaving a daughter (or daughters) but no male issue. An endogamous marriage between the deceased's daughter and his next of kin would provide an heir who was as closely related as possible to the deceased. It was apparently not compulsory, however, for the next of kin to marry the *epiklēros* (although if he declined to do so he would have to find her a suitable alternative husband)[31] and it certainly cannot be assumed that a daughter's sons would have no right to inherit if she had not been in the position of *epiklēros* because she had predeceased her father.

In the absence of conclusive evidence, the strongest point in favour of Isaios and his client is the theoretical one that since Athenian law permitted an inheritance to be transmitted through a female collateral to her descendants, it is unlikely that it would have placed a female descendant and her issue in a less favourable position.[32] Isaios's case is also indirectly supported by the argument deployed by Demosthenes when he tries to prove that his maternal grandfather was not in debt to the state when he died.[33] If liability for a debt could be transmitted through the debtor's daughter to her sons, even when the daughter had been married by *enguē* rather than *epidikasia*, it is a reasonable inference that an inheritance could descend by the same route. There is a further reference to

30 Lentzsch (1932), 32: "Wenn die Ausführungen des Redners richtig wären, so würde die ganze Erbtochterinstitution, zur Erhaltung des Hauses, vollkommen unsinnig sein...." ("If the speaker's explanations were correct, the whole institution of the epiklerate, for the preservation of the lineage, would be completely meaningless....")

31 Cf. the law on *epiklēroi* of the thetic class, cited at [Dem.] 43.54 and discussed by Harrison (1968), 135–136.

32 The argument in this paragraph follows Rubinstein (1993), 100–104. Rubinstein, 102, also cites Men. *Aspis* 270–273 as "perhaps the best indication that grandsons born in marriages contracted by *enguē* could inherit from their maternal grandfathers". Smikrines, in this play, wants to marry his 'heiress' niece so that he can take control of her fortune. When he is offered the chance to keep the property for himself, provided he lets her marry the husband of her choice, he anticipates a legal challenge from a son of the marriage. The 'heiress' in question, however, did not inherit her fortune directly from her father, but from a brother who had died without issue, so it is likely that Smikrines's hypothetical rival would have claimed the estate as the nephew, rather than the grandson, of its previous legitimate holder.

33 Dem. 28.1–7.

the status of daughters' sons at Isa. 6.56, where the speaker implies that, had the dispute been about Euktemon's estate rather than that of his son Philoktemon, Khaerestratos would have had a claim to it as the son of Euktemon's legitimate daughter.

So we may reasonably conclude that a daughter's son, whatever the form of the daughter's marriage, did have a better claim to an intestate's estate than a nephew. But it does not necessarily follow that the son of a daughter married by *enguē* enjoyed the same procedural advantages as a descendant through a male line, or a daughter's son whose mother had been *epiklēros*. Wyse, reluctant as always to accept that Isaios might be in the right, asks why, if the speaker's claim to be Kiron's legitimate heir was valid, he did not make use of a lineal descendant's right of **embateusis*, blocking any rival claim with a **diamarturia*.[34]

One suggested explanation is that the speaker wanted to avoid the financial risk of issuing a *diamarturia*, for which he would have been required to pay a deposit (*parakatabolē*) of ten percent of the value of the estate, to be forfeited if his opponent prosecuted him in a *dikē *pseudomarturiōn*.[35] It is possible, however, that the speaker had to pay the deposit in any event, since he was challenging a claimant to the estate who had already submitted a **lēxis*.[36] An alternative explanation is that the speaker did not

---

34 Wyse, 609. In the circumstances described by the speaker, it might have been more appropriate to use a *dikē exoulēs* to evict Diokles from Kiron's property.

35 This possibility is suggested by Rubinstein (1993), 103. The authority for the amount of the deposit in public and private cases is Pollux 8.39: παρακαταβολὴ δ'ἦν ἐπὶ μὲν τῶν πρὸς τὸ δημόσιον ἀμφισβητημάτων τὸ πέμπτον, ἐπὶ δὲ τῶν ἰδιωτικῶν τὸ δέκατον 'the deposit was one fifth in public cases and one tenth in private cases' (cited by Harrison (1971), 180, n. 4).

36 Wyse, 374, identifies twelve occurrences of *parakatabolē*, or the verb *parakataballein*, in inheritance speeches: Isa. 4.4, 6.12, 11.13, 15, 27; and [Dem.] 43.5, 16; 44.39, 40, 42, 52, 53. He points out that all these cases refer to a claimant who was either coming forward against an earlier claimant, or challenging the occupant of an estate who had been successful in an earlier legal action. He concludes, however, that "it is not logical to deduce from this evidence that the competitor who was the first to bring his petition before the Archon was on a different footing from subsequent pretenders, and was not compelled to make a deposit, when a conflict of claims rendered a trial necessary." Harrison (1971), 181–182, who is followed by Rubinstein on this point, suggests the alternative interpretation that there were probably only three specific circumstances in which the *parakatabolē* was required in inheritance cases: when the claimant was opposing a *lēxis* by means of a *diamarturia*, or when he was asserting his right to succeed as an adopted son, in the face of a *lēxis*, or when he was starting a new *epidikasia* by means of an *antigraphē*, when the estate was already occupied by a claimant who had been successful at an *epidikasia*. While conceding that Wyse's interpretation may be the correct one, Harrison suggests that "The *a priori* objections to such a rule are strong; for it entails the belief that in all cases which came to court there was in effect a court fee of one-tenth of the value of the estate, since one or other party was bound to forfeit the *parakatabolē*."

in fact have the option of using a *diamarturia*, since the procedural position of a daughter's son whose mother was not *epiklēros* was equivalent to that of a collateral kinsman, who had to claim the estate by *epidikasia* or contest a rival claim by *diadikasia*.[37] Against that view, it appears from the speaker's argumentation in Isa. 3.59–62 that a legitimate daughter could proceed by way of a *diamarturia*, but there is no known case in which a daughter actually did so; and even if she could, we cannot be sure that the right extended to a daughter's son as well as the daughter herself.

According to the available evidence, it appears that most inheritance cases in the Athenian courts turned on questions of fact, such as, in the present case, the legitimacy of one of the claimants to an estate. Since the law excluding bastards from inheritance rights was clear and well known, Isaios could not argue that his client had a good claim to Kiron's property irrespective of his status, but had to mount a defence against the opponent's allegations. What makes this case unusual is that it also raises a purely legal question about the respective claims of a daughter's son and a brother's son. It is possible that Kiron's nephew raised the issue chiefly as a diversionary tactic, but it would hardly have been worthwhile for him to raise it at all if it had been covered by a clear and unambiguous law.

From a modern perspective, one would not expect a legal issue of this kind, which is unaffected by the facts of any particular case, to be litigated on a case by case basis. In a common law jurisdiction such as England and Wales, a lacuna or ambiguity in the law could, at least until the relevant legislation had been amended, be clarified by an authoritative judgment from an appellate court. In the Athenian context, unless we accept the speaker's disingenuous protestation that he does not know whether a similar case has ever been brought before,[38] we must assume that the issue did at least occasionally come before a **dikastērion*. Isaios would have been in a good position to know of such cases, and may even have written speeches for some of the litigants involved. Why, then, does he make no reference here to previous cases?

In a legal system with no reasoned judgments or appellate courts, and consequently no concept of legally binding precedent, litigants did not refer to previous cases as a matter of routine, but only when they perceived

[37] Rubinstein (1993), 44 points out that the son of an *epiklēros* could take his grandfather's estate without claiming it through a court, because his mother, together with the estate, had already been the object of an *epidikasia*.

[38] Cf. on καὶ οὐκ οἶδ' …, §34.

a rhetorical advantage in doing so.[39] Such references occur in only about one fifth of the extant forensic speeches; they are more common in public than in private speeches, and are frequently concerned with the severity of the prescribed or expected penalty—a factor that did not arise in inheritance cases. The fact that the cases cited as 'precedents' often involved high profile litigants may reflect the difficulty of obtaining information about court cases. There may also have been a perception among litigants and speechwriters that detailed discussion of previous cases would alienate the *dikastai*, because it would appear unduly technical and legalistic.[40] That would have been important in the present case, where the speaker is characterized as an inexperienced litigant, and it would be consistent with Isaios's reluctance to engage in his opponent's legal argument.

The Strength of the Speaker's Case

It is reasonable to conclude that Isaios's client did have a better claim to the estate than Kiron's nephew, provided he was indeed the son of Kiron's legitimate daughter. This is an issue on which he was clearly vulnerable to attack. His opponent apparently had witnesses from within Kiron's household who said the the speaker's mother was not the daughter of Kiron's lawful wife, claiming either that she had been born to him by a foreign **hetaira* or that she was the child of an unrelated *metic family. These witnesses probably included Kiron's second wife, whose evidence would have been given by Diokles as her **kurios*. It is impossible to tell whether the story was true or whether it had been fabricated by Diokles and his sister, but it appears that the speaker had no witnesses who could counter it directly (despite his claims that Kiron's slaves could have done so if his opponent had allowed them to be interrogated under torture). The speaker's witnesses make a convincing case that his mother was treated during her lifetime as a legitimate Athenian citizen, and that Kiron regarded the speaker and his brother as his grandsons and legitimate heirs, but it remains possible that Kiron and his family were covering up the true circumstances of his supposed daughter's birth.

The speaker's opponents have clearly attacked him on a weak point, and his struggle to find sufficient evidence of his mother's status arouses

---

39 See Lanni (2006), 118–128, for a full discussion of twenty-one speeches in which references to previous cases occur.

40 Litigants in private cases sometimes apologize for displaying detailed legal knowledge, blaming their opponents for reducing them to this necessity. Cf., e.g., Dem. 54.17; Hyp. 3.13.

suspicion, especially because of his excessive reliance on the rhetoric of **basanos* to undermine his opponent's account. But we cannot be sure whether he adopted these tactics because his mother really was illegitimate, or whether he was forced to do so because his opponents had concocted a story that they knew he would find extremely difficult to refute.

Commentary

**Proem (1–6)*

The comparatively lengthy introduction combines the conventional plea of the inexperienced speaker, and plea for the good will of the **dikastai*, with an extended attack on the speaker's opponents. This both prepares the *dikastai* for a different version of the story from the one they have heard from the other side, and sows the *seed for the later character assassination of Diokles. The speaker also identifies, in typically tendentious terms, the points at issue in the case: his mother's legitimacy, and the respective claims to inherit of a daughter's son and brother's son.

1 Ἐπὶ τοῖς τοιούτοις . . . ἐλπίζωσιν ('It is impossible, gentlemen, not to feel indignation against people who not only have the effrontery to claim the property of others, but also hope by their own arguments to abolish the rights conferred by the laws'). The speech opens with an appeal to the indignation of the **dikastai*, which, although it is never stated, also implies the indignation of the speaker. His allusions to his opponents as 'people of this kind' and to 'their own arguments' refer back to the opponent's speech (cf. on ὅθεν οὖν ἤρξαντο, §6) and also point forward to the sustained attack on Diokles later in the speech.

For 'gentlemen', cf. on Ὦ ἄνδρες...

For 'gentlemen', cf. on Ὦιμην, 7.1. There are nine addresses to the *dikastai* in the forty-six sections of this speech: one, following convention, in the opening sentence, and two more in the *proem (§5); one at the opening of the first section of narrative (§7); one to mark the resumption of the narrative after the reading of testimony (§21) and one after the reading of a law (§35); two in the course of argumentation (§§12 and 40); and one in the course of the narrative (§22). The frequency is comparable to that in Isa. 7 (eight addresses in forty-five sections), and significantly lower than in Isa. 10 (twenty-two in twenty-six sections) and Isa. 9 (nineteen in thirty-seven sections). The relatively sparing use of the device in this speech may be explained, at least in part, by the preponderance of narrative over argumentation, and it contributes to the generally restrained and matter of fact tone assumed by the speaker. This makes his occasional outburst of emotion all the more effective.

The tendentious language, used by the speaker to dismiss his opponent's claim from the outset, is characteristic of Athenian forensic oratory. In particular, rival claimants to an inheritance are often accused of stealing the property of others. The point is repeated at §4; cf., e.g., Isa. 4.11, 29; 10.2, 22; Lys. 32.25; [Dem.] 44.28, 35.

The speaker's emphasis on his opponent's use of argumentation to subvert justice plays to the Athenians' prejudice against legalism and mistrust of excessively clever speakers.

τοῦ γὰρ ἡμετέρου πάππου Κίρωνος οὐκ ἄπαιδος τελευτήσαντος ('for our grandfather, Kiron, did not die without issue'). The speaker's opponent is a collateral relation (nephew) of Kiron, whose claim to the estate would be sustainable only in the absence of lineal descendants. The speaker is claiming as Kiron's grandson, so *apais*, in this context, means 'without issue' rather than 'childless'.

ἀλλ' ἡμᾶς ... καταλελοιπότος ('but has left us behind him, his legitimate daughter's sons'). Kiron had two grandsons through his daughter (cf. on ἵν' ἐλπίζων ..., §36), but the speaker's brother is a shadowy figure, who plays no part in the narrative except for his attendance with Kiron at the festivals (§15). His death is not explicitly mentioned in the speech, but the speaker's account of Kiron's death and funeral implies either that his brother was no longer alive by that time or, perhaps, that he had dissociated himself from the speaker's claim to Kiron's estate and thus played no part in the dispute. Cf. on ἧκον γὰρ ἐγώ, §21.

οὗτοί τοῦ τε κλήρου λαγχάνουσιν ('our opponents claim the estate'). The wording makes it clear that Kiron's nephew had initiated the legal action by submitting a **lēxis*, which was challenged by Isaios's client. Cf. on καὶ πρὶν μὲν ληχθῆναι τοῦ κλήρου, 9.24. The procedures available to the speaker, as a lineal descendant of Kiron, are discussed in the introduction to this speech, pp. 101–102.

ὡς ἐγγυτάτω γένους ὄντες ('as being the next of kin'). The Athenian law of intestate succession (see p. 5) set out the order in which a deceased's collateral relations would inherit in the absence of lineal descendants, the closest of kin being a brother or brother's son (cf. Isa. 11.1). In this case, the speaker's opponent is Kiron's brother's son, which implies that the brother was already dead.

ὡς οὐκ ... τὸ παράπαν ('that we are not his daughter's issue, and in fact that he never had a daughter at all'). Isaios apparently thought it would not be in his client's interest to repeat the precise allegations which the

**dikastai* have already heard from his opponents, in order to avoid giving them too much credibility or encouraging the *dikastai* to think more seriously about them. Cf. on πρὸς τὰς αἰτίας…, §9, and εἰ τοιαύτη…, §20. The general nature of the allegations is, however, implicit in Isaios's narrative and argumentation: the opponents may have said that the speaker's mother was Kiron's daughter by a **hetaira* or a **pallakē* rather than a legitimate wife, or that she was not his offspring at all, but the child of a *metic introduced into the family.

2 ἡ τούτων πλεονεξία ('their greed'). It might be expected that claimants in inheritance cases would routinely characterize their opponents as being motivated by greed (*pleonexia*). This is, however, one only of two instances of the word *pleonexia* in Isaios's speeches. The other is at 11.36. Cf. [Dem.] 44.28, 35, 38.

το πλῆθος τῶν χρημάτων ('the high value of the property'). In fact, Kiron's estate appears to have been relatively modest, although its full extent is impossible to determine from the speech (cf. on σὺν ἱματίοις…, §8, and δανείσματα οὐκ ὀλίγα, §35). It must, at least, have been sufficiently large to justify the expense of litigation, but there is no suggestion that he was a member of the *liturgical class. (On the possibility of liturgy avoidance, see on οὐχ ὥσπερ Προνάπης…, 7.39.)

οὗτοι δ' ἔχουσι βιασάμενοι καὶ κρατοῦσι ('which they have taken by force and still hold'). This seems inconsistent with the speaker's earlier statement that his opponent has submitted a formal claim to the estate through the courts. Later, it emerges that it is Diokles whom he accuses of seizing the property by force, and of putting Kiron's nephew forward as the legal claimant. As discussed in the introduction to this speech, it is likely that the opponent had told an alternative version of the story in which Diokles had lived in Kiron's house with Kiron's consent.

καὶ τολμῶσιν…ἀμφισβήτησιν ('and they have the effrontery both to assert that he has left nothing and at the same time to lay claim to the estate'). In §37 the speaker spells out his allegation that Diokles, while grooming Kiron's nephew to make a formal claim to the estate, concealed its true value from him with a view to allowing him to take only a small part. And at §43 the amount given by Diokles to the nephew is specified as two minas.

3 τὸν εἰληχότα τοῦ κλήρου ('the man who has submitted a claim for the estate'). Cf. on οὗτοι…, §1. The speaker never refers to his opponent by name, and only twice (§§17 and 26) mentions his relationship to Kiron. At

§25 the opponent is 'the claimant to the estate'. Elsewhere he is referred to more dismissively as 'this man' (*houtos*, §§ 22, 43) or 'that man' (*ekeinos*, §38). For the rhetorical tactic of marginalizing an opponent by not naming him, see on ταύτην τε…, 7.18.

ἀλλὰ πρὸς Διοκλέα τὸν Φλυέα ('but against Diokles of Phlya'). At an early stage the speaker makes the point that his real enemy is not his legal opponent, Kiron's nephew, but Diokles of Phlya, who is later identified as the brother of Kiron's second wife.

τὸν 'Ορέστην ἐπικαλούμενον ('nicknamed Orestes'). The name Orestes was apparently not common in Attica. (*LGPN Attica* cites only three examples, of which only one is from the fourth century.) The precise origin and significance of the alleged nickname are obscure, but it presumably refers in some way to Diokles's reputation for violence and lawlessness. As Dunbar notes in her commentary on Aristoph. *Birds* 1490–3, it was considered dangerous to meet a dead hero, especially at night. An Orestes, identified in a scholion to *Birds* 1484b as the son of Timokrates, had a reputation for assault and clothes stealing. Diokles is not said to have killed his mother, although his alleged offences were committed against members of his family rather than strangers, so there is no obvious connection with either the legendary hero Orestes or a notorious robber. There may, however, have been a link between the madness of Orestes in tragedy and the manic or wild behaviour of Diokles (cf. Wyse, *ad loc.*). Whatever the exact allusion, the speaker is clearly using the nickname, which does not recur until §44, to blacken the character of his opponent's key witness (or possibly **sunēgoros*). When the speaker of Antiph. 1 refers to his stepmother as 'this Klytemnestra' (Antiph. 1.17), the allusion is more obvious because the stepmother is accused of killing her husband—the crime for which Klytemnestra was notorious.

παρασκευάσας ('groomed'). The verb *paraskeuazein*, 'to prepare', often has pejorative connotations in forensic oratory, because unduly careful preparation for litigation was regarded with suspicion in a system with no professional judges or advocates. Cf. on πρὸς παρασκευὰς λόγων, §5. It is used specifically of Diokles's 'grooming' or 'priming' of Kiron's nephew to claim the estate in opposition to the speaker (§§3, 25, 37). It has a more neutral meaning at §39, where it refers to the speaker's preparations for the ninth day offerings. For the pejorative usage, cf. Isa. 1.7, 17, where the speaker accuses his opponents of 'procuring orators' and 'concocting false arguments', and 10.1.

ἀποστερῶν ('trying to rob us'). This tendentious use of *aposterein*, implying robbery or fraud, is characteristic of speeches from inheritance cases.

It recurs four times in this speech, at §27, §43 (twice) and §45; cf. Isa. 1.18; 4.21; 7.7, 25; 9.2, 23, 31; 10.6, 15, 17, 18, 25.

Κίρων ὁ πάππος ('Kiron our grandfather'). By referring to Kiron as his grandfather, the speaker draws attention to his own status as a lineal descendant. (Altogether the word *pappos* occurs twenty-four times in the speech, as compared with twenty-two instances of the name Kiron.) On Isaios's use of relationship terms instead of names, cf. on ὁ δὲ πάππος…, 7.8 and τῶν τἀδελφοῦ, 9.2.

ἐὰν ὑμεῖς…λόγων ('if you are deceived into believing his words'). The suggestion that the **dikastai* will be 'deceived' if they believe the opponent's story, which recurs at §43, is a commonplace of Athenian forensic oratory. Cf. Isa. 4.1, 21; 5.13; 6.62; 9.27; 11.4, 22; and, e.g., Antiph. 6.49; Isok. 19.47; Lys. 5.4; 12.38; 13.70; 27.7; 30.34; Dem. 21.24; 22.4; 23.92; 37.48; 40.21, 39; 46.1, 25. A speaker who disagrees with the decision in a previous trial may avoid direct criticism of the *dikastai* by saying that they were 'deceived' by the winning party (e.g. Isa. 5.8; Dem. 37.48).

4 τούτων τοιαῦτα μηχανωμένων ('Since they have contrived such stories'). The speaker uses another pejorative verb, *mēkhanasthai*, to imply that his opponent's version of events was untrue. Cf. Isa. 10.17; 11.22, 36.

ἀλλὰ σαφῶς εἰδότες περὶ αὐτῶν ('but with clear knowledge of [the facts]'. The speaker's wish for the **dikastai* to 'know clearly' what happened foreshadows his characterization of his witnesses as 'those who know the facts'. Cf. on τοῖς εἰδόσι χρώμενος μάρτυσιν, §6.

εἴ τινι…ὁμοίως ('If, therefore, you have ever listened with scrupulous attention to any other case, I beg you to pay similar attention to this one'). The speaker's appeal to the previous experience of the **dikastai* reflects the fact that individuals often heard many cases in the course of their service in the courts. This careful build-up seems to imply that he expects them to have some difficulty in believing his story.

πολλῶν δὲ δικῶν ἐν τῇ πόλει γενομένων ('Although there are many lawsuits in our city'). The speaker is at pains to suggest that his own case is unique. Later (cf. on καὶ οὐκ οἶδ',…, §34) he claims to know of no other case in which a direct descendant's right to inherit has been challenged.

οὐδένες ἀναιδέστερον…ἀλλοτρίων ('it will be shown that no-one has ever claimed the property of others more shamelessly and openly than my opponents'). The sweeping generalization sounds exaggerated, but the speaker appears to be preparing the ground for his exceptionally vitriolic attack on Diokles later in the speech.

5 πρὸς παρασκευὰς λόγων ('against fabricated stories'). See on παρασκεύασας, §3, and cf. Dem. 30.3 for this exact phrase.

καὶ μάρτυρας οὐ τἀληθῆ μαρτυροῦντας ('and witnesses who give false evidence'). The testimony of the opposing witnesses was clearly damaging for the speaker, although he does not specify which of them he is accusing of lying, or on what points. This sets the tone for the whole of the speech; he does not challenge his opponent on specific 'facts', or engage with the details of his argumentation, preferring to put forward his own alternative story and arguments. Cf. the introduction to this speech, p. 93.

παντάπασιν ἀπείρως ἔχοντα δικαστηρίων ('being completely without experience of litigation'). The attack on the opponent and his witnesses is neatly combined with the conventional plea of the inexperienced speaker.

ἂν μή τι συμβῇ τοιοῦτον ὃ νῦν ὑπ' ἐμοῦ τυγχάνει προσδοκώμενον ('unless something should happen to me of the kind I now expect'). As Wyse notes, the allusion here is obscure, and is not illuminated in the course of the speech. Perhaps the speaker is hinting that he expects to suffer some form of violence at the hands of Diokles, like the latter's brothers-in-law whose fate is described at §§40–41.

δέομαι οὖν ὑμῶν, ὦ ἄνδρες, μετ' εὐνοίας τέ μου ἀκοῦσαι ('so I beg you, gentlemen, to listen to me with good will'). Cf. on δέομαι…, 7.4. In the present case the speaker's position more closely resembles that of a defendant, since he is responding to allegations made by his opponent. He has already explained that he is at a disadvantage because of his opponent's fabrications and his own inexperience of litigation.

6 In the final section of the *proem, as in Isa. 7 and 10, the speaker defines the issues in the case. Here, he also outlines the types of evidence he intends to use in support of his version of the facts.

τὰ μὲν πάλαι γεγενημένα λόγων ἀκοῇ καὶ μαρτύρων ('for events that happened long ago I shall rely on reports and statements heard by witnesses'). Athenian law permitted the use of hearsay evidence for events of which there were no living witnesses ([Dem.] 44.55). In this case the 'events of long ago' were presumably Kiron's first marriage and the birth of his daughter.

τοῖς εἰδόσι χρώμενος μάρτυσιν ('using witnesses who know the facts'). Here and at §42, the speaker's designation of his witnesses as 'those who know the facts' not only contrasts them with the opposing witnesses, whom he accuses of lying, but also underlines the importance of what his own witnesses say, as distinct from their identity as the speaker's supporters.

Cf., e.g., Isa. 9.29; Andok. 1.6; Lys. 26.8; [Dem.] 33.16. The function of witnesses is discussed more fully in the introduction to Isa. 9, pp. 154–156.

ἔτι δὲ τεκμηρίοις ἃ κρείττω τῶν μαρτυριῶν ἐστιν ('and proofs that are stronger than witness testimony'). See on μεγάλα γὰρ τεκμήρια, 7.11. The 'proof stronger than testimony' in this speech is **basanos*, on which the speaker relies very heavily (see on πῶς ἄν τις..., §9).

ὅθεν οὖν ἤρξαντο... διδάσκειν ('I shall try to explain these matters to you from the point at which [my opponents] started their account'). The wording is a clear indication that Isaios's client was replying to a speech by his opponent; cf. on ἀξιώσων, §11. For the metanarrative narratorial intervention, see on ποιήσομαι..., 7.4.

Narrative, Testimony and Argument: The Family History (7–14)

This is the first of four passages in which the speaker attempts to prove that his mother was the legitimate daughter of Kiron. Taken together, these passages form the longest part of the speech. He begins with a brief and fairly plain narrative (§§7–8) covering Kiron's two marriages, the birth of his daughter by his first wife, and the daughter's own two marriages. The rest of the section comprises testimony interspersed with argumentation about the difficulty of finding witnesses to events that happened so long ago. The speaker's trump card is that the most reliable witnesses to events in Kiron's household would have been his slaves. Their testimony is, however, not available because Kiron's nephew has refused the speaker's challenge to produce them for questioning under torture. The inferences he draws from this refusal, about the unreliability of his opponent's evidence, become a recurrent theme in later sections of the speech.

7 Ὁ γὰρ πάππος ὁ ἐμός, ὦ ἄνδρες ('My grandfather, gentlemen'). For 'gentlemen', see on Ἐπὶ τοῖς τοιούτποις, §1; and for 'my grandfather', see on Κίρων ὁ πάππος, §3. On the combination of an address to the **dikastai* with the explanatory particle *gar*, marking the transition from *proem to narrative, see on Εὔπολις γάρ..., 7.5.

ἀνεψίαν, ἐξ ἀδελφῆς τῆς αὑτοῦ μητρὸς ('his first cousin, the daughter of his mother's sister'). Ferrucci suggests that Kiron might have married his cousin as **epiklēros*, but that is clearly out of the question since only her father's next of kin could claim an *epiklēros* in marriage. On marriages between first cousins in classical Athens, see on Εὔπολις γάρ..., 7.11.

One might have expected the speaker to identify the father of Kiron's first wife; cf. Isa. 6.13, where the speaker says that it is not sufficient for his opponents simply to name Kallippe's father without giving any further information about him. In this case, however, the speaker is talking about a woman who was long since dead, and it may not have been considered necessary for him to extend his family tree beyond his grandparents. Cf. on Ξεναινέτου Ἀχαρνέως θυγατέρα, 10.4.

μετὰ ἐνιαυτοὺς τέτταρας τὸν βίον ἐτελεύτησεν ('died after four years'). The ms. reading ἐνιαυτοὺς τριάκοντα (λ'), meaning 'thirty years', is inconsistent with the statement that Kiron's first wife lived with him only a short time, and with the story that he remarried while his daughter was still a child and brought her up together with his sons by his second wife. The substitution of τέτταρας (δ'), i.e. 'four', rests on the possibility of confusion between Λ and Δ. An alternative interpretation, preferred by Thalheim, is that Kiron's first wife lived only thirty *days* after the birth of their daughter, ἐνιαυτοὺς ('years') being a misreading for ἡμέρας ('days'). Wyse concludes that 'Dobree's emendation (δ' for λ') rests on a surer basis'. Whichever is correct, the use of an exact number gives the speaker's account a degree of precision which may in any event have been spurious; the important point is that his mother was no more than a few years old when her mother died and her father remarried.

μιᾶς μόνης οὔσης αὐτῷ θυγατρὸς ('having only one daughter'). The speaker's emphasis on the fact that Kiron had only one child when he remarried rules out the existence of any other potential heirs from his first marriage.

λαμβάνει πάλιν τὴν Διοκλέους ἀδελφήν ('married Diokles's sister as his second wife'). Kiron's second wife is identified as the sister of the man whom already named by the speaker as his real opponent. Cf. on ἀλλὰ πρὸς Διοκλέα τὸν Φλυέα, §3.

ἐξ ἧς αὐτῷ ἐγιγνέσθην ὑεῖς δύο ('who bore him two sons'). If they had survived, Kiron's sons by his second wife would have been his legitimate heirs, excluding his daughter and her sons from the succession.

καὶ ἐκείνην τε ἔτρεφε παρὰ τῇ γυναικὶ καὶ μετὰ τῶν ἐξ ἐκείνης παίδων ('and brought up his daughter in the house with his wife and her sons'). Whether the speaker's mother really was brought up as Kiron's daughter, alongside her two younger half-brothers, was clearly a matter of dispute. Diokles, whether testifying on his own behalf or that of his sister, would have been an important witness on the issue for the speaker's opponent.

8 ἐκεινῶν τε ἔτι ζώντων ... Ναυσιμένει Χολαργεῖ ('while [his sons] were still alive, he gave her in marriage, when she reached the proper age, to Nausimenes of Kholargos'). For *sunoikein*, see on ταύτην τε ..., 7.18. The 'proper age' for a girl to marry was around sixteen, so Kiron's sons at that

time were probably no more than ten or eleven years old. The fact that they were still alive when their half-sister married is probably mentioned to explain why Kiron married her exogamously, not expecting her to become **epiklēros* after his death.

The marriage of Kiron's daughter to a named Athenian citizen adds credibility to the claim that she herself was legitimate. Listed in *LGPN Attica* as *Ναυσιμένης* (1), this Nausimenes may have been a son of Nausikydes of Kholargos who, according to Davies (1971), 315, is probably "to be identified with the slave-owning miller Nausikydes, whom Xenophon's Socrates quoted as the prime example of a man whose success in business had carried him into the liturgical class".

σὺν ἱματίοις καὶ χρυσίοις πέντε καὶ εἴκοσι μνᾶς ἐπιδούς ('with a dowry of twenty-five minas including clothes and jewellery'). The speaker's opponent had probably tried to cast doubt on the legitimacy of Kiron's daughter by referring to the meagreness of the two dowries he gave her. Cf. Isa. 3.51, where the speaker asks how a legitimate Athenian woman could possibly be given in marriage with a dowry amounting to less than a tenth of her father's fortune. The speaker does not quantify his mother's dowries as a proportion of Kiron's wealth, but gives a valuation of twenty-five minas (2,500 drachmas) for her dowry on her marriage to Nausimenes. Davies (1971), 314, points out that this is "just under the average figure of 2,650 *dr.* yielded by the dotal horoi". Cox (1998), 117–118, argues that the dowry, when defined as a percentage of Kiron's estate (twenty-eight percent), was in fact generous. As Cox concedes, however, her estimate is based on the value of Kiron's real estate; his total wealth may have been considerably more than this, because he had an unspecified amount of money out on loan. Cf. on δανείσματα οὐκ ὀλίγα, §35. If the chronology suggested at p. 90 is correct, the amount of the dowries could have been affected by temporary impoverishment in the final years of the Peloponnesian War.

For the dowry as a woman's 'patrimonial inheritance', equivalent (though not necessarily in financial value) to a man's share in his deceased father's estate, see Foxhall (1989), 32.

πρὶν αὐτῷ γενέσθαι παῖδας ἐκ τῆς ἡμετέρας μητρός ('without leaving any children by our mother'). This again excludes the possibility of other potential heirs to Kiron's estate.

διὰ τὴν Ναυσιμένους ἀπορίαν ('because of Nausimenes's difficulties'). The state of Nausimenes's financial affairs is used by the speaker to explain why Kiron did not recover his daughter's first dowry after Nausimenes's death. The elliptical reference does, however, raise unanswered questions about what had happened to Nausimenes in the three or four years since the marriage, given that Kiron would presumably not have married his daughter to a man who was impoverished. Again, if the chronology suggested at p. 90 is correct, the economic aftermath of the Peloponnesian War would be a possible explanation.

πάλιν ἐκδίδωσι τῷ ἐμῷ πατρὶ ('gave her in a second marriage to my father'). The speaker mentions his father nine times without identifying him by name (§§9, 14, 18 (twice), 19, 20, 21, 36, 43). Since the father was not in the line of succession to Kiron, and was therefore not directly involved in the inheritance dispute, this might appear unremarkable; cf. Isa. 10, another dispute about matrilineal succession where the speaker's father also remains unnamed. Isaios was, in any event, habitually sparing in his use of personal names, and in ordinary discourse it is more natural to refer to a parent in terms of the relationship than by name. The speaker of Isa. 9, nevertheless, names his father, Theophrastos, several times, emphasizing his affectionate relations with the deceased Astyphilos (cf. on πολλὰ κἀγαθὰ παθὼν…, 9.23). In the present case one would have expected the speaker to use his father's identity and status (and, if appropriate, character) as further evidence of his mother's legitimacy, but in fact he tells us virtually nothing about either of his parents. We may perhaps infer that the opponent's case involved an attack on the character of the speaker's father, including specific allegations that he had designs on Kiron's property, perhaps making him a counterpart to Diokles in the speaker's narrative. Cf. on καὶ τὸν πατέρα…, §36.

καὶ χιλίας δραχμὰς προῖκ' ἐπιδίδωσι ('with a dowry of 1,000 drachmas'). The reduced amount of the second dowry is explained, according to the speaker, by Kiron's failure to recover the first dowry from the family of Nausimenes.

9 πρὸς τὰς αἰτίας, ἃς νῦν οὗτοι λέγουσι ('in face of the allegations which my opponents are now making'). See on ὡς οὐκ…, §1.

πῶς ἄν τις δείξειε γεγενημένα φανερῶς; ('how can one prove clearly that all these events occurred?'). It is clear that the speaker's opponents have given an account of events that is seriously detrimental to the speaker's case, denying that Kiron ever had a legitimate daughter, or that she was brought up and married in the way that he claims. The problem for Isaios is to find a way of undermining the other side's testimony, so that the **dikastai* will prefer his client's account. His difficulty appears to be a lack of eyewitnesses to the disputed facts and events, so he resorts to the device of challenging his opponents to allow Kiron's slaves to give evidence under torture.

The evidence of slaves was not admissible in the Athenian courts unless they had been questioned under torture. As a type of **pistis*, **basanos* was formally distinguished from **marturia* (Ar. *Rhet.* 1355b). Slaves could not be submitted for torture without the consent of both parties to the case, so a litigant who wanted to use their evidence had to issue a formal challenge to his opponents to produce them (or, in appropriate circumstances, an offer to produce his own slaves). For a summary of the procedure, with references to the relevant cases, see Harrison (1971), 147–150.

There are no known cases in which a challenge to produce slaves actually resulted in their being interrogated under torture. According to Gagarin (1996), 9, there are about forty references in the orators to a challenge by the speaker which his opponent rejected, and two cases (Dem. 37.40 and Isok. 17.15) in which a challenge was accepted but the torture was not carried out because one of the parties later withdrew his consent. In four speeches (Lys. 4.15–17; Dem. 29.38; 53.22–25; 54.27) the speaker refers to his own refusal of a challenge from his opponent, and Gagarin conjectures that there may be many more cases in which a speaker simply remains silent about his refusal of such a challenge.

Modern scholars have proposed differing explanations of the fact that no evidence of slaves under torture is ever actually produced in the surviving speeches. The view that such evidence was never intended for use in court proceedings, but as a means of achieving an out of court settlement, was first put forward by Headlam (1893) and revived, with some modification, by Mirhady (1996). An alternative view is that, while the evidence of slaves under torture was in principle admissible in court, in practice the challenge was normally worded in such a way that it would be unacceptable to the recipient. There were obvious risks to both parties in allowing the evidence of slaves to be admitted, since no-one could predict exactly what they would say, and so the challenge became a procedural device used by litigants and *logographers to put their opponents in the wrong. See, e.g. Thür (1977), Todd (1990b) and Gagarin (1996).

Johnstone (1999), 70–92, gives a more nuanced account, describing the variety of ways in which challenges could be used to resolve or sometimes inflame disputes. He casts doubt on the suggestion that challenges were invariably designed to be refused, but concludes (75): "The idea that the acceptance of a dare [i.e. challenge] terminated a legal claim most economically accounts for the complete absence of the evidence from any completed oaths or tortures introduced as the result of a dare." It remains, nevertheless, surprising that there are no references in the extant speeches to previous disputes that were resolved by this method, while some of the sources do seem to imply that slaves' evidence could be adduced in court. Cf. on πρὸς τοῖς ὑπάρχουσι μάρτυσιν…, §10.

In this case the challenge probably included an undertaking by the speaker to withdraw his claim if the slaves' testimony did not support his account, coupled with a demand for Kiron's nephew to withdraw if it did. Cf. the terms of the challenge cited at [Dem.] 59.124. This could have been unacceptable to the nephew either because he was uncertain what the slaves would say, or because he knew they would discredit his story about the origins of the speaker's mother. In either event he would still have hoped to persuade the **dikastai* that his account was the true one, or, failing that, to succeed in his claim that a brother's son had priority over a daughter's son.

εἴτε θυγάτηρ ἦν Κίρωνος εἴτε μή ('whether she was Kiron's daughter or not'). This introduces a series of indirect questions, enumerating the 'facts' the speaker expects Kiron's slaves to know, which reflects the wording of his challenge. Typically, this would have included a list of questions to be put to the slave(s) under torture, each in the form of a simple statement which the slave was required either to confirm or to deny (Thür (1977), 111). The reference to the challenge has a rhetorical advantage for the speaker, in that the neutral formulation of the questions gives an impression of balance while enabling him implicitly to summarize the main points of his own case: his mother *was* Kiron's daughter; she *was* brought up in his household; Kiron *did* give her twice in marriage. Cf. Gagarin (1996), 13: '*Basanos* [i. e. the evidence of the rejected challenge]…allows the facts in question to be introduced to the court with the assumption that they would have been confirmed by the requested slaves'.

καὶ προῖκα ἥντινα ἑκάτερος επ' αὐτῇ τῶν γημάντων ἔλαβε ('and what dowry each of her husbands received with her'). For the last item on his list, the speaker departs from the model of a question in the alternative requiring a 'yes or no' answer. The wording of the challenge probably included the actual sums of the two dowries, but since the speaker has only just mentioned these, he can afford to present the questions here in a more summary form. Cf. Thür (1977), 114.

πάντα ταῦτα εἰδέναι τοὺς οἰκέτας καὶ τὰς θεραπαίνας ('all these things must be known to the male and female slaves'). It is certainly true that, in the absence of surviving family members willing to testify on the speaker's behalf, the household slaves would be most likely to know about private family affairs. They may, indeed, have known more than family members who did not actually live in Kiron's house. (Hunter (1994), 94–95, identifies three broad categories of information that slaves were expected to know in Athenian forensic oratory: "occurrences in the life of the master", "relationships in the master's household", and "business and financial matters".) The events with which the speaker is concerned may have taken place fifty years or more before Kiron's death, but if he had slaves who were children or young adults at that time it is possible that at least some of them were still alive.

Given the relative lack of visibility of female citizens in Athenian public life, the evidence of slaves could have been particularly important as a means of confirming or denying the presence of a woman in a household. Cf. Isa. 6.16; Dem. 30.27; also [Dem.] 59.124, where Apollodoros challenges Stephanos to produce his slaves for questioning under torture about the parentage of Neaira's children; and Antiph. 1.6, where the speaker claims that the household slaves would have known the truth about his stepmother's rôle in the murder of his father. What distinguishes Isaios's use of the **topos* in the present speech is the frequency with which the speaker reverts to his opponent's refusal of the challenge, from which he infers that the opponent's witnesses are lying.

ἃς ἐκεῖνος ἐκέκτητο ('whom [Kiron] had acquired'). This phrase may be an abbreviated reference to the actual wording of the challenge. Cf. the text of the challenge preserved at [Dem.] 59.124: 'and those [female slaves] whom he later acquired from Stephanos, Xennis and Drosis'. According to Thür (1977), 128, the features regularly found in a challenge included the name(s) of the slave(s) in question and an indication of how they were qualified to provide the information required.

10 πρὸς τοῖς ὑπάρχουσι μάρτυσιν ('in addition to the witnesses I already had'). The speaker claims that he challenged his opponent to produce Kiron's slaves for torture so that he could use their evidence to support that of his free witnesses, not as a substitute for it. Although it is possible that the speaker did not really expect his opponent to accept the challenge, this implies that evidence given by slaves under torture could be used in court, not just as a means of achieving an out of court settlement. In fact, if the speaker's story was true, the slaves' testimony would have been more useful to him than the inferences he draws from his opponent's refusal of the challenge—provided, of course, that he could rely on them to tell the truth.

ἔλεγχον ἐκ βασάνων ('proof by evidence given under torture'). The word **basanos*, when used of an **atekhnos pistis* (cf. on πῶς ἄν τις..., §9) frequently equates to 'challenge to torture', reflecting the reality that it was the challenge and its rejection, rather than the testimony of tortured slaves, that was put in evidence before the court. Cf. Gagarin (1996), 13, and see on ἐκ μαρτυριῶν…, §45. But despite the lack of evidence that torture was ever actually carried out, it is difficult to believe that *basanos* could have been effective as a means of persuasion if it was purely, as Gagarin suggests, a "legal fiction".

καὶ περὶ τῶν ἄλλων ἁπάντων ὅσα τυγχάνουσι συνειδότες ('and any other matters that they knew about'). Slaves, like free witnesses, 'know the facts'; cf. on τοῖς εἰδόσι χρώμενος μάρτυσιν, §6. According to Thür (1977), 114, this passage does not imply that the slaves could be interrogated on matters not listed in the challenge, but simply that the speaker's enumeration of his questions was not exhaustive. Cf. Lys. 4.10–11, where the speaker lists a number of questions in the alternative, concluding with 'and the rest'. The speaker implies at §17 that he also wanted the slaves to be questioned about Kiron's attendance with his grandsons at sacrifices and festivals.

11 ἀξιώσων ('will demand'). As Wyse notes, the future participle is "difficult": the natural inference, that the opponent had not yet spoken, is precluded by the reference at §6 to 'the point at which they started their account'. Wyse's solution is that *axiōsōn* "denotes…the adversary's attitude of mind, which will only be changed, if at all, by an unfavourable verdict". So the speaker means: "This man, who will expect you (as you cast your vote)…". Cf. ἀξιώσει, §13, which Wyse explains, in the context of a rhetorical question, as "a terse and vigorous way of saying ἀξιοῦν ἔξεσται; ['will it be possible for him to demand?']".

ἔφυγε τὴν βάσανον ('refused the examination under torture'). The speaker extends his argument from his opponent's refusal of the challenge to cast doubt on the credibility of the opponent's evidence. The verb *pheugein*, with its pejorative overtones, is commonly used by litigants of an opponent's refusal to accept a challenge to torture slaves. This usage occurs seven times in the present speech: twice in §11, twice in §13, and in §§14, 28 and 29. Cf., e.g., Dem. 30. 27, 29.

ἀλλὰ μὴν ὡς ἀληθῆ λέγω ('but to prove that I am telling the truth'). These words are too vague to link the speaker's first piece of testimony with any specific points in the preceding narrative, although he has claimed to have at least hearsay evidence of all the events he describes. He may have been trying to conceal the weakness of his evidence on certain points by bringing together all the testimony on several issues.

λαβέ μοι πρῶτον ταύτην τὴν μαρτυρίαν καὶ ἀνάγνωθι ('please first take and read this testimony'). This is the first of eight witness statements produced in the course of the speech. Four of them are introduced by formulae relating to the testimony as documentary evidence, using the imperatives *labe* ('take') and *anagnōthi* ('read'); cf. §§13, 17 and 46. The formulae used for the remaining four refer to the witnesses, with *kalei* ('call'); cf. §§20, 24, 27 and 40. On the change from oral to written testimony in the Athenian courts, see on τούτων πρῶτον..., 7.10.

12 Ὑμεῖς ('You'). The second person plural pronoun conveys the sense of a dialogue between the speaker and his audience. Cf. Denommé (1974b), 137: "Le pronom *humeis*, surtout lorsqu'il figure au nominatif et en tête de la phrase, renforce de façon étonnante le contact que l'orateur vise à maintenir avec les juges." ("The pronoun *humeis*, especially when it occurs in the nominative and at the beginning of a sentence, wonderfully reinforces the contact which the orator aims to maintain with the judges.") In fact, Isaios uses *humeis* relatively sparingly. It occurs forty-one times in his extant speeches: six times in 1, once in 2, ten times in 3, five times in 4, once in 5, six times in 6, once in 7, four times in 8, twice in 9, once in 10, and four times in 11. Apart from this instance, there is only one other (1.18) where it occurs at the beginning of a sentence.

καὶ ἰδίᾳ καὶ δημοσίᾳ ('in both public and private matters'). The use of the challenge to torture (*proklēsis eis basanon*) was permitted in private cases, and in public cases where both parties were individuals, but not when the prosecutor was the state or a public official (Headlam (1893), 1). The speaker's meaning, however, may not be confined to litigation, since **basanos* was used by the state to extract information in matters of public interest.

ἀκριβέστατον ἔλεγχον ('the strictest test'). The idea that the evidence of slaves under torture was superior to the testimony of free witnesses is described by Harrison (1971), 147, as a 'commonplace' of Athenian oratory. Cf. especially Dem. 30.37 where, rather than direct imitation, the similarity of the wording may indicate that both orators were drawing on a common rhetorical **topos*. Other examples cited by Harrison include Dem. 47.8; Antiph. 1.8; 6.25; Isok. 17.54; Lyk. 1.29. In any event, it appears that the speaker is not really voicing a universally accepted view, but taking a rhetorical stance. Arist. *Rh.* 1376–1377a and *Rh. Al.* 1432a provide arguments both for and against the evidential value of **basanos*, but there are no extant examples of the negative arguments in forensic oratory.

Cf. Gagarin (1996), 7: "To be sure, most handbooks and commentaries report that orators argue on both sides of the issue depending on the needs of their case, but this view is probably inspired by Aristotle and fostered by the modern conviction that torture is not generally effective...."

εἰκότως, ὦ ἄνδρες ('That is reasonable, gentlemen'). By addressing the **dikastai* (cf. on Ἐπὶ τοῖς τοιούτοις, §1), the speaker seeks to draw them into his argument and persuade them to see things from his point of view. This may indicate that he did not feel himself to be on very strong ground, or that he was uncomfortable about his excessive reliance on the **basanos* argument.

σύνιστε...μαρτυρῆσαι ('for you know that before now witnesses have appeared not to be giving true evidence'). The speaker is referring to the *dikē *pseudomarturiōn*, a procedure which enabled an unsuccessful litigant effectively to reopen the case by prosecuting one or more of his opponents and their witnesses for giving false testimony.

τῶν δὲ βασανισθέντων...εἰπόντες ('whereas no-one who has been questioned under torture has ever been convicted of giving false evidence as the result of being tortured'). The antithesis is disingenuous: the reason why no slaves had ever been convicted of giving false evidence under torture is that there was no procedure, equivalent to the *dikē *pseudomarturiōn* for free witnesses, under which slaves could be prosecuted. Cf. Todd (1990b), 35, and Thür (1977), 310.

13 οὗτος δ' ὁ πάντων ἀναισχυντότατος ἀνθρώπων ('And my opponent, the most shameless of men'). Most of Isaios's clients deplore the 'shamelessness' of their opponents' behaviour, using either the adjective *anaiskhuntos*, the participle *anaiskhuntōn* or the noun *anaiskhuntia*. The superlative recalls the tone of the speaker's denunciation of his opponents in the *proem ('none more shamelessly than these people', §4), and is otherwise found only in Isa. 3 (§§4, 40 and 72).

ἀξιώσει ('will demand'). On the future tense, see on ἀξιώσων, §11.

φεύγων οὕτως ἀκριβεῖς ἐλέγχους ('while he refuses so sure a method of proof'). See on ἔφυγε τὴν βάσανον, §11, and ἀκριβέστατον ἔλεγχον, §12.

οὕτως οἰησόμεθα δεῖν ὑμᾶς τοῖς ἡμετέροις μάρτυσι πιστεύειν ('in these circumstances we shall consider that you ought to believe our witnesses'). The conclusion, that the speaker's evidence is more trustworthy than his opponents' because he was willing to put the slaves to torture, seems unpersuasive to the modern reader, but presumably it carried more weight with an Athenian audience.

λαβὲ οὖν αὐτοῖς ταυτασὶ τὰς μαρτυρίας καὶ ἀνάγνωθι ('Take, then, the depositions on these points and read them out'). On the formulae used to introduce testimony in this speech see on λαβέ μοι πρῶτον . . ., §11.

14 Τίνας εἰκὸς ειδέναι τὰ παλαιά; . . . ἀκοὴν οὗτοι ('Who are likely to know best about the events of the distant past? Clearly those who were intimate with my grandfather; they, then, have given evidence of what they were told'). Cf. on τὰ μὲν πάλαι γεγενημένα, §6.

τοὺς ἐγγυησαμένους καὶ τοὺς ἐκείνοις παρόντας ὅτε ἠγγυῶντο ('Those who betrothed her and those who were present when they betrothed her'). Formal marriage by **enguē* was a procedure open only to Athenian citizens. Only children born of such a marriage (or of a marriage by **epidikasia*, if the mother was **epiklēros*) were regarded as legitimate and eligible for citizenship. A litigant facing a challenge to his legitimacy (as in this case) or his citizenship (as in Dem. 57) therefore needed proof of his parents' marital status. Marriage by *enguē* was a private contractual arrangement between the woman's **kurios* and the husband, in which the **polis* played no part, and of which there was no official record. So it was important that the betrothal was witnessed by people (usually family members or fellow *phratry members or *demesmen) whose testimony could be relied on in case of a dispute.

οἵ τε Ναυσιμένους προσήκοντες καὶ οἱ τοῦ ἐμοῦ πατρός ('the relations of Nausimenes and of my father'). These would have been credible witnesses, since they had no personal interest in the disputed estate. Their number is unspecified, and the cousin mentioned at §21 may have been the only witness from the family of the speaker's father.

τίνες δὲ . . . Κίρωνος; ('Who knew best that my mother was brought up in Kiron's house as his legitimate daughter?'). Apart from the slaves, it was actually Kiron's second wife, the sister of Diokles, who was in the best position to know whether, on their marriage, Kiron brought with him a daughter by his first wife. Her evidence was no doubt put before the court by Diokles, acting as her **kurios*, and it must have been crucial to the case against Isaios's client. Even if the story she told was entirely fabricated, she would have appeared a convincing witness to the **dikastai*, and her evidence would have been difficult for the speaker to refute.

οἱ νῦν ἀμφισβητοῦντες . . . ἀληθῆ ('The present claimants give clear evidence of the truth of these facts'). The speaker's evasive reply to his own question, resorting yet again to his opponent's refusal of the challenge, underlines his difficulty in producing credible testimony to his own version of events. By describing his opponents as 'those who are *now* claiming the estate', he draws attention to what he wants to be seen as a contradiction in their behaviour: by refusing the challenge, they implicitly recognized the speaker's superior claim, but now they are disputing it. Cf. on ὁ νῦν ἀμφισβητῶν τοῦ κλήρου, §25.

ἔργῳ φανερῶς μαρτυροῦσιν ('clearly testify by their action'). On the idea that the speaker's opponents have 'testified' by their actions, cf. on ἔργοις φανερῶς μεμαρτυρήκασιν, 7.18.

φεύγοντες τὴν βάσανον ('in refusing the examination by torture'). See on ἔφυγε τὴν βάσανον, §11.

ὥστε... μάρτυσιν ('so that I think you have much better reason for disbelieving their witnesses than mine'). Again, the logic is forced: even if Kiron's nephew did refuse the challenge because he was afraid of what the slaves might say, that does not prove that the speaker's story is true.

Narrative and Testimony: Religious Observance (15–17)

The speaker describes how he and his brother were always Kiron's preferred companions at both public festivals and private sacrifices. He clearly intends this to be taken as indirect evidence of their legitimacy, since Kiron would not have treated the boys in such a way if they had not been the children of his legitimate daughter. Cf. Isa. 1 and 9, where references to shared religious observances support the claims of a litigant challenging a will that he was not only more closely related to the deceased but also on terms of closer intimacy and affection. It may be inferred from the speaker's graphic account of the family cults that his opponent has made a convincing claim to have been intimate with Kiron and treated by him as his prospective heir. The weakness of the speaker's case is that he appears to have no evidence of his more recent relations with Kiron, a point which Isaios does his best to gloss over.

15 ἄλλα τεκμήρια πρὸς τούτοις ('other proofs, in addition to these'). See on μεγάλα γὰρ τεκμήρια, 7.11. As the speaker moves on to events within his own lifetime, his evidence is likely to be more reliable, but it is also more remote from the real issue of his mother's birth.

οἷα γὰρ εἰκὸς [παίδων] ὑέων <ὄντων> ἐξ ἑαυτοῦ θυγατρός ('as was natural, since we were the sons of his own daughter'). The plural shows that Kiron had more than one grandson who accompanied him at the sacrifices, but the exact number is not specified at this point. Cf. on ἀλλ' ἡμᾶς, §1, and ἵν' ἐλπίζων, §36. On relations between children and their maternal grandfathers, cf. Hdt. 3. 50 (cited by Bremmer (1983), 177), where

Prokles summons his daughter's children after her death and treats them kindly, "as was natural since they were his daughter's children". Bremmer argues that in patriarchal and patrilineal societies there was often a "special relationship" between a mother's father and daughter's son; passages such as these, while not necessarily an accurate historical record, provide an indication of "what people expected" of such a relationship. (On the similarly close ties between mother's brother and sister's son, see on εἴς τε γὰρ…, 7.34.)

On the various attempts to reconstruct the corrupt text (reproduced here from Wyse's edition), Jebb (1888), 395 conjectures "that the ms. υἱέων referred to the two sons, now dead, born to Ciron by his second wife.…" The meaning of the passage, according to Jebb's reconstruction, would be "as was natural, [since he had no] sons, [but we] were his daughter's sons". This is perfectly plausible, but it is perhaps unlikely that Isaios would have spelt it out, given his habitual economy of language.

πανταχοῦ παρῆμεν ἡμεῖς καὶ συνεθύομεν. (we were always there and took part in the sacrifices'). Shared sacrifices in fourth century Athens were a means of creating and cementing bonds of intimacy both within family units and in wider social groups. Parker (2005), 37–49, discusses the evidence not only from literary sources but also from votive reliefs, which often depict worshippers approaching the shrine of a god in family groups including children. Some of the surviving dedicatory inscriptions mention the individual dedicator's children and grandchildren. In one example, which Parker (2005), 40, describes as "a spectacular demonstration of the bilateral strand in Athenian kinship", the dedicators are Autophilos, three sons, and three grandsons who are all sons of daughters.

ἀλλὰ καὶ εἰς Διονύσια εἰς ἀγρὸν ἦγεν ἀεὶ ἡμᾶς ('but also he always took us into the country for the Dionysia'). On the Rural Dionysia, including the performance of plays there, see Parker (2005), 316–317.

16 καὶ μετ' ἐκείνου τε ἐθεωροῦμεν καθήμενοι παρ' αὐτόν ('and we always accompanied him at public spectacles and sat at his side'). The speaker's picture of himself and his brother sitting with their grandfather to watch the spectacle would have made a strong emotional appeal.

τῷ Διί τε θύων τῷ Κτησίῳ ('sacrificing to Zeus Ktesios'). On Zeus Ktesios as the god associated with household wealth, see Parker (2005), 15–16.

καὶ οὔτε δούλους προσῆγεν οὔτε ἐλευθέρους ὀθνείους ('and he admitted neither slaves nor free men outside his own family'). The speaker emphasizes Kiron's refusal to admit non-kinsmen to his sacrifices to Zeus Ktesios in order to show that he and his brother had privileged access. The implication that heads of household were not always so exclusive is confirmed by the speaker of Isa. 1, who singles out his opponent Pherenikos as the one person not invited by Kleonymos to share in his sacrifices to Dionysios (1.31, cited by Parker (2005), 43). Cf. also 9.30, where the speaker emphasizes the fraternal bond between himself and his half-brother, Astyphilos, by pointing out that his father always took both of them to religious festivals.

17 καίτοι εἰ μὴ θυγατριδοῦς ἡμᾶς ἐνόμιζεν εἶναι ('Yet if he had not considered us his daughter's children'). Cf. 9.21, where the speaker argues that Astyphilos would have attended the sacrifices with Kleon if he had intended to adopt Kleon's son.

μόνους ἐκγόνους ('his only descendants'). After the death of Kiron's sons by his second wife, his daughter's sons were his only living descendants. One might have expected Isaios to mention when they died, if only to rule out the possibility that they might have left sons who were Kiron's potential heirs, but the lack of precision on this point may have suited his rhetorical strategy. Cf. on ἐπειδὴ τάχιστα..., §36.

ὃς ἀδελφιδοῦς αὐτοῦ νῦν εἶναί φησί ('who now claims to be his nephew'). See on τὸν εἰληχότα τοῦ κλήρου, §3. The speaker is not yet prepared to admit that his opponent actually is Kiron's nephew. Cf. §26, where he claims to have shown his opponent the courtesy due to a nephew at Kiron's funeral.

οὓς οὗτος παραδοῦναι εἰς βάσανον οὐκ ηθέλησεν ('whom my opponent refused to hand over for questioning'). The speaker continues to labour his point; cf. on πάντα ταῦτα..., §9.

ἴσασι δὲ... τινές ('some of his intimate friends know the same facts perfectly well'). Cf. on τοῖς εἰδόσι χρώμενος μάρτυσιν, §6.

καί μοι λαβὲ τὰς μαρτυρίας καὶ ἀνάγνωθι ('And please take and read out the depositions'). Cf. on λαβέ μοι πρῶτον..., §11.

Narrative, Argument and Testimony: The Model Athenian Wife (18–20)

The speaker introduces further indirect proofs of his mother's status, first arguing that his father would not have publicly celebrated his marriage to a woman who was illegitimate, and then pointing out that she was accepted by her husband's fellow citizens as his legitimate wife. Evidence that the speaker's mother was accepted by others as the legitimate daughter of Kiron does not actually prove that she was. Cf. Wyse, 603, on the "inconclusiveness" of the speaker's reasoning. Such evidence would, nevertheless, have been highly persuasive in an Athenian court, where, in the absence of the more conclusive documentary and scientific evidence available in the modern world, litigants had to rely heavily on circumstantial 'proofs' of their legitimacy. Evidence that the speaker's mother had been publicly recognized as the legitimate wife of an Athenian citizen would have particularly helpful to him, although it could still have been undermined by his opponents if they were able to challenge him with testimony on the circumstances of her birth or introduction into Kiron's household.

18 τοῖς τε φράτορσι γαμηλίαν εἰσήνεγκε ('and he gave a marriage banquet to the members of his phratry'). The celebration of a *gamēlia*, or marriage banquet, marked the acceptance of a woman's citizen status by her husband's phratry. Cf. Isa. 3.76, 79; Dem. 57.43, discussed by Lambert (1993), 181–184.

κατὰ τοὺς ἐκείνων νόμους ('according to their rules'). This suggests that each phratry had its own way of conducting the *gamēlia*; in this context, *nomous* may perhaps imply 'customs' rather than 'laws' or 'rules'.

19 μετὰ ταῦτα ('after that'). The chronology is characteristically vague: there is no indication of the length of time that elapsed between the marriage of the speaker's parents and the events he is about to describe. Cf. on μετὰ δὲ ταῦτα, 10.6.

προὔκριναν αὐτὴν ('chose her out'). The wording implies a system of sortition from pre-selected candidates; cf. Whitehead (1986), 114, n. 147. Isaios does not explicitly say that the speaker's mother actually performed the *liturgy, but the pre-selection in itself would be sufficient proof that her status as a citizen was accepted by the community. (The introduction of sortition from pre-selected candidates for appointments to public office in Athens was attributed to Solon; see *Ath. Pol.* 8.1, with Rhodes's commentary. For the transition from election to sortition for appointments in the *demes, starting in the fifth century, see Whitehead (1986), 115–116.)

μετὰ τῆς Διοκλέους γυναικὸς τοῦ Πιθέως ('with the wife of Diokles of Pithos'). On the conventional non-naming of women in forensic oratory see on Κυρωνίδης καὶ …, 10.4. A Diokles of Pithos is listed in *LGPN Attica* as Διοκλῆς (164). As discussed by Davies (1971), 158–159, he belonged to "one of the more important mining families of the fourth century", and was apparently active in the 370s and 360s, serving as trierarch in 377. It is likely that either he or an older member of the same family was the Diokles mentioned here, but Isaios's characteristically vague chronology makes a positive identification impossible. As Davies (1971), 315, points out, this passage makes it clear that the speaker and his father were also members of the *deme Pithos. The demotic indicates, however, that this Diokles was not Kiron's brother-in-law, who was identified at §3 as Diokles of Phlya.

ἄρχειν εἰς τὰ Θεσμοφόρια ('to preside at the Thesmophoria'). For a detailed account of the Thesmophoria, an annual festival for citizen women lasting three days, see Parker (2005), 270–282. The speaker implies that his mother would not have been allowed to participate in the festivities, let alone considered eligible to preside, if she had not been accepted as legitimate by the wives of the *demesmen. His account also gives a rare hint of his father's status, since the husband of a woman chosen to preside at one of the festivals is likely to have been wealthy.

ὅ τε πατὴρ ... εἰσήγαγεν ('our father, at our birth, introduced us to his phratry'). The introduction of the speaker and his brother to their father's *phratry is the most significant evidence of their legitimacy. In this case it is clear that they were introduced in infancy, but there is evidence from other sources that some introductions took place in later childhood or adolescence. It appears most likely that there were in fact two admission ceremonies for boys: the first (the *meion*) in infancy or early childhood, and the second (the *koureion*) during adolescence. See Lambert (1993), 161–162.

ὀμόσας ... εἰσαγειν ('having sworn, in accordance with the established laws, that he was introducing the children of an Athenian mother duly married'). The exact terms of the oath sworn by the introducer may have varied from *phratry to phratry, but the legitimacy of the prospective member would have been an important common feature, excluding any children born to a male citizen by a **hetaira* or **pallakē*. Cf. 7.16 for the wording of the oath.

τῶν δὲ φρατόρων ... εἶναι ('and none of the phratry members made any objection or disputed the truth of his statements'). Members of the *phratry present at the admission ceremony would have had the opportunity to object to an introduction by leading the sacrificial victim away from the altar. Cf. Isa. 6.22, where Philoktemon objects to his father Euktemon's attempt to introduce his younger 'sons'. For 'no-one objected', cf. Dem. 19.136; 20.139.

πολλῶν ὄντων καὶ ἀκριβῶς τὰ τοιαῦτα σκοπουμένων ('although many of them were present and they always look into such matters carefully'). Given that this was evidently a point worth mentioning, it is likely that the degree of strictness in the examination of potential members' credentials varied from *phratry to phratry.

20 εἰ τοιαύτη τις ἦν ἡ μήτηρ ἡμῶν οἵαν οὗτοί φασι ('if our mother had been such as our opponents allege'). See on ὡς οὐκ ἐξ ἐκείνου ..., §1.

μήτ' ἂν ... ταῦτα πάντα ('our father would neither have given a wedding banquet ... but rather hushed up the whole matter'). A similar point was made by the speaker of Isa. 3 about the marriage of Pyrrhos and the sister of Nikodemos (3.27). Probability arguments based on general patterns of socially acceptable behaviour, rather than individual personalities and circumstances, were more likely to be credible to an Athenian court than they would be to a modern one.

καὶ ταῦθ' ὡς ἀληθῆ λέγω, κάλει τούτων τοὺς μάρτυρας ('And to prove that I am telling the truth about this, please call the witnesses'). Cf. on λαβέ μοι πρῶτον ..., §11.

Narrative and Testimony: The Burial of Kiron (21–27)

This part of the narrative is brought forward in the chronological sequence because it belongs with the speaker's 'proofs' of his mother's legitimacy. A claimant in a **diadikasia* would gain an important advantage over his opponent if he could prove that he had conducted the funeral of the deceased; or, if he had not done so, that there were good reasons for this (cf. 9.3–6). The speaker's aim is to show that his opponents recognized him as Kiron's legitimate grandson, despite their attempts to take over the funeral arrangements themselves. It becomes clear that there was a bitter quarrel after Kiron's death, and that Kiron's nephew has claimed to have paid for and conducted the funeral himself, allowing the speaker to participate as a courtesy (cf. on οὐχ ὅπως ..., §25). At this stage Isaios does not confront the opponent's version of events directly, but puts forward an alternative story. The **dikastai* had to decide not only which version was true, but also how much evidential value to place on what was no more than indirect evidence of the speaker's entitlement to the estate. The narrative of the funeral is resumed at §§38–39, with some changes of detail.

21 Ἔτι τοίνυν, ὦ ἄνδρες ('Furthermore, gentlemen'). For addresses to the **dikastai* in this speech, see on Ἐπὶ τοῖς τοιούτοις, §1.

καὶ ἐξ ὧν ... θυγατριδοῖ Κίρωνος ('the conduct of Diokles when our grandfather died clearly shows that we were acknowledged as the grandchildren of Kiron'). The speaker focuses the minds of the **dikastai* by explaining at the outset that this part of his narrative is an indirect proof of his mother's legitimacy, showing that he was accepted by Diokles as Kiron's legitimate grandson.

ἧκον γὰρ ἐγὼ ('I presented myself'). After including his brother, by using the plural *thugatridoi* ('daughter's sons') in the previous sentence, the speaker reverts to the first person singular for the narration of his rôle in the events immediately following Kiron's death. Cf. on ἀλλ' ἡμᾶς . . ., §1.

ὡς θάψων ἐκ τῆς οἰκίας τῆς ἐμαυτοῦ ('intending to conduct the funeral from my own house'). This is what the speaker, since he claimed to be Kiron's legitimate heir, would have been expected to do.

οἰκείων τινὰ ἔχων, ἀνεψιὸν τοῦ πατρός ('with one of my relatives, a cousin of my father'). Presumably in anticipation of a dispute, which might result in litigation, the speaker took the precaution of asking a witness to accompany him when he went to collect the body. Cf. Isa. 3.19 for the practice of using witnesses in such circumstances. As an older member of the family, but one who had no possible claim to Kiron's inheritance, a cousin of his father's would have been accepted as a reliable and impartial witness. Cf. Humphreys (1986), 84. In the opponent's version of the story, the speaker's visit to Kiron's house had probably been presented as an ill-timed act of aggression.

καὶ Διοκλέα μὲν οὐ κατέλαβον ἔνδον ('And I didn't find Diokles at home'). The negation suggests that the speaker expected to find Diokles in Kiron's house, while the use of *endon* ('inside') rather than *ekei* ('there') implies that Diokles actually lived there. Cf. Lys. 1.23: 'and I called on one [friend] and another, and some of them I found at home [*endon*]'; and Men. *Dys.* 259: 'but I didn't find Getas at home [*endon*]'.

22 δεομένης δὲ τῆς τοῦ πάππου γυναικὸς ('But when my grandfather's widow requested'). The speaker uses **pathos* to explain why he did not carry out his intention, but was persuaded by the wishes of Kiron's widow.

ὅτι βούλοιτ' . . . καὶ κοσμῆσαι ('that she herself would like to help us lay out and deck the corpse'). On the customary rôle of women in preparing a corpse for burial, cf. Isa. 6.41. The presentation of the grief-stricken widow seems at odds with the allegations later in the speech that she colluded with Diokles in a calculated plot to deprive Kiron of his property. See the introductory note to §§35–39 on Isaios's manipulation of the 'facts' to his client's advantage.

καὶ ταῦτα ἱκετευούσης καὶ κλαιούσης ('and entreating me and weeping'). The participles are piled up to convey a conventional picture of a woman's lack of emotional restraint.

ἐπείσθην, ὦ ἄνδρες ('I was persuaded, gentlemen'). This is the only point in the speech at which the speaker interrupts his narrative with an address to the **dikastai*. (See on Ἐπὶ τοῖς τοιούτοις, §1.) This not only underlines the importance of the point he is making, but also invites them to share his point of view, playing on the Athenians' fear of the perceived irrationality of women: like him, they would have given in to the pleas of Kiron's widow. The use of *peithein* ('persuade') in the passive voice recalls the wording of the Solonian law on wills (cited at [Dem.] 46.14), which provides that a will is invalid if the testator made it under the influence of a woman (*gunaiki peithomenos*). It is noticeable here that the woman does not become the *focalizer; Isaios is simply using a female stereotype as a rhetorical device to engage the audience's sympathy.

καὶ τούτῳ προσελθὼν ('and went to my opponent'). On the use of the pronoun *houtos* with reference to Kiron's nephew, see on τὸν εἰληχότα τοῦ κλήρου, §3. Presumably the speaker left Kiron's house and went to the nephew's.

μαρτύρων ἐναντίον ('in the presence of witnesses'). The witnesses who heard the speaker's conversation with Kiron's nephew presumably included the cousin of his father's who accompanied him to Kiron's house. Cf. on οἰκείων τινὰ ἔχων…, §21.

ἡ τούτου ἀδελφή ([Diokles's] sister'). By thus identifying Kiron's widow, the speaker implicates her in his accusations against Diokles, anticipating her rôle in the plot described at §§35–39.

23 καὶ ταῦτα Διοκλῆς ἀκούσας οὐδὲν ἀντεῖπεν ('Diokles, hearing this, made no objection'). If Diokles heard the speaker's conversation with Kiron's nephew, he must have been at the latter's house. The implication is that they were colluding in the plot to 'rob' the speaker of Kiron's property. For the presentation through negation, see on ἐκείνῳ…, 7.17. Diokles would have been expected to object to the speaker's taking charge of the funeral if he had not accepted him as Kiron's grandson.

ταῦτα ἠξίου παρ' ἐμοῦ λαβεῖν ('demanded that I should pay him for these'). There was clearly a quarrel over Kiron's funeral expenses, but the speaker's account leaves the exact circumstances obscure. Cf. on οὐχ ὅπως…, §25 and ἐξ ὧν ὁ πάππος…, §38.

εὐθὺς οὖν…χρημάτων ('Immediately afterwards he casually remarked that Kiron had left nothing at all, although I had said nothing at all about his money'). This may suggest that, on the opponent's account, there was a disagreement instigated by the speaker.

24 σὺ δὲ τίς εἶ; ('Who are you?'). Isaios very rarely uses direct speech, a rhetorical device for making a narrative more vivid. Apart from this one, the only other examples (cited by Denommé (1974b), 135) are at 2.11–12,

where Menekles discusses with his wife's two brothers the possibility of adopting one of them, and 6.53, where the speaker suggests a question to be put to his opponent. In this instance Isaios is not reporting an actual conversation, but imagining what Diokles ought to have said in order to prevent the speaker from carrying out Kiron's burial. The argument is syllogistic: this is what Diokles would have said if he had not recognized me as Kiron's grandson; he did not say it; therefore he did recognize me as Kiron's grandson. Examples of direct speech in the works of other orators include, e.g., Lys. 32.15–17 and Dem. 54.20. Trevett (1992), 89, notes a 'marked taste' for the device in the speeches of Apollodoros, and also its frequent use in Lys. 1.

οὐ μὴ εἰσίῃς τὴν οἰκίαν ('You will not enter the house'). Wyse (followed by Forster) adopts Bekker's emendation of the ms. εἰσίῃς to εἴσει εἰς because "the future is not predictive but prohibitory, expressing the *will* of the speaker". Cooper (1974), 411–412, persuasively defends the ms. tradition, arguing that the emphatic negative *ou mē* with the future indicative expresses "a shrill stringency which proceeds from fear on the part of the speaker that the prohibition may not be complied with". With the aorist subjunctive, on the other hand, the tone is one of "absolute security and confidence in the prediction", which, as Cooper argues, is "precisely [the] tone which our passage requires".

A further argument in favour of the emendation, also rejected by Cooper, is that *eisienai* ('enter') with a direct object would be inappropriate in the present context because it was an archaism, used in the classical period only in poetry. Agreeing that the construction is "typically tragic", Cooper (1974), 413, points out that this, in combination with the *ou mē* construction, is perfectly in keeping with the tone of the passage: "The mocking irony ... is clear, and the paratragic diction is part of the intended effect."

ταῦτ' εἰπεῖν προσῆκεν 'This is what he should have said [if he did not accept me as Kiron's heir].'

νῦν δὲ τοιοῦτον μὲν οὐδὲν εἶπεν ('but as it is, he has said nothing of the kind'). The speaker has set up an expectation of what Diokles ought to have said if he had not accepted the speaker as Kiron's grandson, so that he can now point out that he did not say it. This is a common feature of argumentation from probability in forensic oratory, repeated at §25. Cf., e.g., Isa. 9.7–9; 10.5.

εἰς ἕω δὲ τἀργύριον ἐκέλευεν εἰσενεγκεῖν ('but told me to bring the money the next morning'). Not only did Diokles fail to say what he might have been expected to say; the only words he did speak were to remind the speaker to bring the money. The speaker's casual reference to this characterizes

Diokles as a greedy man, as well as 'proving' that he accepted it was the speaker's duty to pay for the funeral.

καὶ ταῦτα ὡς ἀληθῆ λέγω, κάλει μοι τούτων τοὺς μάρτυρας ('And to prove that I am telling the truth about this, please call the witnesses'). For the identity of these witnesses, see on μαρτύρων ἐναντίον, §22. Their testimony apparently covered the behaviour of Diokles after Kiron's death, supporting the speaker's interpretation that Diokles recognized him as Kiron's grandson. Cf. on λαβὲ μοι πρῶτον, §11.

25 Οὐ τοίνυν ἐκεῖνος μόνος ('Yet [Diokles] was not the only one'). Having dealt with the behaviour of Diokles, the speaker now moves on to consider that of his legal opponent, Kiron's nephew. See on τὸν εἰληχότα τοῦ κλήρου, §3.

ὁ νῦν ἀμφισβητῶν τοῦ κλήρου ('the present claimant to the estate'). See on τὸν εἰληχότα τοῦ κλήρου, §3. 'Now' makes the point that (according to the speaker) Kiron's nephew has changed his stance since the funeral: whereas he then did not deny the speaker's status as Kiron's grandson, he has now decided (under the influence of Diokles) to claim the estate for himself. Cf. on οἱ νῦν ἀμφισβητοῦντες . . ., §14.

τοιοῦτον εἶπεν οὐδέν ('said nothing of the kind'). Cf. on νῦν δὲ τοιοῦτον μὲν οὐδὲν εἶπεν, §24. Not only did Diokles say nothing of the kind, but neither did Kiron's nephew.

ὑπὸ τούτου παρασκευασθεὶς ('suborned by Diokles'). See on παρασκευάσας, §3.

κἀκείνου . . . ἀπολαβεῖν ('Although Diokles refused to accept the money I brought'). According to the speaker, Diokles had changed his mind since he demanded reimbursement for what he had spent.

οὐχ ὅπως . . . ἀναλωμάτων ('so far from having been borne by my opponent or Diokles, being paid from the property left by [Kiron]'). The speaker's opponent has presumably said that he paid for Kiron's funeral, using this to emphasize the closeness of his emotional ties with Kiron and thus to support his claim to the estate. So the speaker tries to undermine his opponent by pointing out that neither Diokles nor Kiron's nephew actually paid for the funeral, because the money came from Kiron's estate.

26 ἐγὼ μὲν γὰρ εἴων αὐτὸν ἀδελφιδοῦν ὄντα τοῦ πάππου ('for I allowed him since he was my grandfather's nephew'). Cf. on τὸν εἰληχότα τοῦ κλήρου, §3. The speaker tries to convey that it was he who was in control of proceedings at the funeral, while his opponent occupied a passive rôle.

27 ἀλλ' οὕτω τῇ τοῦ πράγματος ἀληθείᾳ κατεπέπληκτο ('But he was so embarrassed by the true state of affairs'). The speaker ostensibly lets his opponent off the hook by identifying Diokles as the real villain, but his language is extremely prejudicial.

ἐπὶ τοῦ σήματος ἐμοῦ ποιουμένου λόγους ('while I was speaking at the tomb'). In the context of the narrative on Kiron's funeral, the ms. *bēmatos* ('platform' or 'rostrum') requires emendation. Wyse, Roussel and Ferrucci accept Schömann's *mnēmatos* ('memorial' or 'monument'), while Forster prefers Photiades's *sēmatos* ('tomb'), which I have adopted here. On either reading the speaker again presents himself in a position of control, making a speech at the graveside; but the fact that he publicly accused Diokles of illegally detaining Kiron's property, and inciting Kiron's nephew to claim the estate, is the clearest indication of dissension and hostility between the two sides.

Jebb (1888), 400, comments on Schömann's text: "But the phrase is strange, and the supposed conduct stranger still. If bēmatos is right, it prob. means the tribune from which the speaker addressed a law-court, when claiming the inheritance in some proceedings previous to this case." Jebb's suggestion, however attractive, is not sustainable on the available evidence. First, it conflicts with the speaker's description of himself as 'completely inexperienced in litigation' (§5), and secondly, it is unclear what kind of legal proceedings might have preceded the present **diadikasia* in the dispute about Kiron's estate. (Diokles has apparently not yet been tried for **hubris* or for the wrongful possession of his nephew's land, and in any event the speaker was not the prosecutor in either of these cases; see on καὶ γραφὴν ὕβρεως…, §41 and καὶ κατέχει τὸν ἀγρόν…, §42.)

ἀποστερῶν ('removing'). See on ἀποστερῶν, §3.

οὐκ ἐτόλμησε γρῦξαι τὸ παράπαν οὐδὲν ('did not dare to mutter a sound'). The colloquial *gruxai* ('mutter', 'mumble') adds colour to the formal narrative, and contributes to the characterization of Kiron's nephew as a timid, ineffectual person who was dominated by Diokles. (Wyse describes the word as a "homely colloquialism, not often found outside the comedians." The other instances he cites are Plato *Euthyd.* 301, Xen. *Oik.* 2.11, and Dem. 19.39.)

οὐδ' εἰπεῖν ἃ νῦν τολμᾷ λέγειν ('or say what he now has the effrontery to say'). Cf. on ὁ νῦν ἀμφισβητῶν…, §25. The implication is that Kiron's nephew was emboldened to make his claim through being coached by Diokles.

καὶ ταῦθ' ὅτι ἀληθῆ λέγω, κάλει μοι τούτων τοὺς μάρτυρας ('And to prove that I am telling the truth, please call the witnesses to these events'). Cf. on λαβέ μοι πρῶτον…, §11.

Summary (28–29)

In these two paragraphs the speaker sums up the evidence he has produced to show that his mother was the legitimate daughter of Kiron, before moving on to address the order of intestate succession. The summary is introduced by a series of questions, to which the speaker provides his own answers. Despite the inconclusive nature of his evidence (see the introductory note to §§18–20), there is some force in the his contention that he has done the best he can with the resources available to him. Cf. Lentzsch (1932), 30–31 and Avramovič (1997), 83. It was easier to cast doubt on someone's legitimacy than to prove it; and a woman's status was particularly difficult to defend because women were not members of *demes or *phratries and were less publicly visible than male Athenians. But there are some additional forms of evidence which he might have been expected to use. He does not say, for example, whether Kiron celebrated a *dekatē* ('tenth day festival' at which a child was customarily named) after his daughter's birth. Cf. Isa. 3.30, where the speaker says that Phile's uncles claim to have been present at her *dekatē*. Nor does he mention his mother's place of burial or the rituals observed at her grave. There are no extant speeches where such evidence is actually produced, but cf. Isa. 6.64–65, where the speaker challenges his opponents to provide these details as evidence that Kallippe was formally married to Euktemon. The speaker's language is noticeably more heated and emotional in this section of the speech than in the narrative.

28 A rapid sequence of three short questions and answers, creating the impression of a dialogue, leads and gives emphasis to the conclusion that Isaios wants the **dikastai* to reach. The whole passage, with some slight variations of wording, is also found in Isa. fr. 23 (Thalheim). A similar question and answer sequence occurs at §33; cf. also 2.21; 5.45–46; 6.63; 11.12, 25–26. Denommé (1974b), 101–102, argues that Isaios uses this technique sparingly but "toujours dans les moments importants pour donner plus de brillant à l'une ou l'autre de ses preuves" ("always at important moments to add brilliance to one or other of his proofs").

οὐκ ἐκ τῶν βασάνων; ('Is it not by evidence given under torture?'). Cf. on ἔλεγχον ἐκ βασάνων, §10.

οὐκ ἐκ τοῦ φεύγειν τοὺς ἐλέγχους; ('Is it not their refusal to put the matter to the test?'). See on ἔφυγε τὴν βάσανον, §11.

πῶς οὖν ἄν … ἐπιδεικνύς; ('How, then, could anyone prove more clearly that my mother was a legitimate daughter of Kiron than in the way that I have proved it?'). The rhetorical question, to which the expected answer is obvious, is a disguised statement. By casting it in interrogative form, the speaker invites his listeners to consider for themselves what someone in his position was able to do. The same formulation was used by Demosthenes in two of his speeches against his guardian Aphobos (Dem. 27.47 and 29.55), while the speaker of Isa. 9 expresses a similar idea in different words; cf. on καθ' ὅσον ἐδυνάμην, 9.27.

29 τῶν μὲν παλαιῶν ἀκοὴν μαρτυρούντων παρεχόμενος ('For events in the distant past I have produced hearsay evidence vouched for by witnesses'). Cf. on τὰ μὲν πάλαι…, §6.

τῶν δὲ ἔτι ζώντων τοὺς εἰδότας ('where living witnesses are available, I have produced those who know the facts'). Cf. on τοῖς εἰδόσι χρώμενος μάρτυσιν, §6.

ἔτι δὲ περὶ πάντων…ᾔδεσαν ('I have further shown that on all these points my opponents have refused to allow the testimony of slaves under torture, who knew all the facts'). See on ἔφυγε τὴν βάσανον, §11. Isaios has been so vague about the content of the testimony that it is difficult to tell whether the slaves' account would simply have supported the evidence given by the free witnesses, or whether he is glossing over gaps in that evidence which he claims the slaves would have been able to fill.

μὰ τοὺς θεοὺς τοὺς Ὀλυμπίους ('By the Olympian gods'). This is the only occurrence of the phrase in Isaios's extant speeches, where invocations to the gods are relatively rare, but cf. 'by the gods', 11.36 and 'by the gods of Olympus', 6.58; also 'by Zeus', 7.33. Here, combined with the emphatic first person pronoun *egōgē*, it adds great emphasis to the speaker's contention that he has proved his mother's legitimacy as clearly as possible. The tone is in keeping with his (feigned) indignation at his opponents' failure to produce the slaves, but it may, nevertheless, betray a hint of (genuine) desperation. By way of contrast with Isaios's more restrained style, 'by the gods' occurs twenty-two times in the Demosthenic corpus, including three in Dem. 54.

οὐκ ἂν ἔχοιμι πίστεις μείζους τούτων εἰπεῖν ('I could not give stronger proofs than these'). This rounds off the argument begun at §28, in which the speaker has mentioned three kinds of **atekhnoi pisteis*: witness testimony (*marturia*) torture (*basanos*) and hearsay (*akoē*). Cf. Arist. *Rh.* 1355b.

ἀλλ' ἱκανὰς εἶναι νομίζω τὰς εἰρημένας ('but I think those I have produced are sufficient'). Cf. on ἔχετε δὲ πίστεις ἱκανὰς, §45.

Argument and Law: The Order of Intestate Succession (30–34)

The legal point at issue—whether a daughter's son had precedence over a brother's son, even when the daughter had been married by **engué* rather than **epidikasia*—has been discussed in the introduction to this speech, pp. 98–102. On the basis of the arguments put forward in that discussion, I am assuming in the following notes that there was no law dealing explicitly with this question, but that Kiron's nephew had cited a law which, according to his argument, supported his case. I am also assuming that this argument was spurious, and that Isaios's client, provided he was legitimate, did have a good claim. These assumptions raise questions about Isaios's rhetorical strategy; why, in particular, did he not dispute his opponent's interpretation of the law, instead of adducing other laws that were at best peripheral to his case?

The only possible answers are speculative, but they have to do with the understanding an experienced *logographer would have acquired of the types of argumentation most likely to appeal to a panel of adjudicators in a **dikastērion*. First, the approach in this section is consistent with Isaios's overall preference in the speech for counterattack rather than defence. He may have feared that engaging directly with his opponent's legal argument would be counterproductive, reminding the **dikastai* of what Kiron's nephew had said and perhaps reinforcing their acceptance of it; cf. on ὡς οὐκ…, §1. Perhaps, too, the *dikastai* were more likely to be impressed by a litigant who could produce his own citations from the law rather than merely attack his opponent's. Most importantly, however, Isaios must have been conscious of the Athenians' mistrust of extensive legal knowledge and technical argumentation. It would have been particularly inappropriate for his client in this case to display such skills, given that he had characterized himself as being entirely inexperienced in litigation, and condemned his opponents for excessive preparation of their case.

30 καὶ νομίζω…ἐξ ἐκείνου γεγονότες ('I suppose you accept it in principle as obvious that Kiron's collateral relations are not closer to him in the **ankhisteia* than those who are descended from him'). At the outset, the speaker states the basis of his legal argument: that descendants are closer of kin than collaterals. Sositheos, the speaker of [Dem.] 43, uses a similar argument in his attack on Makartatos's claim to the estate of Hagnias. Cf. on Κίρωνος…, §33.

ἐξ αὐτῶν τῶν νόμων ('from the laws themselves'). This emphatic phrase, repeated at §45, implies that the speaker expected the **dikastai* to attach particular evidential value to citations from the law. Here, as at 10.15, Isaios uses it when he is about to adduce laws which in fact are no more than indirectly relevant to his client's case. Cf. also Isa. 3.35; Dem. 38.9; Aiskhin. 3.30, 46; Hyp. 3.13.

31 εἰ γὰρ ἔζη μὲν ἡ ἐμὴ μήτηρ … ('For if my mother were still alive …'). The first stage of the speaker's argument is based on a hypothetical scenario in which his mother had survived her father Kiron, who had died intestate, in order to show how Kiron's brother or nephew would have been treated by the laws on the epiklerate.

ἦν δὲ ἀδελφὸς οὗτος αὐτῷ, μὴ ἀδελφιδοῦς ('and even if my opponent had been Kiron's brother, not just his nephew [and therefore a more distant relation]'). The logic of the argument becomes clear at the end of §34.

συνοικῆσαι μὲν ἂν τῇ γυναικὶ κύριος ἦν, τῶν δὲ χρημάτων οὐκ ἂν ('he would have the right to marry the daughter, but not to claim the estate'). A similar argument is put forward by the speaker of Isa. 10, who contends that his uncle and cousin have deprived his mother of her rightful inheritance as **epiklēros*.

ἀλλ' οἱ γενόμενοι παῖδες ἐκ τούτου καὶ ἐξ ἐκείνης ('which would go to the children of their marriage'). The speaker equates his claim to his grandfather's estate with that of the hypothetical offspring of a union between his mother (if she had been **epiklēros*) and his paternal uncle. For those who take the view that an Athenian could not inherit from his maternal grandfather unless his mother was *epiklēros*, this is a crucial flaw in his argument. (See the introduction to this speech, pp. 98–99.)

οὕτω γὰρ οἱ νόμοι κελεύουσιν ('for so the laws ordain'). The speaker wants the **dikastai* to accept that the law applies to his own case as well as to that of the son of a hypothetical **epiklēros*.

32 ἀλλὰ καὶ ἐκ τοῦ περὶ τῆς κακώσεως νόμου ('but also the law about neglect'). The speaker moves on to draw an analogy from the law on neglect of parents, which places the responsibility for care of the elderly not on collateral relations but only on descendants.

οὐκ ἂν οὗτος ὑπόδικος ἦν τῆς κακώσεως ἀλλ' ἡμεῖς ('we, not our opponent, would be liable to prosecution for neglect'). See on τὸν εἰληχότα τοῦ κλήρου, §3.

γονεῖς δ' εἰσὶ … ἐὰν ἔτι ζῶσιν ('the word 'parents' includes father, mother, grandfather, and grandmother, and their father and mother, if they are still alive'). Wyse points out that in Attic prose *goneis* nearly always means simply 'parents', citing Hdt. 1.91 as an example of the "strained use" extending it to remoter ancestors. Despite this objection it would be reasonable to expect that the duty to provide care for the elderly would pass down to grandchildren if children predeceased their parents.

33 Κίρωνος πότερον θυγάτηρ ἢ ἀδελφὸς ἐγγυτέρω τοῦ γένους ἐστί; ('Is Kiron's daughter or his brother more closely related to him?'). On the rhetorical use of questions and answers, see the introductory note to §§28–29. Thompson (1976), 76, comments on the similarity between this passage and [Dem.] 43.22, where Sositheos employs the same technique. He rightly points out that the real issue in both speeches is not the correct interpretation of the law but the status of the women who are held out as being the legitimate daughters of, respectively, Kiron and Hagnias.

34 δέδοικα δὲ μὴ λίαν ὁμολογούμενα λέγων ἐνοχλεῖν ὑμῖν δόξω ('But I am afraid I may seem tiresome in repeating facts so universally recognized'). Introducing a doubtful proposition with a claim that everyone 'knows' or 'agrees' that it is right is a commonplace of Athenian forensic oratory, relying on the likelihood that the hearer would be ashamed to admit his ignorance; cf. Arist. *Rh.* 1408a. These words, therefore, could be taken as a signal that the statement following them may be in some way inaccurate or misleading. But Sositheos, at [Dem.] 43.22, makes a similar point in stronger terms: the closer kinship of descendants than collaterals is recognized not only by the Athenians, but also by other Greeks and even barbarians. Cf. Carey (1996), 43, on the Athenians' respect for laws which "can be shown to be in agreement with laws elsewhere in Greece, and even beyond". So, although Isaios does not use the same formulation, it appears that he was making a valid point.

πάντες γὰρ ὑμεῖς τῶν πατρῴων, τῶν παππῴων, τῶν ἔτι περαιτέρω κληρονομεῖτε ('for you all inherit the property of your fathers, grandfathers, and more remote ancestors'). Cf. Isa. 3.59, where the speaker argues that Phile, had she really been the legitimate daughter of Pyrrhos, would have entered directly on his estate rather than claiming it through the courts. Both speakers have an interest in equating the rights of a daughter and her offspring with those of a son and his offspring, so it may be that the right of **embateusis* applied (or was interpreted as applying) only to descendants in the male line, and that a daughter's son would have to claim his inheritance by **epidikasia*. (See the discussion of *embateusis* in the introduction to this speech, pp. 101–102.) In each of these cases the speaker, by addressing the **dikastai* directly in the second person, is effectively inviting them to support his argument. Cf. on Ὑμεῖς . . ., §12.

ἐκ γένους παρειληφότες τὴν ἀγχιστείαν ('by right of lineal descent'). Collateral kinsmen have no claim to the estate of someone who has left lineal descendants.

καὶ οὐκ οἶδ'... συμβέβηκεν ('and I do not know whether such a case as this one has ever been brought against anyone before'). It is impossible to know whether the speaker was simply being disingenuous in this statement, or whether it really was unheard of (or at least unusual) for a direct descendant's claim to an estate to be challenged by a collateral kinsman. At this point we may suspect that there is some truth in Wyse's contention that Isaios deliberately conflates the inheritance rights of a daughter's son with those of a son's son, but it does not necessarily follow that the daughter's son had no claim to his maternal grandfather's estate. It is likely, nevertheless, that daughters' sons did find themselves in a less secure position, especially since they were vulnerable to attacks on their legitimacy through the female line. Cf. Wyse, *ad loc.*, and, for the contrary view, Rubinstein (1993), 104.

Narrative and Argument: Diokles's Attempts to Take Control of Kiron's Property (35–39)

The extent of Kiron's property, which the speaker enumerates immediately before his allegations of a conspiracy between Diokles and his sister to defraud Kiron and take over the estate after his death, is intended to provide the motivation for their alleged offences. The speaker gives a one-sided account of a family quarrel, with Diokles presented as the driving force, his sister a willing but relatively passive accomplice, and Kiron their helpless and gullible victim. We may assume that his story has some basis in fact, but the extent to which Isaios may have embellished or distorted it for rhetorical purposes is impossible to determine. It is, however, legitimate to question how the speaker could have known about some of the details, especially since he brings no testimony in support of this part of his narrative. The chronology is also characteristically vague: Diokles started planning to take over the property after Kiron's sons died, 'a long time ago'. The speaker's father, who plays a part in the feud against Diokles, had died before the court case, but we have no idea how long before. The speaker's mother and brother, who are not mentioned at all in this section, may or may not have witnessed or participated in the events the speaker describes.

In a modern trial, not only would a litigant or advocate be required to support his story with evidence, but the witnesses would be subject to questioning by the opponent on any apparent omissions, exaggerations or discrepancies. Such inconsistencies would have been less obvious under Athenian procedure, with its reliance on a single speech by each party, and a *logographer would have had less need for concern about detailed factual accuracy and consistency in his efforts to make the best possible case for his client. In this part of the speech, even if it was based on fact, Isaios may well have exploited familiar story patterns, and cultural stereotypes of the scheming woman and gullible old man, in order to enhance his client's credibility with the **dikastai*. In particular, although the extant sources do not exactly parallel the situation portrayed here, faked pregnancies and miscarriages would have been familiar to an Athenian audience from both the tragic and the comic stage (as discussed by Hall (2006), 60–98).

It is also noticeable to a reader that the continuation of the narrative about Kiron's funeral at §§38–39 differs in some significant respects from the account given at §§21–27, but these discrepancies were probably less obvious to those who heard rather than read the speech. The splitting of the narrative has thus enabled Isaios to manipulate the 'facts' to his client's advantage.

35 Κίρων γὰρ ἐκέκτητο οὐσίαν, ὦ ἄνδρες ('For Kiron had acquired property, gentlemen'). For the address to the **dikastai*, see on Ἐπὶ τοῖς τοιούτοις, §1.

ἀγρὸν μὲν Φλυῆσι ('a farm in Phlya'). It may be no more than coincidental that Kiron owned a farm in Phlya, his brother-in-law's *deme; there is no indication in the speech of his own deme. Cf. Davies (1971), 314.

δανείσματα οὐκ ὀλίγα ('considerable sums on loan'). It would be interesting to know how much money Kiron had out on loan, since this would provide a more accurate assessment of his total wealth against which to evaluate the dowries he gave his daughter on the occasion of her two marriages. Cf. on σὺν ἱματίοις…, §8.

36 Διοκλῆς μετὰ τῆς ἀδελφῆς πάλαι ἐπεβούλευεν ('Diokles, with his sister, started plotting a long time ago'). The speaker presents Diokles and his sister in a highly prejudicial light: they had been scheming for a long time to gain possession of Kiron's wealth.

ἐπειδὴ τάχιστα οἱ παῖδες οἱ Κίρωνος ἐτελεύτησαν ('as soon as Kiron's sons died'). The implication is that Diokles expected to take control of the property after Kiron's death, if it was inherited by one or both of Kiron's sons by Diokles's sister. Once the two sons had died, Kiron's grandsons (the sons of his daughter by his first wife) became his heirs, so Diokles had to find some other way of gaining control. By omitting to mention *when* Kiron's sons died, Isaios enables the speaker to give what must be a very selective account of events over a period of probably more than twenty years. Cf. the introduction to this speech, pp. 93–95.

οὐκ ἐξεδίδου ('did not give her in marriage'). For the presentation through negation, see on ἐκείνῳ ..., 7.17. An Athenian woman in the position of the elderly Kiron's second wife would have been expected to remarry after their sons had died, while she was still able to bear children to another husband. Diokles, as representative of her paternal **oikos*, would have been responsible for arranging a new marriage. For other examples from the orators of a brother's concern with his sister's childlessness, see Cox (1988), 381.

ἔπειθε δὲ μένειν ('but kept persuading her to stay [with Kiron]'). Diokles is presented as the instigator of the deception, with his sister acting under his direction.

φάσκουσαν ... ἄκουσαν ('and to claim that she thought she was pregnant by him and then pretend to have had an accidental miscarriage'). One wonders how the speaker knew about this, and other details of the conspiracy between Diokles and his sister. If they were not pure invention, he may have deduced them from Kiron's side of the story, which he could have heard during his visits to his grandfather.

ἵν' ἐλπίζων ... ὑόν ('so that he would continue hoping for children to be born to him and not adopt either of us as his son'). The point of the speaker's story now becomes clear: it was because he still hoped to father another natural son that Kiron did not adopt one of his daughter's sons. (The word *mēdeteron*, 'neither' (of two), is the only positive indication in the speech that there were no more than two.) Presumably this is the speaker's response to a question raised by his opponent, or perhaps he thought it was something the **dikastai* were likely to question on their own account.

καὶ τὸν πατέρα ... ἐκείνου ('and he was always slandering my father, alleging that he was intriguing against Kiron's property'). It is reasonable to infer that Kiron's nephew has given a damaging account of the rôle played by the speaker's father in the family feud. Isaios puts the father in the right by claiming that he was 'slandered' by Diokles, but, in keeping with his overall strategy, he chooses to respond to the attack by making counter-accusations against Diokles rather than by defending the father at greater length. The speaker's reticence about his father's rôle, and even his identity (cf. on πάλιν ἐκδίδωσι τῷ ἐμῷ πατρί, §8) may suggest that he had something to hide.

37 εἰδὼς... ὁπότε ὁ πάππος τελευτήσειεν ('knowing that I would seek to take control of all this property, as was my right, when my grandfather died'). Isaios makes Diokles the *focalizer, using the participle to impute knowledge and motivation to him in a prejudicial way. Cf. on εὖ εἰδότες..., 9.4.

The ms. ὁπότε ὁ πάππος ἐτελεύτησεν, 'since my grandfather had died', would imply that Diokles prevented the speaker from entering the dead Kiron's house. The context, however, makes it clear that, throughout §37, the speaker is talking about what happened before Kiron's death, when he wanted to look after Kiron and spend time with him, so that the aorist indicative in the ms. sources requires emendation. Wyse rejects the substitution of the optative *teleutēseien* for the aorist indicative *eteleutēsen* on syntactical grounds and points out that, elsewhere in the orators, *hopote* ('since') normally has causal rather than temporal force. Despite these arguments it is impossible to make sense of the unemended text, and Wyse's judgment appears to have been clouded by his prejudice against Isaios. ("But correcting the MS. to strengthen Isaeus' reasoning is perilous work. His client may have been a rogue and an impostor, the weakness of whose case could not be entirely concealed by his advocate.")

οὐκ ἐκώλυε ('did not try to prevent'). For the presentation through negation, see on ἐκείνῳ..., 7.17. A violent character such as Diokles might have been expected to prevent the speaker from visiting Kiron. There may also be a hint of polemic: perhaps Kiron's nephew had said something like, 'What does my opponent have to complain about? Diokles treated him fairly, and never stopped him visiting Kiron.'

δεδιὼς μὴ τραχυνθεὶς εἰς ὀργὴν κατασταίη ('Fearing that [Kiron] might become exasperated and angry with him'). The *focalization remains with Diokles as the subject of the participle 'fearing', but there is disagreement as to whether it was Kiron or the speaker who might have become exasperated and angry. Some editors (Wyse, Edwards, Ferrucci) have retained the first person verb, *katastaiēn*, from the manuscript, while others (Forster, Roussel) prefer the third person *katastaiē*. The first person cannot be ruled out, since Diokles may have been postponing confrontation with the speaker, but the third person makes better sense. Diokles would have had more reason to fear Kiron's anger than that of the speaker, and by making the point Isaios implies that the speaker was on good terms with Kiron. It might be objected that no subject is expressed in the third person, but the intended reference to Kiron is clear enough.

παρεσκεύαζε δέ μοι τὸν ἀμφισβητήσοντα τῆς οὐσίας ('was preparing the claimant to dispute my right to the property'). See on παρασκευάσας, §3. The speaker implies that Diokles, knowing he had no legal claim to the estate because he was unrelated to Kiron, had to prepare a rival to the speaker who had a plausible claim to the property.

μέρος πολλοστὸν τούτῳ μεταδιδοὺς εἰ κατορθώσειεν ('promising to give him a small share, if he were successful'). Cf. on καὶ τολμῶσιν ... ἀμφισβήτησιν, §2.

38 καὶ ἐπειδὴ τάχιστα ἐτελεύτησεν ('and as soon as [Kiron] died'). The subject, though unexpressed (cf. on δεδιὼς μὴ ..., §37), cannot be anyone but Kiron; the sentence marks the transition from events during his lifetime to those after his death. The narrative 'catches up' with Kiron's funeral, which has already been described at §§21–27. There is no suggestion here that the pleading of Kiron's widow persuaded the speaker to allow the funeral to be conducted from Kiron's own house, and the overall impression given at this stage of the speech is that the speaker was acting under compulsion at the funeral, not that he was in control of events.

ὡς τῶν μαρτύρων ἠκούσατε μαρτυρησάντων ('as you have heard the witnesses testify'). The speaker reminds the **dikastai* of the testimony he has adduced about the conduct of the funeral, but it is not clear precisely which details of his story were covered by it. Cf. on καὶ ταῦτα ὡς ἀληθῆ λέγω, §24.

ἀπειληφέναι δὲ παρὰ τοῦδε προσεποιεῖτο ('pretended to have received [the money] from my opponent'). See on τὸν εἰληχότα τοῦ κλήρου, §3. According to the speaker, Diokles 'pretended' to have received the money from Kiron's nephew as part of his plan to put the nephew forward as claimant to the estate.

παρ' ἐμοῦ δὲ οὐκέτι ἤθελεν ἀπολαβεῖν ('and no longer wanted to accept payment from me'). If Diokles had been working on his plan for a long time, it is hardly plausible that he should change his mind in the way that the speaker claims he did: rather than demand the money from the speaker, why would he not have pretended from the start that it was Kiron's nephew who was paying for the funeral? This kind of inconsistency appears to reflect the difficulty that Isaios faced in refuting the evidence put forward by his client's opponent.

ὑποπαρωθῶν 'stealthily pushing me aside'.

ὅπως ἐκεῖνος δοκοίη θάπτειν ἀλλὰ μὴ ἐγὼ τὸν πάππον ('so that it might appear that my opponent, not I, was burying my grandfather'). See on τὸν εἰληχότα τοῦ κλήρου and Κίρων ὁ πάππος, §3.

βιάσασθαι μὲν ... οὐκ ᾤμην δεῖν ('I did not think ... that in these painful circumstances I should use violence to carry off my grandfather's body'). The speaker no longer mentions the details given at §§21–22, presenting himself simply as a reasonable man who drew the line at resorting to violence in pursuit of his rights.

τῶν φίλων μοι ταῦτα συγγιγνωσκόντων ('and my friends agreed with me'). It is not clear how the speaker had time to consult his friends before deciding not to take Kiron's body away by force, but his claim to have secured their support helps to present him in a positive light.

ἐξ ὧν ὁ πάππος κατέλιπε τῶν ἀναλωμάτων γιγνομένων ('the expenses of which were paid out of my grandfather's estate'). The speaker repeats the claim first made at §25.

39 καὶ ταῦτα μὲν οὕτως ἀναγκασθεὶς ἔπραξα τοῦτον τὸν τρόπον ('Thus I acted in this way under compulsion'). By admitting that he was forced to act as he did, the speaker implicitly concedes that his conduct fell short of what was expected of him as Kiron's heir.

τὸν ἐξηγητὴν ἐρόμενος ('consulting the *exegetēs*'). On the function of the *exēgētai* as interpreters of the sacred laws, see Parker (2005), 90–92. By referring to his consultation with an *exegetēs*, the speaker demonstrates his own piety and adds a religious dimension to what was essentially a materialistic dispute.

καὶ τὰ ἔνατα ἐπήνεγκα ('and offered the ninth day sacrifices'). The speaker of Isa. 2 claims to have buried his adoptive father Menekles and carried out the third and ninth day ceremonies and all the other appropriate rituals after his death (2.37). Kiron's grandson, having been thwarted in his wish to conduct the funeral himself, makes the best of his situation by celebrating the ninth day ritual as lavishly as possible.

καὶ ἵνα μὴ δοκοῖεν οὗτοι μὲν ἀνηλωκέναι πάντα ('and so that it might not seem that they had paid for everything'). If the speaker cannot claim to have paid for the funeral himself, it is important that he can at least show that he shared in the expense.

Narrative and Testimony: The Character of Diokles (40–42)

Instead of mounting a detailed rebuttal of the case against him, Isaios adopted the bold strategy of deflecting the attack on his client by launching a counterattack against a third party whose rôle in the family feud appears largely irrelevant to the legal issues between the speaker and his opponent. His account of Diokles's criminal record, although it takes up only three paragraphs towards the end of the speech, is the most direct and savage example of **diabolē* in any of his surviving **diadikasia* speeches. It is noteworthy, however, that the target is not the speaker's legal opponent. This enables the speaker to show a degree of moderation by avoiding a direct attack on a member of his own family, while portraying his opponent as an instrument rather than an agent. Cf. Rubinstein (2005), 134–135, on the characteristically restrained tone of speeches from *diadikasiai*. Whether or not the speaker was in the right, the story of Diokles's villainy must have been a highly effective way of persuading the **dikastai* that his opponent's version of the facts was unreliable.

40 ὦ ἄνδρες ('gentlemen'). See on ὦ ἄνδρες, §1.

εἴ δὲ εἰδείητε … οὐκ ἂν ἀπιστήσαιτε τῶν εἰρεμένων οὐδενί ('If you understood the impudence of Diokles, and how he has behaved on all other occasions, you would not disbelieve anything I have said'). This sentence explains why, for Isaios and his contemporaries, Diokles's track record of fraud and violence, if true, was not a "side issue" (as Wyse, 587, asserts). Diokles's bad character is not, of course, conclusive proof that he was complicit in a plot to deprive Kiron's grandson of his inheritance, but it does show that he was capable of the kind of behaviour of which the speaker accuses him.

ἀδελφῶν τριῶν ὁμομητρίων ἐπικλήρων καταλειφθεισῶν ('when his three half-sisters, the daughters of his mother, were left as *epiklēroi*'). The speaker describes the crimes allegedly committed by Diokles against two of these half-sisters, but there is no further mention of the third. Baiter and Sauppe (1850), 230 (cited by Wyse), assume that she was the wife of Kiron. Wyse himself remains neutral on the question, but Ferrucci has no doubt that the third sister was Kiron's widow. There is nothing in the text to support such a firm conclusion, and it is equally possible that Diokles and Kiron's second wife were full siblings.

αὑτὸν τῷ πατρὶ αὐτῶν εἰσποιήσας ('made himself their father's adopted son'). The speaker claims that Diokles 'adopted himself', or 'had himself adopted', as the son of his stepfather, after the latter's death, not that he merely "represented himself as the adopted son" (Forster; cf. "en se donnant comme fils adoptif" (Roussel) and "egli si pretese figlio adottivo" (Ferrucci)). The meaning is better expressed by Edwards's "made himself the adopted son". For this reflexive use of *eispoiein*, cf. [Dem.] 44.19, 51, where the connotations are similarly pejorative. The passing reference to Diokles's 'adoption' is tantalizingly obscure, yielding no information about the procedure that was followed or the qualifications for adoption. Wyse argues that, in the circumstances as described, an adoption would have been illegal, because an adopted son was required to marry his adoptive father's daughter, but marriage between *homometric half-siblings was prohibited. According to more recent scholarship, however, it may not have been obligatory for an adopted son to marry the adopter's daughter; see the introduction to Isa. 10, pp. 206–207.

οὐδεμίαν ἐκείνου περὶ τούτων ποιησαμένου διαθήκην ('although [their father] had left no will to that effect'). This has been taken (notably by Rubinstein (1993), 121) as indicating an example of posthumous adoption. We cannot, however, rule out the possibility that the adoption, if it took place at all, was testamentary, but that the will was contested (or, at least, not recognized by the speaker).

41 καὶ γραφὴν ὕβρεως γραφεὶς οὐδέπω τούτων δίκην δέδωκε ('and although he has been prosecuted for *hubris*, he has not yet been punished'). This is supported by Harpokration's reference to a speech written by Isaios for the prosecution of Diokles for **hubris*, Isa. fr. VII (Thalheim), although titles given by lexicographers do not always accurately reflect the nature of the proceedings. The only other attested prosecution for *hubris*, mentioned at [Dem.] 45.4, was brought by Apollodoros against Phormio, but apparently never came to court. Cf. Osborne (1985b), 50.

42 καὶ κατέχει τὸν ἀγρόν, φελλέα δὲ [χωρία ἄττα] δὲ ἐκείνῳ δέδωκε ('and he is still in possession of the land and has only given him some stony ground'). The piece of land allegedly retained illegally by Diokles was the subject of another legal action, Isa. fr. IX (Thalheim). The prosecutor was Menekrates, the son of Diokles's younger half-sister and her husband Lysimenes.

τοὺς εἰδότας παρέξομαι μάρτυρας ('I shall produce as witnesses those who know the facts'). Cf. on λαβέ μοι πρῶτον . . ., §11; and, on the designation of witnesses as 'those who know the facts', see on τοῖς εἰδόσι χρώμενος μάρτυσιν, §6.

Epilogue (43–46)

In the concluding paragraphs Isaios raises the stakes by treating the case as one of disputed citizenship, not just a disputed inheritance. Through his choice of language and rhetorical **topoi* he places his client in the position of a litigant who is forced to defend himself against prosecution, rather than one who has decided to challenge a claim to an estate.

43 ἀπεστερηκὼς ('robbed'). See on ἀποστερῶν, §3. Diokles is not presented simply as a bad character in general terms, but as someone who 'stole' his half-sisters' inheritance, just as he is trying to 'steal' Kiron's estate from the speaker.

καὶ τὰ τοῦ πάππου χρήματα ἡμᾶς ἀποστερήσων ('to rob us of our grandfather's property'). The repetition of *aposterein* ('rob'), first with a perfect and now a future participle, reinforces the link between Diokles's treatment of his half-sisters and the speaker's allegation that he is the instigator of the claim by Kiron's nephew.

καὶ τούτῳ δύο μνᾶς, ὡς ἀκούομεν, μόνας δεδωκὼς ('and having given our opponent, as we have heard, only two minas'). Cf. on καὶ τολμῶσιν . . . ἀμφισβήτησιν, §2. On the marginalization of the speaker's opponent, see on τὸν εἰληχότα τοῦ κλήρου, §3.

ἀλλὰ καὶ περὶ τῆς πατρίδος ('but also our country'). Isaios begins to shift the argument from the private to the public sphere: it is not just property that is at stake for the speaker, but (so he says) citizenship.

εἰς κινδύνους καθίστησιν ('is placing us at risk'). Isaios presents his client as if he were a defendant in a **graphē*, put 'at risk' by a prosecutor whose case he is forced to answer. In fact the case is a **diadikasia*, and it was the speaker himself who opted to challenge his opponent's claim to Kiron's estate.

ἐὰν γὰρ ἐξαπατηθῆτε ὑμεῖς ('For if you are misled'). See on ἐὰν ὑμεῖς . . ., §3.

πεισθέντες ὡς ἡ μήτηρ ἡμῶν οὐκ ἦν πολῖτις ('persuaded that our mother was not a citizen'). Framing his argument in terms of citizenship rather than legitimacy enables the speaker to consider the wider implications of his mother's status.

οὐδ' ἡμεῖς ἐσμεν ('neither are we [citizens]'). There are adversarial cases where defendants appeal for mercy from the **dikastai* on the grounds that the expected penalty would have a disproportionately harsh impact on them or their families (Lys. 9.21; 18.1; 19.33; 20.34; 21.24–25; Dem. 28.19; Isok. 16.45–48, discussed by Lanni (2006), 56–57). There was no formal penalty for the unsuccessful claimant(s) in a **diadikasia*, and it seems unlikely that an adverse result for the speaker in this case would have led directly to a loss of citizenship, especially since the case is complicated by the opponent's claim that a brother's son had a better claim than a daughter's son. The *dikastai* did not give reasons for their decisions, and neither did they have to reach agreement, so even if the majority did vote against the speaker, they did not necessarily accept that he was illegitimate. It is possible, nevertheless, that if the speaker had lost the case he would have been more vulnerable to attacks on his citizenship from members of his *deme or *phratry.

μετ' Εὐκλείδην γὰρ ἄρχοντα γεγόναμεν ('for we were born after the arkhonship of Eukleides'). Perikles's law of 451/450 BC, restricting Athenian citizenship to those of Athenian parentage on both sides, apparently fell into disuse during the later years of the Pelopponesian War and was re-enacted during the *arkhonship of Eukleides (403/402 BC), applying to anyone born subsequently. (For discussion, see Harrison (1968), 125–126, and cf. Todd (1993), 177: "... the fact that this law was re-enacted but without retroactivity in 403/2 BC may suggest that it had at least ceased to be effectively applied.") On the assumption that the speaker must have been at least twenty, this implies that the earliest possible date for the speech is 383 BC.

κατεσκεύακε ('trumped up'). "It is not easy to find passages in the orators in which [*kataskeuazein*] is used without any suggestion of fraud"; it is "an invidious word much affected by Athenian pleaders" (Wyse, 523). Cf. Isa. 4.6; 6.35; 9.2; 11.37; and parallels from other orators cited by Wyse.

44 καὶ ζῶντος μὲν τοῦ πάππου καὶ τοῦ πατρὸς οὐδεμίαν αἰτίαν εἴχομεν ('While our grandfather and father were alive, no charge was brought against us'). If the speaker's mother really was illegitimate, he and his brother were at risk of being ejected from their *deme as non-citizens. By pointing out that no such accusations were made against them while their father and grandfather were alive, the speaker draws attention to his own isolation and seems to imply that Diokles has waited until he was in a more vulnerable position before launching his attack. This is the only positive indication that the speaker's father was already dead (as, probably, was his brother; cf. on ἀλλ' ἡμᾶς ..., §1.)

διὰ τὸν Ὀρέστην τοῦτον ('thanks to this Orestes'). Cf. on τὸν Ὀρέστην ἐπικαλούμενον, §3. In the concluding sections the main focus is again on Diokles rather than Kiron's nephew.

καὶ παθὼν ὅ τι προσήκει τοὺς τὰ τοιαῦτα ποιοῦντας ('and having suffered the treatment appropriate for those who do such things'). This presumably refers to the punishments to which an adulterer was liable, which included having a radish pushed up his anus (Aristoph. *Clouds*, 1083, with Dover's note; and cf. Carey (1993)).

ὅταν κατ' αὐτοῦ τὴν δίκην ἡμεῖς εἰσίωμεν ('when our case against him comes on'). This could refer to the prosecution for **hubris* mentioned at §41, if the word **dikē* is being used as a generic term for any legal action, or to a private action for the recovery of the piece of land mentioned at §42. If so, the speaker would be using the first person plural somewhat loosely, since he was not the victim in either case, though he might have aligned himself with the other victims of Diokles. Or the reference could be to a separate legal action, as Baiter and Sauppe, (1850), 231, suggest.

45 ὑμῶν δ' ἐγὼ δέομαι καὶ ἱκετεύω ('But I beg and implore you'). Cf. on δέομαι οὖν ὑμῶν ..., §5, and ἀντιβολῶ ὑμᾶς ..., 9.37. This is the only speech

of Isaios to include both a plea for good will in the introduction and a supplication to the *dikastai* in the conclusion.

μή με περιίδητε... ὑβρισθέντα ('do not allow me to be treated with *hubris*'). For the verb *perioran* (lit. 'overlook' or 'disregard'), used by litigants pleading with the judges not to ignore their plight, cf., e.g., Isa. 9.37. By implying that the speaker has been treated with **hubris*, Isaios presents him as the victim of a very serious crime.

ἀποστερηθέντα ('robbed'). See on ἀποστερῶν, §3.

ἀλλὰ βοηθήσατε καθ' ὅσον ὑμῶν ἕκαστος τυγχάνει δυνάμενος 'but help me so far as each of you is able'). The speaker intensifies his appeal to the **dikastai* by addressing it to each of them individually. Cf., e.g., Isa. 4.26; Dem. 21.1; 25.11; 57.50; [Dem.] 59.110.

ἔχετε δὲ πίστεις ἱκανὰς ('and you have sufficient proof'). See on οὐκ ἂν ἔχοιμι..., §29, and cf. Dem. 28.23.

ἐκ μαρτυριῶν, ἐκ βασάνων, ἐξ αὐτῶν τῶν νόμων ('from depositions, challenges to torture, and the laws themselves'). The speaker has already referred (§28) to his use of **marturiai* and **basanoi* in relation to his mother's legitimacy, and in §30 he promised to justify his claim to be Kiron's intestate heir 'from the laws themselves'. Again, *basanoi* refers to the challenge and its rejection; cf. on οὐκ ἐκ τῶν βασάνων;, §28.

46 μνησθέντες οὖν καὶ τῶν ὅρκων οὓς ὀμόσαντες δικάζετε... ταύτῃ τὴν ψῆφον τίθεσθε (Remember, then, the oaths under which you sit in judgment... and cast your vote as justice demands'). This is one of three speeches of Isaios in which the conclusion includes a reference to the dikastic oath. Cf. 2.47; 4.31. Despite some variations of wording, each of the speakers follows essentially the same formula: the **dikastai* are invited to cast their votes in accordance with justice (or the laws), mindful of the law(s), the oaths they have sworn, and the arguments (or testimony) they have heard. Similarly worded appeals to the dikastic oath occur at Lys. 10.32 and Dem. 27.68; cf., e.g., Andok. 1.9, 31; [Dem.] 45.87.

The exact wording of the dikastic oath, which probably varied over time, is not known, but it certainly included a requirement that the *dikastai* should reach their decisions 'in accordance with the laws'. The scholarly debate over the precise meaning of this is summarized by Johnstone (1999), 33–42. In the light of Johnstone's finding that references to the oath occur significantly more often in public than in private speeches, Isaios's decision to mention it here may be seen as a further indication that he was trying to broaden the issues in the case from the private to the public sphere.

Οὐκ οἶδ... εἰρημένων ('I do not know of anything I ought to add, for I think that nothing I have said has escaped your attention'). See on Οὐκ οἶδ..., 7.45.

λαβὲ δ' αὐτοῖς τὴν μαρτυρίαν τὴν λοιπήν, ὡς ἐλήφθη μοιχός, καὶ ἀνάγνωθι ('Now take the remaining deposition, proving that [Diokles] was taken in adultery, and read it out'). Cf. on λαβέ μοι πρῶτον..., §11. Here, in a highly unusual ending (Isa. 3 is the only other speech of Isaios to end with the reading of testimony) the speaker continues to exploit the character of Diokles, and to make him the focus of the audience's attention, by calling testimony to prove that he was taken in adultery.

ISAIOS 9: ON THE ESTATE OF ASTYPHILOS

Introduction

Isaios's client is a *homometric brother of Astyphilos, who died while on military service in Mytilene. The speaker tells us that he was himself abroad on military service at the time of Astyphilos's death, and the funeral was conducted by Astyphilos's friends and fellow soldiers. Theophrastos, the speaker's father and stepfather of Astyphilos, was, on the speaker's account, too ill to conduct the funeral, but was taken there by friends in order to show his respect for his stepson. The speaker returned to Athens after an unspecified interval, and found that Kleon, a patrilineal first cousin of Astyphilos, had installed his son on the estate without legal authority, claiming that Astyphilos had adopted him in a will made just before his departure for Mytilene and left for safekeeping with Hierokles, the maternal uncle of both Astyphilos and the speaker. The speaker contests the adoption, denying that Astyphilos ever made a will and claiming the estate for himself as Astyphilos's next of kin.

Kinship Patterns and Family History

According to the speaker, Astyphilos and Kleon were enemies because of a family feud dating back to their parents' generation: Euthykrates (father of Astyphilos) died as a result of injuries inflicted on him by his brother Thoudippos (father of Kleon) in a fight over the division of their paternal estate. The existence of a third branch of the family is revealed by the speaker's identification of one of his witnesses as the husband of Astyphilos's aunt, i.e. probably a sister of Thoudippos and Euthykrates.[1] The speaker tells us nothing about his mother, beyond the basic genealogical facts: she was a sister of Hierokles, and married first to Euthykrates and then to Theophrastos.

Kleon, son of Thoudippos, is recorded as a *tamias* (treasurer) of Athena in 377/6.[2] Thoudippos had another son, Anaxippos, who is not mentioned

[1] See on τὸν ἔχοντα…, §19.

[2] *IG* ii² 1410, 1–2; 1411, 6; cited by Davies (1971), 229. The *tamiae*, one from each of the 10 tribes, were chosen annually by lot from among the richest property class, the *pentakosioimedimnoi* (*Ath. Pol.* 47).

in Isa. 9 but who is known from epigraphic evidence to have served as a Superintendent of the Dockyards in 356/5 BC.[3] Given that Thoudippos was an uncommon name,[4] it is possible that the brother of Euthykrates is to be identified with the proposer of the reassessment decree of 425/4 BC, an associate of the demagogue Kleon of Kydathenaion. That would be consistent with the further possibility that Thoudippos, who named his son Kleon, was married to a daughter of Kleon of Kydathenaion.[5]

As a patrilineal first cousin of Astyphilos, Kleon ranked higher than the speaker in the order of intestate succession to Astyphilos's estate. So the speaker's claim to be next of kin to Astyphilos depends on his assertion that Kleon's father, Thoudippos, had been adopted into a different **oikos* and had not returned. Isaios gives no information about the timing of this adoption, or the identity of Thoudippos's adoptive father, and it is not easy to see how it fits into the sequence of events. Thoudippos was still a member of his natural father's *oikos*, and of the *deme Araphen, when he quarrelled with his brother Euthykrates over the partition of their paternal estate, which might suggest that he was not adopted until after his natural father's death.[6] But Euthykrates died within days of the fight, and Thoudippos is unlikely to have been adopted after the deaths of both his father and his brother unless there was another brother who is not mentioned in the speech. This casts doubt on the theory, considered by some modern scholars, that Thoudippos was not the son-in-law but the adopted son of Kleon the demagogue, who died in 422 BC,[7] a suggestion which can be

---

[3] *IG* ii² 1622, 417; cited by Davies (1971), 229.

[4] *LGPN Attica* records only two other instances, and there is also one from Boiotia. One of the Athenians is a Thoudippos of Araphen who served as trierarch in the late fourth century (*IG* ii² 1631, 470–3, 592f. and 678–9; cited by Davies (1971), 229). He was probably a son of either Kleon or Anaxippos, and grandson of the Thoudippos who features in Isa. 9.

[5] The possible identification of Thoudippos as a political associate and son-in-law of Kleon was first proposed by Wade-Gery and Merritt (1936), 392, and adopted by Davies (1971), 228–229. It was challenged by Bourriot (1982), partly on chronological grounds and partly because he thought an alliance between two such different families unlikely. Meiggs and Lewis (1988) dispute Wade-Gery and Merritt's chronology of events in 425/4, but not the identity of Thoudippos or the possibility that he married a daughter of Kleon.

[6] Bourriot (1982), 416; cf. Wyse on §17.4.5: "It is implied that the adoption of Thudippos took place after their father's death." Davies (1971), 229, comments that "the fact, if it is a fact, remains mysterious".

[7] See, e.g., Edwards (2007), 151, n. 9: "It has been suggested that … Thudippos was the son-in-law of … Cleon; but it is also possible that this was the family into which the speaker claims that Thudippos had been adopted."

definitively ruled out by the fact that Kleon had a legitimate son.[8] Given that it would have been risky for Isaios to invent the adoption completely, perhaps the most likely explanation is that Thoudippos had been adopted as a young man, but had already returned before his natural father died.

Diagram 3 shows the blood relations of Astyphilos, assuming that Kleon had either remained in or returned to the *oikos* of Thoudippos.

Background and Chronology

Isaios tells us (§14) that before Astyphilos's final expedition to Mytilene, he had first served in Corinth (i.e., presumably, in the Corinthian War of 394–386 BC), then in Thessaly, then 'through the whole of the Theban War', and 'wherever else he heard that an army was being assembled'. The wording makes it clear that he served, at least on some occasions, as a mercenary, but it is possible that his military career also included spells of official service for the **polis*.[9]

From this relatively meagre information approximate dates have been suggested for Astyphilos's birth and death. The traditional view is that he was born at the latest in 413/2 BC, and that his father, Euthykrates, died around 410.[10] Astyphilos's death, and consequently the speech, is generally dated to the mid 360s on the assumption that Astyphilos's final expedition must have taken place after 371, when the Theban War ended. There is no firm evidence of an expedition to Mytilene around this time, but it is possible that Athenian troops under Timotheos landed at Mytilene during operations in the eastern Aegean in 366. More recent scholars have put forward alternative theories, raising the possibility of either an earlier or a later date for the speech.[11] There is, however, no overall consensus, and the evidence is inconclusive.

---

[8] Bourriot (1982), 416. Kleomedon, son of Kleon, married the daughter of Polyaratos of Kholargos who later became the wife of Mantias and mother of Mantitheos, who prosecuted his half-brother Boiotos in Dem. 39 and [Dem. 40] ([Dem.] 40.6, 25).

[9] On the concept of the 'citizen mercenary', who might also fight for his own *polis*, see Hornblower (2002), 194. Athenians who served as mercenaries in the fourth century were not always driven by extreme poverty; cf. Van Wees (2004), 40, citing Xen. *An.* 6.4.8: "Xenophon was probably optimistic in claiming that 'most' of his comrades were like him in fighting to enrich their already respectable estates... but people in that category were certainly not uncommon. One example is Astyphilos... despite owning a sizeable estate in Athens over which his half-brother and cousin proceeded to fight."

[10] Wade-Gery and Merritt (1936), 394, n. 36; their dating is followed by Davies (1971), 229.

[11] Burnett and Edmonson (1960) suggest that Astyphilos served on a garrison at Mytilene which was either established or visited by the mercenary general Khabrias in 375. The theory that Astyphilos died while on garrison duty is developed by Welsh (1991).

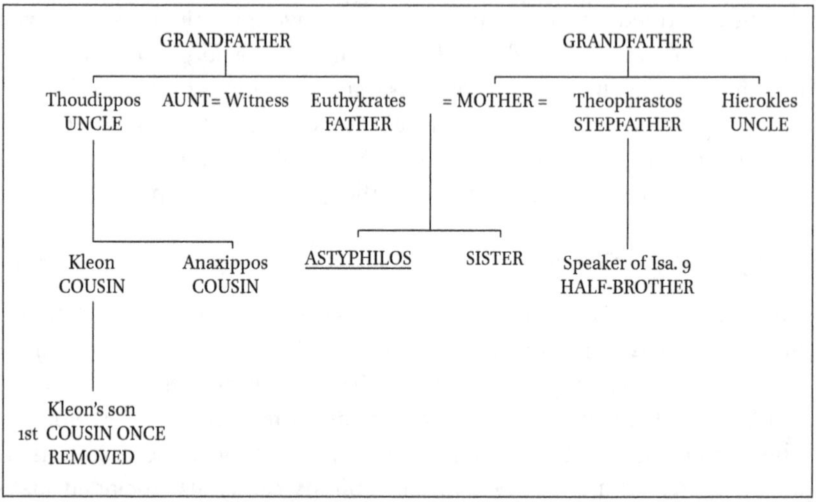

Diagram 3: The family of Astyphilos

The Issues in Dispute and the Order of Intestate Succession

In order to make good his claim, the speaker needs to persuade the **dikastai* not only that Astyphilos did not leave a will adopting Kleon's son (or, if he did, that the will was invalid) but also that he himself has a better claim than Kleon to be Astyphilos's next of kin. The speech is almost entirely devoted to an attack on the will, which the speaker claims is a forgery produced in collusion between Kleon and Hierokles. His strongest line of attack is the accusation that Hierokles went round to Astyphilos's friends offering to produce a forged will in favour of anyone who would give him a share in the estate. He also produces evidence that Kleon's son has been rejected by Astyphilos's *phratry, despite several attempts by Kleon to enrol him as Astyphilos's adopted son. The direct attack on the will is supported by an elaborate series of arguments from probability in which three main points are made. First, it is unlikely that Astyphilos made a will at all, in the circumstances described by the speaker's opponents. Secondly, he is most unlikely to have adopted a son of Kleon, his lifelong enemy following the allegedly fatal quarrel between their fathers.

Rosivach (2005) argues that, from an Athenian perspective, the 'Theban war' may have referred only to the period 378–376, when the war was fought in or near Thebes, or possibly to a later period of warfare after Thebes's defeat of Sparta in 371, in which Athens was aligned with Sparta *against* Thebes.

Finally, if Astyphilos did make a will adopting Kleon's son, he cannot have been in his right mind, so the will is not legally valid.

Towards the end of the speech (§32) the speaker reveals that he is expecting Kleon not only to produce the will but also to stake a claim to the estate on grounds of kinship. Despite the speaker's confidently repeated claim that he alone is entitled to inherit the estate, his status as Astyphilos's intestate heir is in fact open to question. The principle of male precedence gave Kleon, as a patrilineal cousin of Astyphilos, a higher position in the **ankhisteia* than the speaker, a homometric half-brother. The speaker does not deny this, but claims that Kleon has lost his legal relationship with Astyphilos as a result of the adoption of Kleon's father, Thoudippos, into a different *oikos*. No details are given of this adoption and no evidence is offered in support of it. The speaker mentions it only twice, in terms suggesting that it was a fact so well known to everyone that there was no need of proof.[12] It is difficult to believe, however, that Isaios would not have produced testimony on a point that was so fundamental to his client's case, if he could find anyone who was willing to testify to it, especially in a speech where he adduces testimony on so many relatively unimportant issues. So there is a strong suspicion that he was trying to mislead the *dikastai* about the timing of Thoudippos's adoption, and to suppress the fact that he had returned to his natal *oikos*.[13]

Apart from the speaker and Kleon, there may have been other potential claimants to be Astyphilos's intestate heir. Astyphilos's sister, or any legitimate descendant of hers, would have been his closest of kin, but she is mentioned only in passing at §29, and nothing is known of her after she was given in marriage by Theophrastos.[14] A possible inference from Isaios's silence is that she had predeceased Astyphilos, leaving no children. Alternatively, she may have declined to put in a claim to the estate because she accepted that Astyphilos had validly adopted Kleon's son. (If that were the case, it would clearly not be in the speaker's interest to mention it.)[15] A further possibility is that she did survive Astyphilos, but

---

[12] Avramovič (1990), 44, accepts that there was no need for Isaios to dwell on the adoption, arguing that if Thoudippos had not been adopted, Kleon would have been able to claim as Astyphilos's intestate heir instead of following the 'indirect' route of producing a will. This, however, overlooks §32 (on which see commentary), where the speaker anticipates a claim from Kleon on grounds of kinship.

[13] Cf. Isa. 10.7, where witnesses testify that Kyronides had been adopted into the *oikos* of Xenainetos senior, and remained there until his death.

[14] Wyse, 626, thinks it "remarkable that we hear nothing about her or her children".

[15] This contrasts with the position in Isa. 7, where the speaker exploits the fact that Thrasyboulos, a first cousin once removed of Apollodoros, has made no claim to the estate, in support of his own claim as adopted son.

had died before the litigation between Isaios's client and Kleon. She may, in that case, have challenged Kleon's occupation of the estate in an unsuccessful **diadikasia*,[16] and the speaker may have decided to submit his own claim only after her death.

A second potential claimant, not mentioned in the speech at all, is Kleon's brother, Anaxippos (another patrilineal first cousin), who, if the dating of the epigraphic evidence is correct, must have been alive at the time of the trial. There could have been a number of reasons why he did not assert his own claim to a share in the estate, including, perhaps, that he accepted the adoption, or that he had come to a private arrangement with Kleon.

Witness Testimony[17]

The speaker claims (§35) that everything he has said is supported by witnesses, but this is an exaggeration: he has not produced witnesses to the adoption of Thoudippos, or to the fight in which Euthykrates was said to have been fatally wounded by Thoudippos, both of which are crucial to his case and vulnerable to attack from the opposing side. In fact, although this is among the shortest of Isaios's complete speeches, it contains more individual items of testimony (thirteen, in addition to Hierokles's 'oath of ignorance')[18] than any other. Three of these relate to important and contentious elements in the speaker's story: Euthykrates's death-bed denunciation of Thoudippos and his descendants (§19); Hierokles's attempts to 'sell' a forged will (§25); and the rejection of Kleon's son by Astyphilos's phratry (§33). The rest, though relevant to the speaker's case, deal with facts that may appear peripheral, and are unlikely to have been contested by his opponents: Astyphilos's funeral was conducted by his friends and fellow soldiers (§4); Hierokles told the speaker that he had the will, which Astyphilos had left with him before departing for Mytilene (§6); Astyphilos did not summon kinsmen, **phrateres*, fellow *demesmen or friends to witness his will (§9); Astyphilos remained at variance with Kleon throughout his life (§20); Astyphilos never took Kleon with him to the sacrifices (§21); Astyphilos and the speaker went to school together (§28); Theophrastos cultivated Astyphilos's paternal estate (§28), gave his sister in marriage (§29) and introduced him to the confraternity of Herakles

---

16 See on καὶ πρὶν μὲν . . ., §24.

17 For Isaios's deployment of witness testimony in this speech, cf. Griffith-Williams (2008).

18 See the introductory note to §§17–26.

(§30); the speaker never had a quarrel with Astyphilos, with whom he was brought up and who held him in great affection (§30).

The deployment of testimony and the choice of witnesses in this speech have attracted attention from modern scholars. Humphreys, focusing on the identity of the witnesses, characterizes the case as one where the substance of what the witnesses say is "of little significance"; their function is to demonstrate the local community's support for the speaker.[19] Todd makes a similar point, arguing that the absence from Athenian law of a rule that evidence must be relevant to a fact in issue was "presumably because 'who you are' matters more than 'what you say' ".[20] It is certainly true that the speaker would have hoped to gain credibility with the *dikastai* by showing he had the support of Astyphilos's friends, fellow demesmen and *phrateres*, and of respectable citizens such as his teachers. The husband of Astyphilos's aunt, who attested to the words spoken by Euthykrates on his death-bed, must have been a key witness, demonstrating that the speaker was supported by an independent branch of the family not involved in the feud.[21] It does not necessarily follow, however, that who the witnesses were was more important than what they had to say.

As to the volume of testimony, Todd is clearly right to point out that "we cannot simply add up the number of witnesses in a speech and use this as a test of the speaker's veracity".[22] His conclusion that Isaios aims to bolster a weak case by "producing large numbers of witnesses to confirm uncontested points" is, however, only partly justified. On the one hand, the weight of evidence against the will certainly helps to disguise the speaker's vulnerability on the adoption of Thoudippos. Moreover, Isaios maximizes the impact of the testimony on Astyphilos's good relations with Theophrastos and the speaker by itemizing separately several points that he could have dealt with in a single, composite piece of testimony. On the other hand, both Todd and Humphreys underestimate the potential importance of 'uncontested' testimony in inheritance disputes. An Athenian litigant attacking a will would have been expected to show that he was on better terms than his opponent with the testator, as part of his argument that the will was unlikely to be valid.[23] In the present case

19 Humphreys (1985), 191.

20 Todd (1990b), 31.

21 This assumes that the aunt was a sister of Thoudippos and Euthykrates; see on τὸν ἔχοντα…, §19.

22 Todd (1990b), 31.

23 Cf. General Introduction, pp. 19–20.

the speaker's argument would have been more persuasive if he had been able to bring evidence of his more recent relations with Astyphilos, but he can only make use of what evidence he has. Its omission would have significantly weakened his case.

Structure and Style

Isaios makes a complete break with the conventional structure of a forensic oration in this speech, where there is no clear division into sections. The *proem, which merges with the first section of narrative, comprises simply a brief summary of the speaker's case, with none of the rhetorical features, such as the plea of the inexperienced speaker or an appeal for the attention or good will of the *dikastai*, which characterize the introductions to Isaios's other *diadikasia* speeches (1, 7, 8 and 10).[24] Each of these other speeches contains at least two separate passages of narrative: two each in Isa. 1 and 10, three in Isa. 7, and six in Isa. 8, with the beginning of each narrative section marked by the particle *gar*.[25] In Isa. 9, where there are as many as eleven separate narrative passages, *gar* marks the opening of only two: on the death of Euthykrates (§17) and on Astyphilos's upbringing by Theophrastos (§27). Metanarrative interventions along the lines of 'I will try to tell you the facts from the beginning', which regularly signal the opening of the first or main narrative in the other speeches, are also lacking here. The remaining narrative passages in Isa. 9, some of them very short, are interwoven seamlessly with argument, and blocks of narrative (especially in §§27–30) are broken up by testimony. Changes of *focalization, found in all of Isaios's speeches, are at their most frequent here; Kleon, Hierokles, Astyphilos's friends and Astyphilos himself all become focalizers at various points in the narrative.

Another striking feature of the speech is the speaker's tone, which, after a confident and businesslike beginning, becomes noticeably more urgent and emotive as the speech progresses. The change of tone is marked by an increase in the frequency of addresses to the *dikastai*, and by the use of religious language. The epilogue, in particular, includes rhetorical devices, such as a supplication to the *dikastai* and an appeal for their protection

---

[24] Isa. 4 also comes from a *diadikasia*, but its structure is different because it is a supplementary speech delivered by a **sunēgoros*.

[25] Cf. Edwards (2004), 319: Antiphon does not always introduce his narratives with *gar*, but "Narratives in later orators regularly begin with the particle *gar*".

against a more clever speaker, which would more commonly be found in the proem of a conventionally structured speech.[26]

The Strength of the Speaker's Case

The overall effect (and perhaps the intention) of these structural and stylistic features is to obscure the distinction between objective fact and subjective comment or interpretation, making it difficult for the audience at an oral presentation to form an accurate assessment of the strength of the speaker's case. For the modern reader, with more time for analysis and reflection, the style and structure of the speech combine with Isiaos's argumentation and deployment of testimony to suggest that the factual basis of his client's case may have been less impressive than he wants it to appear. It is impossible to judge whether the story of Hierokles and the forged will is factually true, but it is persuasively told and supported by testimony, and may well have convinced the *dikastai* that the will was invalid. It is clear, however, that the speaker would still have been vulnerable on the issue of intestate succession. Isaios's strategy, which must have been highly risky, was apparently to say as little as possible directly on the isssue, in the hope that he had successfully undermined Kleon's credibility in his attack on the will.

Commentary

**Proem (1–2)*

The short, abrupt introduction, which incorporates the opening of the narrative, is unparallelled in Isaios's surviving speeches. Dispensing with the plea of the inexperienced speaker, it conveys the impression of a competent, businesslike man of affairs. The speech is the first at the hearing, and the speaker sets the tone at the outset by giving the **dikastai* no more than the basic facts of his kinship with Astyphilos, without dwelling on them or spelling out the legal implications. Cf. Isa. 11, which begins with a detailed exposition of the law of succession, in order to show how the rule on male precedence operates in the speaker's favour. So, until they hear the opposing case from Kleon, the *dikastai* will have to rely on their own

[26] Cf. Usher (1999), 149.

previous knowledge of the law, which may have varied from individual to individual, for their interpretation of the facts supplied by the speaker.

1 Ἀδελφός μοι ἦν ὁμομήτριος, ὦ ἄνδρες, Ἀστύφιλος ('Astyphilos, gentlemen, was my half-brother, my mother's son'). By admitting straightaway that he and Astyphilos were *homometric half-brothers, which would appear to put him at a disadvantage against Kleon, the speaker creates an impression of openness and honesty. Later he frequently refers to Astyphilos as his brother, but conveniently drops the word 'homometric'. Cf. on ἀνεψιὸς Ἀστυφίλῳ πρὸς πατρός and τῶν τἀδελφοῦ, §2.

On addresses to the **dikastai* in Isaios's speeches, see on Ὤιμην, 7.1. In this speech, in addition to seventeen instances of his preferred mode of address, he twice uses *ō andres dikastai* (§§16 and 37). The resumption of the speech after the reading of testimony is marked by an address at §§7, 26, 28 and 31. The speaker also addresses the *dikastai* four times to engage them in his argumentation about the will (§§11, 12, 14 and 16).

μετὰ τῶν εἰς Μυτιλήνην στρατιωτῶν ἐτελεύτησε ('went abroad with the force that sailed to Mytilene, and died there'). The manner of Astyphilos's death is not clear from this extremely compressed formulation. Cf. Isa. 6.27, where the speaker specifies that Philoktemon died at the hands of the enemy. Since Astyphilos had a private funeral, and since there is no eulogy in the speech of his military prowess, it is more likely that he died accidentally or through illness than that he fell in battle. This is also consistent with the hypothesis that he was stationed at Mytilene on garrison duty. Cf. on καὶ μάλιστα ..., §15.

πειράσομαι δ' ὑμῖν ἐπιδεῖξαι ('I shall try to prove to you'). Cf. on ποιήσομαι ..., 7.4, for the metanarrative narratorial intervention.

ὅπερ ἀντώμοσα ('what I said in my preliminary oath'). The speaker refers to the declaration he made at the **anakrisis*, the truth of which was confirmed by an oath. (See Wyse, 294 on the shift in meaning of *antōmosia*, 'preliminary oath'.) Such references are used by the Athenian orators either to reaffirm what the speaker said in his own declaration or to attack the veracity of his opponent's. Cf., e.g., Isa. 3.6; 5.1; Lys. 23.13; Isok. 16.2; 18.37.

ὡς οὔτε ἐποιήσατο ... κατέλιπεν ('that [Astyphilos] did not adopt a son, did not bequeath any property, and left no will'). For the presentation through negation, here polemical, see on ἐκείνῳ ..., 7.17.

οὐδενὶ ἄλλῳ ἢ ἐμοί ('to no-one else but me'). This emphatic way of saying 'to me' (repeated at §24) also suggests, through negation, that the speaker is denying a right asserted by someone else. He may be referring simply to Kleon and his son, or perhaps he implies the existence of other past or potential claimants. Cf. on καὶ πρὶν μὲν…, §24. Alternatively, it may be that he simply wishes to eliminate the possibility of any counterclaim.

2 [ὁ] Κλέων οὑτοσί ('Kleon here'). The emphatic form of the demonstrative pronoun, which implies that the person referred to was physically present, is commonly used by Athenian litigants of their opponents. It recurs three times in this speech in relation to Kleon (§§3, 10, 17); and cf. 10.1. With reference to the speaker's opponent, it was perhaps spoken in a contemptuous tone, or accompanied by a dismissive gesture, but it was not inherently pejorative; cf. Isa. 4 and 6, where the speakers, both **sunēgoroi*, use it with reference to their own 'clients'; also 2.36, where it refers to the speaker's father-in-law who had testified for him in a **diamarturia*. If it is rarely used elsewhere of a speaker's friends or associates, this may be less because it would be inherently inappropriate than because forensic speakers did not often need to refer to supporters who were present in court.

ἀνεψιὸς Ἀστυφίλῳ πρὸς πατρός ('a first cousin of Astyphilos on his father's side'). Although Kleon was only a cousin of Astyphilos, the patrilineal relationship gave him a higher ranking in the **ankhisteia* than a *homometric half-brother, according to the order of intestate succession set out at Isa. 11.1–2.

ὃν εἰσποιεῖ ἐκείνῳ ('whom he pretends Astyphilos adopted', lit. 'whom [Kleon] is trying [conative present] to adopt for [Astyphilos]'). The speaker uses tendentious language to reflect his denial of the adoption. When *eispoiein*, 'to adopt', is used in the active voice, the subject is not the adoptive father but someone (usually the prospective adoptee's natural father or **kurios*) arranging an adoption or conducting the formalities. Cf. 7.44; 8.40; 10.14, 16, 17; 11.49.

εἰς ἄλλον οἶκον ('into another *oikos*'). It is remarkable that Isaios did not seek to enhance the credibility of his client's story by providing more detailed information about the alleged adoption of Kleon's father. As it is, we are not told either by whom Thoudippos was adopted, or when. Cf. on εἰς τὸν οἶκον τὸν Ἱππολοχίδου, 7.23. From the internal evidence of the speech it may be inferred that, if he was indeed adopted, he had returned to his natal **oikos* before the death of his natural father, since he and Euthykrates were dividing the paternal estate when they quarrelled (§17).

καὶ οὗτοι… Ἀστυφίλῳ ('and they still belong to that *oikos*, so that legally they have no relationship with Astyphilos'). It is crucial to the speaker's case not only that Thoudippos was adopted, but also that he did not return to his natal **oikos*, so that Kleon and his son have no legal relationship to Astyphilos. Cf. on ἐξεποιήθη . . . , 10.4; and, for the conditions under which an adopted son was permitted to return to his natal *oikos*, see on ἐὰν μὴ ἐπανέλθῃ . . . , §33. The implications of Isaios's evasiveness on this matter are discussed in the introduction to this speech, pp. 150–151.

ἐπειδὴ δὲ κατὰ ταῦτα οὐκ ἦν ἀμφισβήτησις ('since they had no claim on these grounds'). The reasoning imputed to Kleon is tendentious. It suits the speaker's argument to imply that Astyphilos would have had no need to adopt Kleon's son if he had known that his estate would pass to Kleon as next of kin. There is some force in this, but not enough to prove that the will must be forged. Adoption of an intestate heir, which had the advantage of preserving the adopter's **oikos* as well as transferring his property, was apparently not uncommon (Rubinstein (1993), 79–80). But even if Kleon's position in the family was unaffected by adoption, he may not have been Astyphilos's intestate heir. We know that Astyphilos had a *homopatric sister (see on μετὰ δὲ ταῦτα . . . , §29), and, in the absence of lineal descendants, she, or a son of hers after her death, would have been Astyphilos's next of kin. So it is possible that, after Kleon's seizure of the estate, he was faced with a challenge which he could not defend on the basis of closer kinship. If that were the case, his only hope of establishing a better claim would have been by pretending that Astyphilos had adopted his son.

διαθήκας, ὦ ἄνδρες, ψευδεῖς ('a forged will, gentlemen'). The formulaic address to the **dikastai* is often used parenthetically, but its interpolation between a noun and its qualifying adjective is striking, and more than usually disruptive to the natural flow of the sentence. The effect is strongly emphatic.

ὡς ἐγὼ οἶμαι ἐπιδείξειν ('as I think I shall prove'). Instead of 'I shall try', as at §1, the speaker here says 'I think', implying a stronger belief in his powers of persuasion. The effect of the parenthesis, nevertheless, is rather to undermine the confidence of his assertion that the will was forged; this is characteristic of the relatively restrained tone in which Isaios attacks his client's opponents throughout this speech.

κατεσκεύασαν ('concocted'). See on κατεσκεύακε, 8.43.

ἀποστερῆσαί ('to rob'). See on ἀποστερῶν, 8.3.

τῶν τἀδελφοῦ ('of my brother's property'). The speaker refers to Astyphilos seven times as 'my brother' instead of using his name (cf. §§4, 7, 24, 29, 30, 34). His emphasis on their relationship supports his claim to the estate, especially since he avoids repeating the point that they were in fact only half-brothers. On Isaios's use of relationship terms instead of names, cf. on ὁ δὲ πάππος…, 7.8 and Κίρων ὁ πάππος, 8.3.

Narrative: The Death and Burial of Astyphilos (*3–6*)

So important was the social obligation to bury one's closest kin and carry out all the appropriate ceremonies, that claims that one party had done so while the other had not were an important feature of Athenian inheritance cases, amounting almost to supplementary evidence that the party in question either was or was not the deceased's legitimate heir or next of kin. (See General Introduction, pp. 21–22.) In this case, at least according to the speaker, neither of the opposing parties buried Astyphilos; the fact that he was buried by friends and fellow soldiers requires the speaker to explain why neither he nor his father did so, and enables him to cast doubt on his opponents' claim to the estate. It is worth remembering that the speaker had no firsthand knowledge of these events, since (as he loses no opportunity to remind the **dikastai*) he was not in Athens at the relevant time.

3 οὐδένα ἄλλον…ἢ αὑτόν ('no-one but himself'). The speaker adapts the words he used to assert his own entitlement to the estate (cf. on οὐδενὶ ἄλλῳ ἢ ἐμοί, §1) in order to present Kleon in a bad light. The difference, as he presents the situation, is that he is pursuing his claim through the courts, whereas Kleon is trying to circumvent the legal process.

ἐπειδὴ τάχιστα ἠγγέλθη ('as soon as the news was reported'). The speaker emphasizes Kleon's undue haste in occupying the estate of Astyphilos. He may have heard about this from the friends and colleagues of Astyphilos who testify at §4, although it is not clear how detailed their evidence was. The speaker's own parents may have been another source of information, if either of them was still alive when he returned to Athens.

τοῦ μὲν πατρὸς τοῦ ἐμοῦ ἀσθενοῦντος ('since my father was ill'). The speaker's father, Theophrastos, was not formally a party to litigation about the estate of a *homometric half-brother, but he has an important rôle in this speech as the benevolent stepfather, and probably former guardian, of Astyphilos. (See on καὶ ἐπαιδεύθη…, §27.) This contrasts with the anonymity of the speaker's father in Isa. 8; cf. on πάλιν ἐκδίδωσι τῷ ἐμῷ πατρί, 8.8.

The speaker mentions three times that his father was ill at the time of Astyphilos's death (cf. on ὁρῶντες τὸν πατέρα…and καὶ τὸν ἐμὸν πατέρα…, §4). The picture of a frail old man, who had to be carried to the funeral to pay his respects to his beloved stepson, both appeals to the sympathy of the **dikastai* and also explains why Theophrastos did not challenge Kleon's right to take possession of the estate, perhaps in anticipation of an argument from Kleon that he encountered no opposition when he entered the estate.

ἐμοῦ δὲ οὐκ ἐπιδημοῦντος ἀλλὰ στρατευομένου ('and I was not at home but on military service abroad'). The speaker's absence from Athens on military service (which he mentions again at §7) explains why he, like his father, was unable to challenge Kleon or to conduct the funeral. It also contributes to the speaker's characterization of himself as a good citizen, playing his part in the defence of the city. The speaker does not say how long he has been away, and it is possible that he is glossing over an interval of several years since the death of Astyphilos. Cf. on οὗτοι μέντοι . . ., §33.

εἰς τὸ χωρίον ἐνεβάτευσε ('entered into possession of the land'). Only a direct descendant of the deceased, or a son adopted *inter vivos*, had the right of **embateusis*, and could meet any challenge from a rival claimant with a **diamarturia*. Cf. Isa. 6.4; [Dem]. 44.46, discussed by Harrison (1968), 156. Any other claimant, including a son adopted by will, had to apply to the court in order to establish his claim by **epidikasia* (cf. Isa. 3.60; [Dem.] 44.19). The implication in the present case is that Kleon acted illegally in installing his son on Astyphilos's property, but it is not clear from the sources whether *embateusis* by a claimant who lacked the proper qualifications was strictly illegal in the sense of being punishable. Cf. Todd (1993), 220. Such a claimant would not, however, have benefited from the procedural protection afforded by the *dikē *exoulēs* or the *diamarturia*, and so would have been vulnerable to challenge by a rival with a better claim.

πρίν τι ὑμᾶς ψηφίσασθαι ('before you had the opportunity to vote'). In what appears to be part of a straightforward statement of the legal position, that Kleon had failed to submit a formal claim to the property through the process of **epidikasia*, there is also a hint that Kleon's action was insulting to the authority of the **dikastai*. The second person plural was conventionally used in references to the *dikastai* who heard (or might have heard) a previous case, with no implication that the composition of the panel was the same. This reflects the Athenian perception of a specific dikastic panel as representatives of the citizenry as a whole, with its collective responsibility for the making and interpretation of laws and the dispensation of justice.

4 τὰ ὀστᾶ τοῦ ἀδελφοῦ ('my brother's remains'). On the speaker's references to Astyphilos as 'my brother', see on τῶν τἀδελφοῦ, §2.

προσποιούμενος πάλαι ὑὸς εἰσπεποιῆσθαι ('who pretends to have been long ago adopted as his son'). This is another example of tendentious language, enabling the speaker to dissociate himself from the claim that Astyphilos had adopted Kleon's son. Isaios plays on the repetition of the syllable *-poi*—in the two verbs (*prospoiesthai*, 'pretend' and *eispoiesthai*, 'adopt') and uses the characteristically vague *palai* to obscure the time-scale of his narrative. Welsh (1991), 138–139, notes that *palai* ('long ago') in Isaios's speeches normally means at least twenty years ago, but that its precise meaning in particular contexts is "elastic".

οὐ προὔθετο οὐδ' ἔθαψεν (did not lay out [the remains] or bury them'). For the presentation through negation, see on ἐκείνῳ ..., 7.17. It is unlikely that Kleon could have claimed that he or his son did bury Astyphilos, as an adopted son would have been expected to do. The speaker's account, if true, makes it more likely that Kleon did not claim that Astyphilos had adopted his son until after the funeral.

οἱ δὲ φίλοι Ἀστυφίλου καὶ οἱ συστρατιῶται ('Astyphilos's friends and fellow soldiers'). These were, presumably, members of Astyphilos's company (*lokhos*); see on λοχαγῶν, §14, for the suggestion that they may have felt a special bond with him, which would explain why they organized the funeral.

ὁρῶντες τὸν πατέρα τὸν ἐμὸν ἀρρωστοῦντα, ἐμὲ δὲ οὐκ ἐπιδημοῦντα ('seeing that my father was ill and I was abroad'). Cf. on τοῦ μὲν πατρὸς ..., §3. The *focalization switches here to Astyphilos's friends and fellow soldiers, but the motivation attributed to them suits the speaker's own purpose.

καὶ τὸν ἐμὸν πατέρα ἀσθενοῦντα ('my father, ill as he was'). Cf. on τοῦ μὲν πατρὸς ..., §3.

εὖ εἰδότες ὅτι ἀσπάζοιτο αὐτὸν Ἀστύφιλος ('well aware that Astyphilos was fond of him'). The speaker is sowing the *seed for his later, more detailed portrayal of the affectionate relationship between Astyphilos and Theophrastos, giving greater authority to his account of his father's relations with Astyphilos by attributing the relevant knowledge to Astyphilos's friends. In the course of the speech 'well aware' is used once (§5) in relation to the speaker himself, and three times to impute knowledge to others: §15 (referring to Astyphilos); §24 (Hierokles), and §35 (the 'weaker parties' to litigation generally). Cf. also the more emphatic 'knowing precisely', §33 (referring to the speaker's opponents). The formulation does not occur elsewhere in Isaios's speeches.

αὐτοὺς τοὺς ἐπιτηδείους τοὺς ἐκείνου μάρτυρας παρέξομαι τῶν παρόντων. ('I shall produce [Astyphilos's] friends, who were among those present, as witnesses'). The identification of these witnesses as 'friends' or 'acquaintances' of Astyphilos indicates that they were not related to him.

For Isaios's deployment of testimony in this speech, see the introduction, pp. 154–156. The unusually large volume of testimony is matched by a wider than usual variety of formulae to introduce it, the majority of which refer to the witnesses rather than their written depositions (cf. on τούτων πρῶτον…, 7.10). Formulae involving the verb *parekhesthai* ('produce') are the most frequent, occurring at §§4, 9, 19, 20 25. This sequence is interrupted, at §§6 and 21, by formulae using *anagignōskein* ('read'); and the remaining testimony is introduced by formulae with *lambanein* ('take') at §§28, and 33, *anabainein* ('come up') at §§28, *anabibazein* ('bring up'), at §30, or *marturein* ('testify') at §§29 and 30.

5 οὐδ' <ἂν> αὐτὸς ἔξαρνος γένοιτο ('even he himself would not deny'). This is the first of several points in the speech at which the speaker anticipates Kleon's response. Even if Kleon cannot deny his failure to bury Astyphilos, he will certainly be expected to explain it.

καρπουμένους τούτους τὰ ἐκείνου ('my opponents enjoying his property'). The tendentious language implies that Kleon and his son were enjoying the benefits of property that did not legally belong to them.

ὁ [δὲ] ὑὸς αὐτοῦ ποιηθείη ὑπὸ Ἀστυφίλου ('his son had been adopted by Astyphilos'). The lacuna preceding this sentence makes the identity of the speaker's interlocutor unclear. Dobree's plausible conjecture, '[Adii Cleonem, qui dixit] suum filium ab Astyphilo adoptatum esse' ('[I went to Kleon, who said that] his son had been adopted by Astyphilos'), was adopted by Wyse and Forster. Given that the events narrated are all denied by the speaker, it is unlikely that he would attribute such statements to a friend or a member of his own branch of the family, so Kleon is the most likely source.

The speaker uses indirect speech to report his conversation. For Isaios's more sparing use of direct speech, see on σὺ δὲ τίς εἶ;…, 8.24.

καὶ τούτων διαθήκας καταλίποι παρὰ Ἱεροκλεῖ Ἰφιστιάδῃ ('and that [Astyphilos] had left a will to that effect with Hierokles of Iphistiadai'). This is the speaker's first reference to Hierokles, who, as the pretended depositary of Astyphilos's will, will be Kleon's principal witness. Undermining the credibility of Hierokles's testimony was a significant challenge for Isaios in writing this speech.

εὖ μὲν εἰδὼς… Κλέωνι ('well aware that he was on very friendly terms with Kleon'). In the first half of an antithesis, the speaker prepares the ground for his allegations of collusion between Kleon and Hierokles. The wording makes the point that Hierokles was not actually related to Kleon, as he was to both the speaker and Astyphilos. This is the first hint of a theme developed throughout the speech: that Hierokles was careless of the ties of kinship, to which the speaker attaches so much importance.

At this point it is the speaker himself who is 'well aware' (cf. on εὖ εἰδότες ..., §4), but he does not explain how he knows about Kleon's friendship with Hierokles, or when or how it originated.

6 τολμῆσαί τι ψεύσασθαι κατὰ Ἀστυφίλου τετελευτηκότος ('dare to lie against the wishes of Astyphilos now he was dead'). The tendentious use of the verbs 'dare' and 'lie' is a typical oratorical device, enabling the speaker to adopt a tone of outraged incredulity at his opponent's temerity. Cf. the opening of Lys. 3, where the speaker launches directly into an indignant attack on his opponent, Simon. In this instance the fact that Astyphilos was dead, and therefore vulnerable, seems to magnify the injury allegedly done to him. The speaker's words may be an oblique reference to the Solonian law forbidding slander against the dead (μὴ λέγειν κακῶς τὸν τεθνεῶτα, Dem. 20.104, discussed by MacDowell (1978), 126–127). In objective terms, it is hard to see that the speaker has any specific grounds for such an accusation, but from his point of view Hierokles's claim that Astyphilos had made a will in favour of his lifelong enemy would constitute 'speaking ill' of the dead. Cf. on Ἀστυφίλου δὲ ..., §23 and Τί οὖν χρή ...., §26.

καὶ ταῦτα θεῖον ὄντα καὶ ἐμοῦ καὶ ἐκείνου ('especially since he was [Astyphilos's] uncle as well as mine'). Isa. 9, according to Cox (1998), 124, is "one of the rare instances of a public dispute between nephew and maternal uncle". (On the traditionally strong bond of affection in ancient Greece between mother's brother and sister's son, see on εἴς τε γὰρ ..., 7.34.) On the speaker's account, therefore, the behaviour of Hierokles is all the more shocking in view of his relationship as maternal uncle not only to the speaker but also to Astyphilos himself. Isaios's pursuit of this line is a risky strategy; he was clearly aware of the possible counter-argument that if Astyphilos did make a will in favour of Kleon's son, it would have been perfectly natural for him to entrust it to Hierokles, but perhaps he hoped to secure the support of the *_dikastai_ by being the first to allude to the point.

ὡς δὲ ταῦτ' ἔλεγεν, ἀνάγνωθί μοι ταύτην τὴν μαρτυρίαν ('And to prove that he said this, please read this testimony'). This witness was, presumably, not a chance bystander but a 'formal witness' invited by the speaker to accompany him when he went to speak to Hierokles. Cf. on οἰκείων ..., 8.21. The anonymity of this witness may suggest that he was not a member of the family. The testimony seems to add little to the speaker's case, since it is unlikely that Hierokles would challenge his account of what was said.

On the formulae used to introduce testimony in this speech, see on αὐτοὺς τοὺς ἐπιτηδείους..., §4. On the imperative 'read' as an indication of the change from oral to written testimony in the Athenian courts, see on τούτων πρῶτον..., 7.10.

Argument: The Will (*7–16*)

The speaker has no direct evidence that the will was forged, so he has to resort to arguments from probability. He makes three points. First, if Astyphilos had really made a will, he would have had it witnessed by his close relations and friends—none of whom, in fact, know anything about it. Secondly, since Astyphilos had served on several previous campaigns without leaving a will, it would be a remarkable coincidence if he had made one just before the campaign on which he died. Thirdly, Astyphilos would never have made a will in favour of Kleon's son because Kleon was his lifelong enemy.

7 οὐδεὶς τῶν οἰκείων ('none of [Astyphilos's] relatives'). The implication is that the speaker would have called on Astyphilos's relations as witnesses if any of them had been present when he died. Cf. on ἀλλὰ πρῶτον..., §8. This reflects the Athenians' preference for testimony from family members on matters concerning the family, although in other circumstances neutral witnesses would have carried more conviction. Cf. Humphreys (1986), 88.

ὅτε ὁ ἀδελφὸς ἐτελεύτησεν ('when my brother died'). Cf. on τῶν τἀδελφοῦ, §2.

οὔτε ἐγὼ ἐπεδήμουν ('and I was abroad'). Cf. on ἐμοῦ δὲ οὐκ..., §3. *Pace* Wyse ("I cannot discover any force in the speaker's statement that he was not in Athens when the bones arrived") this repetition serves to remind the **dikastai* that the speaker cannot be blamed for not having buried Astyphilos.

εἰκὸς γὰρ ('for it is reasonable'). Isaios starts the argument with an explicit premise, building up an idealized picture of the precautions Astyphilos ought to have taken in order to ensure that his will would be accepted as valid before arguing that, because these precautions were not taken, the will cannot be genuine.

καὶ ἐπὶ τοὺς βωμοὺς... τὰ νομιζόμενα ποιήσει ('and to have access to his ancestral altars and perform the customary rites after his death for him and his ancestors'). Cf. on καὶ πάντα τὰ νομιζόμενα, 7.30.

8 εἰ μὴ…ποιοῖτο ('if he did not make his will without the presence of his relatives'). This somewhat awkward example of presentation through negation (see on ἐκείνῳ…, §7.17), using 'not without' instead of the more straightforward 'with', makes the point that, according to Kleon, Astyphilos did make his will without the presence of family members.

ἀλλὰ πρῶτον…πλείστους ('but having first summoned his kinsmen, then the members of his *phratry and *deme, and then as many as possible of his other acquaintances'). The speaker lists, in descending order of importance, the kinds of people who would carry most weight as witnesses to a will. By carefully amassing details of this kind, he sets up a demanding ideal against which to judge his opponents' statements.

9 οὐδὲν φαίνεται τοιοῦτον ποιήσας ('clearly did nothing like this'). This is a form of presentation through negation (see on ἐκείνῳ…, 7.17) characteristic of forensic oratory: the speaker sets up an expectation of what Astyphilos ought to have done, then denies emphatically that he did it in order to make his point. Cf. Isa. 10.5; Lys.15.6; Dem. 20.94; 24.19, 25; 27.61; 54.29; [Dem.] 48.45.

εἰ μή τις ἄρα ὑπὸ τούτων πέπεισται ὁμολογεῖν παρεῖναι ('unless, indeed, anyone has been suborned by them to say that he was present'). The speaker is hedging his bets: having confidently claimed that none of Astyphilos's friends and relations knew anything about a will, he now says that if any of them does claim to have witnessed it, he or they must have been suborned by Kleon. This is a potentially damaging concession; the speaker must have known or feared that Kleon would produce a credible witness to the will. There is a further possibility that Kleon will turn the accusation of false testimony against the speaker's own witnesses.

αὐτὸς ('myself'). The pronoun is strongly emphatic: the speaker asserts that he—unlike his opponent—has the testimony of Astyphilos's family and friends on his side.

πάντας τούτους μαρτυροῦντας παρέξομαι ('I shall produce all these people as witnesses'). Cf. on αὐτοὺς τοὺς ἐπιτηδείους…, §4. Here, the speaker claims to produce all the people who, in his view, ought to have witnessed the will if it was genuinely made by Astyphilos. This might be more credible if he said who they were, and if it did not contradict his concession in the previous sentence. It seems, in any event, unlikely that Astyphilos's surviving kinsmen were numerous, so most of the speaker's witnesses were probably friends or fellow *demesmen rather than relations. It is also possible that some of them testified on more than one issue, so that the speaker had fewer witnesses in total than might appear at first reading of the speech. Cf. comments on [Dem.] 43 in Humphreys (1986), 65–66.

10 Ἴσως τοίνυν Κλέων οὑτοσὶ φήσει ('Perhaps Kleon here will say'). The future tense indicates that this was the first speech at the court hearing: the speaker anticipates Kleon's argument that negative evidence from people who know nothing about Astyphilos's will is worthless. (On the disingenuous use of 'perhaps', and on **prokatalēpsis* generally, see the introductory note to 10.8–17.) The speaker's witnesses cannot positively testify that Astyphilos did not make a will; they can only cast doubt on the existence of a will by saying that they did not know of one. Cf. Isa. 6.11 where the speaker brings witnesses to attest that they knew nothing of Euktemon's supposed second marriage.

τεκμηρίοις ('proofs'). See on μεγάλα γὰρ τεκμήρια, 7.11.

βεβαιοτέραν ... οἱ μηδὲν προσήκοντες ('you should attach more weight to the evidence of his intimate friends ... than to those who have no connection with him'). The speaker, in reply, emphasizes the standing of his witnesses as friends and relations of Astyphilos; even their negative evidence is of more value than the positive testimony of the strangers who, according to Kleon, did witness the making of the will. This is one example of the importance attached by the speaker to kinship; cf. his description of those to whom Hierokles allegedly made his offer of a forged will as unrelated to Astyphilos (§24). His deployment of this argument illustrates the way in which each side chooses the arguments that best support its case.

11 ὦ ἄνδρες ('gentlemen'). Cf. on Ἀδελφός ..., §1.

καὶ τοὺς ἄλλους, ὅτῳ περ ἔμβραχυ ᾔδει Ἀστύφιλον χρώμενον ('and any other people with whom he knew Astyphilos was at all intimate'). The speaker places a heavy responsibility on Kleon: if none of Astyphilos's friends or relations were available to witness the will, he should still have made sure it was witnessed by someone who knew him. The implication is that those who did witness the will (according to Kleon) were complete strangers, and therefore completely unreliable.

κωλῦσαι ... τὰ ἑαυτοῦ ('For no-one could have prevented him from giving his property to whoever he wished'). The speaker makes it clear by this indirect reference to the law of Solon that his argument is directed specifically against the validity of the will produced by Kleon, not against Astyphilos's right to dispose of his property as he wished. Cf. General Introduction, pp. 14–15.

οὐ λάθρᾳ ('not in secret'). Isaios plays to the Athenians' suspicion of secrecy; a good citizen conducted his business openly. For *lathra* ('in secret') in association with shameful or dishonest actions, cf., e.g., Antiph. 6.18; Dem. 24.48; 34.6; 57.3; Aiskhin. 1.90.

12 ἔτι δ', ὦ ἄνδρες ('Furthermore, gentlemen'). Cf. on Ἀδελφός…, §1. In this and the following section the argumentation is carefully loaded to make the opponents' version of events (as the speaker presents it) appear incredible. At one extreme, if Astyphilos had wanted to keep his will secret, he would not have asked anyone to witness it. On the other hand, he might have invited kinsmen, but there would have been no point at all in having a will witnessed by strangers. In fact, it is unlikely that the opponents were going to say that he did so, and this again suggests that they did have credible witnesses to the will, including, presumably, Hierokles. Cf. on εἰ μή τις…, §9.

13 οὐ γὰρ <ἂν> ἡγοῦμαι…καταλιπεῖν ('For my part, I do not believe that anyone adopting a son would have ventured to summon as witnesses anyone except those with whom he was about to leave that son'). The sweeping generalization is characteristic of argumentation in forensic oratory; see on οὐδεὶς γὰρ πώποτε…, §33 and cf., e.g., Isa. 3.14, 61; 6.28. This particular argument fits well with the speaker's repeated emphasis on the importance of kinship, but it makes no allowances for individual character or circumstances. If Astyphilos did make a will immediately before his last campaign, he may not have had time to bring the 'best' witnesses together: perhaps some of them were away, or ill, or perhaps he preferred not to involve them because he knew that his choice of adopted son would upset them.

καὶ ἱερῶν…χρόνον ('to participate in their religious and civic acts in the future in his place'). The speaker emphasizes the religious as well as the civic aspects of adoption: if Astyphilos had adopted a son, he would have been appointing not just an heir to his property, but someone to take over his own place in the shared rites of his family. On the importance of this in fourth century Athens, see, e.g., Harrison (1968), 123.

νόμου γε ὄντος ἐξεῖναι ὅτῳ βούλοιτο δοῦναι τὰ ἑαυτοῦ ('since there is a law permitting a man to bequeath his property to anyone he wishes'). Cf. on κῶλυσαι…, §11, where the reference to Solon's law on freedom of testamentary disposition was less direct.

14 ἐξέπλει στρατευόμενος ('when he was sailing on military service'). Rosivach (2005), 195 points out that the "language of soldiers and soldiering" in this and the following two sentences (*strateuomenos, estrateusato, strateuma, strateia*) "suits either citizen or mercenary soldiering, and so blurs the distinction between the two, a useful confusion since it subtly suggests that there was something patriotic about Astyphilos' soldiering".

ἔπειτα εἰς Θετταλίαν ('then to Thessaly'). There is no surviving record of Athenian military activity in Thessaly between 390 and 378 BC, but Astyphilos may have served as a mercenary under Jason, tyrant of Pherai, whose military activities are first recorded in 379 and who was assassinated in 370. Cf. Rosivach (2005), 196.

ἔτι δὲ τὸν Θηβαϊκὸν πόλεμον ἅπαντα ('and in addition throughout the Theban war'). Most commentators have taken this as a reference to the war of 378–371 in which Athens joined forces with Thebes against Sparta, but Rosivach (2005), 197, points out that this is the period in which Astyphilos is most likely to have been in Thessaly. He argues that from an Athenian perspective, 'the Theban war' may have referred only to the years 378–376, when the war was fought in or near Thebes; alternatively, it may refer to a later period of warfare after Thebes's defeat of Sparta in 371, in which Athens was aligned with Sparta against Thebes. The chronology is important, since 'the end of the Theban war' provides the *terminus a quo* for Astyphilos's final expedition to Mytilene.

καὶ ἄλλοσε … συλλεγόμενον ('and wherever else he heard that an army was being collected'). This is the strongest indication that Astyphilos fought as a mercenary.

λοχαγῶν ('as a *lokhagos*'). A *lokhagos*, or 'company commander', was the leader of a *lokhos*, "a body of some hundred men and the principal subunit within a mercenary corps, to judge from Xenophon's *Anabasis*" (Rosivach (2005), 198). Rosivach argues that Astyphilos's status as *lokhagos* "says something about his competence as a soldier, a competence presumably developed with experience over time. Indeed it is also possible that Astyphilos recruited his *lokhos* himself, and that his men thus felt a special bond with him".

καὶ οὐδ' ἐν μιᾷ τούτων τῶν ἐξόδων διαθήκας κατέλιπεν ('yet he did not leave a will on departure for any of these campaigns'). Isaios could not credibly argue that no-one would think of making a will immediately before setting off on military service. (Six out of the ten attested Athenian cases of testamentary adoption were carried out by men who later died in war or while travelling; cf. Rubinstein (1993), 23.) Instead, he tries to convince the **dikastai* that Astyphilos would not have done so just before the very expedition which resulted in his death, focusing on specific aspects of the military situation that made it less dangerous than Astyphilos's earlier campaigns. In reality—if, indeed, it is true that he had never previously made a will (cf. Wyse, 635)—there may have been something in Astyphilos's personal circumstances that affected the timing of his will. Perhaps he had been ill, or was simply becoming more conscious of his mortality with advancing age. He may have been influenced by the death of a friend or fellow soldier, especially if intestacy had caused problems. Since we are told nothing about Astyphilos's marital status in the speech, it is possible that he had had hopes of producing a natural heir, or even that he had a son who had recently died. The death of his intestate heir (perhaps his sister or a son of hers) is another possible reason, as is a wish to disrupt the intestate succession because of a recent quarrel within the family.

15 τῷ οὖν ἂν ὑμῶν φανείη πιστόν ('which of you could believe it possible?'). The tendentious question (cf. Dem. 30.20, 33) encourages a sceptical attitude among the **dikastai* towards all the propositions in this single, long sentence.

εὖ εἰδότος ('well aware'). Cf. on εὖ εἰδότες ..., §4.

καὶ μάλιστα ἐκ ταύτης τῆς στρατείας ἐλπίζοντα σωθήσεσθαι ('with every hope of returning safely from this campaign'). The claim that Astyphilos was at less risk than on previous campaigns and expected to return safely is consistent with the hypothesis, proposed by Burnett and Edmonson (1960) and elaborated by Welsh (1991), that he was stationed at Mytilene on garrison duty.

16 ὦ ἄνδρες δικασταί ('judges') See on Ἀδελφός ..., §1. Isaios, when addressing the **dikastai* in his inheritance speeches, shows a marked preference for the formula *ō andres* ('gentlemen'). This is the first of two instances in this speech of *ō andres dikastai* ('judges', equivalent to 'gentlemen of the jury' in a modern criminal court). There is apparently no substantive difference in meaning, but it may be significant that he reminds his audience of their specifically judicial function at a point where the speech is approaching a crux, and again, just before the end of the whole speech (§37). Cf. Isa. 4.30 and 9.27, where *ō andres dikastai* also occurs near the end of the speech; and the highly unusual *andres dikastai* (without the interjection) at 3.1. Other *logographers, including Lysias and Demosthenes, use *ō andres dikastai* routinely to address a dikastic court, but Plato's Socrates tendentiously reserves it for those of the *dikastai* who have shown themselves worthy of the title by voting for his acquittal (*Apol.* 40a, discussed by Dickey (1996), 177–180). Martin (2006) argues that *ō andres dikastai* in the Demosthenic corpus is consistently used in passages where the *dikastai* are specifically reminded of their judicial tasks.

ἔτι μείζω τεκμήρια ('yet stronger proofs'). See on μεγάλα γὰρ τεκμήρια, 7.11.

καὶ οὕτω σφόδρα καὶ δικαίως μισοῦντα τοῦτον ('and hating him so much and with such justification'). The speaker twice describes Astyphilos as 'hating' Kleon; cf. on Δοκεῖ..., §31. The verb *misein* ('hate') does not occur elsewhere in Isaios's **diadikasia* speeches (but cf. 3.66). Here, the adverb 'justly' puts a tendentious slant on the description.

Narrative and Testimony: The Death of Euthykrates and the Family Feud (17–21)

The allegation that Thoudippos caused the death of Euthykrates, leading to an irreconcilable enmity between Astyphilos and Kleon, is central to the speaker's case. Yet he can produce no witnesses to the assault, although he claims that it was seen by a number of fellow demesmen of Euthykrates and Thoudippos, and by Euthykrates's brother-in-law, Hierokles (a member of a different *deme), whom he attempts to call as a witness. Following the usual procedure, the speaker has drafted a witness statement which Hierokles must either affirm or 'swear away' (*exomnumai*) at the trial. The 'oath of ignorance' (*exōmosia*) probably took the form of a statement that the witness had no knowledge of the events to which he was invited to testify (cf. Carey (1995)). The procedure was presumably designed to protect witnesses against prosecution for false testimony, but it was clearly open to abuse by litigants. Martin (2008), 66, notes the use of the *exōmosia* as an anticipatory device, pointing out that each of the five extant examples comes from the speech delivered first at a trial.

17 λέγεται ('is said'). The speaker expresses the allegation in terms of rumour rather than fact.

ἐν τῇ νεμήσει τοῦ χωρίου ('in the division of their land'). According to the speaker, Thoudippos and Euthykrates apparently quarrelled over the division of their father's land, which, under the Athenian system of partible inheritance, they would have inherited in equal shares when he died. (See General Introduction, pp. 12–13, and cf. Wyse, *ad loc.*, on the division of the paternal estate as "a proverbial source of strife among brothers".) It may not be accidental that the speaker depicts both Kleon and his father as men prepared to go to any length in pursuit of an inheritance dispute.

οὐ πολλαῖς ἡμέραις ὕστερον ('a few days later'). The interval between the assault and Euthykrates's death, and the speaker's vagueness as to its duration, may perhaps suggest some doubt about causation.

18 καὶ Ἀραφηνίων καὶ πολλοὶ τῶν τότε συγγεωργούντων ('many of the Araphenians who were working on the land with them at the time'). The

speaker suggests that fellow *demesmen who were working in the fields were potential witnesses to the fight between Thoudippos and Euthykrates. This implies that it took place while they were actually in the process of inspecting the land or marking out the boundaries between their holdings.

διαρρήδην δὲ ... παρασχοίμην ('but I could not find anyone to give positive testimony to you in so grave a matter'). The speaker implies that there are many potential witnesses to the assault on Euthykrates, but he struggles to find a convincing explanation of their unwillingness to come forward. Perhaps he is hinting at a reluctance among Thoudippos's fellow *demesmen to testify against a member of such an influential family, or even at intimidation of potential witnesses (cf. Whitehead (1986), 228). It is open to question how many of these there really were; whatever lies behind the speaker's story, it would have been easy for him to argue, like the speaker of Isa. 8, that it was difficult to find witnesses to events that happened more than forty years ago. In this case, however, it appears to be part of Isaios's strategy to minimize the length of time elapsed, to discourage speculation about more recent relations within the family.

καὶ γὰρ αὐτὸν τυπτόμενον ἰδὼν Ἱεροκλῆς ('Hierokles saw him being struck'). The speaker has the difficult, and self-imposed, task of persuading the **dikastai* that Hierokles saw the fight between Thoudippos and Euthykrates, knowing that Hierokles himself will deny it. The advantage of this tactic is that it enables him to present Hierokles as an inveterate liar, but he does not explain how Hierokles, who was not a fellow *demesman of Euthykrates and Thoudippos, came to witness the event.

φάσκων ('asserting'). The speaker is careful to distance himself from Hierokles's claim that Astyphilos deposited a will with him. The concision with which he achieves this, using a participial construction, is typical of Isaios's economical use of language.

ἐναντία ταῖς διαθήκαις ('against the will'). The speaker's imputation of motive to Hierokles is highly tendentious, insinuating that Hierokles has a vested interest in rejecting the testimony. Isaios's reasoning is that the will must be a forgery because of the enmity between Astyphilos and Kleon, and that Hierokles would effectively be conceding this if he admitted that he had witnessed the fight between Euthykrates and Thoudippos. The forced logic is an indication of the difficulty for Isaios of proving his client's case, in the absence of any solid evidence.

καὶ κάλει Ἱεροκλέα ('and call Hierokles'). Formulae based on the verb *kalein* ('call') are among those most commonly used by Isaios, as by the other orators, to introduce witnesses. In this speech it occurs only here, where it is natural to use the imperative *kalei* with the name of a specific witness. No witnesses are summoned by name in Isaios's other **diadikasia* speeches, but Protarkhides is summoned at 5.27, and Nikodemos is named, in Isa. 3, as a witness who testified in the proceedings that gave rise to the *dikē *pseudomarturiōn*.

ἵνα ἐναντίον τούτων μαρτυρήσῃ ἢ ἐξομόσηται ('so that he may either testify before the court or swear the oath of ignorance'). In accordance with regular Athenian procedure, Hierokles as witness would have had no opportunity to modify the statement prepared for him by the speaker, or to substitute his own version of events. He must either accept the statement as written or take the oath of ignorance. The refusal of a key witness to testify must have been potentially damaging, but Isaios has manipulated the procedure (like the challenge to produce slaves for torture in Isa. 8) to create an illusion of evidence that does not actually exist. Cf. Martin (2008), 67, on the "psychological value" of having the evidence read out even though the witness does not accept it: "the speaker can draw on 'artless proofs' without actually having them." The stratagem also contributes to Isaios's aim of discrediting Hierokles's testimony, by enabling the speaker to denounce him as a liar.

19 τοῦ γὰρ αὐτοῦ . . . γενόμενα ('for it is quite in character for the same man to swear that he is ignorant of facts he really knows and to be willing to testify to the truth of what has never really happened'). The speaker wants the **dikastai* to believe that Hierokles has refused to testify to the fight between Thoudippos and Euthykrates because it would undermine his claim that Astyphilos left a will in favour of Kleon's son. (See on ἐναντία ταῖς διαθήκαις, §18.) It is, of course, equally possible that Hierokles did not witness the assault, and that in taking the oath of ignorance he is simply telling the truth.

πίστιν ἐθέλειν ἐπιθεῖναι ('to be willing to testify'). Both Forster's translation, 'to be willing to pledge his oath', and Edwards's 'swear an oath' imply that Hierokles would have had to take an oath before giving positive testimony (as distinct from the 'oath of ignorance' discussed above). But the word *pistis* is not normally associated with oath-taking, and there is no independent evidence that Athenian witnesses testified on oath except in homicide cases.

ἐπέσκηψε ('solemnly enjoined'). There are four other instances in the Attic orators (all cited by Karabélias (1992), 62) of the verb *episkēptein* used of someone conveying his wishes to friends and family in the event of his death. The subject of such a solemn injunction (*episkēpsis*) may be the provision of a dowry for a daughter or surviving wife (Lys. 32.6), arrangements for a daughter's marriage (Isa. 3.69), the posthumous adoption of a daughter's as yet unborn son (Isa. 3.73), or the renting of an orphan's house (Dem. 28.15).

τὸν ἔχοντα τὴν τηθίδα τοῦ Ἀστυφίλου ('the husband of Astyphilos's aunt'). The Greek word *tēthis*, like the English 'aunt', can be used of either a father's sister or a mother's sister (cf. Thompson (1971), 111), but it seems most likely that Astyphilos's aunt was a sister of Euthykrates and Thoudippos (and therefore also the aunt of Kleon). If she had been the sister of Astyphilos's mother, and of Hierokles, the speaker might have been expected to refer to his own kinship with her, but the possibility that she was a maternal aunt of both Astyphilos and the speaker cannot be entirely ruled out; cf. Griffith-Williams (2008), 257. Her husband is the only witness apart from Hierokles to be identified as a member of the family, albeit he is not actually named, and this probably reflects the importance to the speaker of his testimony. It is not clear whether the witness was present at the scene himself, or whether his evidence was given on behalf of his wife, but in either event her implicit support for the speaker's case, against that of her nephew Kleon, could have weighed heavily in his favour with the **dikastai*. On an objective view the evidential value of this testimony, confirming that the dying Euthykrates forbade Thoudippos and his descendants to approach his tomb, is considerably less than that of Hierokles's statement that Astyphilos deposited a will with him. In the context of Isaios's argument, however, it is intended to undermine the validity of the will.

μάρτυρα παρέξομαι ('I shall produce as a witness'). Cf. on αὐτοὺς τοὺς ἐπιτηδείους…, §4.

20 Ἀκούων…ἐκ παιδίου ('hearing in childhood'). Astyphilos was too young to remember the circumstances of his father's death, but heard about them from members of his family.

οὐδὲ πώποτε διελέχθη Κλέωνι, ἀλλὰ πρότερον ἐτελεύτησεν ('never spoke to Kleon for the rest of his life'). The literal meaning is 'never spoke to Kleon, but first died'. Wyse points out the illogicality of this expression, which he compares to the construction using *prin* ('before') with the infinitive to denote an event that could not or did not happen.

οὐχ ἡγούμενος ὅσιον εἶναι ('thinking that it was impious'). Isaios makes Astyphilos the *focalizer, without explaining how the speaker knew what Astyphilos was thinking. It is conceivable, though, that Astyphilos might have told his brother and other members of the family that he thought it would be impious for him to speak to Kleon. The religious vocabulary underlines the strength of the enmity between the cousins; the word *hosion* is not used in this way elsewhere in Isaios's speeches.

τὸν ἅπαντα χρόνον ('the whole time'). The vague phrase is intended to convey that Astyphilos remained at enmity with Kleon for the rest of his life. Cf. §27, where the same words clearly refer to a period shorter than a whole lifetime.

μάρτυρας παρέξομαι ('I shall produce witnesses'). Cf. on αὐτοὺς τοὺς ἐπιτηδείους..., §4. Given the importance that the speaker attaches, elsewhere in the speech, to kinship, one might have expected him to identify these particular witnesses if they had been related to Astyphilos. It is reasonable to assume, therefore, that they were friends or acquaintances. (In fact, the witnesses in Isaios's inheritance speeches are seldom positively identified as kinsmen of the deceased, but cf. Isa. 12.5–6, where Euphiletos's claim to Athenian citizenship is said to have been supported by his brothers-in-law and maternal uncle, and three named kinsmen whose relationship to him is not specified. Cf. also the identification of witnesses at Dem. 57.20–22, another citizenship case.) The substance of this testimony is unclear, but the witnesses could probably say little more than that they knew of no contact between Astyphilos and Kleon. If they had been able to provide positive evidence of quarrels or hostility, Isaios would surely have said so.

21 Εἰς τὰς θυσίας ('to the sacrifices'). For the significance of attendance at sacrifices, see the introductory note to 8.15–17, and cf. on Εἰς τοίνυν..., §30.

ἔπειτα ἀνεψιόν ('and also his cousin'). The speaker was careful to point out in his introduction that, following the adoption of Thoudippos into a different **oikos*, Kleon was no longer legally related to Astyphilos. It seems here that he has overlooked this point to suit his own convenience, unless Thoudippos had not yet been adopted at the time to which he is referring, or had already returned to his natal *oikos*.

ἔτι δὲ τὸν ὑὸν τὸν τούτου μέλλοντα ποιεῖσθαι ('and, moreover, intending to adopt his son'). Perhaps it is true that Astyphilos would have been all the more likely to attend the sacrifices in Kleon's company if he intended to adopt his son, but we do not know either the date of the sacrifices in question or when Astyphilos decided on the adoption. He may not have thought of adopting Kleon's son until shortly before his departure for Mytilene, when he is said to have made the will. In any event it is unlikely that the speaker would have had the knowledge he claims about Astyphilos's state of mind, and this seems like a detail invented to make his story sound more convincing.

ὁπότε περ ἐπιδημοίη ('whenever he was at home'). We do not know how often Astyphilos's military career gave him the opportunity to return to Athens and attend the sacrifices. Cf. Isa. 4.8, where it is said that Nikostratos had been away on service as a mercenary for eleven years before his death.

ὡς τοίνυν οὐδέποτ' ἦλθε μετ' αὐτοῦ ('that he was never accompanied by him'). The evidential value of this negative testimony may be questionable (cf. on Ἴσως τοίνυν . . ., §10), but it does serve more than one tactical purpose. First, even if Kleon does not dispute the speaker's account, he may feel obliged to explain why he did not accompany Astyphilos to the sacrifices, using up some of his allotted time on a relatively insignificant point. Secondly, the **dikastai* may take it as a point in the speaker's favour that he has persuaded at least some of Kleon's fellow *demesmen to testify, even on an uncontentious issue. Finally, it contributes to Isaios's strategy of using as much testimony as possible (cf. on καὶ μάρτυρας . . ., §35.)

μαρτυρίαν ἀναγνώσεται ('will read out the testimony'). See on αὐτοὺς τοὺς ἐπιτηδείους . . ., §4, and, on the use of *anagignōskein*, cf. on ὡς δὲ ταῦτ' ἔλεγεν . . ., §6.

Argument, Narrative and Testimony: The Attack on Hierokles (22–26)

The speaker deliberately turns his attention from Kleon to Hierokles, whom he accuses of touting a forged will in return for a share in the estate. Like Diokles in Isa. 8, Hierokles, although not formally the speaker's opponent, is presented as the real villain. In this case, however, Isaios's blackening of his character does not go beyond the circumstances of the case. Perhaps this relative restraint is explained by the speaker's own kinship with Hierokles, but there may have been something about the people involved in this case that made it advantageous for the speaker to deflect his attack away from his main opponent. Perhaps it was considered dangerous to confront a member of such a powerful family, or Kleon himself may have been a popular figure whom the **dikastai* would have been inclined to support. Cf. the reluctance of potential witnesses to testify, discussed at §18.

22 καὶ τί δεῖ τοῦτον λέγειν; ('Yet why should I speak of [Kleon]?'). The rhetorical question formally marks the beginning of the speaker's attack on Hierokles.

θεῖος ὢν καὶ <ἐκείνῳ καὶ> ἐμοί ('the uncle of both [Astyphilos] and me'). The speaker again draws attention to Hierokles's relationship both to himself and to Astyphilos.

23 καίτοι, Ἱερόκλεις ('And yet, Hierokles'). As mentioned in the General Introduction pp. 9–10, *apostrophe to an opponent is a rhetorical device used sparingly by Isaios. Apart from this, the only examples are 3.40, 69–71; 5.43; 6.53 (all cited by Denommé (1974b), 136–138); and 6.25. Here the speaker accuses Hierokles directly of ingratitude for (unspecified) favours received from Astyphilos and Theophrastos, of trying to deprive the speaker of what is lawfully due to him, and of slandering the memory of Astyphilos. The diatribe adds nothing of substance to the speaker's allegations against his opponents, but raises the emotional tone of the speech and makes Hierokles rather than Kleon the centre of attention.

πολλὰ κἀγαθὰ παθὼν ὑπὸ Θεοφράστου τοῦ πατρὸς τοῦ ἐμοῦ ('having received many kindnesses from my father Theophrastos'). In contrast to the list of Theophrastos's kindnesses to Astyphilos (§§28–30), the nature of his favours to Hierokles is unspecified. The speaker has already mentioned his father three times, and now refers to him by name (twice in §23 and once in §27). Isaios is generally sparing in his use of personal names, recording only those which are essential for his narrative (cf. Blass (1892), 503). In this case he wants the jury to remember Theophrastos as the benefactor of Hierokles and Astyphilos, and the object of the latter's affection and loyalty. Cf. on πάλιν ἐκδίδωσι…, 8.8, for the very different approach in Isa. 8.

οὐδετέρῳ αὐτοῖν τὴν ἀξίαν χάριν ἀποδίδως ('not making the appropriate repayment to either of them'). The speaker accuses Hierokles of violating "an important structuring principle in ancient Greek social relationships. The ideology of *kharis* insisted that a gift obligated the recipient until they returned the favor" (Johnstone (1999), 100). Aristotle, in a discussion of reciprocity and justice, says that the recipient of *kharis* is obliged not merely to repay it, but to give it on his own initiative in the future (*Nic. Eth.* 5.5.7). Cf. ταύτην τὴν χάριν ἀποδοῖτε, 7.41.

ἐμὲ…ἀποστερεῖς ('you are trying to rob me'). See on ἀποστερῶν, 8.3. The present tense is conative.

ἅ μοι οἱ νόμοι ἔδοσαν ('which the laws have given me'). The conventional appeal to 'the laws' (rather than to any specific law relevant to the issues in dispute) gives the speaker a spurious authority; whether his claim is in accordance with the law is precisely what he has to prove. It also implies a criticism of Hierokles for flouting the law.

Ἀστυφίλου δὲ τεθνεῶτος καταψεύδῃ ('and you are slandering the dead Astyphilos'). Cf. on τολμῆσαί τι ψεύσασθαι…, §6.

24 καὶ πρὶν μὲν ληχθῆναι τοῦ κλήρου ('before any claim was made to the estate'). The phrase *langkhanein tou klērou* ('claim the estate') is a tech-

nical term referring to the *lēxis submitted to the *arkhōn by someone making a claim to a deceased person's estate. The impersonal construction with the passive infinitive led Wyse to assume, in his tendentious note, that Isaios was deliberately concealing the identity of a specific claimant, who must have been either the speaker or Kleon. An alternative possibility is that after Kleon had taken possession of the estate, his entitlement to it was challenged by another member of the family, most probably Astyphilos's sister, or, if she had predeceased Astyphilos, a son of hers. At that point, Kleon would have been in an extremely vulnerable position. He could not have blocked the sister's claim by means of a *diamarturia, because his son was neither a natural descendant of Astyphilos nor adopted by him *inter vivos. He could not have relied on a higher ranking within the *ankhisteia, even if he remained in or had returned to his natal *oikos, because a *homopatric sister had precedence over a cousin (cf. Isa. 11.1.) So his only recourse would have been to produce a will in favour of his son. If this interpretation is correct, Isaios's silence about the earlier litigation can be explained as reluctance to prejudice his client's case by mentioning that Astyphilos's adoption of Kleon's son had been upheld in a previous court case. He would, however, have had no prospect of concealing this information altogether from the *dikastai: at least some of them might already have known about it, especially in view of the notoriety of Kleon's family, and Kleon himself would undoubtedly refer to it in his response.

ὦ ἄνδρες ('gentlemen'). At this point the address to the *dikastai makes it clear that the speaker is no longer speaking to Hierokles personally.

εὖ εἰδὼς ('well aware'). Cf. on εὖ εἰδότες…, §4.

οὐδενὶ ἄλλῳ γίγνοιτο τὰ Ἀστυφίλου ἢ ἐμοί ('the property of Astyphilos was coming to no-one but me'). Cf. on οὐδενὶ ἄλλῳ ἢ ἐμοί, §1. The use of *gignesthai* (lit. 'become'), an ingressive equivalent to *einai* ('be'), indicates that the estate was not actually in the speaker's possession but was (in his view, at least) 'on its way' to him.

ἐν μέρει ('in turn'). Isaios conveys extremely economically that Hierokles approached each of his potential 'clients' separately, and that he spoke to several of them without finding a positive response. The people in question, though not related to Astyphilos (§24), were his friends or acquaintances. It is possible that some or all of them were among those who buried Astyphilos, and who had already testified to the conduct of the funeral.

πωλῶν τὸ πρᾶγμα (lit., 'trying to sell the affair'). The conative sense of the present participle, and the pejorative connotations of *pragma*, are nicely conveyed in Forster's translation "hawking his scheme". The story of Hierokles's efforts to 'sell' the forged will would have belonged more logically in the earlier part of the narrative, where the speaker has already explained (§§5–6) how he found out about Hierokles's claim that Astyphilos had deposited a will with him. The narrative postponement enables Isaios to build up a picture of Hierokles as an untrustworthy witness before launching this all out attack at the climax of the speech.

τοὺς οὐδὲν προσήκοντας ('those who were unrelated [to Astyphilos]'). These people would include Kleon, if his father really had been adopted and had not returned to his natal **oikos*.

πείθων ἀμφισβητεῖν ('trying to persuade [them] to dispute the case'). Again, the present participle is conative. It is not clear whether Hierokles succeeded in persuading one of Astyphilos's friends to submit a claim for the estate, or whether the threat of such an action was sufficient to induce Kleon to reach an agreement with him.

λέγων ὅτι θεῖος εἴη Ἀστυφίλῳ ('saying he was Astyphilos's uncle'). By introducing himself as Astyphilos's uncle, Hierokles would have established his credentials as a potential custodian of the will. The implication that those whom he approached did not already know of his kinship with Astyphilos emphasizes economically that they were not related to him, except that Kleon, whether or not he was legally related to Astyphilos at the relevant time, would certainly have known.

ἐπειδὴ δὲ ('and since'). This introduces the second half of the antithesis started six lines above (πρὶν μὲν, §24).

πρὸς Κλέωνα διωμολογήσατο ('he has reached an agreement with Kleon'). The fact that Kleon is mentioned last suggests that he was not among those originally approached by Hierokles with the offer of a forged will. The implication may be that he came to terms with Hierokles under the threat of a rival claim from one of Astyphilos's friends.

καὶ τῶν τοῦ ἀδελφοῦ ἐμερίσατο ('and divided my brother's property'). See on τῶν τἀδελφοῦ, §2.

νυνὶ ὡς ἀληθῆ λέγων ἀξιώσει πιστεύεσθαι ('now he will ask you to believe that he is speaking the truth'). Cf. on Ἴσως τοίνυν . . . , §10. The speaker now explicitly anticipates Hierokles's rôle as a witness for Kleon, whose evidence he seeks to discredit.

25 καὶ ἐμοὶ μὲν συγγενὴς ὢν ('And for me, although he is my kinsman'). See on καὶ ταῦτα θεῖον ὄντα . . . , §6.

οὐδὲ τὰ γενόμενα ἐθέλει μαρτυρεῖν ('he refuses to testify even to what has actually happened'). The language is tendentious, making the assumption that the alleged fatal attack to which Hierokles was invited to testify actually happened.

ᾧ δ'οὐδὲν προσήκει ('to whom he is not related at all'). Hierokles's willingness to testify for Kleon, to whom he is not even related, underlines his neglect of the obligations of kinship in refusing to support his nephew's case.

τὰ ψευδῆ ... φέρων ('co-operates in lying and has brought a document to prove events that never occurred'). In the second half of the antithesis, the speaker claims that Hierokles not only denies real events, but is prepared to testify to fictitious ones. The reference here to a document seems to play on the Athenians' suspicion of documentary evidence.

αὐτοὺς ὑμῖν οἷς προσῆλθε μάρτυρας παρέξομαι ('I shall produce for you as witnesses those whom he approached'). Cf. on αὐτοὺς τοὺς ἐπιτηδείους ..., §4. It would be interesting to know the number and identity of those who claimed that Hierokles had tried to 'sell' them a will, and the capacity in which they knew Astyphilos. Cf. the situation described in Isa. 4.7–10, where six named individuals are said to have come forward, with claims based either on collateral kinship or on adoption, in response to news of the death of Nikostratos (who, like Astyphilos, died abroad on military service). Such claims may have been prompted by information which the **prutaneis* posted about vacant estates (*Ath. Pol.* 43.4). In this case, however, if the speaker's account is true, any rival claimants came forward at the instigation of Hierokles rather than on their own initiative.

26 Τί οὖν χρή ... καταψεύδεσθαι; ('What name should be given, gentlemen, to this man, who is so readily willing for his own profit to slander one who is dead?'). Cf. on τολμῆσαί τι ψεύσασθαι ..., §6. The rhetorical question is addressed to the **dikastai* immediately after a witness statement "dans l'intention d'assurer le triomphe de l'orateur" ("to assert the orator's victory"), Denommé (1974b), 139.

οὐ μικρὸν τεκμήριον ('no small proof'). See on μεγάλα γὰρ τεκμήρια, 7.11.

Narrative and Testimony: The Ties of Friendship and Affection (*27–30*)

The speaker's portrayal of harmonious relations within the household of Theophrastos complements his claims about the enmity of Astyphilos and Kleon as a means of demonstrating how unlikely it was that Astyphilos would have adopted Kleon's son. Like the speaker of Isa. 1, though in different terms, this speaker aims to show that he has a better claim to the estate than his opponents because he was closer to the testator both by blood and through bonds of intimacy and affection. The legal basis for this form of argumentation emerges more clearly at the end of the speech, when the speaker argues (again like the speaker of Isa. 1) that if Astyphilos did make a will in favour of Kleon's son, then, given his animosity towards Kleon and his affection for Theophrastos and the speaker, he cannot have been in his right mind (cf. on πῶς οὐ δόξει…, §37).

So it would be misleading to characterize this part of the speech, as some scholars have done, as a 'moral' or 'non-legal' argument: the speaker does not invite the **dikastai* to ignore Astyphilos's will, but seeks to undermine its authenticity from every possible angle. Some of the *dikastai* may, nevertheless, have found this part of the argument persuasive at an emotional rather than a rational level, and Isaios undoubtedly exploits the sentimental appeal of his narrative to influence those who may not have been convinced on strictly legal grounds. There may, in particular, have been a perception that the strict application of the rule of male precedence would be unfair in a case such as this, where (according to the speaker) Astyphilos was in practice much closer to his *homometric half-brother than to his patrilineal cousin.

The characteristically Isaian technique of breaking down narrative into very short sections, each followed by testimony on detailed points, is particularly apparent in this part of the speech. Witnesses testify separately to five facts designed to illustrate the close relationship between Theophrastos, his son and his stepson, which could have been dealt with in a single, composite piece of testimony (cf. the introduction to this speech, p. 155). Dionysios's explanation, that Isaios used this technique when he feared that a speech might become difficult to follow because of the diversity of the topics covered by testimony (Dion. Hal. *De Isaeo* 14), clearly does not apply in this instance. Rather, it appears that Isaios wanted to maximize the impact of the available testimony and impress the *dikastai* with its volume.

27 ἀλλὰ Κλέων καὶ Ἱεροκλῆς βούλονται ὑμᾶς ἐξαπατῆσαι ('but Kleon and Hierokles want to deceive you'). See on ἐὰν ὑμεῖς…, 8.3.

καθ' ὅσον ἐδυνάμην ('to the best of my ability'). The speaker's claim, to have proved as conclusively as he can that the will was forged, appears to be justified. Cf. on πῶς οὖν ἄν…, 8.28. Given that he could not make use of modern scientific evidence and that there was no systematic official record-keeping in fourth century Athens, he has had no choice but to rely heavily on argument from probability. The testimony he has produced from those to whom Hierokles allegedly tried to 'sell' a will would also count in his favour.

ὡς δ'... ἢ οὗτοι ('that even if I had been unrelated to Astyphilos, I would have a better right to his property than these men'). An example of *hyperbolē* or rhetorical exaggeration, not intended to be taken literally. Cf. εἰ καὶ δεκάκις..., §31, where the impossibility of the protasis is more obvious. Although it is clear that close ties of affection and friendship could influence the **dikastai* in an inheritance case, evidence on such matters was always integrated into the legal argument. There is no surviving speech from an inheritance case in which a litigant's claim is based on 'moral' grounds alone. (Cf. General Introduction, p. 17.)

ὅτε γὰρ ἐλάμβανε... Ἀστυφίλου ('for when my father received my mother, and the mother of Astyphilos, in marriage'). One might have expected the verb *elambane* ('received') to be in the aorist tense; cf. Isa. 3.55; 5.5; 10.4. The imperfect is, however, found in a similar context at 8.18. Here, perhaps, the emphasis is on the process of negotiation with the woman's **kurios*, Hierokles.

The name Theophrastos occurs here for the third time (cf. on πολλὰ κἀγαθὰ..., §23); but this is the speaker's only reference to his mother, and he emphasizes that she was also the mother of Astyphilos. We cannot be sure whether she was still alive at the time of the speech, but it is tempting to infer from Isaios's silence about her that she had already died. Otherwise, one might have expected her to appear in the list of people (with Theophrastos, Astyphilos, and the speaker himself) who had been wronged by her brother Hierokles. Cf. the repeated references, in Isa. 10, to the speaker's mother as a victim of his opponents' wrongdoing.

παρὰ Ἱεροκλέους ('from Hierokles'). As Wyse points out, *ad loc.*, Hierokles became his sister's **kurios* after the death of Euthykrates, and gave her in marriage to her second husband. The speaker's reference to this fact emphasizes Hierokles's treachery.

μικρὸν ὄντα ('then a small child'). Isaios is apparently trying to create the impression that Astyphilos was a baby when his father died and that his mother remarried soon afterwards, but emotive words such as 'small' (also at §29) and 'child' (§§20, 30) are vague, and may suggest that there was a larger age gap between Astyphilos and the speaker than he wants the **dikastai* to infer. Cf. on μετὰ δὲ ταῦτα..., §29.

τὸν ἅπαντα χρόνον ('the whole time'). Cf. on τὸν ἅπαντα χρόνον..., §20.

καὶ ἐπαιδεύθη ὑπὸ τοῦ πατρὸς τοῦ ἐμοῦ ('and was brought up by my father'). An Athenian widow had the option, until she remarried, of remaining in her deceased husband's **oikos* or returning to that of her father, while any children of the marriage would normally have remained in their natural father's *oikos*. Cf. the position of Apollodoros in Isa. 7, who remained in his paternal *oikos* under the tutelage of his uncle Eupolis, until he was 'rescued' by his stepfather Arkhedamos. For further examples and discussion, see Harrison (1968), 44. The fact that Astyphilos's mother took him with her into the *oikos* of her new husband, Theophrastos, suggests that Theophrastos was the legal guardian of Astyphilos. In that case he would have been obliged, with sanctions for default, to bring up the boy and look after his interests. In Wyse's view, Isaios does not mention Theophrastos's position as guardian because he wants to convey the impression that Theophrastos was acting out of the kindness of his heart, not under a legal obligation. But even if Isaios avoided spelling this out, the language in this part of the speech would have made it sufficiently clear to the **dikastai* that Theophrastos was Astyphilos's guardian. The question of guardianship raises the possibility that Theophrastos was a kinsman of Euthykrates, although Isaios does not mention a relationship. Whether he was a kinsman or a friend, it is possible (though not mentioned in the speech) that the dying Euthykrates designated Theophrastos to be both his son's guardian and his wife's second husband.

28 μετ' ἐκείνου συνεπαιδευόμην ('I was educated with him'). The fact that the speaker and Astyphilos went to school together is presented as a sign of their closeness. A similar point is made in the papyrus fragment P.Oxy. 2538, which contains part of the narrative section of a forensic speech (tentatively attributed to either Lysias or Isaios; Carey (2005) argues for Isaios) in which the speaker defends his legitimacy. There, the speaker calls his brother to attest that they were educated at the same school and by the same teacher.

λαβὲ δέ μοι ταύτην τὴν μαρτυρίαν ('Please take this deposition'). Cf. on αὐτοὺς τοὺς ἐπιτηδείους…, §4.

Τὸ τοίνυν χωρίον τὸ ἐκείνου πατρῷον, ὦ ἄνδρες ('his paternal estate, gentlemen'). Here, as at §§7 and 26, the address to the **dikastai* marks the resumption of the speech after a witness statement. The language in this section suggests that Theophrastos was acting in an official capacity as Astyphilos's guardian, but whether he was or not, it is possible that he had taken out a lease on the land during the minority of Astyphilos. Cf. Wyse, 642.

ἀνάβητέ μοι καὶ τούτων μάρτυρες ('Let the witnesses on these matters also come forward'). Cf. on αὐτοὺς τοὺς ἐπιτηδείους…, §4. The formula used here, evidently a survival from the period when witnesses testified orally, is commonly used by Lysias (cf. Wyse, *ad loc.*) but not found elsewhere in Isaios. (In this case, however, the witnesses were presumably expected to come forward simply to affirm their agreement with the written testimony.) Carey (2005) discusses its use in P.Oxy. 2538, and mentions further instances in Isok. 17. For the transition from oral to written testimony, see on τούτων πρῶτον…, 7.10.

29 Ἐπεὶ τοίνυν ἐδοκιμάσθη ὁ ἀδελφός ('when my brother came of age'). See on τῶν τἀδελφοῦ, §2.

μετὰ δὲ ταῦτα…ὅτῳ ἐδόκει αὐτῷ ('after that my father gave [Astyphilos's] *homopatric sister in marriage to the man of his choice'). According to Wyse, Astyphilos, when he came of age, became his sister's **kurios* and was under a moral obligation to find her a suitable husband, but: "So great was the confidence that he reposed in the affection of his stepfather that he left this important duty entirely in the hands of Theophrastus…". It is possible, however, that Theophrastos, if he was guardian to both Astyphilos and his sister, would have remained the sister's *kurios*. Cf. Wyse's discussion, at Isa. 3.2.3, of the law cited at [Dem.] 46.18. An alternative possibility, that Astyphilos was still under age when his sister was married, is ruled out by 'after that'. Isaois thus makes it clear that the sister married after Astyphilos came of age and received his patrimony from Theophrastos, while leaving the interval characteristically vague.

This is the only reference in the speech to Astyphilos's sister, who, as I have argued (see on ἐπειδὴ δὲ…, §2 and καὶ πρὶν μὲν…, §24) may have unsuccessfully challenged Kleon's tenure of the estate. An alternative possibility, if indeed she was still alive at the time of her brother's death, is that she refrained from making a claim because she accepted that Astyphilos had legally adopted Kleon's son. In either case, it would not have been in the speaker's interest to bring her position to the attention of the **dikastai*. Cf. Isa. 7, where the speaker uses Thrasyboulos's silence to his own advantage. The possibility that she was only a half-sister of Astyphilos, as some critics have suggested (cf. Wyse, 643) would not affect her position as next of kin to Astyphilos, since a homopatric half-sister and her sons would still have had a stronger claim than a *homometric half-brother.

ἐκ μικροῦ παιδίου τεθραμμένος παρ' αὐτῷ ('brought up by him from early childhood'). Cf. on μικρὸν ὄντα, §27.

μαρτυροῦσι…οἱ εἰδότες ('those who know the facts will testify'). For the designation of witnesses as 'those who know the facts', see on τοῖς εἰδόσι χρώμενος μάρτυσιν, 8.6. On the formulae used to introduce testimony in this speech, see on αὐτοὺς τοὺς ἐπιτηδείους…, §4.

30 Εἰς τοίνυν ... πανταχῇ. ('My father took Astyphilos with him when he was a child, as well as me, to the religious ceremonies on every occasion'.) This emphasizes both the close fraternal ties between Astyphilos and the speaker and Theophrastos's benevolence towards his stepson. Cf. on Εἰς τὰς θυσίας, §21; and, on the more general significance of shared religious observances, see the introductory note to 8.15–17.

εἰς τοὺς θιάσους τοὺς Ἡρακλέους ('to the *thiasoi* of Herakles'). As discussed by Lambert (1993), 81–93, *thiasōtai* were members of a *thiasos*, a term that could refer to any group or association, including, as here, an organized cultic association of citizens. There is evidence that some *thiasoi* were sub-groups of a phratry.

Wyse justifies his emendation of the ms. θιάσους to θιασώτας on the grounds that, although there may well have been many *thiasoi* associated with Attic shrines of Herakles, "it is hard to believe that Theophrastos belonged to all or even several of them". Lambert (1993), 89 n. 138, disagrees: " 'He introduced him to the Heraklean thiasoi' is perfectly acceptable in English, as in Greek, implying introduction to one of a group of thiasoi." Isaios's use of the plural *thiasoi* would, according to Lambert, imply the existence of a number of Heraklean *thiasoi* associated with one another, "possibly with some sort of collective membership".

ἵνα μετέχοι τῆς κοινωνίας ('so that he might become a member of the association'). The reason given for the introduction of Astyphilos to the *thiasoi* of Herakles is vague, giving no indication that these particular *thiasoi* might have been subdivisions of a *phratry or phratries. The fact that Astyphilos's membership of the *thiasoi* is "not mentioned as evidence of legitimacy" leads Lambert (1993), 89, n. 141, to the conclusion that "These Heraklean thiasoi sound much more like the thiasoi of other cults which were clearly not subdivisions in that foreigners and women were members." Since, however, Astyphilos's status was not at issue, the passage would perhaps be better regarded as inconclusive on this point.

αὐτοὶ ... μαρτυρήσουσιν ('the *thiasōtai* themselves will testify'). Cf. on αὐτοὺς τοὺς ἐπιτηδείους ..., §4.

Ἐγὼ δὲ, ὦ ἄνδρες, ... σκέψασθε ('consider, gentlemen, my relationship with my brother'). See on τῶν τἀδελφοῦ, §2.

πρῶτον μὲν ... ἠσπάζετό με ('first, I was brought up with him from infancy; secondly, I never had a quarrel with him and he had great affection for me'). The speaker has already made the point that he went to school with Astyphilos (cf. on μετ' ἐκείνου συνεπαιδευόμην, §28) but apart from that he has no specific evidence of their supposedly close fraternal relationship. In fact, there is stronger evidence of good relations between Astyphilos and Theophrastos than between Astyphilos and the speaker. (This is reminiscent of Isa. 7, where there is little indication of a close relationship between the speaker, Thrasyllos, and his deceased uncle Apollodoros, but more emphasis on Apollodoros's debt of gratitude to his stepfather and half-sister, the speaker's grandfather and mother.) The reader may suspect that the reality was somewhat different from the idealized picture which the speaker aims to present. It is questionable whether anyone could attest that the two half-brothers *never* quarrelled, and even if they did get on well as children, it is possible that they fell out, or simply drifted apart, later in life. The speaker brings no evidence that would convincingly refute this possibility.

οὓς βούλομαι ὑμῖν μάρτυρας ἀναβιβάσαι ('whom I wish to come forward and testify to you'). Cf. on αὐτοὺς τοὺς ἐπιτηδείους…, §4.

Epilogue (31–37)

The speech concludes with an unusually detailed, albeit selective, summary of the speaker's case, in which he also introduces new argument and evidence, and anticipates some of the points he expects Kleon to make. His tone at this stage of the speech is markedly less confident and businesslike than it was at the beginning, and his language again takes on a religious flavour as he pleads for the indulgence of the **dikastai*.

31 Δοκεῖ… ἀποστερήσας; ('Can you imagine, gentlemen, that Astyphilos, who hated Kleon so much but had experienced so many kindnesses from my father, would have adopted a son of one of his enemies, depriving his benefactors and relatives?') There are no fewer than six addresses to the **dikastai* in these final sections of the speech, perhaps a sign of the speaker's desperation. The interrogative form of the sentence gives the appearance of drawing the *dikastai* into the speaker's argument and inviting them to form their own conclusions. The question is, however, loaded in favour of the conclusion that the speaker wants them to reach. He seems to be making the point that those who already have a good claim through their relationship with the deceased are all the more deserving if they have treated him well.

For 'hating Kleon so much', cf. on καὶ οὕτω σφόδρα…, §16. The emphasis in the second half of the antithesis is on Astyphilos's good relations with the speaker's father, Theophrastos, rather than with the speaker himself. Cf. on πρῶτον μὲν…, §30.

ἐγὼ μὲν οὐκ ἂν οἴομαι ('I think not'). The answer expected by the speaker to his rhetorical question is obvious enough, but he gives his own reply for the avoidance of any possible doubt (using the emphatic first person pronoun *egō* in antithesis to the second person *humin* at the beginning of the sentence).

εἰ καὶ δεκάκις ὁ Ἱεροκλῆς διαθήκας ψευδεῖς ἀποδεικνύει ('even if Hierokles produces a forged will ten times over'). For the *hyperbolē*, see on ὡς δ'..., §27.

καὶ διὰ τὸ ἀδελφὸν εἶναι καὶ διὰ τὴν ἄλλην οἰκειότητα ('both because I am his brother and because of our other family ties'). The speaker does not remind the **dikastai* that he and Astyphilos were not full siblings. His argumentation is reminiscent of Isa. 1, where the speaker argues that he has a better claim than his opponents because of his greater intimacy with Kleonymos as well as his closer kinship.

32 τὰ δὲ ὀστᾶ οὐκ ἔθαψαν ('did not bury his remains'). Cf. on οὐ προὔθετο οὐδ' ἔθαψεν, §4.

ἀλλὰ πρότερον...ποιῆσαι ('but entered on the estate before carrying out the funeral rites for him'). The construction *proteron...prin* is not necessarily temporal, and does not here imply that Kleon ever did conduct the funeral rites. The wording is reminiscent of the speaker's earlier contention, that Kleon took posssession of the estate without seeking an adjudication to establish his claim. (See on πρίν τι ὑμᾶς ψηφίσασθαι, §3.) The earlier formulation emphasizes the illegality of Kleon's behaviour, the later its impiety. The exact chronology, which remains obscure, was probably not Isaios's main concern.

ἀλλὰ καὶ...πρὸς πατρός ('but additionally on the grounds of kinship, because Kleon was [Astyphilos's] first cousin on his father's side'). The speaker has never denied that Kleon, as a patrilineal kinsman of Astyphilos, would have had a stronger claim to the estate, but has based his own claim on the unsubstantiated assertion that Kleon has had no legal relationship to Astyphilos since his father's adoption. It is imperative for the speaker to persuade the **dikastai* of this point, and in the closing section of the speech he gives his first and only hint that it is likely to be disputed. At this point he gives the impression of being less confident than he at first appeared.

33 ὑμᾶς δέ...τὸν νοῦν ('But it is unlikely, gentlemen, that you will pay any attention to his degree of kinship'). The address reflects the increasing urgency of the speaker's need to get the **dikastai* on his side. He is, in effect, inviting them to ignore what was probably the fatal flaw in his case.

οὐδεὶς γὰρ πώποτε ἐκποίητος γενόμενος...ἐξεποιήθη ('for no-one, after being adopted, has ever inherited from the *oikos* out of which he was adopted'). Cf. on ἐκποίητος, 7.23, and, for the sweeping generalization ('no-one ever'), on οὐ γάρ…, §13. This is only the second reference in the speech to the alleged adoption of Kleon's father, Thoudippos, into a different **oikos*; cf. on καὶ οὗτοι…, §2. As discussed in the introduction to this speech, p. 153, the speaker alludes to it casually, as something the **dikastai* already know about, even though he has made no attempt to prove it.

ἐὰν μὴ ἐπανέλθῃ κατὰ τὸν νόμον ('unless he returned in accordance with the law'). The law permitting an adopted son to return to his natal **oikos*, provided he left behind a legitimate son in the *oikos* of his adoptive father, is cited at Isa. 6.44 and 10.11. Cf. [Dem.] 44.21, 44, 46. The speaker's case would collapse entirely if Kleon could prove either that his father was not adopted, or that he had returned to his natal *oikos* after being adopted. Isaios may be expecting Kleon to argue that Thoudippos did return, leaving his other son, Anaxippos, behind. In that case Isaios's failure to mention Anaxippos would be highly significant.

οὗτοι μέντοι…ἐληλυθότι ('Yet these men, well aware that Astyphilos never adopted Kleon's son, though he has often presented himself'). A lacuna in the text after κατὰ τὸν νόμον ('in accordance with the law') leads to an apparently abrupt change of subject: after closing off his argument against the will at §32, then brushing aside Kleon's anticipated claim on grounds of closer kinship, the speaker now reverts to the supposed adoption by Astyphilos of Kleon's son, bringing witnesses to attest that Kleon had failed to get his son accepted by Astyphilos's *phratry. There must be at least a line of text missing, in which the speaker presumably says that Kleon tried to introduce his son to the *phrateres*, to whom 'these men' apparently refers.

We may wonder how the members of Astyphilos's phratry knew that he had never adopted Kleon's son. Cf. on εὖ εἰδότες…, §4. Wyse thinks this simply an invention of Isaios, but it is possible that some of the *phrateres* were among the friends of Astyphilos who testified (§25) that Hierokles had offered to sell them a forged will.

It is, in any event, surprising to find new evidence on so important and contentious an issue so late in the speech. Logically, it belongs with the speaker's earlier attack on the validity of Astyphilos's purported will, where the relatively unconvincing argumentation could have been strengthened by testimony, but the postponement may have helped to ensure that the *dikastai* did not forget about it.

The passage raises questions about the respective rôles of the courts and the phratries in the Athenian testamentary adoption procedure. Wyse argues that Kleon had jumped the gun by trying to introduce his son without first obtaining authority from the court; the *phrateres* were acting properly by refusing to admit him before the outcome of the **diadikasia* was known, and their refusal does not carry the significance attributed to it by Isaios. Avramovič (1997), 53–54, attempts a rebuttal by citing Isa. 7.28 as an example of an adoption ratified by a *deme or phratry before trial. This, however, overlooks the difference between testamentary and **inter vivos* adoption: Thrasyllos in Isa. 7 claims to have exercised his legitimate right of **embateusis* after being adopted *inter vivos* by Apollodoros.

The speaker's assertion that Kleon and his son had approached the phratry more than once provides some insight into the chronology of the case. The admission of new phratry members normally took place on Koureiotis, the third day of the festival of Apatouria. Cf. on καὶ ἐπειδὴ Θαργήλια ἦν, 7.15. Whatever the exact date of the admission ceremony there is no evidence that an unsuccessful candidate could return within the same year, so, if Kleon had made repeated attempts to have his son accepted as the adopted son of Astyphilos, this would seem to indicate that several years had elapsed between Astyphilos's death and the speaker's claim to his estate. Cf. on ἐμοῦ δὲ οὐκ..., §3.

αὐτῷ οὐδεπώποτε κεκρεανομήκασι ('have never given him a share in the victims'). Isaios alludes very cursorily to the procedure for the introduction of new *phratry members. In the course of the ceremony the introducer (in this case, presumably, Kleon as the natural father) would lead a sacrificial victim to the phratry altar. Provided there were no objections from members, the victim was slaughtered, relevant parts of it were burnt on the altar, and the remaining meat was distributed among the *phrateres*. In this case, presumably, there was an objection from a phratry member, who interrupted the proceedings by leading the sacrificial victim away from the altar (cf. Isa. 6.22 and [Dem.] 43.14.) After that, some attempts would have been made to resolve the issue; but if the phratry voted against the admission of the applicant, it would appear that their decision was not regarded as final. See Lambert (1993), 170–178, for a full discussion of the available evidence on phratry admission procedures.

λαβέ μοι καὶ ταύτην τὴν μαρτυρίαν ('Please take this deposition too'). Cf. on αὐτοὺς τοὺς ἐπιτηδείους..., §4.

34 ἀδελφὸς ὢν ἐκείνου ('being his brother'). Cf. on τῶν τἀδελφοῦ, §2. In the second half of the antithesis, anticipating Kleon's case, the speaker once again emphasizes his relationship to Astyphilos, without mentioning that it was only of the half blood. His summary of the issues is selective, and

he does not explain how his kinship with Astyphilos affects the rival claim about the adoption of Kleon's son.

ὡς καὶ αὐτοὶ οὗτοι ἴσασι ('as they themselves know'). The implication is that it is wrong for the speaker's opponents to press their claim, knowing that he was Astyphilos's brother. In reality their claim is better than his, unless he can persuade the **dikastai* both that Astyphilos did not validly adopt Kleon's son and that Kleon and his son no longer have a legal relationship with Astyphilos.

μὴ τοίνυν … ἐποιήσατο ('So do not, gentlemen, give Astyphilos an adopted son whom he himself never in his life adopted'). This is a stereotypical reminder to the **dikastai* of the effect their decision will have if they vote against the speaker. He could have made this point by asking them not to 'ratify' the adoption, but the chosen wording also reinforces his contention, expressed in the next clause, that no adoption had actually taken place.

ἀλλὰ τοὺς νόμους οὓς ὑμεῖς ἔθεσθε βεβαιώσατέ μοι ('but confirm in my favour the laws that you have enacted'). The speaker's appeal to the **dikastai* is not simply a plea for mercy, but is based on the legality of his case. The use of the second person pronoun *humeis* reflects the collective responsibility of the Athenian citizens for lawmaking. Cf. on πρίν τι ὑμᾶς ψηφίσασθαι, §3.

ὁσιωτάτην δέησιν δεόμενος, ὦ ἄνδρες ('making a most pious request, gentlemen'). The speaker uses religious language in his final plea to the **dikastai.* The repetition of the address, after only a few lines, contributes to the rise in the emotional temperature.

τῆς τοῦ ἀδελφοῦ οὐσίας ('of my brother's property'). Cf. on τῶν τἀδελφοῦ, §2.

35 καὶ μάρτυρας ἁπάντων ὧν εἶπον παρεσχόμην ('and I have produced witnesses to all my statements'). This, as has been shown, is not quite true: the speaker has not produced witnesses to the adoption of Thoudippos, or to the fight in which Euthykrates was said to have been fatally wounded by Thoudippos, both of which are crucial to his case and vulnerable to attack from the opposing side.

καὶ εἰ λέγειν ἐμοῦ δύναται Κλέων μᾶλλον ('and if Kleon can speak better than I can'). The words of the speaker's appeal to the **dikastai* are conventional enough, but his tone has become noticeably less confident than it was at the beginning of the speech. The suggestion that Kleon is a more able speaker, if it is not simply false modesty, is consistent with his being a member of a prominent political family.

ἄνευ τοῦ νόμου καὶ τοῦ δικαίου ('without the law and justice'). The speaker again makes the point that the case must be judged within a legal framework: it is not enough for Kleon to be a more able speaker, unless he also has the law and justice on his side.

οἱ δὲ ἀδυνατώτεροι ('the weaker parties'). For the portrayal of the **dikastai* as upholders of justice for the weak, or those who are less skilled in oratory, cf., e.g., Dem. 24.190; [Dem.] 52.2; Lys. 30.24.

εὖ εἰδότες ('well aware'). Cf. on εὖ εἰδότες . . . , §4.

36 ἅπαντες οὖν, ὦ ἄνδρες, μετ' ἐμοῦ γένεσθε ('Therefore, all of you, support me, gentlemen'). Throughout the final two sections, the speaker addresses the **dikastai* directly in the second person.

ἐάν τι ἄλλο ψηφίσησθε Κλέωνι πειθόμενοι ('if you are persuaded by Kleon to vote differently'). Like the more tendentious 'deceive' (see on ἐὰν ὑμεῖς . . . , 8.3, and cf. on ἀλλὰ Κλέων καὶ Ἱεροκλῆς . . . , §27), 'persuade', in this context enables the speaker to avoid any suggestion that the **dikastai* are to be blamed for a wrong decision.

Ἀστύφιλον παρανοίας αἱρήσετε ('you will convict Astyphilos of insanity'). This not only introduces the argument that a will made by Astyphilos in favour of Kleon would have been invalid (see following note), but also seems to refer to the *graphē paranoias*, apparently an action against someone who was wasting his family property through mental incapacity. (Forster's "consummate folly" does not adequately convey the legal implications of *paranoia*.) There are no extant cases, but see *Ath. Pol.* 5.6.6, with Rhodes's note.

37 πῶς οὐ δόξει . . . διεφθάρθαι; ('surely those who hear of it will think that he was insane or under the influence of drugs?'). The speaker has already gone to considerable lengths to persuade the **dikastai* that the document produced by Kleon and Hierokles was not really Astyphilos's will, but in case any of them remain unpersuaded he now attacks it from a different angle. Boiled down to its essentials, the argument (which closely parallels the line taken by the speaker of Isa. 1) now runs as follows: 'Astyphilos got on very well with me, and with my father, but he hated Kleon. It is highly unlikely, therefore, that he would have made a will in favour of Kleon's son. But if the document produced by Hierokles really is Astyphilos's will, then he cannot have been in his right mind when he wrote it, so it is invalid.' Cf. the Solonian law cited at [Dem.] 46.14. Provided the *dikastai* accept the speaker's account of Astyphilos's enmity with Kleon (and there are good reasons why they should treat it with scepticism),

the weakness of his other arguments against the will no longer matters. Nor, more importantly, does any testimony that Kleon may bring about the genuineness of the will.

ὦ ἄνδρες δικασταί ('judges'). See on ὦ ἄνδρες δικασταί, §16.

ἐκτραφέντα … καὶ ἀδελφὸν ὄντα ('brought up in the same household and educated with Astyphilos and being his brother'). These domestic details are now detached from their legal context and aimed directly at the emotions of the **dikastai*.

ἀποστερηθέντα ('to be robbed'). See on ἀποστερῶν, 8.3.

ἀντιβολῶ ὑμᾶς καὶ ἱκετεύω ἐκ παντὸς τρόπου ψηφίσασθαί μοι ('I beg and implore you by every means I can to vote in my favour'). The speech concludes on a highly emotional note with a plea to the **dikastai* using two verbs of supplication. Cf. on δέομαι …, 7.4.

ISAIOS 10: ON THE ESTATE OF ARISTARKHOS

Introduction

Background and Chronology

Aristarkhos junior has died in battle, leaving a will in favour of Xenainetos junior, whose claim to the estate is challenged by Isaios's client. Aristarkhos junior and Xenainetos junior were brothers, grandsons of Aristarkhos senior, but the family's relationships have been changed by two adoptions: first, their father Kyronides was adopted by his maternal grandfather Xenainetos senior, and later Aristarkhos junior became the son of Aristarkhos senior by posthumous adoption. The effect of these adoptions is discussed in detail below. Diagram 4 shows the family of Aristarkhos senior before either of the adoptions took place.

The speaker was, and remained at the time of the trial, the grandson (daughter's son) of Aristarkhos senior. His opponent, Xenainetos junior, claims to be the testamentary heir of Aristarkhos junior, but the speaker presents his case in terms of a claim to the estate of Aristarkhos senior, asserting that the estate should have passed to him through his mother, whom he portrays as a defrauded **epiklēros*.

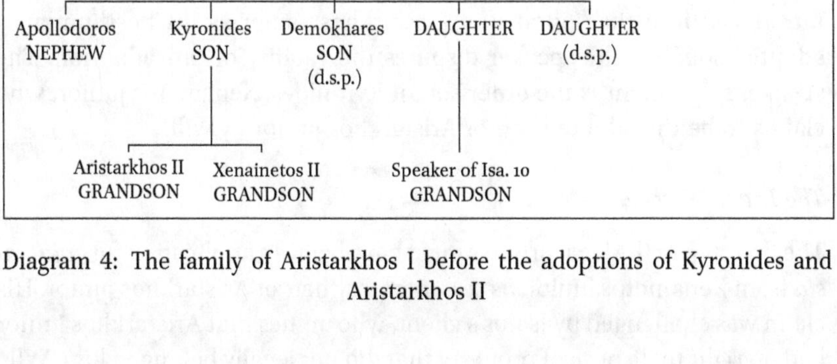

Diagram 4: The family of Aristarkhos I before the adoptions of Kyronides and Aristarkhos II

Internal references enable us to date the speech between 378 and 371 BC. The speaker and his father served in the Corinthian War (394–386 BC), and Aristarkhos junior died in the course of a war that was still in progress, which must have been the Theban War of 378–371 BC. Even if the speaker's service started only halfway through the Corinthian War, that would place his birth no later than 410 BC, so that he would have been at least in his mid to late 30s at the time of the speech. So, on the speaker's own account, at least 35 or 40 years must have elapsed since the death of Aristarkhos senior.

The Speaker's Story

Aristarkhos senior married a daughter of Xenainetos senior. They had two sons, Kyronides and Demokhares, and two daughters, one of whom was the mother of Isaios's client. Kyronides was the natural father of Aristarkhos junior and of Xenainetos junior, the speaker's opponent. The speaker tells us that Aristarkhos senior died leaving Demokhares as his sole legitimate heir. Kyronides, who was presumably the older son, had already been adopted into the **oikos* of his maternal grandfather, Xenainetos senior, and so had no claim to the estate. Demokhares and his two sisters were under age when their father died, and Aristomenes, their paternal uncle, became their guardian. Demokhares and one of the sisters died while they were still minors, so that the other sister, the speaker's mother, became *epiklēros* to the whole estate (§4). Once she was old enough to marry, either Aristomenes or his son Apollodoros should have claimed her in marriage, along with the estate of Aristarkhos senior, by **epidikasia*. Instead, Aristomenes gave her in marriage with a dowry (§19), presumably to a non-kinsman, although her husband is not identified in the speech. Aristomenes also gave his own daughter in marriage to Kyronides, with the inheritance which, according to the speaker, belonged to his mother (§5). After the death of Kyronides one of his sons, Aristarkhos junior, was introduced into the *phratry of Aristarkhos senior as his posthumously adopted son, but the speaker disputes the validity of this adoption. The speaker's opponent is the other son of Kyronides, Xenainetos junior, who claims to be the adopted son of Aristarkhos junior by will.

The Legal Proceedings

The first step in the legal process must have been an application for *epidikasia* from Xenainetos junior, as testamentary heir of Aristarkhos junior. His claim was challenged by Isaios's client, who argues that Aristarkhos junior had no right to dispose of property that did not legally belong to him. Why did the speaker, presumably on Isaios's advice, effectively reopen the succession of his grandfather, Aristarkhos senior, instead of attacking the will of Aristarkhos junior? In a direct attack on the will, he might (like the speaker of Isa. 9) have chosen to expose the document produced by his opponent as a forgery, or to assert that Aristarkhos junior made the will while under the influence of drugs or a woman. Isaios may have anticipated problems with that approach, especially if Aristarkhos junior had forestalled any accusation of forgery by taking care to have the will authenticated by plausible witnesses and depositing it with a reliable custodian. Alternatively, it is possible that the will might have been open to challenge on the ground that Aristarkhos junior, as an adopted son, was not himself entitled to adopt, although the prohibition may have applied only to sons adopted **inter vivos*.[1] But even if Isaios could have successfully attacked the will, there would have been no advantage in doing so unless he could also prove that his client had a better claim than his opponent to be the intestate heir of Aristarkhos junior. Diagram 5 shows the family of Aristarkhos junior following his adoption as the son of Aristarkhos senior.

Who, then, would have had the best claim to the estate of Aristarkhos junior if he had not left a valid will? The question is complicated by the adoptions of both Kyronides and Aristarkhos junior. On the one hand, it is clear that the speaker (a first cousin of Aristarkhos junior by birth,

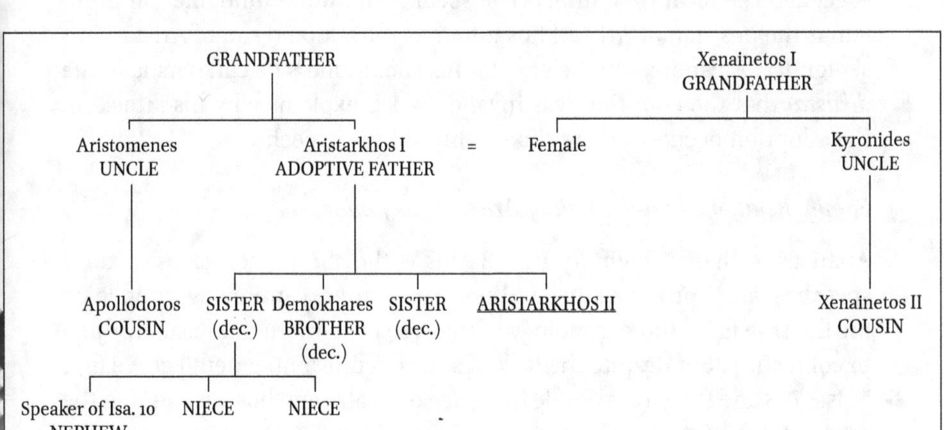

Diagram 5: The family of Aristarkhos II after his adoption

[1] The precise limits of an adopted son's testamentary capacity are disputed; for discussion, see Harrison (1968), 84–87.

and first cousin once removed after the adoption of Kyronides) became legally Aristarkhos junior's nephew (sister's son) following the latter's adoption into the *oikos* of Aristarkhos senior. The position of the speaker's opponent, Xenaenotos II, is more obscure. He was the natural brother of Aristarkhos junior, and retained that relationship after the adoption of their father, Kyronides, into the *oikos* of Xenainetos senior. After the adoption of Aristarkhos junior, on the other hand, Xenainetos junior was no longer his full brother, but became legally a matrilineal first cousin, who would have been outranked in the **ankhisteia* of Aristarkhos junior by the speaker as a matrilineal nephew (as shown in Diagram 5). It is possible, nevertheless, that Athenian law also regarded Xenainetos junior and Aristarkhos junior as *homometric half-brothers, given that an adopted son did not lose his legal relationship with his mother.[2] If that was the case, it would have been Xenainetos junior who occupied the higher place in the *ankhisteia* of Aristarkhos junior (as shown in Diagram 4).

So Isaios's approach to the case is probably explained by his awareness, as an expert in Athenian inheritance law, that his client would have stood little chance of success in a claim to be Aristarkhos junior's intestate heir. But his chosen strategy, to present his client's case in terms of a claim to the estate of the long-deceased Aristarkhos senior, poses problems of its own. First, as the speaker acknowledges in §18, the **dikastai* will want to know why he delayed so long in bringing the claim (although he has not exceeded the legal time limit). The second and more fundamental problem is the position of Aristarkhos junior as the adopted son of Aristarkhos senior. Isaios cannot win the case for his client unless he can persuade the *dikastai* that the adoption was invalid, which explains why his attack on the adoption occupies more than a third of the speech.

Family Relations and the Will of Aristarkhos Junior

Apart from the fragmentary Isa. 12, this is the shortest of Isaios's extant speeches, and both narrative and testimony are exceptionally brief, leaving the true facts and chronology of the case even more than usually open to conjecture. But despite the lack of such circumstantial detail as we find in Isa. 7, 8 and 9, there is ample evidence of rivalry and hostility among the descendants of Aristarkhos senior. The family of Kyronides (apparently aligned with Aristomenes and Apollodoros), on the one side, is opposed

---

2 Cf. on μητρὸς δ'οὐδεὶς…, 7.25.

to that of the speaker's mother on the other. The speaker's attitude to his maternal uncle, Kyronides, carries echoes of the attack on Hierokles in Isa. 9, but in this case Kyronides was no longer alive at the time of the trial, and we do not have sufficient information to reconstruct the family feud with any certainty. But the speaker evidently had a strong sense of grievance, and perhaps a legitimate one, about the exclusion of his branch of the family from the succession to Aristarkhos senior, although there is no indication that the adoption of Aristarkhos junior into the *oikos* of Aristarkhos senior had been seriously contested before the present case.

Whether or not he was personally involved in it, Aristarkhos junior must have been aware of the family feud, and presumably would not have wanted his estate (including what he had inherited from Aristarkhos senior) to devolve to the speaker's branch of the family. Why, though, did he think it necessary to make a will in favour of Xenainetos junior, if the latter would have inherited anyway under the law of intestate succession? One possible reason is that he foresaw a challenge from the speaker if Xenainetos claimed the estate as intestate heir, and was not confident of the result if the dispute went to court. This may have reflected the general uncertainty about the outcome of litigation, especially in a case where the facts were as complex as they appear to have been in this one. But it was not unusual in Athens for an adopted son to be the kinsman who would normally have inherited under the rules of intestate succession,[3] and perhaps the most likely explanation is that he wanted to prevent the line of succession of Aristarkhos senior from dying out.

The Adoption of Kyronides

There are evasions and omissions in the speaker's account which give rise to the suspicion that Isaios was suppressing 'inconvenient' facts, and distorting the sequence of events, in order to enhance his client's chances of success. The adoption of Kyronides is an aspect of the speaker's case on which his evidence seems to be particularly weak.

The speaker's witnesses testify that Kyronides was adopted into the *oikos* of Xenainetos senior, his maternal grandfather, and that he remained there until his death, but the testimony does not say when the adoption took place. This is a surprising omission, given the emphasis placed on the speaker's contention that, in consequence of the adoption, Kyronides was

[3] See General Introduction, p. 11.

not entitled to a share in the estate of Aristarkhos senior. The omission cannot plausibly be explained by a lack of witnesses with the relevant knowledge, since anyone who could testify to the fact of the adoption must have known something about its timing—if not the exact date, then at least where it stood in relation to other events in the family's history.

The significance of this omission may be related to a claim that the speaker anticipates from his opponent, that Kyronides paid a judgment debt on the estate of Aristarkhos senior. The speaker denies that the estate was insolvent, implying that this is simply a story put forward by Xenainetos junior to provide moral justification for Kyronides's acceptance of the fortune given to him by Aristomenes on his marriage. But if Xenainetos did make such a claim, and if it was true, it may more plausibly be interpreted as an indication that Kyronides had not yet been adopted when Aristarkhos senior died, since as legitimate heir he would have been under a legal obligation (not just a moral one) to pay off any debts on the estate before entering on his inheritance.[4]

The Status of the Speaker's Mother

The speaker gives the impression that his mother was unmarried when Demokhares died, but he brings no testimony on the marriage and says nothing about its timing apart from the vague 'after that' (§6). So one cannot exclude the possibility that she was in fact already married; but, as I shall argue below, it is unlikely that an existing marriage would have made any difference to her entitlement to claim her father's estate.

It is central to the speaker's case that his mother was an *epiklēros* defrauded by her father's next of kin. The defining feature of the epiklerate is that an Athenian woman was *epiklēros* (and, therefore, available to be claimed in marriage through an *epidikasia* initiated by her father's next of kin) if she was the sole surviving representative of her paternal *oikos*. (This reflects the fact that a woman's marriage did not completely sever her connection with the *oikos* into which she was born.)[5] By definition she had no living father or brothers; and, if a brother or brothers had predeceased her, she would not become *epiklēros* if they had left a

[4] On the question of liability for the debts of a deceased, including a discussion of the sources, see Harrison (1968), 125–129.

[5] Cf. Just (1989), 74–75. On the economic implications of a married woman's holding a 'stake' in two households, see Foxhall (1989), 34. Hunter (1993), 103, stresses the contrast between Athenian law and the Roman *patria potestas*, whereby marriage severed a woman's link with her natal family and made her a full member of her husband's inheritance group.

son or sons, because the latter would then become their father's legitimate heirs and automatically continue their paternal grandfather's line of succession.

It is likely that a woman who had already been married by **enguē* before her father died could still be treated as *epiklēros*, at least if she did not yet have a son, and that her father's next of kin could still claim her in marriage, forcing a divorce from her existing husband. The main evidence for this is at Isa. 3.64: 'The law ordains that those women who have been betrothed by their fathers, even if they are married, if their father dies without leaving them legitimate brothers, are adjudicable to the next of kin.'[6] The speaker's additional comment, that there are many men who have been divorced from their wives because of this law, is not supported by any other sources; but the majority of modern scholars have, despite the absence of more direct evidence, accepted that the law referred to by Isaios applied at least to a married *epiklēros* who had no sons.[7] If she did have sons, it is likely that they would automatically become her father's legitimate heirs, and that the rules of the epiklerate did not apply.[8]

So the sons of a woman with no father or male collaterals on her father's side, whether she had been married by *epidikasia* to her father's next of kin or by *enguē* to an outsider, would inherit their maternal grandfather's estate as his only male descendants. Since, however, they belonged from birth to their father's *oikos*, they would not continue the maternal grandfather's line of succession unless they were transferred into his *oikos* by posthumous adoption.

It is clear, then, that a woman became *epiklēros* on the death of her father if he left no sons or descendants of sons; but what if the father's estate had originally been inherited by a son, who subsequently died childless leaving his sister as his next of kin? Was she then regarded as

---

[6] τὰς μὲν ὑπὸ τῶν πατέρων ἐκδοθείσας καὶ συνοικούσας ἀνδρασι γυναῖκας... καὶ τὰς οὕτω δοθείσας, ἂν ὁ πατὴρ αὐτῶν τελευτήσῃ μὴ καταλιπὼν αὐταῖς γνησίους ἀδελφούς, τοῖς ἐγγύτατα γένους ἐπιδίκους ὁ νόμος εἶναι κελεύει.

[7] See, e.g., Hafter (1887), 24; Gernet (1921), 349; Paoli (1976a), 346; Karabélias (2002), 80–81. Maffi (1990), on the other hand, argues that the evidence is inconclusive. (See the introductory note to §19.)

[8] So Gernet, Paoli and Karabélias, who adds that even a woman who had only daughters could not be claimed by her father's next of kin. The law cited at [Dem.] 46.20 provides that the sons of an *epiklēros* inherited their maternal grandfather's estate two years of coming of age. It is not clear whether this applied to the sons of a daughter who had married by *enguē*, or whether they would inherit only after their mother's death.

epiklēros, or simply as her brother's intestate heir?[9] Hafter, accepting the evidence of Isa. 10, would include her in his comprehensive definition of *epiklēros*.[10] Wyse and Lentzsch, taking the opposite view, have argued that Isaios deliberately misrepresented the legal position of the speaker's mother in order to gain the sympathy of the *dikastai*.[11] My conclusion, as discussed below, is that she did become *epiklēros* on the death of her brother Demokhares, even if the family's situation was not exactly as Isaios presents it, but that Isaios probably manipulated some of the factual details in order to present his client's case in the most favourable possible light.

As Wyse points, out there are instances in Isa. 7 and 11 of women who have inherited from a brother without being described as *epiklēroi*.[12] We cannot necessarily conclude, however, that the sisters of Apollodoros Eupolidos in Isa. 7, and the sister of Makartatos in Isa. 11, were not *epiklēroi* simply because Isaios does not use the term in relation to them. In neither case was their position as heiresses central to his client's claim, and he may simply have regarded the legal details as unimportant. A different point is made by Lentzsch, who takes it as read that an *epiklēros* must inherit directly from her father: if, as he accepts, it is true that Demokhares outlived Aristarkhos senior, then what he calls the '*epiklēros* fiction' (Erbtochterfiktion)[13] is simply a rhetorical tactic used by Isaios to discredit his client's opponents. On his interpretation, the *dikastai* would have been incensed by any suggestion of wrongdoing against an *epiklēros*, but they were unclear about the precise scope and meaning of the term because the strict letter of the law was no longer observed in the fourth century.

Wyse and Lentzsch are right to point out that Isaios exploits his portrayal of the defrauded *epiklēros* to solicit the audience's sympathy and put the speaker's opponents in a bad light, but it does not follow that he

9 Under Athenian law a woman could inherit from her brother as next of kin if he left no legitimate offspring and had not made a will appointing a male heir, and if there were no homopatric brothers or brothers' sons. It is quite conceivable that this might happen while the father of the heiress and her deceased brother was still alive, if it is correct to assume that ascendants did not inherit. (The evidence on this point is inconclusive. For a summary of the argument on both sides, see Harrison (1968), 138–142.) In that case, however, it is clear that the woman would not become *epiklēros* until the death of her father—and then only if he had not in the meantime acquired a legitimate male heir, or appointed one by will.

10 Hafter (1887), 24.

11 Wyse, 655–656; Lentzsch (1932), 35–38.

12 Wyse, 656.

13 Lentzsch (1932), 37.

was distorting the legal position. The status of the speaker's mother as *epiklēros* after the death of her brother has a parallel in Men. *Aspis*, where Kleostratos is reported to have died on military service. He is unmarried, his father is already dead, and his only surviving sibling is a sister who is about to be married. One of their paternal uncles, Smikrines, wants to cancel his niece's betrothal and claim her in marriage as *epiklēros* so that he can take control of the property left by Kleostratos.

The evidence of *Aspis* needs, of course, to be treated with caution. It is unclear how far the action (to the extent it reflects reality at all) is based on custom rather than law, and MacDowell's attempt to use the details of the plot as a supplementary source of information on Athenian law has, rightly, been called into question.[14] But those who would deny the status of *epiklēros* to the sister of Demokhares and to the sister of Kleostratos in Menander's comedy must, nevertheless, explain how Isaios and Menander were able to present these women as *epiklēroi* in the expectation that this would be accepted by their respective audiences. Hypotheses based on the supposed ignorance of Athenian *dikastai* are always questionable,[15] and it is safe to assume that Isaios and Menander, and their contemporaries, were in a better position than we are to understand the implications of the term *epiklēros*. So, from the available evidence, it is reasonable to conclude that the speaker's mother in Isa. 10 did become *epiklēros* on the death of Demokhares. But if, as I have argued above, Kyronides had not been adopted before his natural father's death, but had shared the estate with Demokhares, then she could not have inherited the whole estate,[16] but only the half of it left to her by Demokhares.

The Legal Basis of Posthumous Adoption

Isaios might have been expected to choose a specific reason for his attack on the adoption, such as a procedural irregularity or an allegation that Aristarkhos junior was not eligible for adoption. Instead, he argued that the only valid form of adoption (at least after the death of the adoptive father)[17] was testamentary; and sought to prove that, since Aristarkhos was not adopted by will, he could not have been legally adopted at all. Despite this, although the details are sparse, there

---

14 MacDowell (1982); Brown (1983).
15 Cf. Harrison (1968), 122, n. 1.
16 See on ἡ μήτηρ . . ., §4.
17 See on ἄλλως δὲ οὐκ ἔξεστιν, §9.

is sufficient evidence from other sources that a son could be 'adopted' posthumously into the *oikos* of a man who had died intestate and without leaving legitimate heirs. Indeed, the criticism directed by the speaker of Isa. 7 against the sisters of Apollodoros Eupolidos, for failing to give their brother an heir by posthumous adoption, suggests that it may, in appropriate cases, have been regarded as a moral obligation to provide an heir for a man whose *oikos* would otherwise remain empty.[18] Isaios's insistence that Aristarkhos junior's adoption was 'not in accordance with any law' seems, therefore, to indicate that there was no law expressly authorizing posthumous adoption, but that it had developed as a matter of custom.[19] That hypothesis is strongly supported by his confident challenge to Xenainetos, later in the speech, to produce the law under which Aristarkhos junior was adopted, since it would be a remarkably reckless tactic if his opponents could respond by citing a specific legal provision.[20]

If it is right to suppose that the practice of posthumous adoption was founded in custom rather than statute, it is not surprising to find no evidence that such an adoption had to be approved by a **dikastērion*. There are, nevertheless, some speeches in which the *dikastai* are expected to accept the validity of a posthumous adoption as part of the speaker's argument. One is Isa. 11, where Theopompos explains that his wife persuaded him to have one of their sons adopted into the *oikos* of her deceased brother. The situation in Isa. 10 also has some similarities with that described by Sositheos, the speaker of [Dem.] 43, who had one of his sons posthumously adopted into the *oikos* of the boy's maternal grandfather, Euboulides II. Sositheos emphasizes that the adoption was carried out in accordance with the wishes of Euboulides II, but makes no mention of a will. We may infer from this, first, that the adoption was posthumous rather than testamentary, since Sositheos would certainly have mentioned a will if there had been one; and, secondly, that evidence of the deceased's wishes, though not necessarily essential, could be expected

---

18 See on τὸν δὲ οἶκον . . ., 7.31, and cf. Gernet (1930), 274.

19 It is worth noting that the law of England and Wales made no provision for the adoption of children until the Adoption of Children Act 1926. Before that date informal adoptions were common, and not 'illegal' in the sense of violating the law, but the lack of statutory regulation meant that there was no legal security for the adoptive parents if, for example, the natural parents demanded the return of their child once it was old enough to become economically active. Cf. Cretney and Masson (1997), 876–878.

20 See commentary on §§14, 21, 22. The origin of posthumous adoption cannot be known with certainty, but Gernet (1930), 271–272, argues plausibly that it was a survival from the archaic period before Solon introduced his law on freedom of testamentary disposition.

to impress the *dikastai* in a case of posthumous adoption. There may, nevertheless, have been cases where a posthumous adoption was the most convenient way of dealing with a situation that could not have been foreseen by the deceased.

It seems clear from this speech, and from [Dem.] 44, that an Athenian could be enrolled into the phratry of a deceased member as the latter's adopted son, whether or not the 'father' had expressed his intention to adopt in a will. So, even if there was no strictly legal authority for the practice, it seems reasonable to assume that the phratries had a rôle in its regulation, to prevent abuse and protect the rights of other potential claimants to the deceased's estate. In the absence of evidence to the contrary, it would appear that the procedure for introduction was similar to that for other forms of adoption, including an opportunity for other family members to raise objections.[21] Although we know nothing about the qualifications for carrying out a posthumous adoption, it is more than likely that Apollodoros, as nephew of Aristarkhos senior, would have been regarded as an appropriate person to introduce an adopted son into his uncle's phratry, especially if Aristomenes was already dead.[22] Another possibility is that a posthumously adopted son, provided he was an adult, could simply present himself to the phratry for enrolment, without the need for a formal sponsor.[23] On the question of eligibility for posthumous adoption, we may tentatively conclude that a posthumously adopted son had to be within the *ankhisteia* of the deceased (though not necessarily the next of kin) and accepted by the remaining family members as a plausible intestate heir.[24]

The Epiklerate and Adoption

This case, as presented by Isaios, involves a conflict between the rights of an adopted son and those of an *epiklēros*. The situation is similar to that in Isa. 3, where Phile claims to be a legitimate daughter of Pyrrhos whose rights as *epiklēros* were violated by Endios, Pyrrhos's nephew whom he

21 See on ὥστε οὐκ ἐπὶ τῷ δικαίως…, §15.

22 As Wyse, 661, suggests, the death of Aristomenes may have taken place "in the interval between the marriage of the speaker's mother and the death of Cyronides".

23 As discussed in the introduction to Isa. 7, the possibility of 'self-enrolment' is suggested (though not in a case of posthumous adoption) by the wording of Dem. 39.5. Cf. also Isa. 8.40 and [Dem.] 44.51.

24 Rubinstein (1993), 44, places posthumous adoption within a more strictly legal framework, concluding that "the right to be adopted posthumously was restricted to those intestate heirs who had already had the inheritance awarded to them by *epidikasia*".

had adopted by will. There is, however, no extant example of a forensic dispute in which a daughter and an adopted son are direct opponents.

Athenian law appears to restrict the testamentary freedom not only of a man who died without issue, but also of one who left legitimate daughters but no sons:

> The law expressly says that a man may dispose of his property as he wishes if he leaves no legitimate sons, but if he leaves daughters, with them.[25]

The precise meaning of 'with them' is unclear, but the speakers of both Isa. 3 and 10 paraphrase the law in terms which state more plainly that a man could not give his estate to an adopted son without giving his daughter, if he had one, as well: 'Anyone who dies leaving legitimate daughters may not dispose of or give any of his property to anyone without the daughters'; 'And it would not have been permissible for her father, if he had no sons, to dispose of his property without her'.[26]

On the basis of these passages the majority of modern scholars agree that the adoption of a son by an Athenian who had a legitimate daughter was conditional on marriage between the adoptive siblings,[27] and it is certainly reasonable to assume that the interpretation proposed by the speakers of Isa. 3 and 10 was commonly accepted in the fourth century. In practice, nevertheless, there must have been cases in which it would have been inconvenient, if not impossible, for an adopted son to marry his adoptive father's daughter. In such circumstances, it is likely that the application of the law was more flexible than Isaios, in the interest of these clients, would have wanted to concede. For example, one explanation sometimes put forward of the situation in Isa. 3 is that Phile was a

[25] ὁ γὰρ νόμος διαρρήδην λέγει ἐξεῖναι διαθέσθαι ὅπως ἂν ἐθέλῃ τις τὰ αὔτου, ἐὰν μὴ παῖδας γνησίους καταλίπῃ ἄρρενας· ἂν δὲ θηλείας καταλίπῃ, σὺν ταύταις, Isa. 3.68. Cf. the law on intestate succession, cited at [Dem.] 43.51: Ὅστις ἂν μὴ διαθέμενος ἀποθάνῃ, ἐὰν μὲν παῖδας καταλίπῃ θηλείας, σὺν ταύτῃσιν… 'If anyone dies without having disposed of his property, if he leaves daughters, with them…'. The law conferring the right to dispose of one's property, attributed to Solon, is cited verbatim at [Dem.] 46.14, but the passage cited does not include a reference to daughters.

[26] οὔτε γὰρ διαθέσθαι οὔτε δοῦναι οὐδενὶ ουδὲν ἔξεστι τῶν ἑαυτοῦ ἄνευ τῶν θυγατέρων, ἐάν τις καταλιπὼν γνησίας τελευτᾷ, Isa. 3.42; καὶ τῷ μὲν πατρὶ αὐτῆς, εἰ παῖδες ἄρρενες μὴ ἐγένοντο, οὐκ ἂν ἐξῆν ἄνευ ταύτης διαθέσθαι, Isa. 10.13.

[27] Rubinstein (1993), 95–96, dissents, suggesting that an Athenian with daughters may have been required simply to make adequate provision for them and their descendants if he adopted a son, and that what constituted adequate provision would be for a *dikastērion* to decide on a case by case basis.

small child when her father Pyrrhos, died, and by the time she reached marriageable age Endios was considered too old to father children.[28]

An exception to the rule would also have been needed when a man chose to adopt his stepson, in which case a marriage with the adoptive father's daughter (a *uterine sister of the adopted son) would have been prohibited as incestuous. This is what happens in Men. *Dys.*, where Knemon adopts his former wife's son, whom he explicitly instructs to find a husband for his daughter. The legal details are not spelt out, but the audience is apparently expected to find the situation a credible reflection of one that might arise in real life, whether or not it was strictly in accordance with the law.[29]

If, then, it was possible in some circumstances for a man to be adopted without marrying his adoptive father's legitimate daughter, what were the respective claims of the daughter and the adopted son to their father's estate? The position seems most straightforward in the case of a son adopted *inter vivos*, who immediately took on the legal status of a natural legitimate son. On the death of the father, the son would presumably inherit his estate, leaving the daughter, if she was not yet married, to be married by *enguē*. It would be possible for any apparent injustice to the daughter to be redressed by giving her a larger than usual dowry; this appears to be the position in Men. *Dys.*, where Knemon gives half his estate to his daughter as a dowry and the other half to his adopted son, Gorgias. Even allowing for an element of comic exaggeration this arrangement is, by normal standards, generous to the daughter,[30] treating her in effect like another son.

The potential for conflict between the rights of a daughter and those of an adopted son is more apparent when the adoption was testamentary. At the time of the testator's death his only surviving descendant would be the daughter, because the adoption could not take effect without *epidikasia*. Whether or not the deceased left a daughter, a testamentary adoption could be challenged on the grounds that the will itself was invalid. An unmarried daughter would not be in a position to act independently of her father's next of kin; but they, presumably, could challenge the will and, if successful, take the deceased's estate, along with the daughter, under the law of intestate succession. It is possible that a married daughter could

[28] See, e.g., Carey (1997), 126.
[29] For another example, cf. on αὑτὸν τῷ πατρὶ αὑτῶν εἰσποιήσας, 8.40.
[30] Cf. on σὺν ἱματίοις…, 8.8.

challenge the will in her own right, acting through her husband as **kurios*. It is unlikely, however, that a daughter could block an adopted son's claim by way of a **diamarturia*, since that would effectively deny a father of daughters the right to adopt by will at all.[31]

It is not clear from the sources what would happen if the will was unchallenged, or if it was successfully defended by the adopted son. Was the son strictly obliged to marry the *epiklēros* himself, or did he, like the next of kin, have the option of marrying her to someone else? Crucially, if he did not marry her, would he then (again like the next of kin) sacrifice his own right to the paternal estate, or at least put himself at risk of being disinherited by the daughter's eventual male issue?[32] The evidence from the speeches on this question is hardly conclusive. The speaker of Isa. 3 relies on the supremacy of the daughter's lineal descent from her father: Phile, he says, cannot have been a legitimate daughter of Pyrrhos because Endios (whom Pyrrhos had adopted by will) allowed her to be given in marriage to someone else, instead of marrying her himself. No adopted son would be silly enough to do this, knowing that the offspring of a legitimate daughter are entitled to inherit their grandfather's estate.[33] It is not, however, clear that the law itself was explicit and unambigous on this point.[34] If not, it would have been equally possible to construct a counter-argument based on the principle of male precedence, given that an adopted son (whether or not he was related by blood to the adopter) was normally considered to have the same legal rights as a natural legitimate son.

The argument, on a theoretical level, appears to be finely balanced. On the one hand, the adoption of a son might seem pointless if he did not become his adoptive father's successor. On the other hand, it might appear anomalous if a daughter's legitimate sons, who were direct descen-

---

31 Phile's use of the *diamarturia* in Isa. 3 is not directly relevant, since she did not attempt to reclaim her father's estate during Endios's lifetime, and her opponent is Endios's brother (her cousin) who claims as next of kin.

32 There can be no doubt that a daughter and her offspring, whether or not she was claimed in marriage as *epiklēros*, had precedence over the collateral relations of her deceased father (cf. the introduction to Isa. 8, pp. 96–97). This explains why Smikrines rejects the bargain offered to him in Men. *Aspis*: if he kept his brother's estate, but allowed his niece to marry the husband of her choice, she and her husband might have a son who would take legal action to recover the estate from him at a later date.

33 ἀκριβῶς γὰρ <ἂν> ᾔδει ὅτι τοῖς γε ἐκ τῆς γνησίας φυγατρὸς παισὶ γεγονόσιν ἁπάντων τῶν παππῴων κληρονόμια προσήκει, Isa. 3.50.

34 The law cited at [Dem.] 46.20, which establishes the inheritance rights of the son of an *epiklēros*, does not envisage the presence of an adopted son.

dants of her father and would have inherited his estate if she had been *epiklēros* at his death, were to be passed over in favour of an adopted son and his offspring who were at best collateral relatives of the deceased and need not be his blood relations at all.[35] So, in the absence of firm evidence to the contrary, it is at least conceivable that an Athenian with no legitimate sons could, in effect, disinherit his daughters and their offspring by adopting a son, either *inter vivos* or by will, without giving him one of the daughters in marriage.

The issue in Isa. 10, however, is different: when a woman became her father's only surviving descendant after the death of her brother, could her claim to the paternal estate be excluded by a son whose adoption adopted as the father's successor was posthumous? This seems highly doubtful, and it is likely that a posthumous adoption would have been open to challenge if it interfered with the rights of any natural descendant of the deceased. In some circumstances, nevertheless, it may have been the most acceptable and practical solution for the family concerned.

The Succession of Aristarkhos Senior

I have made the assumption that Kyronides was adopted at some time after the death of Aristarkhos senior, leaving his brother Demokhares to continue their father's *oikos*. The subsequent death of Demokhares must, then, have placed the family in some difficulty if they wanted to prevent the *oikos* of Aristarkhos senior from dying out. The lack of detail makes it difficult to reconstruct the family's situation at the time of Demohkares's death, but it is clear that the only surviving descendant of Aristarkhos senior was a daughter (the speaker's mother) who, according to the speaker, was not yet married. If that is correct, she became *epiklēros* when her brother died, and could have been claimed in marriage by her father's next of kin. (Even if she was already married, they could probably

---

[35] But see Karabélias (2002), 74: "Si le fils adoptif n'épousait pas la fille légitime du défunt ... les descendants du chef défunt de l'*oikos*, à savoir la progéniture de la fille légitime, ne pouvaient être exclus de la succession du défunt ... Car le fils adoptif ne semblait pas intervenir dans l'*oikos* du défunt en vertu de l'adoption, mais plutôt en sa qualité de mari de la fille légitime du défunt, en tant que partenaire de cette fille pour la procréation d'une descendance *kata phusin*." ("If the adopted son did not marry the legitimate daughter of the deceased ... the descendants of the deceased head of the *oikos*, namely the offspring of the daughter, could not be excluded from the succession of the deceased ... For the adopted son seemed to intervene in the *oikos* of the deceased by virtue of the adoption, but in his capacity as husband of the deceased's legitimate daughter, as partner of that daughter for the procreation of natural descendants.")

have forced a divorce from her existing husband, at least if she did not yet have a son.) The next of kin was either Aristomenes or, if he was already dead, his son Apollodoros (although there is no conclusive evidence in the speech that either of them was still alive when Demokhares died).

What, then, were the family's options? One course, which the speaker implies was the only strictly legal one, would have been for Aristomenes or Apollodoros to claim the *epiklēros* by *epidikasia*, if necessary forcing the dissolution of her first marriage. Alternatively, if they were content to renounce any claim to Aristarkhos senior's estate, or perhaps to rely on an informal arrangement with her present or future husband, they could have arranged an exogamous marriage, or allowed an existing marriage to continue, in the expectation that any male offspring would eventually take up the inheritance transmitted through their mother (and perhaps that one of them would be posthumously adopted as successor to his grandfather, Aristarkhos senior). We may conjecture that this is what the speaker would really have liked to happen, since the advantage to him is obvious, although it is not consistent with his criticism of Aristomenes and Apollodoros for failing to marry his mother.[36]

For reasons which are now impossible to determine, the family rejected these options in favour of having Aristarkhos junior posthumously adopted into the *oikos* of Aristarkhos senior, legally his great-uncle (although in fact the adoption returned Aristarkhos junior to his natural place in the succession of his paternal grandfather). If it was legal at all, such an adoption could, presumably, take place only with the consent of all the interested family members. Isa. 10.19 may be taken as an indication that the speaker's father raised an objection to the adoption, pointing out that he and his wife might produce a son who could in due course become her father's successor, but that he grudgingly acquiesced under the threat of an enforced dissolution of his marriage to the speaker's mother.

The details of the 'arrangement' remain obscure, but it is likely that they included a generous dowry for the speaker's mother, or, if she was already married, a substantial payoff for her husband in cash or landed property. A further possibility is that there may have been an agreement that Aristarkhos junior would occupy the estate for his lifetime, on the

---

36 The speaker expressly says that Kyronides had died before the adoption of Aristarkhos junior (§6). Had that not been the case it might have been possible for Kyronides to return to his natal *oikos* after the death of Demokhares, leaving one of his own sons behind in the *oikos* of his adoptive father, Xenainetos senior. In fact the speaker denies, with the support of testimony, that Kyronides returned at any stage (§7).

understanding that he would be succeeded by the speaker. If Aristarkhos junior had broken such an agreement by making a will in favour of Xenainetos junior, the speaker would have found himself in a difficult position: he could not invite a court to uphold a private arrangement that was not strictly legal, so his only recourse was to persuade the *dikastai* that the adoption was invalid. He does not deny that Aristarkhos junior had been introduced to the phratry of Aristarkhos senior, and the absence of any reference to objections by the phratry members strongly suggests that the procedure had not been formally challenged. In short, since there was no way of overturning the phratry's decision, the posthumous adoption of Aristarkhos junior was a major obstacle for the speaker, whatever the strength of his complaints about the treatment of his mother.

The Strength of the Speaker's Case

The lack of detail in this speech makes it exceptionally difficult to construct a coherent account of the speaker's factual and legal position. As the commentary will show, it seems likely that Isaios manipulated the early history of the family to give the impression that the whole of the estate of Aristarkhos senior should have gone to the speaker's mother as *epiklēros*. But even if the *dikastai* were persuaded that his story was true, it is difficult to see how they could have overturned an adoption that had been approved by Aristarkhos senior's phratry and accepted for many years as valid. Isaios contrives, nevertheless, not only to make an arguable case but also, taking advantage of his client's position as first speaker at the trial,[37] to create a dilemma for his opponent. By focusing on the succession of Aristarkhos senior instead of the will of Aristarkhos junior he has, in effect, made the entire speech into a digression from the real issue. If Xenainetos junior attempts a detailed reply to the speaker's attack on the adoption of Aristarkhos junior, he may fail to convince the *dikastai* and miss the opportunity to validate his claim as Aristarkhos junior's testamentary heir. If, on the other hand, he ignores what the speaker has said and focuses on proving the validity of the will, he runs the risk of appearing evasive.

---

[37] Cf. introductory note to §§8–17.

Commentary

**Proem (1–3)*

In a typically tendentious introduction, the speaker attempts to prejudice the **dikastai* against the 'professionalism' of his opponents. Without giving any detail of the substance of the dispute, he makes two key points to which he will revert later: that the opponents have acted illegally, and that the disputed property lawfully belonged to his mother.

1 Ἐβουλόμην <μέν>, ὦ ἄνδρες ('I could wish, gentlemen'). On addresses to the **dikastai* in Isaios's speeches, see on Ὤιμην ..., 7.1. Although this is the shortest of Isaios's extant speeches, it contains twenty-two addresses, more than any of his other inheritance speeches, including one instance of *ō andres dikastai* (§25). In this speech, as in Isa. 9, the frequency of addresses appears to be associated with a heightening of the emotional tone, and perhaps reflects a lack of confidence on the speaker's part in his own arguments.

ὥσπερ Ξεναίνετος οὑτοσὶ ... δυνηθῆναι ('just as Xenainetos here finds it easy to lie with boldness, I could with equal confidence speak the truth to you in presenting my claim'). Isaios neatly combines the conventional plea of the inexperienced speaker with his client's wish to speak the truth, representing the opponent as an eloquent and shameless liar. The theme will be taken up in the argument; cf. on οὐκ ἀληθῆ λέξει and καὶ ταῦτα ψεύσονται, §9 and ἢ ἐὰν φῶσι, ψεύσονται, §11. On the demonstrative *houtosi*, see on [ὁ] Κλέων οὑτοσί, 9.2.

εἴθ' ἡμεῖς ἀδίκως ... ταῦτα εἰλήφασι ('whether we have come forward unjustly to claim the estate, or whether our opponents have been wrongfully in possession of the property for a long time'). Despite the specious balance, the alternatives are loaded; there is no doubt that the speaker wants the **dikastai* to accept the second, which supersedes the first and is expressed at greater length.

πάλαι ('long ago'). Cf. on προσποιούμενος ..., 9.4.

νῦν δὲ οὐκ ἐξ ἴσου διακείμεθα, ὦ ἄνδρες ('but now, gentlemen, we are not on an equal footing'). The speaker appeals to the Athenians' prejudice against those who have too much experience of litigation, and, like the speakers of Isa. 1 and 8, tries to secure the sympathy of the **dikastai* by presenting himself as at a disadvantage. This is consistent with his portrayal of himself and his mother as victims.

καὶ παρασκευάσασθαι ἱκανοί ('and skilled at concocting cases'). See on παρασκευάσας, 8.3. The speaker's slur against his opponents is not supported by any evidence, and the vagueness of his allegations enables him to hint at a range of corrupt activities without specifying any particular offence.

καὶ ὑπὲρ ἑτέρων πολλάκις ἐν ὑμῖν ἠγωνίσθαι ('and have often contested cases before you on behalf of others'). The speaker's opponents are all the less deserving of indulgence from the **dikastai* because they have spoken frequently in the courts, not only on their own account but also on behalf of others. The language is too vague to determine whether he means that they were acting as **sunēgoroi* or *sykophants.

οὐδὲ ὑπὲρ ἐμαυτοῦ πώποτε δίκην ἰδίαν εἴρηκα ('I have never even spoken on my own behalf in a private suit'). The conventional plea of the inexperienced speaker is adapted to suit the present speaker's circumstances. Wyse takes the reference to private litigation as leaving open the possibility that the speaker could have been involved in a public action. This, however, overlooks the force of 'nor', which conveys the sense '[So far from having spoken as a **sunēgoros*] I have never even spoken on behalf of myself in a private case'. Having already said that his opponents have spoken in court on behalf of others, the speaker implies through this antithesis that they did so in public cases.

πολλῆς δεῖ με συγγνώμης ('I deserve great indulgence'). The speaker asks for the indulgence (*sungnōmē*) of the **dikastai* because his skill in public speaking is inferior to that of his opponent, not because he admits any substantive weakness in his case. Cf. Isa. 6.2, the only other example of a plea for *sungnōmē* in Isaios's speeches.

2 Ἠνάγκασμαι ... προσγράψασθαι ('It is true that I was obliged, gentlemen, because I could not obtain justice from my opponents, to add to my claim at the *anakrisis* that my mother was the sister of Aristarkhos junior'). The **anakrisis* (on which see Harrison (1971), 94–105) is not mentioned explicitly in any of Isaios's other **diadikasia* speeches, but cf. 6.12, 13, 15. In this case it seems that the basis of the speaker's claim was discussed, and that he had to make some concessions to get it admitted. His mother was by birth the aunt (father's sister) of Aristarkhos junior, but when the latter was adopted into her father's **oikos* she became *de jure* his sister. Formally the speaker made his claim as the *de jure* nephew of Aristarkhos junior, which implies that he recognized the posthumous adoption of Aristarkhos junior by Aristarkhos senior. He presents this as a concession that he was forced to make; the passive 'was obliged' enables him to avoid saying by whom. Perhaps the **arkhōn* refused to accept his claim on any other basis, or perhaps his opponent tricked him. Alternatively

(as suggested in the introduction to this speech, pp. 196–198) it may be that the speaker himself was initially content to describe himself as Aristarkhos junior's nephew, but later changed the basis of his claim. Whatever the reason for the concession, it appears that it did not prevent him from trying to persuade the **dikastai* that the supposed adoption was illegal (cf. Harrison, (1971), 95–96). The admission does, nevertheless, suggest some embarrassment on the speaker's part, and his opponent will be able to exploit the fact that he has accepted the adoption in writing.

The combination of particles *men oun* ('it is true') may be either adversative or affirmative (Denniston (1954), 479–480). Here it appears to have a concessive force, anticipating the emphatic negation *ou mēn* at the beginning of the following sentence.

The speaker's complaint that he could not obtain justice from his opponents probably refers to a breakdown of informal negotiations, showing that he clearly had some opportunity to find out about his opponent's case; cf. the introductory note to §§8–17.

εἰ τὰ ἑαυτοῦ δέδωκε τούτῳ Ἀρίσταρχος ἢ τὰ μηδὲν προσήκοντα ('whether Aristarkhos junior gave his own property to [my opponent] or whether it was property to which he was not entitled'). The speaker explains the basis of his claim from the outset: he is not challenging Aristarkhos junior's capacity to make a will, nor does he claim that the will in which Aristarkhos junior left his estate to Xenainetos junior is a forgery. His point is rather that the estate did not lawfully belong to Aristarkhos junior in the first place, because his adoption into the **oikos* of Aristarkhos senior was invalid. Possible reasons for Isaios's choice of this strategy are discussed in the introduction to this speech, pp. 196–198.

ὁ γὰρ νόμος κελεύει ('for the law ordains'). At an early stage the speaker seeks to establish that the law is on his side, and that his opponents have acted illegally.

τῶν δὲ ἀλλοτρίων οὐδένα κύριον πεποίηκε ('but it has given no-one power over the property of others'). For 'the property of others', see on Ἐπὶ τοῖς τοιούτπος…, 8.1. Isaios's interpretation of the law on testamentary disposition is tendentious; it is self-evident that no-one can make a will disposing of someone else's property. The truism will have had some persuasive force, but it begs the question about the rightful ownership of the property at issue. The point is repeated at §22.

3 ἐάν μου μετ' εὐνοίας ἀκοῦσαι ἐθέλητε ('if you will listen to me with good will'). Using a different formula (cf. 'I deserve great indulgence' in §1) the speaker again solicits the sympathetic attention of the **dikastai*, perhaps

as an indication of the difficulty he is experiencing. On pleas for good will, see on δέομαι…, 7.4.

ἀλλὰ τῆς ἐμῆς μητρὸς πατρῷος ('but my mother's inheritance from her father'). The idea that the estate of Aristarkhos senior rightly belonged to the speaker's mother becomes a *leitmotif* of the speech, recurring at §§7, 11, 14 and 26. By portraying his client as a dutiful son seeking to redress an injustice against his mother, Isaios gives him a creditable motive for claiming the estate, deflecting any suspicion that he was acting out of personal greed.

οὐδὲ καθ' ἕνα νόμον ('not in accordance with any law'). This emphatic negative, used to deny the legality of Aristarkhos junior's supposed adoption into the **oikos* of Aristarkhos senior, is repeated at §§6 and 8. The repetition of the negative phrase at key points in the speech is reminiscent of the way in which the speaker of Isa. 9 deploys the phrase 'to no-one but me'. Cf. on 9.1 and 24.

παρὰ πάντας τοὺς νόμους ('against all the laws'). This phrase, repeated at §13, is not used elsewhere in Isaios's extant speeches, but occurs thirteen times in the Demosthenic corpus (e.g. Dem. 21.27; 24.19, [Dem.] 44.41) and once in Aiskhines (Aiskhin. 3.212). Here it reinforces 'not in accordance with any law', but is not merely tautologous since it carries a stronger sense of illegality. Isaios's use of the two phrases blurs the distinction between actions which are tolerated, though not explicitly sanctioned by law, and those which actually contravene the law. His purpose may be less to make a legal point than to generate emotion in order to obfuscate factual considerations.

ἀδικεῖ μετὰ τῶν οἰκείων τὴν ἐμὴν μητέρα ('he, with members of his family, wronged my mother'). Since the subject of *adikei* (lit. 'wrongs') is the deceased Aristarkhos junior, it must be a historic present (cf. on πάσχει δεινότατα, §5). By implicating Aristarkhos's relations in the offence against the speaker's mother, Isaios presents her as a victim isolated within the family.

ὅθεν…πειράσομαι διδάσκειν ('I shall try to explain things to you, going back to the point from which you will most clearly understand the facts'). For the metanarrative narratorial intervention, see on ποιήσομαι…, 7.4.

Narrative (4–6)

In an exceptionally brief main narrative, the speaker appears to give a simple and straightforward account of events, but closer analysis shows that he is mingling objective fact with subjective and biased interpretation, and omitting some important details. Later in the speech, when he anticipates some of the arguments to be put forward by his opponent, a fuller picture begins to emerge, but there is none of the circumstantial detail provided in Isaios's other **diadikasia* speeches.

4 Ἀρίσταρχος γὰρ ... ὦ ἄνδρες ('For Aristarkhos, gentlemen'). On the combination of an address to the **dikastai* with the explanatory particle *gar*, marking the transition from *proem to narrative, see on Εὔπολις γὰρ ..., 7.5.

Ξεναινέτου Ἀχαρνέως θυγατέρα ('a daughter of Xenainetos of Akharnai'). This is one of only three speeches where Isaios names an ancestor of the claimant to an estate earlier than his grandfather; cf. Isa. 5 and 11, both of which belong to long-running dynastic disputes involving distinguished Athenian families. Xenainetos senior is identified as the father-in-law of Aristarkhos senior and adoptive father of Kyronides (§7) but the speaker tells us nothing more about him. This is consistent with the view that 'family memory' in classical Athens rarely extended back beyond the speaker's grandparents, and that when earlier generations are mentioned for genealogical purposes, information about them tends to be sparse. Cf. Thomas (1989), 123–131, on "the limits of family memory" in classical Athens.

Κυρωνίδης καὶ ... ἀδελφή ('Kyronides and Demokhares and my mother and another sister of theirs'). The speaker names his two maternal uncles, but not his aunt or maternal grandmother, and not even his mother, whose position in the inheritance dispute is at least as important as that of her brothers. This anonymity reflects the general convention that women of citizen status are not named in forensic speeches, especially while they are still alive. Women who are named are likely to be non-citizens (e.g. Alke in Isa. 6, Neaira in [Dem.] 59) or presented by an opponent as being non-citizens or of dubious reputation (e.g. Plangon in Dem. 39 and [Dem.] 40, Phile in Isa. 3, Phano in [Dem.] 59). In a few cases there is a positive reason for naming a female citizen without casting any slur on her character. One example is the speaker's mother, Nikarete, in Dem. 57, a case of disputed citizenship where positive identification of both of the speaker's parents is essential. Another is the aristocratic Agariste, one of the alleged informants in Andok. 1, where it is important for Andokides to give the fullest possible information if his defence is to be credible. Kleitarete, the mother of Pyrrhos in Isa. 3, is named because of a dispute about her granddaughter's name, but was not alive at the time of the speech. It is possible that the Athenians' reluctance to name respectable women in forensic speeches was more than simply a mark of respect; in a society where female citizens had no public rôle in civic affairs, a woman may have been more easily identifiable by her relationship to a husband, father or brother than by her own name. For more examples and a detailed discussion, see Schaps (1977). Sommerstein (1980) argues that a similar convention is observed in Greek and Roman comedy.

ὁ τοῦδε πατὴρ ('this man's father'). Kyronides was the father of the speaker's opponent, Xenainetos junior. Typically, the speaker uses a pronoun instead of a personal name to marginalize his opponent. Cf. on ταύτην τε ἣ νῦν ἀμφισβητεῖ…, 7.18.

καὶ θατέρου τοῦ τόνδε τὸν κλῆρον ἀδίκως ἔχοντος ('and of the other one who held the estate illegally'). The speaker does not name Aristarkhos junior, Kyronides's other son, perhaps in order to avoid confusion with Aristarkhos senior; but he takes the opportunity to refer to him, in highly prejudicial terms, as the illegal possessor of the property of Aristarkhos senior.

ἐξεποιήθη … προσῆκεν ('was adopted into another **oikos*, so that he had no further claim to the property'). Cf. on ἐκποίητος, 7.23. The speaker does not specify when Kyronides was adopted by Xenainetos senior, but it is implicit in the narrative that the adoption took place before the death of Kyronides's father, Aristarkhos senior, whose estate, according to the speaker, passed to Demokhares alone. Isaios may have been trying to mislead the **dikastai* on this point; cf. on ἐπὶ τοῖς της ἐμῆς μητρὸς χρήμασι, §5, καὶ ἐν ἐκείνω ἐτελήυτησεν, §7 and Κυρωνίδου μὲν…, §8.

Ἀριστάρχου δέ τοῦ πατρὸς <τοῦ> τούτων τελευτήσαντος ('On the death of Aristarkhos, the father of these two'). The involvement in this case of two men called Aristarkhos, and two called Xenainetos, is a potential source of confusion which Isaios sometimes exploits. Here, however, he is careful to distinguish the speaker's grandfather Aristarkhos from his recently deceased namesake.

τούτου δὲ παιδὸς ἀποθανόντος καὶ τῆς ἑτέρας ἀδελφῆς ('but when he died while a child and the other sister also died'). On the speaker's account, the deaths of both Demokhares and his other sister while under age left the speaker's mother as sole claimant to the estate.

ἡ μήτηρ ἡ ἐμὴ ἐπὶ παντὶ τῷ οἴκῳ ἐπίκληρος ἐγένετο ('my mother became *epiklēros* to the whole of the family estate'). See the introduction to this speech, p. 196. Despite the speaker's insistence on his mother's entitlement to her father's estate, he uses the term **epiklēros* only three times (cf. §§12 and 21).

If Kyronides had not been adopted before his natural father's death, but had shared the estate with Demokhares, then the speaker's mother would not have inherited the whole estate, but only the half of it left to her by Demokhares. The speaker's emphasis may imply that this was a point disputed by his opponents.

5 πάσχει δεινότατα ('she was [lit. 'is'] treated very badly'). The present tense might be taken as implying that the speaker's mother was still alive, or even that he was acting as her **kurios* to claim the estate on her behalf. The context suggests, however, that it could be read as a historic present, representing the aorist *epathen deinotata*: 'she was treated very badly [on the occasion when she was given in marriage by **enguē* instead of being claimed as **epiklēros*]'. See on ἀδικεῖ…, §3, and cf. 'gives' and 'introduce' in §6. Although the evidence is inconclusive, the overall impression conveyed by the speech is that the speaker was claiming the estate for himself after his mother's death. (See on κατὰ τὸν νόμον…, §12 and εἰρήνης τ'αὖ γενομένης…, §20, and cf. Wyse, 650.) The ambivalence contributes to Isaios's strategy of engaging the sympathy of the **dikastai* on her behalf.

ὦ ἄνδρες ('gentlemen'). See on Ἐβουλόμην…, §1. In the course of what is presented as a straightforward, objective narrative, the address adds emphasis to the statement and engages the attention of the **dikastai.*

ἀμελήσας… ἐπιδικάσασθαι ('neglected either to make her his own wife or to have her married to his son by an adjudication of the court'). The tendentious language implies that Aristomenes was neglecting a duty by not claiming the speaker's mother in marriage for himself or his son, Apollodoros. In fact, although the father's next of kin were entitled to claim the hand of an **epiklēros*, they were not obliged to do so, provided they were prepared to forfeit any property that came with her. The rules of the epiklerate are discussed in the introduction to this speech, pp. 205–209.

τούτων μὲν οὐδὲν ἐποίησε ('he did neither of these things'). For the presentation through negation, see on ἐκείνῳ…, 7.17, and οὐδὲν φαίνεται…, 9.9. The speaker conveys the impression that what may have been perfectly reasonable behaviour on Aristomenes's part was a transgression against a social or moral obligation, if not actually illegal.

ἐπὶ τοῖς τῆς ἐμῆς μητρὸς χρήμασι ('with the property that belonged to my mother'). Cf. on ἀλλὰ τῆς ἐμῆς μητρὸς πατρῷος, §3. It is significant that Kyronides was the beneficiary of this 'dowry'. On the speaker's account (§15), his opponents will claim that Kyronides was entitled to what remained of Aristarkhos senior's estate, because he cleared an outstanding debt on it. The real explanation may have been more simple: that

Kyronides had not been adopted in his father's lifetime, and so became joint heir to the estate with his brother Demokhares. (See the introduction to this speech, p. 203, and cf. on ἐξεποιήθη …, §4, καὶ ἐν ἐκείνῳ ἐτελεύτησεν, §7, and Κυρωνίδου μὲν …, §8.)

ἐξ ἧς ('by whom'). Xenainetos junior and Aristarkhos junior were full brothers, both born to Kyronides by the daughter of Aristomenes.

ὁ Ξεναίνετος οὗτος καὶ Ἀρίσταρχος ὁ τελευτήσας ('Xenainetos here and Aristarkhos, who has now died'). The use of *houtos* distinguishes 'this' Xenainetos (i.e. Xenainetos junior) from Xenainetos senior; and *ho teleutēsas* ('the one who has died') distinguishes Aristarkhos junior from Aristarkhos senior. It appears that Kyronides showed his piety, and respect for the ties of kinship, by naming his two sons respectively after his own natural father and adoptive father. It is possible, however, that the names were taken after adoption.

6 ἀπεστερήθη ('was robbed'). See on ἀποστερῶν, 8.3.

μετὰ δὲ ταῦτα ('and after that'). One effect of the extremely compressed narrative is that the sequence of events, and the length of the intervals between them, are unclear. The speaker implies that his mother's marriage took place after the death of her brother Demokhares, as well as that of their father, so she was not married when she became **epiklēros*, but it may be significant that he does not produce testimony on this point. As Harrison (1968), 311, suggests, it is possible that she was in fact married before the death of Demokhares, "and that on the latter event a composition was reached between the speaker's father and his mother's family of which §19 is a distorted account." Cf. Roussel (1922), 176–177, and see the introductory note to §19.

ἐκδίδωσι ('gave [lit. "gives"] in marriage'). Instead of seeking to marry her as **epiklēros*, Aristomenes gave his niece, the speaker's mother, in marriage by **enguē*. At this stage the speaker does not mention his mother's dowry, but cf. on ἐπὶ προικὶ ἐγγυησάμενος, §19. The historic present makes the highly compressed narrative more vivid.

τῷ ἐμῷ πατρί ('to my father'). All we know about the speaker's father, who is not named in the speech, is that he fought during the Corinthian War of 394–386 BC (§20), and that he died leaving unmarried daughters who were later given in marriage by the speaker (§25). This latter fact suggests that he must have been dead some considerable time—probably at least ten years—before the trial.

Κυρωνίδου … ὑὸν ('After Kyronides had died, they introduced Xenainetos's brother as the adopted son of Aristarkhos senior'). Here and elsewhere (§§8, 15, 21) the speaker uses the verb *eisagein* ('introduce') as if it were synonymous with *eispoiein* ('adopt'). This suggests, as argued by Rubinstein (1993), 43, 'that the enrolment in the *phratry of the adoptive father could sometimes be construed as the actual procedure of adoption.' Again, the historic present is used for vividness, but the subject of the verb is left deliberately vague, in keeping with the speaker's later argument that there was no-one who could legally have carried out an adoption. The speaker does not, however, deny that the introduction took place, or that the phratry acquiesced in the introduction of Aristarkhos junior, which implies that there was a reasonable legal and factual basis for his adoption as the son of Aristarkhos senior.

Why did the death of Kyronides, rather than that of Demokhares, become the occasion for the posthumous adoption of Aristarkhos junior as son of Aristarkhos senior? If Kyronides had not been adopted, or had returned to his natal **oikos*, it would almost certainly not have been considered necessary to adopt a son for Aristarkhos senior, since the sons of Kyronides would already have been in their paternal grandfather's line of succession. As it was, Kyronides died in the *oikos* of his adoptive father, Xenainetos senior, leaving two sons, and it may be that the family found it convenient to avoid dividing the estate of Xenainetos senior by making one of them the successor to Aristarkhos senior. Whether or not the speaker had been born at the time of the adoption, it is easy to understand how he might have grown up to resent this arrangement, especially if his own father was less affluent than Kyronides and his sons.

οὐδὲ καθ' ἕνα νόμον ('not in accordance with any law'), see on οὐδὲ καθ' ἕνα νόμον, §3.

ὡς ἐγὼ ἐκ πολλῶν τεκμηρίων ὑμῖν ἐπιδείξω ('as I shall demonstrate to you by many proofs'). See on μεγάλα γὰρ τεκμηρία, 7.11.

Witness Testimony (7)

The speaker begins his proof by adducing testimony on the key 'facts' of his story. He calls only one set of witnesses, immediately after the exceptionally brief narrative, bringing together testimony on several points. This contrasts sharply with the structure of Isa. 9, where the narrative is broken down into short sections, each followed by the relevant piece of testimony (cf. introductory note on 9.27–30). Isaios's intention here may have been to disguise a weak point in the testimony; it is also possible that some of his evidence was uncontested, and that he was avoiding the real issues.

μάρτυρας ὑμῖν παρέξομαι ('I shall produce witnesses'). It would be interesting to know the identity of the witnesses, and how many there were. The speaker may have been supported by his sisters' husbands, and we cannot rule out the possibility that he had a brother, but there is no evidence that he had any male blood relations, apart from his opponent, who were living at the time of the speech. It is likely, however, that if the witnesses had been kinsmen of Aristarkhos junior or the speaker, Isaios would have identified them at least by relationship, if not by name. Cf. especially Isa. 9, where the speaker is keen to demonstrate that he has the support of other members of the family and of the wider community. In this case, it is not clear whether there were potential witnesses who were unwilling to testify on the speaker's behalf, or whether there was simply no-one in or close to his family who could have done so.

ὡς Κυρωνίδης ἐκποίητος εἰς τὸν Ξεναινέτου οἶκον ἐγένετο ('that Kyronides was adopted into the **oikos* of Xenainetos'). Cf. on ἐκποίητος, 7.23. Now, for the first time, Isaios identifies Xenainetos senior as the adoptive father of Kyronides. The adoption of Kyronides out of the *oikos* of his natural father, Aristarkhos senior, is a crucial element in the story that the estate of Aristarkhos senior devolved through Demokhares to the speaker's mother. It is likely, however, that the fact of the adoption was not contested by the speaker's opponent, even if the detailed circumstances were contentious, so the weight of this evidence may not be particularly great.

It is not clear whether Xenainetos senior adopted Kyronides *inter vivos* or by will, or whether the adoption was posthumous. The speaker gives no indication of the reasons for the adoption, but it is worth considering why it was thought to be necessary, given that Kyronides would presumably have inherited the estate as his maternal grandfather's intestate heir. The practice of adopting grandsons has sometimes been taken as evidence that a daughter's son did not automatically inherit unless his mother was **epiklēros* (cf. the introduction to Isa. 8, pp. 98–99) but there are other explanations. It is possible that Xenainetos senior had more than one daughter, all of whose sons would have shared his estate equally unless he excluded the others by adopting Kyronides as his preferred heir. Or he may have been concerned about the continuation of his *oikos*, as well as the transmission of his property. The same considerations could have been taken into account by members of the family if the adoption was posthumous, but if it was *inter vivos*, Xenainetos may have felt the need for a son to look after him in old age. Cf. Rubinstein (1993), chapter 4, 'Why did the Athenians adopt?'

καὶ ἐν ἐκείνῳ ἐτελεύτησεν ('and died in that [*oikos*]'). The speaker also excludes the possibility that Kyronides returned to his natal **oikos*, leaving a son of his own in the *oikos* of his adoptive father. Cf. on ἀλλ' αὐτῷ ..., §11, for the legal position. It is possible that the speaker was expecting his opponent to say that Kyronides did return, although it is not clear why it would be in Xenainetos junior's interest to make such a claim. On the other hand, it may be that the speaker was simply trying to bolster his case by bringing testimony on an uncontested issue. A more significant point which is not covered by the testimony is when Kyronides was adopted (cf. on ἐξεποιήθη ..., §4).

ἔπειθ' ὡς Ἀρίσταρχος ... ἐτελεύτησε ('secondly, that Aristarkhos ... died before his son Demokhares'). The reason for the speaker's insistence that Demokhares outlived his father, Aristarkhos senior, is not immediately apparent, but it sows the *seed for his argument that Aristarkhos senior could not have adopted a son by will (cf. on γνησίου γὰρ ..., §9). The survival of Demokhares would also have been regarded as a necessary condition for the adoption of Kyronides, which would otherwise have left Aristarkhos senior without a successor.

οὗ ἦν οὗτος ὁ κλῆρος ('to whom this estate belonged'). Cf. 'to whom the estate originally belonged', Isa. 3.3, where, as in this case, the reference is not to the recently deceased estate holder but his adoptive father. (The present tense at 9.1, 'whose estate this is', identifies Astyphilos as the **de cuius*.) Although the speaker tries to put his case in terms of a claim to the estate of Aristarkhos senior, the legal basis of the action must have been an application for **epidikasia* from Xenainetos junior, as testamentary heir to Arkistarkhos junior.

Δημοχάρης δὲ παῖς ὢν ἀπέθανε καὶ ἡ ἑτέρα ἀδελφή ('and that Demokhares died while a child, as did the other sister'). The speaker is also very insistent that Demokhares died while still a minor, putting beyond doubt that he left no offspring who might have had a claim to the estate of Aristarkhos junior. Cf. on τούτου δὲ παιδὸς ..., §4. Later (see on παιδὸς γὰρ ..., §10), he uses the minority of Demokhares to demonstrate that he could not have left a will adopting Aristarkhos junior. Gernet (1921), 345–346, thought it possible that a woman might not have been treated as **epiklēros* if her brother had already reached the age of majority at the time of his death. On the evidence of Men. *Aspis*, however, this was not a relevant distinction.

ὥστε τὸν κλῆρον ἐπὶ τῇ ἐμῇ μητρὶ γενέσθαι ('so that the estate devolved onto my mother'). Cf. on ἀλλὰ τῆς ἐμῆς μητρὸς πατρῷος, §3. It is unlikely that the speaker expected his witnesses to testify that the estate of Aristarkhos senior devolved to his mother; this is simply his own, tendentious conclusion from the facts to which they will testify.

καί μοι κάλει τούτων τοὺς μάρτυρας ('Please call the witnesses to these facts.') Isaios uses the simplest of the available formulae to summon the only group of witnesses appearing for his client. On the range of formulae available to him, see on τούτων πρῶτον . . ., 7.10.

Argument and Law: The Succession of Aristarkhos Senior (*8–17*)

A distinctive rhetorical feature of this speech is the extensive use of **prokatalēpsis*. In adversarial litigation this was a tactic used by prosecutors not only to dispose in advance of points that they genuinely expected the defendant to make, but also to prejudice the **dikastai* by misrepresenting the defendant's case. (See the introduction to Isa. 8, p. 93.)

It appears that Isaios was not in a position to launch a direct attack on the testimony or character of Xenainetos junior or his witnesses, as he did against the wife of Pronapes in Isa. 7, Diokles in Isa. 8 and Hierokles in Isa. 9. So he found another way of undermining Xenainetos's evidence by adapting the prosecutorial tactic to his client's position as the first speaker in a **diadikasia*, purporting to anticipate some of the opponent's arguments about the adoption of Aristarkhos junior.

The argument proceeds in two stages. First (§§8–11) the speaker seeks to prove that neither Aristarkhos senior nor Demokhares could (legally) have adopted Aristarkhos junior by will, and neither could Kyronides have introduced him to the phratry of Aristarkhos senior. The legal basis of the argument appears, for the most part, to be sound, but in the factual context all these possibilities are somewhat remote and hypothetical. Then (§§12–17), the speaker moves on to consider, and reject, the suggestion that Aristarkhos junior could have been introduced into Aristarkhos senior's phratry by Aristomenes or Apollodoros. At this stage the legal argumentation becomes more suspect, but it appears to reflect (albeit in a rather distorted form) the reality that it was Apollodoros who carried out the introduction to Aristarkhos senior's *phratry.

In the course of the argument Isaios uses a variety of devices (propositions in the alternative, in the conditional tense, or introduced by 'perhaps') which might be thought to imply that the speaker was not entirely sure of his ground. Cf. Dorjahn (1935), 282, citing Lys. 6.42; 12.50; 13.52; Isok. 20.5; 21.16; Lyk. 1.63. Further examples of 'perhaps' in anticipation of the opponent's argument include Isa. 3.24; 5.3, 28, 46; 9.10.) So Avramovič, (1997) 266, takes Isaios's reasoning as an indication that the speaker was uncertain whether his opponent's line of attack would be based on testamentary or posthumous adoption. But Isaios's client had an opportunity to find out about his opponent's case during the preliminary negotiations alluded to at §2, so it seems more likely that the suggestion of uncertainty is disingenuous: Isaios was employing a deliberate strategy to confuse the *dikastai* with a series of improbable and sometimes mutually conflicting points, under the guise of a comprehensive rebuttal. By pretending that he expects Xenainetos to advance such claims, and then discrediting them, he gives his client the opportunity to claim that he has the law on his side, while making his opponent's case look ridiculous.

8 Οὕτω μὲν ἐξ ἀρχῆς ... ὁ κλῆρος ('Thus, gentlemen, the estate belonged to my mother from the beginning'). See on Ἐβουλόμην ..., §1. The parenthetic address marks the transition from testimony to argument, at the same time seeking to secure the support of the *dikastai* for the speaker's biased version of the facts.

Κυρωνίδου μὲν ἐκποιήτου γενομένου εἰς τὸν Ξεναινέτου οἶκον ('since Kyronides had been adopted into the *oikos* of Xenainetos'). Cf. on ἐκποίητος, 7.23. Isaios clearly wants his audience to understand that Kyronides was adopted by Xenainetos senior before the death of Aristarkhos senior, to whose estate he therefore had no valid claim. It may be significant, however, that Isaios avoids stating this directly in a temporal clause, and instead uses the more ambivalent genitive absolute.

οὐδὲ καθ' ἕνα νόμον ('not in accordance with any law'). See on οὐδὲ καθ' ἕνα νόμον, §3.

εἰς τοὺς φράτορας τοὺς ἐκείνου εἰσῆκται ('was introduced into the phratry of [Aristarkhos]'). For the use of 'introduce' instead of 'adopt', see on Κυρωνίδου ..., §6. By using the verb in the passive voice, the speaker avoids saying by whom Artistarkhos junior was, according to Xenainetos and his supporters, introduced into the phratry of his grandfather Aristarkhos senior. In fact this is a question to which the speaker claims not to know the answer, which he challenges his opponents to give. But there is a hint at §13; see on τῷ δὲ μήτε λαβεῖν αὐτὴν....

ἐὰν γὰρ τοῦτο μάθητε ... προσῆκεν ('if you understand this you will clearly know that the man who held the estate illegally had no right to dispose of it either'). This is the crux of the speaker's argument: if Aristarkhos junior had no legal status as the adopted son of Aristarkhos senior, then he had no right to dispose of the estate in his turn. The direct address to the *dikastai* in the second person puts the point across in a highly persuasive way. Cf. on Ὑμεῖς, 8.12.

9 οἶμαι τοίνυν πάντας ὑμᾶς εἰδέναι, ὦ ἄνδρες ('I think you all know, gentlemen'). On the presentation of a doubtful or contentious fact as common knowledge, see on δέδοικα δὲ . . ., 8.34. The 'conversational and lively' particle *toinun* is, in this context, transitional, marking the introduction of a new argument. Cf. Denniston (1954), 569, 574–575.

The address engages the **dikastai* in the speaker's argument, reinforcing the effect of the particle and the second person pronoun earlier in the sentence. Isaios thus takes great care in setting up an argument which is based on a decidedly shaky premise. Cf. on ἐγὼ δ', ὦ ἄνδρες, §16.

ὅτι κατὰ διαθήκας αἱ εἰσαγωγαὶ τῶν εἰσποιήτων γίγνονται ('that the introductions of adopted sons are always carried out in accordance with a will'). The structure of the speaker's argument is syllogistic: his major (and highly misleading) premise is that an adoption is always carried out in accordance with the testamentary dispositions of an adopter who has died. The phrase 'introductions of adopted sons [into their adoptive fathers' *phratries]') is here used synonymously with *eispoiēseis*, 'adoptions'. Cf. on Κυρωνίδου . . ., §6.

διδόντων τὰ ἑαυτῶν καὶ ὑεῖς ποιουμένων ('[the testators] simultaneously disposing of their property and adopting sons'). The two elements of an Athenian will were the disposal of property and the appointment of a son and heir to ensure the continuation of the testator's **oikos*.

ἄλλως δὲ οὐκ ἔξεστιν ('no other method is allowed'). Isaios stops short of claiming explicitly that non-testamentary forms of adoption were against the law (*para tous nomous*) but his formulation is still emphatically negative. The speaker's assertion seems to deny the possibility of adoption *inter vivos* as well as posthumous adoption, which would be a patent misstatement, but the context may suggest that he is concerned exclusively with adoptions that took effect after the adoptive father's death. Even so, the denial of posthumous adoption is difficult to reconcile with evidence from other speeches (discussed in the introduction to this speech, pp. 203–205). It would appear, then, that Isaios was relying on the strict letter of the law, ignoring a practice that had grown up by custom.

Having presented his major premise in a short, unsubstantiated statement, the speaker goes on to expound the minor premise of his syllogism—that neither Aristarkhos senior nor Demokhares could have made a will in favour of Aristarkhos junior—at considerably greater length, pointing to the implicit conclusion that the latter could not have been legally adopted.

εἴτε οὖν Ἀρίσταρχον φήσει τις αὐτὸν διαθέσθαι ('So if anyone says that Aristarkhos himself made a will'). The vague, impersonal 'anyone' can only refer to Xenainetos or his witnesses, whom the speaker purportedly expects to say that Aristarkhos senior left a will providing for the adoption of Aristarkhos junior as his son, but from the facts as they appear in the speech it seems unlikely that Xenainetos junior was going to argue that the adoption of Aristarkhos junior was testamentary.

οὐκ ἀληθῆ λέξει ('he will not be telling the truth'). However improbable it is that Xenainetos or his witnesses will actually say what the speaker pretends he expects them to say, he is able to introduce the idea that their testimony will be untrue.

γνησίου γάρ… [δια]πρᾶξαι ('for while he had a legitimate son, Demokhares, he could not have wished to do so'). The *seed planted at §7 (cf. on ἔπειθ' ὡς Ἀρίσταρχος…) bears fruit here: Isaios wants to convince the **dikastai* that Aristarkhos senior could not legally have left his property to anyone other than his legitimate son, Demokhares. He does this by an indirect reference to the Solonian law on freedom of testamentary disposition—which, as explained below, does not really fit the circumstances of the case. But he starts with the kind of generalization which is characteristic of argumentation from probability: a man with a legitimate son would not want to give his estate to anyone else. Irrespective of the legal position, this may well have struck a chord with the *dikastai*.

οὔτε ἐξῆν δοῦναι τὰ ἑαυτοῦ ἑτέρῳ ('and he was not permitted to give his property to anyone else'). Isaios focuses on only one aspect of testamentary practice, the disposal of property, presumably in order to avoid saying explicitly that an Athenian with a legitimate son could not adopt a son by will. In fact, although an Athenian with legitimate male offspring could not adopt another son *inter vivos*, the law cited at [Dem.] 46.24 permitted him to make a provisional adoption by will, which would come into effect if his legitimate son(s) died in infancy: 'Whatever dispositions a father may make while he has legitimate sons, if the sons die within two years after reaching puberty, the father's will is valid'. In theory, therefore, Aristarkhos senior could have made a provisional will, adopting a son in the event of Demokhares's death, but since (on the speaker's account) Aristarkhos senior predeceased Demokhares, such a will would not have come into effect. There is the further difficulty that he could not have made even a provisional will in favour of Aristarkhos junior, who, according to the speaker, could not yet have been born at the time of Aristarkhos senior's death; cf. §5, where the speaker describes how Aristomenes gave his daughter in marriage to Kyronides, endowing her with the fortune which the speaker claims really belonged to his mother. For that reason it seems unlikely that Xenainetos junior was going to base his case on a testamentary adoption, and this supports the view that Isaios's arguments on the subject were intended as a digression, diverting attention from the real issues and giving the impression that his client's case is supported by the laws which he cites.

εἴτε Ἀριστάρχου τελευτήσαντος Δημοχάρην αὐτὸν ποιήσασθαι ('if [they say that] Demokhares adopted Aristarkhos (II) after Aristarkhos (I) had died'). Again, it is unlikely that Xenainetos intended to argue that Demokhares had adopted Aristarkhos junior (his nephew) by will, but the speaker rules out the possibility for the sake of his argument.

καὶ ταῦτα ψεύσονται ('they will be lying about that, too'). The speaker repeats the slur on his opponent's evidence with a variation on 'he will not be telling the truth'. Grammatically, the subject is still the impersonal 'anyone', but the use of the third person plural shows that the speaker has specific people—Xenainetos's witnesses—in mind.

10 παιδὸς γὰρ ... πέρα μεδίμνου κριθῶν ('for a child is not allowed to make a will, for the law expressly forbids any child or woman to make a contract for more than a *medimnos* of barley'). It would appear self-evident that a minor in the position of Demokhares, who was under the tutelage of a guardian following the death of his father, could not make a will until he had come of age and taken possession of his father's estate. So perhaps the law mentioned here, restricting the legal capacity of women and children to enter into contracts, did not explicitly forbid minors to make wills because such a provision would not have been considered necessary. If this is right, it would seem that Isaios's tactic was to boost his client's case by introducing a law that would be recognized as genuine, even though it was only indirectly relevant. Cf. Wyse, *ad loc.*: 'Isaeus does not mean to assert that making a will is a branch of *to sumballein*. The argument is *a fortiori*; if an infant cannot contract, much less is he able to devise his property by will.'

The scope of the term *sumballein* is extremely broad, covering 'every kind of contract, purchase and sale, letting and hiring, lending and borrowing, bailment ... exchange, partnership, suretyship, etc.'(Wyse, *ad loc.*). As discussed by Todd (1993), 262–268, it is doubtful whether Athenian law recognized a 'doctrine of contract' in the Roman or modern sense. It did, nevertheless, explicitly recognize the concept of a binding and enforceable agreement.

The restriction to no more than a *medimnos* of barley has been taken by some ancient and modern commentators to apply only to women, not children, but the correct interpretation remains uncertain; as Wyse points out, 'we must not overlook the possibility that the order in which the words stood in the law has been altered for the sake of rhetorical emphasis'. On the fluctuating price of a *medimnos* of corn (a bushel and a half, equivalent to twelve gallons or approximately fifty-five litres), see Wyse, *ad loc.*

μεμαρτύρηται ('testimony has been given'). Cf. on ἔπειθ' ὡς Ἀρίσταρχος…, §7.

ἀνάγνωθι δὴ … ποιήσασθαι ('and now read the laws according to which neither of them had the right to make a will'). It would be interesting to know precisely which laws were read out at this point. In the light of the preceding argument, it appears that they dealt with restrictions on the testamentary freedom of a man with legitimate sons, and on the capacity of children and women to conduct business. If so, they would support Isaios's minor premise (that neither Aristarkhos senior nor Demokhares could have adopted Aristarkhos junior by will), but they are irrelevant to his major premise, that valid adoptions were always made by will, and thus do not justify the conclusion that the adoption of Aristarkhos junior was invalid.

So the argumentation on this point illustrates Isaios's skill in deployment of the law as part of a rhetorical strategy, seeking to create the impression that he has proved more than he actually has. In this instance, however carefully the argument was set up and developed, the major premise still looks questionable. It is impossible to know how an Athenian court would have reacted to Isaios's argument, but the practice of posthumous adoption, even if it was not explicitly sanctioned by law, must have been familiar to many of the **dikastai* through the experience of their own families and friends. It cannot be assumed that they would have rejected the validity of such an adoption, especially if it was properly regulated by the appropriate phratry.

11 Οὐ τοίνυν … εἰσποιῆσαι ('Nor again, gentlemen, could Kyronides have given Aristarkhos senior a son by adoption'). After citing the law to prove that neither Aristarkhos senior nor Demokhares had testamentary capacity, the speaker implicitly anticipates a new argument from his opponent: that it was Kyronides who introduced an adopted son into the **oikos* of Aristarkhos senior. This would be incompatible with the speaker's version of the facts, according to which Aristarkhos junior was adopted into the *oikos* of Aristarkhos senior after the death of Kyronides. (See on Κυρωνίδου …, §6.). Isaios seems to be employing the same highly sophisticated strategy as in the argument about the testamentary capacity of

Aristarkhos senior: if any of the **dikastai* noticed the anachronism, this would work to his client's advantage because they would think it was his opponent who was confused.

ἀλλ' αὐτῷ μὲν ... οὐκ ἔστι νόμος ('he could certainly have returned to his father's **oikos* if he had left a son in the *oikos* of Xenainetos senior, but there is no law permitting him to introduce a son of his own to take his place'). The law permitting an adopted son to return to his natal *oikos*, provided he left behind a legitimate son of his own to take his place as the son of his adoptive father, is attested at Isa. 6.44: 'For the law does not allow [an adopted son] to return [to his natural father's *oikos*] unless he leaves behind a legitimate son'. Cf. Isa. 9.33; [Dem.] 44.22, 44, 46. It may also have been true that there was no law expressly permitting an adopted son to remain in his adoptive *oikos* and transfer his own son back to that of his natural father, but there is no reason to think that such an action would actually have been a violation of the law, provided the adoption procedure was properly carried out and the son in question was eligible to be adopted. In this case, Aristarkhos junior was no longer legally a grandson of Aristarkhos senior, but he may have been accepted as a suitable candidate for posthumous adoption because of his continuing relationship as Aristarkhos senior's matrilineal great-nephew. In any event, it cannot have been Kyronides himself who arranged the adoption of Aristarkhos junior, which, on the speaker's account, took place after Kyronides's death.

ἢ ἐὰν φῶσι, ψεύσονται ('if they say [that there is such a law] they will be lying'). This is the third time the speaker has asserted that his opponent and his witnesses will be lying if they make certain claims. Cf. on οὐκ ἀληθῆ λέξει and καὶ ταῦτα ψεύσονται, §9. As noted above, it is unlikely that they would put forward such claims, so this appears to be a tactic designed to prejudice the **dikastai* by casting a slur on the opponent's evidence in general. In each instance the vivid construction for a future open condition, with the verb of the apodosis in the future indicative, makes the accusation look like a direct statement.

τὰ τῆς μητρὸς χρήματα ('my mother's property'), See on ἀλλὰ τῆς ἐμῆς μητρὸς πατρῴος, §3.

12 καὶ μὲν δή, ὦ ἄνδρες ('Furthermore, gentlemen'). See on Ἐβουλόμην ..., §1. The extremely emphatic combination of particles, *kai men dē*, followed by the address to the **dikastai*, indicates that Isaios wants them to pay particular attention to what the speaker is about to say. It is at this point that Isaios's legal argument about the rules of the epiklerate begins.

οὐδὲ Ἀριστομένει γε οὐδὲ Ἀπολλοδώρῳ ('neither Aristomenes nor Apollodoros'). In fact, if anyone did introduce Aristarkhos junior as the posthumously adopted son of Aristarkhos senior, it is most likely to have been either Aristomenes or his son Apollodoros, the brother and nephew respectively of Aristarkhos senior. Isaios turns to them only after diverting the attention of the **dikastai* to the hypothetical claims of three far more unlikely candidates. Knowing, as he probably did, that Xenainetos would say that Apollodoros had introduced Aristarkhos junior as the adopted son of Aristarkhos senior (cf. on τῷ δὲ μήτε λαβεῖν αὐτὴν…, §13), he presumably hoped that they would treat this story with equal scepticism.

οἷς προσῆκε τῆς ἐμῆς μητρὸς ἐπιδικάσασθαι ('who should have had my mother adjudicated to them in marriage'). The speaker argues that, although Aristomenes or Apollodoros would have been entitled to claim his mother in marriage as **epiklēros*, neither of them had the right to deprive her of her inheritance by installing Aristarkhos junior as Aristarkhos senior's adopted son. As discussed in the introduction to this speech, pp. 205–209, this may reflect the position that posthumous adoption would have been regarded as unacceptable if it conflicted with the rights of a legitimate descendant. Cf. the case of Diokles (8.40), who allegedly tried to deprive his *uterine sisters of their inheritance by making himself the adopted son of their father.

θαυμαστὸν γὰρ ἂν ἦν ('for it would be surprising'). From this point the argumentation, although still purportedly based on the law, becomes noticeably vaguer and more rhetorical. This could be taken to reflect the weakness of the speaker's position, but it is possible that there were no specific laws on which he could rely to support his case.

εἰ τὴν ἐμὴν μητέρα…γενέσθαι ('if either Apollodoros or Aristomenes had married my mother he could not have obtained possession of her property'). The essence of the speaker's somewhat convoluted point is that if Aristomenes or Apollodoros had claimed his mother in marriage (as, according to his argument, they ought to have done), they would not have been able to dispose of her property because the estate of an **epiklēros* devolves on her son(s) two years after reaching puberty. It follows from that, as he argues, that they could not legally give her to a husband outside the family, and then introduce an adopted son to inherit from her father the estate that should have been hers. The argument appears legally sound, but he may have been distorting the facts, especially if his mother was already married before she became *epiklēros* and if Kyronides had legitimately taken a share of Aristarkhos senior's estate because he had not been adopted at the time of the latter's death.

κατὰ τὸν νόμον … χρημάτων ('in accordance with the law which allows no-one to dispose of the property of an *epiklēros* except her sons, who obtain possession of it on reaching the second year after puberty'). Cf. on ἀλλ' οἱ γενόμενοι παῖδες …, 8.31. The law to which the speaker alludes is cited at [Dem.] 46.20: 'And if someone is born of an *epiklēros*, he takes control of the property two years after reaching puberty'. Although he does not labour the point, the speaker's self-interest is obvious, and this passage reinforces the impression that he is claiming the estate on his own behalf, not representing his mother.

ἀλλ' ἑτέρῳ … ὑὸν εἰσποιῆσαι ('but if he were going to be allowed, after giving her in marriage to another, to introduce a son to inherit her property'). On the marriage of the speaker's mother, and Isaios's vagueness on the sequence of events, see on μετὰ δὲ ταῦτα, §6. Even if she was already married when Demokhares died, and if she was legally **epidikos* at that stage, it is likely that Aristomenes or Apollodoros could still have claimed her in marriage, forcing a divorce from her first husband. They would not, however, have been obliged to do so, provided they relinquished any claim to the estate, and in that situation there might have been more scope for informal negotiation. Cf. the introduction to this speech, p. 210, and the introductory note to §19. Aristomenes, moreover, could not have been blamed for having married her exogamously at a time when she was certainly not **epiklēros* or *epidikos* because her brother was still living.

13 δεινὰ μέντ' ἂν γίγνοιτο ('It would indeed be extraordinary'). Isaios does not explicitly say that Aristomenes or Apollodoros would have acted illegally in carrying out the adoption, merely that it would be 'astonishing' and 'dreadful' if the law permitted them to do what (his opponent alleges that) they did. His argumentation appears devious, but he may have been forced to argue along these lines because there was no specific law to which he could appeal.

καὶ τῷ μὲν πατρὶ αὐτῆς … τὰ ἑαυτοῦ ('Even her own father, if he had no male heirs, could not have disposed of his estate unless he disposed of her with it'). The law referred to is discussed in the introduction to this speech, pp. 206–207.

κελεύει … τὰ ἑαυτοῦ ('for the law ordains that he may give his property to whoever he wishes, if he gives his daughters with it'). The wording follows very closely that of Isa. 3.68, and of the law cited at [Dem.] 43.51.

τῷ δὲ μήτε λαβεῖν αὐτὴν ἀξιώσαντι μήτε πατρὶ ὄντι, ἀλλ' ἀνεψιῷ ('But when someone has refused to take her in marriage and is not her father but her cousin'). The speaker elaborates his argument that either Aristomenes or

Apollodoros should have claimed his mother as **epiklēros*, but had refused to do so, reasoning that a father was best placed to look after a daughter's interest, therefore what the law does not allow her father to do could not possibly be permitted to a mere cousin. Again, he appears to be arguing by analogy because there was no law directly relevant to the situation he is describing. The *argumentum a fortiori* has, nevertheless, a persuasive basis in common sense.

The 'cousin' in question is Apollodoros, who was a first cousin of the speaker's mother, as well as a nephew of Aristarkhos senior and maternal uncle of Aristarkhos junior. It is probably reasonable to infer that Isaios and his client knew it was Apollodoros who took formal responsibility for the posthumous adoption of Aristarkhos senior (or, at least, that this was the story Xenainetos would put forward) and that Isaios constructed the preceding argument as a smokescreen to divert attention from the real issue. If this is right, it is clearly a tactic that could only have worked in the first speech at the trial.

παρὰ πάντας τοὺς νόμους εἰσαγαγόντι ('introducing [an heir] in violation of all the laws'). See on παρὰ πάντας τοὺς νόμους, §3. Despite the speaker's insistence on the illegality of his opponents' behaviour, he does not accuse them of any specific procedural irregularity, and none of the laws he has cited expressly forbids posthumous adoption in general.

14 οὔτε Ξεναίνετος οὔτε ἄλλος οὐδεὶς ἀνθρώπων ('neither Xenainetos nor anyone else in the world'). For the emphatic negation, cf., e.g., Isa. 12.4; Lys. 13.79; [Dem.] 48.44; [Dem.] 59.38.

ὡς οὐ τῆς ἐμῆς μητρὸς οὗτος <ὁ> κλῆρος ἐστι ('that this estate is not my mother's'). See on ἀλλὰ τῆς ἐμῆς μητρὸς πατρῷος, §3.

τοῦ ἀδελφοῦ αὐτῇ τοῦ Δημοχάρους καταλιπόντος ('her brother Demokhares having left it to her'). In presenting his mother as having received her inheritance through her brother, the speaker does not apparently see any inconsistency with the status he claims for her as **epiklēros*. This supports the view that a woman could be treated as an *epiklēros* if she was the sole surviving representative of her father's **oikos*, even if she did not inherit directly from her father.

νόμον κελεύετε δεῖξαι καθ' ὃν γεγένηται ἡ εἰσποιήσις Ἀριστάρχῳ ('tell them to indicate under which law the adoption in favour of Aristarkhos was carried out'). The speaker has already explained why he thinks the Solonian law on freedom of testamentary disposition would, for different reasons, have excluded both Aristarkhos senior and Demokhares. (It would not, in any event, have expressly permitted a posthumous adoption; cf. Rubinstein (1993), 27.) His confidence that the adoption of Aristarkhos junior was 'not in accordance with any law' seems to reflect the position that the practice of posthumous adoption was not explicitly covered by the law. If (as is suggested in the introduction to this speech, p. 204, n. 20) its origin predated Solon's law on testamentary freedom, it may have survived into the classical period as a substitute for testamentary adoption in circumstances where the adoptive father had not been able to make the appropriate arrangements himself.

καὶ τίς ὁ εἰσποιήσας ('and who was the adopter'). On the verb *eispoiein* in the active voice, see on ὃν εἰσποιεῖ ἐκείνῳ, 9.2. The speaker has already explained why, in his view, neither Aristarkhos senior nor Demokhares could have adopted Aristarkhos junior by will, and neither could Kyronides, Aristomenes or Apollodoros have carried out a posthumous adoption.

ἀλλ' οἶδ' ὅτι οὐχ ἕξουσιν ἐπιδεῖξαι ('but I know that they will not be able to indicate this'). The speaker's confidently repeated assertion, that his opponents will not be able to specify the legal basis of Aristarkhos junior's adoption, is the strongest indication that there was no law explicitly sanctioning posthumous adoption. But neither, presumably, was it expressly forbidden, a point which the opponents may have been able to exploit.

15 ἀπεστερῆσθαι ('robbed'). See on ἀποστερῶν, 8.3.

ἔκ τε τῶν εἰρημένων καὶ μεμαρτυρημένων καὶ ἐξ αὐτῶν τῶν νόμων ('by my arguments, by the testimony, and by the actual laws'). The speaker tries to create the impression of a comprehensive proof by claiming to have proved his case with three different kinds of **pisteis*: argument, testimony and law. (For the special status of the laws, see on ἐξ αὐτῶν τῶν νόμων, 8.30.) The quality of some of this evidence is, as has been shown, highly dubious; see the introductory note to §7.

οὕτω δὲ καὶ … τὰ χρήματα ('Indeed, it is so clear even to them that they are wrongfully in possession of the property'). The tendentious reasoning attributed to the speaker's opponents, who briefly become *focalizers, is designed to prejudice the **dikastai* against the reported claim that follows.

ὥστε οὐκ ἐπὶ τῷ δικαίως … μόνον ('that they do not rely only on the legality of the introduction of Aristarkhos (junior) to the phratry of Artistarkhos (senior))'. This is the second reference in the speech to the fact, not denied by the speaker, that Aristarkhos junior was introduced to the *phratry of Aristarkhos senior. Cf. Κυρωνίδου …, §6. The wording implies that the introduction of an adopted son into his adoptive father's phratry was equivalent to the completion of the adoption itself, and there is a similar emphasis on the phratry introduction in cases of testamentary or *inter vivos* adoption, e.g. in Isa. 7. Cf. Lambert (1993), 39, and Rubinstein (1993), 43. From the available sources there is no evidence that the phratries had specific rules for posthumous adoption, so it may be reasonable to assume that the procedure was the same as for the other types of adoption. The admission procedure would have allowed the *phrateres* an opportunity to object to a proposed new member. Cf. Isa. 6.22; 8.19; [Dem.] 43.82, discussed by Lambert (1993), 171; also Isa. 7.16–17. If any such objection had been raised to the admission of Aristarkhos junior, one would have expected the speaker to mention it, and, if possible, to adduce testimony from those who were present. His omitting to do so may well be significant.

ἀλλὰ καὶ δίκην φασὶν . . . ἐκτετικέναι ('but also claim that Xenainetos's father paid a debt on behalf of the estate'). The speaker anticipates an alternative line from his client's opponents: that Kyronides paid a judgment debt on behalf of the estate of Aristarkhos senior, and that this shows their legitimate possession. Isaios, typically, leaves this potentially damaging disclosure until a late stage in the speech, when his client has already given the **dikastai* his own version of the story. Cf. on ἀλλὰ καὶ . . ., 9.32. The way in which he introduces it—suggesting that Xenainetos junior has so little confidence in the validity of Aristarkhos junior's adoption that he has to rely on a fabrication—may indicate that it was in fact a significant piece of evidence which Isaios is trying to marginalize. Underlying the speaker's argument is the assumption that when Aristarkhos senior died, Kyronides had already been adopted into the **oikos* of Xenainetos senior. If the claim was true, why would he take on the burden of paying a debt on the estate of his natural father, with whom he no longer had a legal relationship? If his opponent accepted the premise about the timing of the adoption, he might argue in response that Kyronides paid the debt because he felt a moral obligation to Aristarkhos senior and his household. Perhaps (as argued in the introduction to this speech, pp. 199–200) the real position, which the speaker cannot afford to admit, was that Kyronides had not yet been adopted, and that he was under a legal obligation to pay off any debt before taking his share of the estate as one of Aristarkhos senior's legitimate heirs.

On the assumption that Aristarkhos senior left his children "a property overwhelmed by debt", Wyse, 651, argues that this would put the actions of Aristomenes in a completely different light: "The daughter of Aristarchus I, far from having a grievance, owed a debt of gratitude to her relatives; the estate could not furnish her with a dowry, and but for the generosity of her guardian and her brother she might have had some difficulty in finding a husband...". This interpretation accepts the speaker's assessment of the extent of the debt, which may well have been exaggerated. Moreover, Wyse's conjecture that Aristarkhos senior was in debt to the state, and therefore **atimos*, at the time of his death, is ruled out by *dikēn*, which refers to a private suit. There is no evidence for the public debt which, according to Wyse, Kyronides paid in order to prevent the confiscation of the family estate and to restore the privileges of citizenship to the heir of Aristarkhos senior.

16 ἐγὼ δ', ὦ ἄνδρες ('but I, gentlemen'). See on 'Εβουλόμην..., §1. Here, as at §9, it may be significant that the speaker addresses the **dikastai* at a point where his argumentation appears noticeably weak.

μεγάλοις ὑμᾶς τεκμηρίοις διδάξω ('shall show you with convincing proofs'). See on μεγάλα γὰρ τεκμηρία, 7.11.

ὡς οὗτοι λέγουσιν ('as they say'). The plural pronoun could in this context be taken to include the opposing witnesses, as well as Xenainetos junior, following the general tendency in forensic oratory to treat the speaker's opponent and his supporters as a group. The speaker may have intended to include Aristarkhos junior and Kyronides among his opponents, referring to them as if they were still alive.

From this point in the speech Isaios increasingly uses pronouns instead of names to refer to the speaker's opponents. This imprecision, combined with his vague chronology, makes it impossible to get a clear picture of the events and their sequence. The obfuscation is almost certainly a deliberate tactic on Isaios's part.

οὐ γὰρ προσῆκεν αὐτοῖς ('for it was not their business to do so'). The pronoun must refer to Kyronides and his sons, although on the speaker's account it is unlikely that Aristarkhos junior and Xenainetos junior had in fact been born at the time to which he is referring (since Kyronides did not marry until after the death of Aristarkhos senior).

ἀλλ' οἷς ἐγένετο ἡ ἐμὴ μήτηρ ἐπίδικος ('but those who were entitled to claim my mother in marriage'). This is a tendentious reference to Aristomenes and Apollodoros, reflecting the speaker's allegation that they wronged his mother by failing to claim her in marriage as **epiklēros*. His assertion that they would have been the people responsible for paying off any debt on the estate would be true only if Kyronides had already lost his right to the succession of Aristarkhos senior through adoption, which again suggests that Isaios is deliberately and carefully obscuring the chronology.

οὔτε ἂν εἰσεποίουν εἰς τοῦτον τὸν κλῆρον ὑὸν Ἀριστάρχῳ ('nor would they have provided an adopted son for the estate of Aristarkhos'). On the verb *eispoiein* in the active voice, see on ὃν εἰσποιεῖ ἐκείνῳ, 9.2. Isaios compresses the timescale of events in order to present the story in the most favourable light for his client: by associating the adoption with the payment of the debt, he implies that Aristarkhos junior was adopted shortly after the death of Aristarkhos senior. On his own account, however, the adoption took place after Kyronides had died. In the meantime, Kyronides had married and had two sons, so there must have been an interval of at least several years, during which the family's financial affairs might have had time to recover, especially if the debt was indeed smaller than the speaker suggests.

17 ἢ ἕτεροι μέν ... τῆς τοῦ πατρὸς ἀτιμίας ('Others, indeed, when they have lost money, have their sons adopted into other **oikoi* so that they do not share in the fathers' **atimia*'). The generalization is typical of arguments from probability in forensic oratory: while many Athenians may have been motivated by financial hardship to have their children adopted into more wealthy households, this was not the only rationale for adoption, and it does not prove that no-one would ever seek adoption into a poorer family. The desire to continue a deceased kinsman's line of descent could have been the main reason for some adoptions.

οὗτοι δὲ ... σφᾶς αὐτούς ('and did they adopt themselves into an **oikos* and an estate that was insolvent?'). There was only one man who, according to the speaker's opponent, was adopted into the succession of Aristarkhos senior, so 'they' is a rhetorical exaggeration. Presumably the speaker intends, by implication, to include both Kyronides and Xenainetos junior, as well as Aristarkhos junior, although on his own account Kyronides was already dead when Aristarkhos junior was adopted. The expression 'adopted themselves' has an ironic flavour, implying that the adoption was not genuine. Cf. on αὐτὸν τῷ πατρὶ αὐτῶν εἰσποιήσας, 8.40.

φιλοχρηματοῦντες ('being avaricious)'. Cf. Isa. 2.29, where the speaker says that he agreed to submit his claim to arbitration, 'so that no-one might say I was avaricious'.

ἀποστεροῦντες ('robbing'). See on ἀποστερῶν, 8.3.

ταῦτα πάντα ἐμηχανήσαντο ('fabricated this whole story'). The speaker's accusation that his opponents have simply fabricated the story of the debt paid by Kyronides is a further indication that he regards it as seriously damaging to his case, and possibly that he lacks confidence in his own more reasoned arguments against it.

Argument: The Speaker's Reasons for Delaying His Claim (18–21)

A claim to a deceased person's estate could be brought under Athenian law at any time during the lifetime of the first heir—in this case, Aristarkhos junior—or within five years of his death (cf. Isa. 3.58). The speaker appears to have submitted his claim immediately after the death of Aristarkhos junior, so there is no suggestion that he has exceeded the time limit. Since, however, he bases his case on his mother's entitlement to the estate of Aristarkhos senior, who had probably died over forty years previously, it would have been natural to ask why the speaker or his father, as **kurios* of the supposed heiress, did not claim the estate earlier on her behalf. Cf. Lys. 3.19, 38, where the speaker makes great play of his opponent's delay of four years before bringing the prosecution; this indicates that delay could be represented as suspicious, even if no legal time limit had been exceeded.

The speaker's explanation goes some way towards justifying his own and his father's inactivity, but does not really answer the question 'Why claim now?' The true reason may have been connected with the terms on which the family had agreed to the adoption of Aristarkhos junior, especially if (as suggested in the introduction to this speech, pp. 210–211) there had been an understanding that he would occupy the estate for his lifetime and be succeeded by the speaker. Alternatively, it may be that the speaker had simply harboured a general feeling of resentment about the adoption, perhaps thinking that he rather than his cousin should have been adopted into the **oikos* of Aristarkhos senior, and saw the death of Aristarkhos junior as an opportunity to stake his claim to the estate.

18 Ἴσως … θαυμάσειε ('Some of you, gentlemen, may perhaps be surprised by the delay'). On the disingenuous use of 'perhaps', see the introductory note to §§8–17.

ἀποστερούμενοι ('being robbed'). See on ἀποστερῶν, 8.3. The plural includes the speaker's father, who, until the speaker came of age, would have been the only person in a position to challenge Kyronides or Aristarkhos junior on behalf of his wife.

ἐγὼ δὲ οἶμαι … κατημέλησεν ('although I think it unjust that anyone should have less than his due rights because he was either unable or neglected to assert them'). The speaker begins his defence with a generalization: it is the justice of the claim that matters, not the time at which it was brought. The first person pronoun is emphatic, contrasting the speaker's own opinion with the view he has just attributed to some of the **dikastai*. He will argue that he and his father were unable to claim the estate at an earlier stage, but he is careful to forestall any suggestion, from his audience or his opponents, that they actually neglected to do so.

19 The speaker claims that his father tried to negotiate with Aristomenes on his wife's behalf, to ensure that she was not deprived of her father's inheritance, but that he was silenced by the threat that if he persisted, Aristomenes would claim her by **epidikasia*. This has been taken by the majority of scholars as evidence of a law permitting the deceased's next of kin to claim an **epiklēros* in marriage even if this involved a divorce from her existing husband. (See the introduction to this speech, p. 201.) Maffi (1990), finding the evidence inconclusive, argues that it is clear from §§4–6 and 14 that the speaker's mother was not married until after the deaths of her father and brother, and that the law in question would apply only to a woman who was already married when she became *epiklēros*. The argument is questionable and would, in any event, be irrelevant if the speaker's mother was in fact married before Demokhares died. (See on ἀλλ' ἑτέρῳ . . ., §12.)

A further issue is the basis of the 'agreement' reached by the speaker's father and Aristomenes. Some earlier scholars saw this passage as evidence of a loophole in the law which allowed an *epiklēros* to avoid being claimed by her father's next of kin provided she relinquished her own claim to his estate. It is now generally accepted that the rules of the epiklerate were binding on the woman (though not on those entitled to claim her) and that the agreement reached here is more likely to have been a private arrangement not strictly in accordance with the law. (Gernet (1921), 350 regards the arrangement as immoral because it breaches the principle that the deceased's next of kin cannot take the property without the daughter; cf. Paoli (1976b), 373, and Karabélias (2002), 81.)

ἐπὶ προικὶ ἐγγυησάμενος ('having betrothed himself with a dowry'). This is the speaker's only reference to his mother's dowry, which he uses to underline his point that she was deprived of her rightful inheritance as **epiklēros*. He does not, however, mention the size of the dowry; cf. on ὅτε γὰρ . . ., below.

The speaker's idealized picture of his parents' marriage, as well as helping to explain their acquiescence in an arrangement of questionable legality, is an important aspect of his attempt to secure the sympathy of the **dikastai*. Since he is dealing with events which must have happened either before his birth or during his early childhood, to which he brings no witnesses, one may reasonably question the reliability of his account. An experienced dikast would no doubt have understood that it was impossible to verify uncorroborated assertions such as these, but they must nevertheless have influenced at least some of his listeners.

τὸν δὲ κλῆρον τούτων καρπουμένων ('while these men were enjoying the estate'). The tendentious 'enjoying' contrasts with 'robbed', implying that the speaker's opponents were benefiting from property to which they were not entitled. Once again, Isaios avoids using names in this sentence, with the effect of smearing the speaker's opponents in general; it is not clear whom, precisely, the speaker meant by 'those who were enjoying the estate', and, as a result, the chronology is also unclear. The reference may be to Kyronides (to whom, according to the speaker, Aristomenes had given Aristarkhos senior's estate) and his sons. Alternatively, it may be Aristarkhos junior's tenure of the estate that the speaker has in mind, so that the plural is either a rhetorical exaggeration or intended to include those who, in the speaker's view, were on the same side (of whom only Xenainetos junior and Apollodoros are likely to have been still alive at the relevant time). We know that several years must have elapsed between the death of Aristarkhos senior and the posthumous adoption of Aristarkhos junior (cf. on οὔτε ἂν εἰσεποίουν …, §16), so we are left uncertain about the timing of the supposed intervention by the speaker's father on behalf of his wife.

ὅτε γὰρ περὶ αὐτοῦ λόγους ἐποιήσατο ('when he discussed the matter'). This is the only direct hint in the speech of quarrels within the family about the position of the speaker's mother (cf. the much more detailed accounts of family feuds in Isa. 7, 8 and 9), and exactly what lies behind it is unclear. The aorist tense, used for 'discussed' and 'threatened' (see below) implies that the matter was resolved (whereas the imperfect would have suggested continuing negotiation), but the speaker does not specify when this happened. It is likely, whether the negotiations concerned a dowry or on additional payment after the marriage, that the settlement was more generous, and more readily accepted by the speaker's parents, than he wants to admit.

οὗτοι ταῦτα αὐτῷ ἠπείλησαν ('they threatened him'). Here, 'they' must refer to Aristomenes and Apollodoros, who, as next of kin to Aristarkhos senior, were the only potential claimants to the hand of the speaker's mother as **epiklēros*.

ὥστε τῆς μητρὸς μὴ στερηθῆναι ('so as not to be deprived of my mother'). This passage expects a sympathetic response from the **dikastai* to a man's expression of affection for his wife. As Just (1989), 102, points out, the speaker's father would have lost not only the wife but also her dowry if she had been claimed in marriage by her uncle or cousin: 'But it is still personal attachment to a wife which is stressed, and even if the argument is dismissed as a piece of pleading designed simply to sway the jury in the speaker's favour, it is still significant that this sort of emotional argument was considered valid.'

καὶ δὶς τοσαῦτα χρήματα εἴασεν ἂν αὐτοὺς καρποῦσθαι ('and he would have allowed them to enjoy twice as much property'). For the *hyperbolē*, cf. on ὡς δ'..., 9.27. The antithesis between 'be deprived' and 'enjoy' reinforces the contrast between the deprivation suffered by the speaker's family and the affluence enjoyed (illegally, as he implies) by his opponents.

20 μετὰ δὲ ταῦτα ὁ Κορινθιακὸς πόλεμος ἐγένετο ('and after that the Corinthian War took place'). Cf. on μετὰ δὲ ταῦτα, §6. Isaios's typically vague chronology provides no reliable indication of the length of time elapsed between the events just described and the beginning of the Corinthian War (394–386 BC). The fact that the war took the speaker and his father away from Athens, and prevented them from making a claim to the estate, seems to be something of a *non sequitur*. If the father had already been deterred from taking action because he was afraid of losing his wife, what difference could it make that he was prevented from doing so by the war? The main point of the reference may be that it prevented the speaker and his father from alienating the sympathy of the **dikastai* by appearing merely timid, and provided an opportunity for him to demonstrate their good character by mentioning their military service.

ἐν ᾧ ἐγὼ κἀκεῖνος στρατεύεσθαι ἠναγκαζόμεθα ('in which he and I were obliged to serve'). The speaker does not mention the length of either his own or his father's military service, and the vagueness about timescale is especially useful to him here. They may not have served for the full duration of the war, and in any event it is unlikely that they would have been constantly on campaign.

ὥστε οὐδετέρῳ ἂν ἡμῶν δίκην ἐξεγένετο λαβεῖν ('so that it was impossible for either of us to obtain justice'). It is not clear why the speaker implies that, had they not been away from home, either he or his father could have submitted a claim. It would have been the father, acting as his wife's **kurios*, who had standing to claim the inheritance on her behalf. After her death her son, but not her husband, could claim it in his own right. A possible explanation is that she died during the course of the war, but there is not enough information in the speech to support a firm conclusion.

εἰρήνης τ'αὖ γενομένης... συνέβη ('when peace returned I had an unfortunate difficulty with the public treasury'). The speaker's difficulties with the treasury would not have prevented his father from making a claim, on his wife's behalf, to the estate of Aristarkhos senior. But the speaker does not mention his father again at this point, perhaps implying that he had died in the course of the Corinthian War, so that the speaker had become his mother's **kurios*. Alternatively, if the mother herself had died, the speaker would have been a potential claimant in his own right to his grandfather's estate.

ὥστε οὐ μικρὰς ἔχομεν αἰτίας περὶ τοῦ πράγματος ('So we have good reasons for our conduct in the matter'). The excuses offered by the speaker are valid as far as they go, but there may have been other opportunities for him or his father to claim the estate.

21 ἀλλὰ νυνὶ δίκαιον εἰπεῖν ἐστιν, ὦ ἄνδρες ('but now it is right for them to say, gentlemen'). Having explained that the **dikastai*, in reaching their verdict, must ignore his delay in bringing the claim, the speaker now summarizes the real issues (as he sees them) in the form of three questions which he claims that his opponent needs to answer. This echoes his challenge to his opponents in §14, but the questions are put in different terms this time.

τίνος δόντος [ἔχει] τὸν κλῆρον 'who gave [Aristarkhos junior] the estate'). The question appears to be put directly to the speaker's opponent, Xenainetos junior, but in fact it is the transmission of the estate from Aristarkhos senior to Aristarkhos junior that is in issue.

κατὰ ποίους νόμους εἰς τοὺς φράτορας εἰσῆκται ('in accordance with what laws he was introduced to the *phratry'). Again, the real subject is Aristarkhos junior, but the question is framed as if it referred to Xenainetos junior. This is the third reference in the speech to the introduction of Aristarkhos junior into the phratry of Aristarkhos senior. Cf. on εἰς τοὺς φράτορας..., §8 and ὥστε οὐκ ἐπὶ τῷ δικαίως..., §15.

καὶ πῶς οὐκ ἐπίκληρος ἦν... μήτηρ ('and how it is that my mother was not **epiklēros* to this estate'). See on ἡ μήτηρ ἡ ἐμὴ..., §4.

ταῦτα γάρ ἐστι περὶ ὧν ὑμᾶς δεῖ τὴν ψῆφον ἐνεγκεῖν ('These are the points on which you must cast your vote'). The real issue for the **dikastai* was the validity of the will of Aristarkhos junior. The speaker would argue that his questions were relevant to that, but they could be seen as part of a strategy to divert the attention of the *dikastai* away from more crucial points on which the speaker's position is weak.

μὴ δυνηθέντων ... ψηφίσαισθε ('If they cannot explain these points, it will be right for you to decide that the estate is mine'). The speaker makes his position clear: if his opponents cannot satisfactorily make their case on his terms, then the **dikastai* should vote for him.

Argument: The Character of the Speaker and His Opponent (22–25)

On the use of character in Athenian litigation generally, and its particular relevance to inheritance disputes, see pp. 20–21. Isaios portrays his client in this case as a worthy citizen who has used his modest resources wisely in the interests of his family and the **polis*, in contrast to his opponent who has already inherited a substantial estate but wasted it. This is not, in a strictly legal sense, relevant to the speaker's claim, and even in a case as apparently weak as this it is hardly his strongest point. But in a dispute involving property (and perhaps especially in an inheritance dispute) it would, nevertheless, have been accepted as part of the 'larger story' that the **dikastai* would take into account (cf. Rhodes (2004), 146), and it is likely to have had a powerful influence on them. (For other elements of **ēthos* in this speech, cf. on μετὰ δὲ ταῦτα ..., §20.)

22 Τοῦτο μὲν οἶδ' ὅτι ποιεῖν οὐχ οἷοί τ' ἔσονται ('I know they will not be able to do this'). The speaker appears fully confident that his opponents will not be able to explain the legal basis of the adoption of Aristarkhos junior. Cf. on νόμον κελεύετε δεῖξαι ... and ἀλλ' οἶδ' ὅτι οὐχ ἕξουσιν ἐπιδεῖξαι, §14.

χαλεπὸν γὰρ πρὸς νόμους καὶ δίκαιον πρᾶγμα ἀντιλέγειν ἐστί ('for it is difficult to make a case against law and justice'). This sententious statement is self-evidently true, in general terms, but it begs the question (which the **dikastai* had to decide) whether the speaker really did have a just case in accordance with the law.

περὶ δὲ τοῦ τεθνεῶτος λέξουσιν ('but they will talk about the deceased'). Johnstone (1999), 112–113, points out that in adversarial litigation it was characteristic of defendants to ask for pity, and of prosecutors to forestall such appeals by invoking the supremacy of the law. Examples cited by Johnstone are Dem. 21.225; Lyk. 1.150; Lys. 14.40; 15.9.

ἐλεοῦντες ὡς ανὴρ ὢν ἀγαθὸς ἐν τῷ πολέμῳ τέθνηκε ('lamenting that he was a good man who died in battle'). The fact that Aristarkhos junior has recently died on military service indicates that the speech was delivered while the Theban War (378–371 BC) was still in progress.

ἐγὼ δὲ ... περὶ τῶν ἑαυτοῦ ('But I myself, gentlemen, think that a will made by a man about his own property ought to be valid'). The speaker demonstrates his respect for the laws of Solon with this tendentious paraphrase of the provision on freedom of testamentary disposition.

τῶν ἀλλοτρίων ('other people's property'). See on τῶν ἀλλοτρίων, 8.1, and cf. on τῶν δὲ ἀλλοτρίων, §2.

23 ὡς διέθετο ἐκεῖνος ('that he made a will'). Isaios creates further confusion in this paragraph by his use of pronouns instead of personal names. From the context, 'he' must refer to Aristarkhos junior, since there is no suggestion that Aristarkhos senior disposed of an estate that did not properly belong to him.

ὄντες ἐξ ἐκείνου ('being descended from him)'. Since the subject of 'being' is explicitly Kyronides and his sons, 'him' here must be Aristarkhos senior.

πλέον ἢ τεττάρων ταλάντων ('more than four talents'). The speaker specifies that the estate of Xenainetos senior, inherited by Kyronides and his sons, was worth more than four talents, but he does not put a value on the estate of Aristarkhos senior, which he is claiming for himself.

ἀλλὰ καὶ τόνδε προσλήψονται ('but they will also receive this estate'). In legal terms, there appears to be no reason why a man should not have inherited from both his father and his maternal grandfather, but for the Athenian prejudice against the inheritance of more than one estate, see on ἔχειν μὲν ..., 7.44.

καὶ ἐκ τῶν αὐτῶν Κυρωνίδῃ γεγενημένος ('and descended from the same ancestors as Kyronides'). This seems to overlook the fact that Kyronides was adopted into the **oikos* of Xenainetos senior, losing his place in the succession of Aristarkhos senior. By making the point that he was 'descended from the same ancestors as Kyronides', the speaker reinforces his sense of injustice at being excluded from the inheritance, perhaps hinting that he, rather than Aristarkhos junior, ought to have become the posthumously adopted son of Aristarkhos senior. Cf. on ἐκ τῶν αὐτῶν, 7.20.

24 καίτοι δίκαιον, ὦ ἄνδρες ('Yet it is just, gentlemen'). As the speech approaches its conclusion the addresses to the **dikastai* begin to pile up: there are two in this section, and one in §25. This enables Isaios to raise the emotional tone of the speech without using too much overtly emotive vocabulary.

πρὸ δίκης ('before any trial has been heard'). The speaker again alludes to his complaint that Aristomenes ought to have claimed his niece in marriage by **epidikasia.*

ἐκ τῶν πατρῴων ἐκβάλλειν ('ejecting from her paternal inheritance'). The emotive verb, implying that the speaker's mother was physically removed from her father's estate, invites the **dikastai* to sympathize with the speaker and condemn his opponents. Cf. Edwards (2007), 164.

25 τὸν Ἀριστομένους οἶκον ('the estate of Aristomenes'). If, as the speaker claims, Kyronides was adopted by Xenainetos senior, his sons would have lost their position in the **ankhisteia* of Aristarkhos senior, but not in that of their maternal grandfather, Aristomenes. Cf. on μητρὸς δ'οὐδείς ἐστιν ἐκποιήτος, 7.25.

καταπεπαιδεραστηκέναι ('used up on his affairs with boys'). A *hapax legomenon*. Compound verbs with the prefix *kata-* denoting exhaustive expenditure on a particular activity may be but are not always pejorative: cf. *kathippotrophēkas* ('spent on horse-rearing'), Isa. 5.43; *katekhorēgēse* ('spent on the office of *khorēgos*'), Lys. 19.42; *katekekubeuto* ('spent on gambling') and *katōpsophagēto* ('spent on gluttony'), Aiskhin. 1.95 (all cited by Wyse). Here, nevertheless, the insinuation is seriously damaging, not because Xenainetos's homosexual behaviour in itself offends against Athenian values but because his excessive expenditure on personal pleasure has brought no benefit to his family or the **polis* (cf. Just (1989), 41) This idea is spelt out explicitly in the extended attack on the character of Dikaiogenes III at Isa. 5.43: 'You, Dikaiogenes, having taken over their estate, have wickedly and disgracefully wasted it... for it is clear that you have spent nothing either on the *polis* or on your friends.' Cf. Dover (1974), 175, on the 'distinction between creditable and discreditable expenditure'.

The object of *katapepaidepastēkenai* is *oikon* ('estate'). Here, as at 5.43 and frequently elsewhere in Isaios's speeches, the word *oikos* is used interchangeably with *ousia* or *klēros* in the sense of 'property' or 'estate'. In the present context there is perhaps also a hint that Xenainetos has damaged the *oikos* ('family' or 'line of succession') of Aristomenes through the sterility of his homosexual relationships. (See MacDowell (1989), 10 on the possibility that two or more senses of *oikos* may overlap.)

On Isaios's use of the 'glancing blow' to blacken the character of his opponents, see on οὐχ ὥσπερ Προνάπης..., 7.39. In the present context his deployment of the technique may indicate that he did not have enough against Xenainetos junior for a more sustained attack (cf., e.g., the more detailed character comparison at Isa. 4.27–30), but the suggestive force of the accusation could, nevertheless, have been very effective.

ἐγὼ δ', ὦ ἄνδρες δικασταί, βραχείας οὐσίας ὑπαρξάσης ('But I, judges, although my means are slender'). For the form of the address to the

**dikastai*, see on ὦ ἄνδρες δικασταί, 9.16. The personal pronoun is emphatic, marking a contrast between the speaker's own lifestyle and what he has told the **dikastai* about that of Xenainetos junior. The speaker never gives any precise indication of his own or his father's financial means, but strives throughout the speech to convey the impression that their circumstances were relatively modest compared with those of his opponents.

ἀδελφὰς μὲν ἐξέδωκα ('gave my sisters in marriage'). By giving his sisters in marriage the speaker, unlike Xenainetos junior, has fulfilled his family obligations and contributed to the perpetuation of the citizen body (cf. Just (1989), 41). The fact that he acted as his sisters' **kurios* indicates that his father had already died.

ὅσα ἐδυνάμην ἐπιδούς ('providing as large a dowry as I could afford'). Although it was not strictly a legal requirement, the speaker has fulfilled another social and moral obligation by providing his sisters with dowries. Again, he emphasizes (though without giving any specific details) that he did what he could within his limited means.

κόσμιον δ' ἐμαυτὸν παρέχων... στρατευόμενος ('as someone who leads an orderly life, performing the duties assigned to him and serving in the army'). In keeping with what he has said about his financial circumstances, the speaker makes no extravagant claims about his services to the **polis*, but portrays himself as an ordinary law-abiding citizen.

ἀποστερηθῆναι ('to be robbed'). See on ἀποστερῶν, 8.3. The speaker is now openly claiming the estate on his own behalf.

Epilogue (26)

The speech concludes with a brief summary of the 'facts' as the speaker wants the **dikastai* to remember them. This, like the narrative in §§4–6, makes his case appear straightforward by omitting any of the more complex issues raised in the argument.

ἀπέδειξα δ' ὑμῖν ('I have proved to you'). The speaker's claim to have proved all the points covered in his summary is disingenuous.

Κυρωνίδην μὲν... ἐκποίητον γενόμενον... ('that Kyronides, my opponents' father, was adopted into another **oikos*'). See on ἐκποιήτος, 7.23. The speaker has indeed brought evidence in the form of testimony that Kyronides was adopted, and that he remained for the rest of his life in the *oikos* of his adoptive father, Xenainetos senior, but this is beside the point if Kyronides was not adopted until after the death of Aristarkhos senior.

τὸν δὲ πατέρα... καταλιπόντα ('that the father of Kyronides and of my mother left this estate to his son Demokhares'). The speaker's claim that

Demokhares was the sole legitimate heir of Aristarkhos senior rests on the assumption that Kyronides had already been adopted out of the *oikos* at the time of Aristarkhos senior's death. Cf. on ἐξεποιήθη . . ., §4.

ἐκεῖνον δὲ παῖδα ὄντα τελευτήσαντα ('that [Demokhares] died while still a child'). The speaker's witness testimony (§7) covered the fact that Demokhares died while still a minor. The ms. ἄπαιδα ('childless') at §26, instead of παῖδα ('a child') suggests the possibility of confusion, but the editorial emendation is clearly necessary in the light of the speaker's argument (§10) about the testamentary incapacity of minors.

καὶ εἰς τὴν ἐμὴν μητέρα τοῦτον τὸν κλῆρον ἐπιγιγνόμενον ('and that this estate then devolved on my mother'). See on ἀλλὰ τῆς ἐμῆς μητρὸς πατρῷος, §3.

APPENDIX

CATALOGUE OF CONTESTED COURT HEARINGS IN ATHENIAN INHERITANCE DISPUTES

Listed in this catalogue, in alphabetical order of the name of the deceased, are all the Athenian inheritance disputes, known from the work of the Attic orators, in which there was at least one contested court hearing. (This may have been a *diadikasia* or a *dikē*, and in some speeches there is evidence of one or more previous hearings.) In addition to all the extant speeches, 'lost' speeches, known only as fragments or by title, are included where the title indicates that the subject of the dispute was an inheritance (*klēros*), or an 'heiress' (*epiklēros*) or daughter (*thugatēr*), or an adoption (*poiēsis*). Other procedures which may or may not have arisen in the course of an inheritance dispute, such as actions for ejectment from a property (*exoulēs*), or for maltreatment of an orphan (*kakōseōs orphanou*) are not included.

Fragments of the orators are cited according to the following editions: Deinarkhos, ed. Conomis (Teubner); Hypereides, ed. Jensen (Teubner); Isaios, ed. Thalheim (Teubner); Lysias, ed. Carey (OCT).

1 Androkleides

On behalf of Pherenikos concerning the estate of Androkleides (ὑπὲρ Φερενίκου περὶ τοῦ Ἀνδροκλείδου κλήρου)—Lys. fr. CXXXV.

2 Antiphon

Concerning Antiphon's daughter (περὶ τῆς Ἀντιφῶντος θυγατρός)—Lys. fr. XII.

3 Apollodoros

Concerning the estate of Apollodoros (περὶ τοῦ Ἀπολλοδώρου κλήρου)—Isa. 7 (*diadikasia* between Apollodoros's adopted son, Thrasyllos, and cousin, the wife of Pronapes).

4 Aristarkhos

Against Xenainetos concerning the estate of Aristarkhos (πρὸς Ξεναίνετον περὶ τοῦ Ἀριστάρχου κλήρου)—Isa. 10 (*diadikasia* between grandson (daughter's son) of Aristarkhos senior and Xenainetos junior, brother of Aristarkhos junior).

5 Aristophon

Diamarturia, *claiming that the daughters of Aristophon are not subject to adjudication* (διαμαρτυρία, ὡς οὐκ επίδικοι <αἱ> Ἀριστοφῶντος θυγατέρες)—Dein. fr. LX.

6 Arkhephon

(i) *Concerning the estate of Arkhephon* (περὶ τοῦ Ἀρχεφῶντος κλήρου)—Dein. fr. LXXX.

(ii) *On behalf of Theodoros, whom Arkhephon adopted as his son* (ὑπὲρ Θεοδώρου, ὃν ἐποιήσατο υἱὸν Ἀρχεφῶν)—Dein. fr. LXXIX.

7 Arkhepolis

Against Aristogeiton and Arkhippos concerning the estate of Arkhepolis (πρὸς Ἀριστογείτονα καὶ Ἄρχιππον περὶ τοῦ Ἀρχεπόλιδος κλήρου)—Isa. fr. III.

8 Arkhiades

Against Leokhares concerning the estate of Arkhiades (πρὸς Λεωχάρη περὶ τοῦ Ἀρχίαδου κλήρου)—[Dem.] 44 (*diadikasia* between Aristodemos and Leokhares).

9 Astyphilos

Concerning the estate of Astyphilos (περὶ τοῦ Ἀστυφίλου κλήρου)—Isa. 9 (*diadikasia* between Astyphilos's patrilineal cousin, Kleon, and unnamed uterine half-brother).

10 Dikaiogenes (a)

(i) *Diadikasia* won by Dikaiogenes III against Polyaratos [mentioned at Isa. 5.8].

(ii) *Dikē pseudomarturiōn* won by Menexenos II against Lykon [mentioned at Isa. 5.12].

(iii) *Dikē pseudomarturiōn* won by Menexenos against Leokhares [mentioned at Isa. 5.17].

(iv) *Concerning the estate of Dikaiogenes* (περὶ τοῦ Δικαιογένους κλήρου)—Isa. 5 (prosecution of Leokhares in an action for the enforcement of a surety (*dikē enguēs*)).

11 Dikaiogenes (b)[1]
Against Glaukon concerning the estate of Dikaiogenes (πρὸς Γλαύκωνα περὶ τοῦ Δικαιογένους κλήρου)—Lys. fr. XXXIII.

12 Diogenes
Concerning the estate of Diogenes (περὶ τοῦ Διογένους κλήρου)—Lys. fr. XXXVII.

13 Euippos
Diamarturia *concerning the estate of Euippos against Khares* (διαμαρτυρία περὶ τοῦ Εὐίππου κλήρου πρὸς Χάρητα)—Dein. fr. LXII.

14 Hagnias
(i) *Diadikasia* won by Phylomakhe [mentioned at Isa. 11.9 and [Dem.] 43, *passim*.
(ii) *Diadikasia* won by Theopompos [mentioned at Isa. 11.18 and [Dem.] 43.8–10.
(iii) *Concerning the estate of Hagnias* (περὶ τοῦ Ἁγνίου κλήρου)—Isa. 11 (defence of Theopompos in an action for maltreatment of an orphan (*kakōseōs orphanou*)).
(iv) *Against Makartatos concerning the estate of Hagnias* (πρὸς Μακάρτατον περὶ τοῦ Ἁγνίου κλήρου)—[Dem.] 43 (*diadikasia* between Sositheos and Makartatos).

15 Hegesander
Concerning the estate of Hegesander (περὶ τοῦ Ἡγήσανδρου κλήρου)—Lys. fr. LXIII.

16 Hippeus
Two speeches concerning the estate of Hippeus (περὶ τοῦ Ἱππέως κλήρου λόγοι Β)—Hyp. frr. XXV, XXVI.

[1] It is unlikely that the *de cuius* in this case was the same as in Isa. 5, given that the latter makes no mention of a claimant known as Glaukon. The possibility cannot, however, be completely excluded.

17 Iophon

Action about an epiklēros *concerning the daughter of Iophon* (ἐπικληρικὸς ὑπὲρ τῆς Ἰωφῶντος θυγατρός) (and second speech)—Dein. frr. LVIII, LIX.

18 Kiron

Concerning the estate of Kiron (περὶ τοῦ Κίρωνος κλήρου)—Isa. 8 (*diadikasia* between Kiron's grandson (daughter's son) and nephew (brother's son)).

19 Kleonymos

Concerning the estate of Kleonymos (περὶ τοῦ Κλεωνύμου κλήρου)—Isa. 1 (*diadikasia* between a nephew and other collateral relations of Kleonymos).

20 Komon

(i) *Diadikasia* won by Olympiodoros [mentioned at [Dem.] 48.31].

(ii) *Against Olympiodoros for damages* (κατὰ Ὀλυμπιοδώρου βλάβης)—[Dem.] 48 (prosecution by Kallistratos).

21 Makartatos

Concerning the estate of Makartatos, or concerning half the inheritance (hēmiklēros) *of the property of Makartatos* (περὶ Μακαρτάτου κλήρου vel περὶ ἡμικληρίου τῶν Μακαρτάτου χρημάτων)—Lys. fr. XCVIII.

22 Menekles

Concerning the estate of Menekles (περὶ τοῦ Μενεκλέους κλήρου)—Isa. 2 (prosecution of Philonides by Menekles's adopted son in *dikē pseudomarturiōn*).

23 Mnesikles

Concerning the estate of Mnesikles (ὑπὲρ [i.e. περὶ] τοῦ Μνησικλέους κλήρου)—Dein. fr. LXIII.

24 Mnesitheos

Concerning the daughter of Mnesitheos (ὑπὲρ [i.e. περὶ] τῆς Μνησιθέου θυγατρός)—Isa. fr. XXXII.[2]

---

[2] Blass (1892), 493, is undoubtedly correct to gloss the first word *huper* ('on behalf of') as *peri* ('concerning'). Cf. also items 17, 23, 29, and (b) under 'Others'.

25 Mneson
Diadikasia won by Apollodoros against Eupolis [mentioned at Isa. 7.10].

26 Nikostratos
Concerning the estate of Nikostratos (περὶ τοῦ Νικοστράτου κλήρου)—Isa. 4 (*diadikasia* between Hagnon and Hagnotheos, cousins of Nikostratos, and Khariades, claiming to have been adopted by will; the speech is delivered by a *sunēgoros* on behalf of Hagnon and Hagnotheos).

27 Onomakles
Concerning the daughter of Onomakles (περὶ τῆς Ὀνομακλέους θυγατρός)—Lys. fr. CXVIII.

28 Philoktemon
Concerning the estate of Philoktemon (περὶ τοῦ Φιλοκτήμονος κλήρου)—Isa. 6 (prosecution by Khairestratos of Androkles and Antidoros in *dikē pseudomarturiōn*, delivered by a *sunēgoros* on behalf of Khairestratos).

29 Phrynikhos
Concerning the daughter of Phrynikhos (ὑπὲρ [i.e. περὶ] τῆς Φρυνίχου θυγατρός)—Lys. fr. CXLI.

30 Polyainos
Concerning the estate of Polyainos (περὶ τοῦ Πολυαίνου κλήρου)—Lys. fr. CXXI.

31 Pyrrhandros
Concerning the estate of Pyrrhandros (περὶ τοῦ Πυρράνδρου κλήρου)—Hyp. fr. XLIX.

32 Pyrrhos
(i) *Dikē pseudomarturiōn* won by speaker of Isa. 3 against Xenokles.
(ii) *Concerning the estate of Pyrrhos* (περὶ τοῦ Πύρρου κλήρου)—Isa. 3 (prosecution of Nikodemos in *dikē pseudomarturiōn*).

33 Theopompos
Concerning the estate of Theopompos (περὶ τοῦ Θεοπόμπου κλήρου)—Lys. fr. LXVIII.

Others (*de cuius* unknown)

(a) *Against Lysibios concerning an* epiklēros (πρὸς Λυσίβιον περὶ ἐπικλήρου)—Isa. fr. XXVI.

(b) *Against Satyros concerning an* epiklēros (πρὸς Σάτυρον ὑπὲρ [i.e. περὶ] ἐπικλήρου)—Isa. fr. XXXIX.

(c) *Concerning the adoption* (περὶ τῆς ποιήσεως)—Isa. fr. XXXVI.

(d) *Supporting speech (*sunēgoria*) for Hegolokhos concerning an* epiklēros (συνηγορία Ἡγελόχῳ ὑπὲρ [i.e. περὶ] ἐπικλήρου)—Dein. fr. LV.

GLOSSARY

This glossary is intended as a basic guide to relevant technical terms (mainly legal and rhetorical) which are used more than once in this book and not glossed in the text; full definitions are not necessarily given if they would go beyond the scope of the book. More detailed explanations of legal terms may be found in Todd (1993), 359–402. For rhetorical terminology, cf. Usher (1999), 364–368.

An asterisk (*) indicates a word for which there is a separate entry in the list. Words included in the glossary are also marked with an asterisk on their first occurrence in the introductions to each of the speeches, and (for the benefit of readers consulting the commentary for guidance on individual passages) on their first occurrence in each note in the lemmatic commentary.

anakrisis A pre-trial hearing before the **arkhōn* at which each party swore an oath (*antōmosia*) as to the truth of his case, and litigants were questioned by the *arkhōn* and one another.

ankhisteia The statutorily defined kinship group whose members (*ankhisteis*, lit. 'those who are nearest') could inherit from an Athenian who died leaving no legitimate descendants (natural or adopted).

antōmosia See *anakrisis*.

apostrophe A comment or question addressed to someone, usually the speaker's opponent, who is not part of the main audience of the speech.

arkhōn/arkhonship The *arkhōn* was a public official whose duties included supervision of the courts and presiding over trials (sometimes translated 'magistrate', but the *arkhōn*'s functions were administrative not judicial).

atekhnoi pisteis 'Artless' or 'inartistic' proofs: forms of proof or means of persuasion not produced by the speechwriter's skill or forming part of the speech itself, i.e. documentary evidence such as witness statements, laws, etc. Cf. *entekhnoi pisteis*.

atimia Loss of civil rights, imposed as a penalty by the courts on conviction for certain offences. The adjective *atimos* describes a man subject to this penalty.

basanos 'Torture'. The evidence of slaves could not be used in Athenian courts unless it had been extracted under torture. *Basanos* often refers to the challenge (*proklēsis*) issued to a speaker's opponent for slaves to be produced for torture. See also *atekhnoi pisteis*.

de cuius A term borrowed from Roman law to refer to the deceased in an inheritance case. ('De cuius hereditate agitur' = 'whose estate is in question').

deme (Gk. *dēmos*) One of 139 districts in Athens and rural Attica, membership of which was a prerequisite for Athenian citizenship after the constitutional reforms of Kleisthenes in the sixth century. Deme membership passed from father to son, whether or not they continued to live in the deme, and members were registered at the age of 18.

demesman A member of a *deme.

diabolē Blackening of [an opponent's] character.

diadikasia (pl. *diadikasia*) Non-adversarial procedure used in the Athenian courts for contested inheritance claims and, more generally, to determine competing claims to a benefit or to avoid performing a duty, including rival claims to guardianship, and disputed claims to privileges among priests.

diamarturia A formal declaration, used in inheritance cases to assert that an estate (**klēros*) was 'not subject to adjudication' because the deceased had left a legitimate natural or adopted son.

dikastērion One of the popular courts, which dealt with the majority of legal actions in Athens apart from special cases such as those of homicide.

dikastai (plur. of *dikastēs*) Citizens serving in a **dikastērion* whose functions combined those of modern judges and jurors. According to the type of case they were hearing, the *dikastai* sat in panels of 200–500, selected by lot. The minimum age for a *dikastēs* was 30.

dikē (pl. *dikai*) A private legal action, which could be brought only by the aggrieved party or his personal representative. Cf. *graphē*. The term can also be used generically of any legal action, and has a broader range of meanings including 'justice', 'judgment' and 'trial'. See also *exoulēs, dikē; pseudomarturiōn, dikē.*

embateusis The right to enter into possession of an estate without legal formality, enjoyed only by a direct descendant of the deceased or a son adopted **inter vivos*.

enguē Lit. 'pledge', 'security'; the formality by which an Athenian woman was given in marriage by her **kurios*. Formal marriage by *enguē* was a prerequisite for the production of legitimate children (unless the mother was an **epiklēros*, given in marriage by **epidikasia*).

entekhnoi pisteis 'Artistic' or 'artificial' proofs: forms of proof or means of persuasion produced by the speechwriter's skill and forming part of the speech itself, such as **ēthos* and **pathos*. Cf. *atekhnoi pisteis*.

epidikasia Formal procedure by which an uncontested claim to an inheritance was approved by the Athenian courts. Cf. *diadikasia*.

epidikos (of an estate or an **epiklēros*) Subject to adjudication; available to be claimed by application to the court.

epiklēros (pl. *epiklēroi*) Sometimes, inaccurately, translated as 'heiress': a girl or woman who became the sole representative of her paternal **oikos* after the death of her father and any brothers. The *epiklēros* could be claimed in marriage, along with her paternal estate, by her father's next of kin, who applied to the court for **epidikasia*. The property inherited by an *epiklēros* passed to her sons two years after puberty.

ēthos 'Character'; in rhetorical theory, one of the **entekhnoi pisteis*. Cf. *pathos*.

*exoulēs, *dikē* A private legal action to eject the occupant from property claimed by the complainant.

focalizer/focalization In narratological theory, a focalizer is the person (narrator or character) through whose eyes the people or events in the story are presented.

gennētēs, pl. *gennētai* A member of a **genos*.

genos, pl. *genē* A kinship group whose members performed certain religious cults for which they provided the priest or priestess. Not every Athenian belonged to a *genos*, and membership had no specific legal significance, but it could be used as evidence of legitimate birth or citizenship. Cf. 'phratry'.

graphē, pl. *graphai* A public legal action which could be prosecuted by any citizen (*ho boulomenos*, lit. 'anyone who wishes') not just by the injured party (cf. *dikē*). See also *hubreōs, graphē*.

gymnasiarch A superintendent of games or athletic contests at festivals; cf. *liturgy.

hetaira Lit. 'female companion'; a courtesan or mistress. Cf. *pallakē*.

homometric Having the same mother. Cf. *homopatric, *uterine.

homopatric Having the same father. Cf. *homometric, *uterine.

hubris A form of aggravated assault involving (according to different scholarly interpretations) either a misuse of the assailant's superior strength or a deliberate attack on the victim's honour (*timē*).

inter vivos Lit. 'between the living': used of an adoption carried out by the adoptive father in his lifetime, as distinct from an adoption by will.

khorēgos The producer of a play at one of the annual dramatic festivals in Athens, payment for which was undertaken as a *liturgy.

klēros 'Estate', 'inheritance' (originally an ancestral plot of land). Cf. *oikos*.

kurios Lit. 'master': the husband, father, brother or other male family member who represented the interests of an Athenian woman (or child) in court.

lēxis The formal written claim submitted by a claimant to an inheritance.

liturgy/liturgical (Gk. *leitourgia*, pl. *leitourgiai*) A public service, such as acting as a trierarch, *gymnasiarch, or **khorēgos*, performed as a duty by the wealthiest Athenian citizens.

logographer (Gk. *logographos*) A professional writer of speeches for litigants to deliver in court.

marturia 'Witness statement', 'testimony'. See also *atekhnoi pisteis*.

metic (from Gk. *metoikos*) a 'resident alien' in Athens (often a citizen of another Greek *polis*), of free (non-slave) status but not enjoying the privileges of Athenian citizenship and subject to a special tax.

nomizomena, ta Lit. 'the customary things'; often refers to the funeral and commemorative rites carried out on behalf of a deceased by his heir.

oikos (pl. *oikoi*) a) 'house', i.e. a building (synonymous with *oikia*); b) 'estate' or 'property' (synonymous with **klēros*); c) 'family' or 'line of descent' (as in 'the house of Bouselos' or 'the house of Windsor').

pallakē 'Concubine', 'mistress', denoting a more permanent relationship than one with a **hetaira*, but not a legally married wife. Cf. *enguē*.

pathos 'Emotion'; 'passion'. In rhetorical theory, the arousal of the audience's emotions was one of the **entekhnoi pisteis*. Cf. *ēthos*.

per stirpes 'By lines of descent', denoting a method of dividing the estate of someone who has died. For example, if an Athenian died childless but leaving two brothers, each of them would receive half of his estate. But if one of the brothers had already died, leaving three sons, the surviving brother of the deceased would still receive half of the estate, with the other half divided equally among the three nephews as 'representatives' of their deceased father. (Under the alternative method of division, *per capita*, each of the beneficiaries would receive an equal share.)

phrateres Members of a *phratry.

phratry (Gk. *phratria*, lit. 'brotherhood') One of a number of Athenian kinship groups, membership of which was passed from father to son. After the reforms of Kleisthenes (see under 'deme'), membership of a phratry was no longer compulsory, but it was still used as evidence of legitimate birth or citizenship. Cf. *genos*.

pistis, pl. *pisteis* Often translated as 'proof' or 'evidence'; more lit., 'means of persuasion'. See also *atekhnoi pisteis* and *entekhnoi pisteis*.

polis, pl. *poleis* 'City', 'city-state'.

proem, proemium In rhetorical theory, one of the formal divisions of a speech: the introduction.

prokatalēpsis Anticipation of opponent's argument.

prutaneis (pl. of *prutanis*) A committee of the Athenian Council (*boulē*), comprising a tribal delegation of fifty men, who collectively served as *prutaneis* for one tenth of the year; they remained on duty at all times in case of emergency.

pseudomarturiōn, **dikē* A prosecution for false testimony (*pseudomarturia*), brought against a witness in a trial or the witness producing a **diamarturia*.

seed In narratological theory, seeding is 'the insertion of a piece of information, the relevance of which will only later become clear. The later event thus prepared for becomes more natural, logical or plausible' (De Jong (2001), xvii–xviii).

sunēgoros (pl. *sunēgoroi*) 'Supporting speaker': one who spoke on behalf of a litigant, delivering either the main speech at a trial or a shorter epilogue after the litigant had spoken for himself.

sykophant (Gk. *sukophantēs*) A term used pejoratively of a vexatious or officious litigant; not to be confused with modern English 'sycophant'. The etymology and precise meaning are unclear.

thesmothetēs Originally 'law-giver', 'legislator'; in the fourth century, a title given to a junior **arkhōn*.

topos pl. *topoi* A standard theme used in forensic oratory.

uterine Having the same mother but not the same father. Cf. *homometric, *homopatric.

BIBLIOGRAPHY

Andrewes, A. 1961, "Philochoros on phratries", *Journal of Hellenic Studies*, vol. 81, pp. 1–15.

Avramovič, S. 1990, "Plaidoyer for Isaeus, or. IX", in *Symposion 1988: Vorträge zur griechischen und hellenistischen Rechtsgeschichte*, G. Nenci & G. Thür, eds., Cologne & Vienna, pp. 41–45.

——. 1997, *Iseo e il diritto attico*, Naples. [Originally published Belgrade, 1988, as *Isejovo sudsko besednistvo I atinsko pravo.*]

Baden, W. W. 1906, *The principal figures of language and figures of thought in Isaeus and the guardianship speeches of Demosthenes*, Baltimore.

Baiter, J. G. and Sauppe, H. 1850, *Oratores attici*, vol. 2, Zürich.

Bar Standards Board. 2004, *Code of conduct*, 8th edn., London.

Blass, F. 1892, *Die attische Beredsamkeit, zw. Abtheilung*, 2nd edn., Leipzig.

Boëthius, A. 1918, *Die Pythaïs: Studien zur Geschichte der Verbindungen zwischen Athen und Delphi*, Uppsala.

Bonner, R. J., 1905, *Evidence in Athenian courts*, Chicago.

Bourriot, F. 1982, "La famille et le milieu social de Cléon", *Historia*, vol. 31, pp. 404–435.

Bremmer, J. 1983, "The importance of the maternal uncle and grandfather in archaic and classical Greece and early Byzantium", *Zeitschrift für Papyrologie und Epigraphik*, vol. 50, pp. 173–186.

Brown, P. G. M. 1983, "Menander's dramatic technique and the law of Athens", *Classical Quarterly*, vol. 33, pp. 412–420.

Burnett, A. P. & Edmonson, C. N. 1961, "The Chabrias monument in the Athenian agora", *Hesperia*, vol. 30, pp. 80–91.

Caillemer, E. 1879, *Le droit de succession légitime à Athènes*, Paris.

Calhoun, G. M. 1919, "Oral and written pleading in Athenian courts", *Transactions of the American Philological Society*, vol. 50, pp. 177–193.

Carey, C. 1993, "The return of the radish, or Just when you thought it was safe to go back into the kitchen", *Liverpool Classical Monthly*, vol. 18, pp. 53–55.

——. 1994, "Legal space in classical Athens", *Greece and Rome*, vol. 41, pp. 172–186.

——. 1995, "The witness's *exomosia* in the Athenian courts", *Classical Quarterly*, vol. 45, pp. 114–120.

——. 1996, "Nomos in Athenian rhetoric and oratory", *Journal of Hellenic Studies*, vol. 116, pp. 33–46.

——. 1997, *Trials from classical Athens*, London.

——. 2005, "An overlooked papyrus of Isaios", *Bulletin of the Institute of Classical Studies*, vol. 48, pp. 15–25.

——. 2007, *Lysiae orationes cum fragmentis* (Oxford Classical Texts), Oxford.

Christ, M. 1990, "Liturgy avoidance and *antidosis* in classical Athens", *Transactions of the American Philological Association*, vol. 120, pp. 147–169.

Cobetto Ghiggia, P. 2002, *Iseo: Contra Leocare (sulla successione di Diceogene) introduzione, testo critico, traduzione e commento*, Pisa.

Cohen, D. 1995, *Law, violence and community in classical Athens*, Cambridge.

Conomis, N. C. 1975, *Dinarchii orationes cum fragmentis* (Bibliotheca Teubneriana), Leipzig.

Cooper, G. L. 1974, "Prepositional problems in Thucydides, Xenophon, Isaeus and Plato", *Greek Roman and Byzantine Studies*, vol. 15, pp. 403–420.

Cox, C. 1988, "Sibling relationships in classical Athens: brother-sister ties", *Journal of Family History*, vol. 13, pp. 377–395.

——. 1998, *Household interests: property, marriage strategies and family dynamics in classical Athens*, Princeton, N. J.

Cretney, S. & Masson, J. 1997, *Principles of family law*, 6th edn, London.
Davies, J. K. 1971, *Athenian propertied families, 600–300 BC*, Oxford.
De Jong, I. 2001, *A narratological commentary on the Odyssey*, Cambridge.
——. 2004, *Narrators and focalizers: the presentation of the story in the Iliad*, 2nd edn, Bristol.
Denniston, J. D. 1954, *The Greek particles*, 2nd edn, Oxford.
Denommé, J. M. 1968, *Index Isaeus*, Hildesheim.
——. 1973, "L'ordre des mots dans les discours d'Isée", *Revue de Philologie*, vol. 47, pp. 281–295.
——. 1974a, "Le choix des mots dans les discours d'Isée", *Les Études Classiques*, vol. 42, pp. 127–148.
——. 1974b, *Recherches sur la langue et le style d'Isée*, Hildesheim.
Dickey, E. 1996, *Greek forms of address from Herodotos to Lucian*, Oxford.
Dorjahn, A. P. 1935, "Anticipation of arguments in Athenian courts", *Transactions and proceedings of the American Philological Association*, vol. 66, pp. 274–295.
Dover, K. J. 1968a, *Lysias and the corpus Lysiacum*, Berkeley, Cal.
——. 1968b, *Aristophanes Clouds, edited with introduction and commentary*, Oxford.
——. 1974, *Greek popular morality in the time of Plato and Aristotle*, Oxford.
Du Cann, R. 1993, *The art of the advocate*, rev. edn., Harmondsworth.
Dunbar, N. 1998, *Aristophanes Birds, with introduction and commentary*, Oxford.
Edwards, M. J. 1994, *The Attic orators*, Bristol.
——. 2004, "Oratory", in *Narrators, narratees and narratives in ancient Greek literature*, I. De Jong, R. Nünlist, & A. Bowie, eds., Leiden, pp. 317–348.
——. 2007, *Isaeus, translated with introduction and notes*, Austin, Tex.
Ferrucci, S. 2005, *Iseo: La Successione di Kiron: introduzione, testo critico, traduzione e commento*, Pisa.
Forster, E. S. 1927, *Isaeus, with an English translation* (Loeb Classical Library), Cambridge, Mass.
Foxhall, L. 1989, "Household, gender and property in classical Athens", *Classical Quarterly*, vol. 39, pp. 22–44.
Gabrielsen, V. 1994, *Financing the Athenian fleet: public taxation and social relations*, Baltimore & London.
Gagarin, M. 1996, "The torture of slaves in Athenian law", *Classical Philology*, vol. 91, pp. 1–18.
Garner, R. 1987, *Law and society in classical Athens*, London.
Gernet, L. 1921, "Sur l'épiklérat", *Revue des Études Grecques*, vol. 34, pp. 337–379.
——. 1930, "La loi de Solon sur le testament", *Revue des Études Grecques*, vol. 33, pp. 123–168 & 249–290.
Griffith-Williams, B. 2008, "'Those who know the facts': witnesses and their testimony in Isaios 9", *Acta Antiqua*, vol. 48, pp. 253–261.
——. 2012, "*Oikos*, family feuds and funerals: argumentation and evidence in Athenian inheritance disputes", *Classical Quarterly*, vol. 62, pp. 145–162.
Hafter, E. 1887, *Die Erbtochter nach attischem Recht*, Leipzig.
Hall, E. 2006, *The theatrical cast of Athens: interactions between ancient Greek drama and society*, Oxford.
Hardcastle, M. 1980, "Some non-legal arguments in Athenian inheritance cases", *Prudentia*, vol. 12, pp. 11–22.
Harrison, A. R. W. 1947, "A problem in the rules of intestate succession in Athens", *Classical Review*, vol. 61, pp. 41–43.
——. 1968, *The law of Athens*, vol. 1, *The family and property*, London.
——. 1971, *The law of Athens*, vol. 2, *Procedure*, London.
Hart, H. L. A. 1994, *The concept of law*, 2nd edn., Oxford.
Headlam, J. W. 1893, "On the πρόκλησις εἰς βάσανον in Attic law", *Classical Review*, vol. 7, pp. 1–5.

Hornblower, S. 1994, "Narratology and narrative techniques in Thucydides", in *Greek historiography*, S. Hornblower, ed., Oxford, pp. 131–166.
——. 2002, *The Greek world*, 3rd edn., London.
Humphreys, S. C. 1985, "Social relations on stage: witnesses in classical Athens", in *The discourse of law*, S. C. Humphreys, ed., London. [Reprinted in *Oxford readings in the Attic orators*, E. Carawan, ed., Oxford, 2007, pp. 140–213, to which page numbers in citations refer.]
——. 1986, "Kinship patterns in the Athenian courts", *Greek Roman and Byzantine Studies*, vol. 27, pp. 57–92.
Hunter, V. J. 1993, "Agnatic kinship in Athenian law and Athenian family practice: its implications for women", in *Law, politics and society in the ancient Mediterranean world*, B. Halpern & D. W. Hobson, eds., Sheffield, pp. 100–121.
——. 1994, *Policing Athens: social control in the Attic lawsuits, 420–320 BC*, Princeton, N. J.
Inns of Court School of Law. 2006, *Advocacy*, Oxford.
Isager, S. 1982, "The marriage pattern in classical Athens: men and women in Isaeus", *Classica et Mediaevalia*, vol. 33, pp. 81–96.
Jebb, R. C. 1876, *The Attic orators from Antiphon to Isaeus*, vol. 2, London.
——. 1888, *Selections from the Attic orators*, 2nd edn., London.
Jensen, C. 1963, *Hyperidis orationes sex cum ceterarum fragmentis* (Bibliotheca Teubneriana), Stuttgart.
Johnstone, S. 1999, *Disputes and democracy: the consequences of litigation in ancient Athens*, Austin, Tex.
Jones, W. 1779, *The speeches of Isaeus in causes concerning the law of succession of property at Athens, with a prefatory discourse, notes critical and historical, and a commentary*, London.
Just, R. 1989, *Women in Athenian law and life*, London.
Kamps, W. 1938, "Une affaire de fraude successorale à Athènes", *Annuaire de l'Institut de Philologie et d'Histoire Orientales et Slaves*, vol. 6, pp. 15–27.
Karabélias, E. 1975, "L'épiclérat dans la comédie nouvelle et dans les sources latines", in *Symposion 1971: Vorträge zur griechischen und hellenistischen Rechtsgeschichte*, J. Modrzejewski, D. Nörr, & H. J. Wolff, eds., Cologne & Vienna, pp. 215–254.
——. 1992, "L'acte à cause de mort (diathèke) dans le droit attique", *Recueils de la Société Jean Bodin*, vol. 59 (Actes à cause de mort), pp. 47–121.
——. 2002, *L'épiclérat attique: recherches sur la condition juridique de la fille épiclère athénienne*, Athens.
——. 2005, "Une nouvelle source pour l'étude du droit attique: le *Bouclier* de Ménandre", in E. Karabélias, *Études d'histoire juridique et sociale de la Grèce Ancienne*, Athens, pp. 17–47.
Kirchner, J. 1901–1903, *Prosopographica Attica*, 2 vols., Berlin.
Körte, A. 1906, "Zum attischen Erbrecht", *Philologus*, vol. 65, pp. 388–396.
Kurtz, D. L. & Boardman, J. 1971, *Greek burial customs*, London.
Labarbe, J. 1953, "L'âge correspondant au sacrifice du κούρειον et les données historiques du sixième discours d'Isée", *Bulletin de la Classe des Lettres de l'Académie Royale de Belgique*, vol. 39, pp. 358–394.
Lacey, W. K. 1968 (repr. with corrections, 1980), *The family in classical Greece*, Auckland.
Lambert, S. D. 1993, *The phratries of Attica*, Ann Arbor, Mich.
Lanni, A. 2006, *Law and justice in the courts of classical Athens*, Cambridge.
Lavency, M. 1964, *Aspects de la logographie judiciare attique*, Louvain.
Lawless, J. M. 1991, *Law, legal argument and equity in the speeches of Isaeus*, Ph.D., Brown University.
Lentzsch. 1932, *Studien zu Isaios*, Leipzig.
Lewis, N. 1959, "Pro Isaeo, 11.50", *American Journal of Philology*, vol. 80, pp. 162–168.
Lincke, E. M. 1884, *De elocutione Isaei*, Leipzig.
Lipsius, J. H. 1905, *Das attische Recht und Rechtsverfahren*, Leipzig.

MacDowell, D. M. 1978, *The law in classical Athens*, Ithaca, N.Y.
——. 1982, "Love versus the law: an essay on Menander's *Aspis*", *Greece and Rome*, vol. 29, pp. 42–52.
——. 1989, "The *oikos* in Athenian law", *Classical Quarterly*, vol. 39, pp. 10–21.
Maffi, A. 1990, "È esistita l'afèresi dell'epikleros?", in *Symposion 1988: Vorträge zur griechischen und hellenistischen Rechtsgeschichte*, G. Nenci & G. Thür, eds., Cologne & Vienna, pp. 21–36.
Maine, H. S. 1861, *Ancient law: its connection with the early history of society and its relations to modern ideas*, London.
Martin, G. 2006, "Forms of address in Athenian courts", *Museum Helveticum*, vol. 63, pp. 75–88.
——. 2008, "The witness's *exomosia* in Athens", *Classical Quarterly*, vol. 58, pp. 56–68.
Meiggs, R. & Lewis, D. 1988, *A selection of Greek historical inscriptions to the end of the fifth century BC*, rev. edn., Oxford.
Miller, M. W. 1936, "Isaeus' vocabulary", *Classical Journal*, vol. 31, pp. 442–444.
Mirhady, D. 1996, "Torture and rhetoric in Athens", *Journal of Hellenic Studies*, vol. 116, pp. 119–131.
Mossé, C. 1989, "Quelques remarques sur la famille à Athènes à la fin du IVe siècle: le témoignage du théatre de Ménandre", in *Symposion 1982: Vorträge zur griechischen und hellenistischen Rechtsgeschichte*, F. J. Fernandez Nieto, ed., Cologne & Vienna, pp. 129–134.
Moy, L. 1876, *Etude sur les plaidoyers d'Isée*, Paris.
Münscher. 1919/1920, "Isaios", *Zeitschrift für vergleichende Rechtswissenschaft*, vol. 37, pp. 32–329.
Mylonas, G. E. 1962, *Eleusis and the Eleusinian mysteries*, Princeton, N.J.
Nicklin, T. 1905, "Wyse's Isaeus", *Classical Review*, vol. 19, no. 6, pp. 305–308.
Osborne, R. 1985a, *Demos: the discovery of classical Attica*, Cambridge.
——. 1985b, "Law in action in classical Athens", *Journal of Hellenic Studies*, vol. 105, pp. 40–58.
Paoli, U. E. 1976a, "L' ἀγχιστεία nel diritto successorio attico", in *Altri studi di diretto greco e romano*, Milan, pp. 323–361.
——. 1976b, "La legitima afèresi dell' *epikleros* in diritto attico", in *Altri studi di diritto greco e romano*, Milan, pp. 363–376.
Parke, H. W. 1939, "The Pythaïs of 355 BC and the Third Sacred War", *Journal of Hellenic Studies*, vol. 59, pp. 80–83.
Parker, R. 1996, *Athenian religion: a history*, Oxford.
——. 2005, *Polytheism and society at Athens*, Oxford.
Raubitschek, A. E. 1949, *Dedications from the Athenian Akropolis*, Cambridge, Mass.
Renehan, R. R. 1980, "Isocrates and Isaeus", *Classical Philology*, vol. 75, pp. 242–253.
Rhodes, P. J. 1981, *A commentary on the Aristotelian Athenaion Politeia*, Oxford.
——. 2004, "Keeping to the point", in *The law and the courts in ancient Greece*, E. M. Harris & L. Rubinstein, eds., London, pp. 137–158.
Robinson, C. A. 1901, *The tropes and figures of Isaeus: a study of his rhetorical art*, Princeton, N.J.
Rosivach, V. 2005, "Astyphilos the mercenary", *Greece and Rome*, vol. 52, no. 2, pp. 195–204.
Roussel, P. 1922, *Isée, texte établi et traduit*, Paris.
Rubinstein, L. 1993, *Adoption in IV. century Athens*, Copenhagen.
——. 2000, *Litigation and co-operation: supporting speakers in the Athenian courts*, Stuttgart.
——. 2004, "Stirring up of dicastic anger", in *Law, rhetoric and comedy in classical Athens: essays in honour of Douglas M. MacDowell*, D. L. Cairns & R. A. Knox, eds., Swansea, pp. 187–203.
——. 2005, "Differentiated rhetorical strategies in the Athenian courts", in *The Cambridge companion to ancient Greek law*, M. Gagarin & D. Cohen, eds., Cambridge, pp. 129–145.

Rudhardt, J. 1962, "La reconnaissance de la paternité, sa nature et sa portée dans la société athénienne", *Museum Helveticum*, vol. 19, pp. 39–64.

Sawyer, C. 1998, *Principles of succession, wills and probate*, 2nd edn., London.

Schaps, D. 1977, "The woman least mentioned: etiquette and women's names", *Classical Quarterly*, vol. 27, pp. 323–330.

Seymour, T. D. 1901a, "Hypophora in Isaeus", *Classical Review*, vol. 15, pp. 108–109.

——. 1901b, "Isaeus as an imitator of Lysias", *Classical Review*, vol. 15, p. 109.

——. 1906, "The speeches of Isaeus", *Classical Philology*, vol. 1, no. 2, pp. 187–190.

Sommerstein, A. 1980, "The naming of women in Greek and Roman comedy", *Quaderni di Storia*, vol. 11, pp. 393–418.

Tangri, D. 2004, *Relevance in Athenian courts*, Ph.D., Australian National University.

Thalheim, T. 1903, *Isaei orationes cum deperditarum fragmentis* (Bibliotheca Teubneriana), Leipzig.

Theodorakopoulos, V. 1972, *A statistical and rhetorical study of Isaeus*, Ph.D., University of London.

Thomas, R. 1989, *Oral tradition and written record in classical Athens*, Cambridge.

Thompson, W. E. 1967, "The marriage of first cousins in Athenian society", *Phoenix*, vol. 21, pp. 273–282.

——. 1970, "Isaeus VI. The historical circumstances", *Classical Review*, vol. 20, pp. 1–4.

——. 1971, "Attic kinship terminology", *Journal of Hellenic Studies*, vol. 91, pp. 110–113.

——. 1972, "Athenian marriage patterns: remarriage", *California Studies in Classical Antiquity*, vol. 5, pp. 211–225.

——. 1976, *De Hagniae hereditate: an Athenian inheritance case*, Leiden.

——. 1981, "Athenian attitudes toward wills", *Prudentia*, vol. 13, pp. 13–25.

Thür, G. 1977, *Beweisführung vor den Schwurgerichtshöfen Athens: die Proklesis zur Basanon*, Vienna.

Todd, S. C. 1990a, "The use and abuse of the Attic orators", *Greece and Rome*, vol. 37, pp. 159–178.

——. 1990b, "The purpose of evidence in Athenian courts", in *Nomos*, P. Cartledge, P. Millett, & S. Todd, eds., Cambridge, pp. 19–39.

——. 1993, *The shape of Athenian law*, Oxford.

Trevett, J. 1992, *Apollodoros, the son of Pasion*, Oxford.

Twining, W. 2006, *Rethinking evidence: exploratory essays*, Cambridge.

Usher, S. 1974, *Dionysios of Halicarnassus, Critical essays*, vol. 1 (Loeb Classical Library), Cambridge, Mass.

——. 1976, "Lysias and his clients", *Greek Roman and Byzantine Studies*, vol. 17, pp. 31–40.

——. 1999, *Greek oratory: tradition and originality*, Oxford.

Van Wees, H. 2004, *Greek warfare: myths and realities*, London.

Wade-Gery, H. T. & Merritt, B. D. 1936, "Pylos and the assessment of tribute", *American Journal of Philology*, vol. 57, pp. 377–394.

Webster, T. B. L. 1952, "Chronological notes on Middle Comedy", *Classical Quarterly*, vol. 2, pp. 13–26.

Welsh, D. 1991, "Isaeus 9 and Astyphilos' last expedition", *Greek Roman and Byzantine Studies*, vol. 32, pp. 131–150.

Wevers, R. F. 1969, *Isaeus: chronology, prosopography and social history*, The Hague.

Whitehead, D. 1986, *The demes of Attica 508/7–250 BC*, Princeton, N.J.

——. 2000, *Hypereides: a commentary on the forensic speeches*, Oxford.

Wilson, P. 2000, *The Athenian institution of the Khoregia: the chorus, the city and the stage*, Cambridge.

Wohl, W. 2010, *Law's cosmos: juridical discourse in Athenian forensic oratory*, Cambridge.

Wyse, W. 1904, *The speeches of Isaeus, with critical and explanatory notes*, Cambridge.

GENERAL INDEX

INDEX OF ANCIENT SOURCES

Literary Sources

Inscriptions and Papyri

www.ingramcontent.com/pod-product-compliance
Lightning Source LLC
LaVergne TN
LVHW010656300926
849161LV00005B/1142